THE LONG ALLIANCE

THE LONG ALLIANCE

THE IMPERFECT UNION OF
JOE BIDEN AND BARACK OBAMA

GABRIEL DEBENEDETTI

HENRY HOLT AND COMPANY

NEW YORK

Henry Holt and Company
Publishers since 1866
120 Broadway
New York, New York 10271
www.henryholt.com

Henry Holt® and Ⓗ® are registered trademarks of Macmillan Publishing Group, LLC.

Library of Congress Cataloging-in-Publication Data is available.

ISBN: 9781250829979

Our books may be purchased in bulk for promotional, educational, or business use. Please contact your local bookseller or the Macmillan Corporate and Premium Sales Department at (800) 221-7945, extension 5442, or by e-mail at MacmillanSpecialMarkets@macmillan.com.

First Edition 2022

Designed by Meryl Sussman Levavi

Printed in the United States of America

10 9 8 7 6 5 4 3 2 1

To my parents

A vice president is totally a reflection of the president. There is no inherent power. None. Zero. And it completely, totally depends on your relationship with the president.

—Joe Biden, 2015

I am president. I am not king. I can't do these things just by myself.

—Barack Obama, 2010

CONTENTS

PREFACE

Barack Obama was almost enjoying himself.

He didn't really mind the pandemic-imposed isolation from basically everyone other than his immediate family. And by September 2020 life on Martha's Vineyard—where he and Michelle, the former first lady, had mostly stayed since leaving DC for roomier environs that spring—was tailor-made for an ex-president who had finally finished the first volume of the memoir he'd taken forever to write, who liked to golf, and who had, at long last, figured out the proper role for himself in his old partner Joe Biden's quest to beat Donald Trump and perhaps save American democracy in the process.

This hadn't been as intuitive as it might seem for the famously close pair, seeing as how Obama started the election cycle by essentially trying (and failing) to make sure Biden understood that he *really* didn't need to run this time. He'd undertaken this act of light dissuasion because of what he perceived to be a mismatch between Biden and the political moment, but mostly out of concern for the former vice president. He'd then proceeded to monitor the Biden campaign but grown plenty interested in a procession of candidates not named Joe. None of this was particularly amusing to the ex-VP, who, despite it all, still insisted to anyone who'd listen that the two were like brothers after their conspicuously tight eight years in office together. Then, as COVID-19 started bearing down, Obama had indeed begun to help Biden behind the scenes with some sub-rosa encouragement and covert political muscle-flexing—a combination that ended up being far more important than the public appreciated as Biden won the nomination. And, more recently, the supposed retiree had begun supplementing his role as the Democratic nominee's most important surrogate on the trail by also becoming one of his top private advisors and an important voice on the phone for Biden's highest-ranking aides, too. For a few months now he'd been way more involved in the campaign than almost anyone outside of that tiny circle knew.

Still, the fall wasn't looking particularly easy to navigate, between the virus's rampage, the ongoing racial reckoning across the country, and, as of late, the growing likelihood that the sitting president might not accept the result of the election if he lost in November. Few people in Biden's inner circle doubted that a democratic crisis might be brewing, and so they hardly needed Obama's repeated warnings to take the prospect seriously. Yet watching from afar, and after discussing the matter repeatedly with friends and allies between campaign rallies and on calls from the Vineyard, the ex-president determined he still needed his own real plan for what to do if Trump refused to admit defeat or in case he sowed doubt about the result if the vote took longer to count than usual, thanks to the increased popularity of mail-in ballots. So, that month, Obama convened a small group of his own advisors to map out his plan for the final stretch of campaign season. They talked through some of these nightmare scenarios and determined that the ex-president—who'd insisted on respecting the polite conventions of the postpresidency even as Trump spent four years pulverizing those kinds of norms, and even as some liberals pined for some sort of implausible Obama-as-savior plot—should be as active as ever for Biden on the trail but again refrain from saying much publicly should one of those dangerous story lines come to pass. Unless things spiraled and it became absolutely necessary, he would step back and let Biden take the lead, as was appropriate.

Further, Obama determined that after the polls opened he shouldn't talk to Biden at all until the result was official, since the last thing either of them wanted was Trump accusing them of some fantastical, corrupt, coordinated scheme to steal the election, and also because Obama wanted to be as cautious as possible to avoid any premature celebration at a delicate moment.

They could handle the distance. They'd been talking plenty recently, but "Joe as Nominee, Barack as Backstage Guru" was really only the latest chapter in the complicated saga of the relationship between the forty-fourth and would-be-forty-sixth presidents. Plus, both of them wished to project the message that a Biden win would mean a return to a normal democratic order. You get congratulated only when you win, period.

Biden understood the outlines of this plan. He'd welcomed Obama's help during the campaign, of course—anything from his longtime friend and ally who remained one of the world's most popular political figures could be useful. But Biden had also slightly surprised some of his other friends with his sensitivity to the idea that his victory would represent a restoration of the Obama years, considering how explicitly he'd run on a return to normalcy, and on his tenure as VP, during the primary especially. Either way, Obama's logistics were hardly top of mind for Biden in the final days of his campaign. It was nearly half a century after he got to Washington, over three decades after he'd started running for president, a dozen years since his public profile had been transformed by the partnership in the White House, and just months since he had correctly gauged the country's exhaustion, despite the supposedly savvy crowd's insistence that he was hopelessly out of touch. And this was it.

In other words, Biden had other things to think about on election night. At home in Wilmington, Delaware, surrounded by his family and his longtime political strategist Mike Donilon, he sat nervously, doing what he always did as he waited for results. He knew he had lawyers on standby in DC monitoring any irregularities and Trump's pronouncements that he couldn't possibly lose, so Biden stuck to flipping between NBC and CNN and working his phone. He called his friend Doug Jones to console him ten minutes after the Alabama senator lost his reelection bid. He checked in with old buddies and allies from past campaigns and past lives who were peppered around swing states like Michigan and Florida. And he stayed away from the one number he knew he couldn't dial.

Biden had entered the night expecting to win but knowing it could take a while. He only started to exhale when Fox News, of all networks, called Arizona, usually a Republican state, for him after 11:00 p.m. eastern time. Still, there went his plan to victoriously address the nation on Tuesday night. It was all trending in the right direction, but it clearly wasn't going to be official quite yet. He stuck to his calls as his top advisors across town in Wilmington checked in with his analytics team in Philadelphia, which kept crunching its numbers. Biden maintained his pace as Wednesday approached. Florida and North Carolina were gone, but even GOP-friendly Georgia was still in play, and it looked like Pennsylvania—his childhood home—might push him over the edge when more votes came in, whenever that was going to be.

Around 1:00 a.m. the candidate called Bob Casey, the state's Democratic senator, to compare notes and vent a bit about the slow process. Biden was doing his best to stay calm. Casey told him it sure looked like he was going to win the state eventually, but that it still might take a while longer. And that was before Trump popped up in the White House trying to declare victory.

Wednesday, Thursday, and Friday proceeded the same way, Biden mostly parked in front of his television, phone in hand, as ballots trickled in across the country and the president veered deeper into the realm of conspiracy to insist that he'd won. Biden's staffers were burning through their phones as much as he was, scavenging for on-the-ground intel from Pennsylvania, in particular, from Casey and other Keystone State friends, allies, and acquaintances who were themselves looking for clues about the timing of the ballot-tallying. Or, really, about anything that might help.

The circumstances could hardly have been more different, but it was the second time in five years that Biden, in a period of most intense political pressure, knew he couldn't call Obama. This time, at least, was more hopeful. In 2015, as the then VP agonized over whether he should launch a presidential campaign after months of painful consideration, he knew Obama didn't want him to run, and that the president had pushed Hillary Clinton to run instead, so that there was no more discussion to be had about it. It had taken them years to get over that experience, and people around them still didn't like to talk about that year, the same one Biden's son Beau died. Now it was self-imposed protocol stopping them from talking—yet another obstacle they'd set for themselves. That didn't make it any less uncomfortable.

Not for Biden, and not for Obama.

The former president, too, was watching closely, dispatching his political and communications advisor Eric Schultz and some other aides to keep in constant touch with Biden's political side for rolling updates on vote counts and expectations in Georgia and Pennsylvania counties. As the days seemed to lengthen, Schultz occasionally reminded Biden's campaign manager Jen O'Malley Dillon and confidants like veteran strategist Anita Dunn, "My boss is a little anxious to know what's going on." Nerves still jangling late into the week, he offered to have Obama call Biden if it would be useful while they all waited, but neither O'Malley Dillon nor Dunn thought it was necessary to deviate from the plan quite yet.

Still, twice between Tuesday and Saturday Obama called O'Malley Dillon directly for the latest updates, uneasy with the prospect of relying on cable news, which he hated, to keep him posted on the agonizingly slow vote-counting. It would determine not just his old partner's next four years and arguably the country's next epoch, but also how he—and his era—would be remembered. He wouldn't put it like this, but it was hard to ignore that vast swaths of his own legacy were hanging in the balance.

Biden was out on the dock behind his home with his wife, Jill, on the afternoon of Saturday, November 7, trying to find peace overlooking the lake, when it happened. He was ambushed by a pack of adult children and young adult grandchildren screaming, "We won!"

Only then did the phone ring, Obama on the line.

* * *

Biden kept Obama on the phone throughout the transition, though the pace of calls slowed from its general election peak as the president-elect built his cabinet from home in Wilmington and the ex-POTUS first published a volume of presidential memoirs, then went on a publicity tour, then retreated to Hawaii for his annual family trip in December. The new president was eager for advice from his old friend—one of the few people on earth who could give it to him—but only to a point.

He'd quickly gotten tired of the commentary about how he was hiring a ton of old Obama team members for his own administration, though he knew it was inevitable to some degree. The process was always destined to be politically delicate, read as a signal of continuity or breakaway from his old boss, just as George W. Bush's selections had been read closely as indications of his loyalty to his father's administration. Bush and Biden both argued—to little avail—that it was only natural to bring on people with senior government experience, no matter who controlled the last

White House of their party. (The younger Bush ended up hiring an array of his dad's former aides, but also some officials with whom he'd famously clashed, like Donald Rumsfeld.)

What even Obama didn't know was that Biden had been bristling slightly when answering the constant questions about his old boss's influence. He'd been wary of the impression that Obama had helped him win any more than the ex-president would have for any Democrat in his position, and he'd loved hearing—then repeating—the news when he first raised more money as the nominee than Obama had during a comparable time period in 2008. When, as president-elect, he then encouraged his teams to aim to confirm cabinet officials and judges more quickly than Obama had, he insisted it was a matter of the urgency of the moment, and not competitiveness. Still, within his inner circle it was noted with arched eyebrows when, during the transition, the former president referred to Biden and his new vice president, Kamala Harris, as having "the ability to pick up where we left off and keep on going."

Biden saw no inconsistencies in the fact that, at the same time as he held these feelings, he still considered plenty about the Obama years to be worthy of intense study, admiration, and imitation. Biden in fact set out twelve characteristics he wanted in the senior team members who would helm his administration, largely focused on their experience, abilities, and ideological agreement with him, and looking especially for uncontroversial bureaucrats who could fulfill his initial pledge of a return to normalcy with their focus on government experience and willingness to collaborate rather than, in most cases, idiosyncratic subject-matter expertise. He nonetheless ended up with a roster that looked like it was pulled from an Obama administration yearbook.

Before December was out, senior Obama officials or allies had agreed to become Biden's Treasury secretary, Veterans Affairs secretary, and COVID response czar. The list grew as the transition did, too: Obama's old agriculture secretary would be reprising his role, the former surgeon general would take back his own old job, Obama's deputy secretary of Homeland Security would assume the top job in that department, and Obama's friend and national security advisor Susan Rice would become the director of Biden's Domestic Policy Council. An old Senate and administration aide to Obama took over at the Agency for International Development. Biden's climate advisor was an Obama alum, as was his climate envoy, as were his legislative affairs director, his choice for Office of Management and Budget director, and his White House counsel. His National Economic Council director was, as well, and so was the Council of Economic Advisers chair. Even Biden's White House press secretary, the face of his administration, would be Obama's former communications director Jen Psaki.

The tone of DC chatter about the crossover struck Biden as a bit overheated, since all those people had worked for him, too—he was the VP!—and the lists describing the overlap often also tended to include his new chief of staff, secretary of state, national security advisor, and director of national intelligence. All of them had indeed worked for Obama, but each was a Bidenite first.

The reality was that Obama himself had been careful to tread relatively lightly as Biden built his team, not wanting to be seen as cynically or inappropriately seeding his friends throughout the administration, even as he did want the best for his close allies and advocated for some of them. (He was especially gratified to learn of Rice's job, the hiring of former senior White House aide and Obama Foundation COO Yohannes Abraham to be the National Security Council's chief of staff, and the choice of Wally Adeyemo—another former White House advisor who'd become the Obama Foundation president—as deputy Treasury secretary.)

But by the final stretch of the transition in early 2021, once he'd rallied for a pair of Democrats still running for the Senate in Georgia, Obama figured his job was done and he could more or less tune out for a while as Biden took over from Trump. He unplugged ahead of those Senate elections, which were set for January 5.

Back from Hawaii two weeks later, the former president and Michelle piled into the heavily protected Capitol building. It was the frigid morning of Biden's inauguration, and the threat of light snow hung in the air around official Washington, which was still traumatized from the January 6 attack.

If you'd asked him how he was feeling, Obama would have simply said he was happy for Joe, but mostly relieved. He also saw some hope ahead—at least some chance for a national reckoning over Trumpism and real overdue progress on the pandemic, too. He was still conscious that he would never quite be able to escape the Washington fray, that Biden might still want his advice, that Trump's threat wasn't quite vanquished, and that the country was still a long way from healed. But he felt a little less like he was destined to a retirement defined by the constant threat of political explosions. Obama was eager, finally, to be the kind of semidisconnected ex-president he'd long envisioned being.

As he brushed past the beefed-up security phalanx protecting the Capitol, he was still ruminating on what it meant that it was Biden, the man with whom he'd been through so much, who would be the one to take up the tasks. The Bidens hadn't arrived yet—they were due last—and the Obamas were ushered into a holding room where they could wait and warm up a bit before the speeches, before the handoff to Biden was official and they could all truly exhale again.

They found that the space was already occupied when they walked in. The Clintons and the Bushes looked up and briefly paused their quiet but joyous joint celebration of Trump's ouster. They then invited the Obamas to join their circle. One of the room's windows was still cracked. The broken glass was still there.

* * *

It's possible to excavate any relationship for clues about its participants' priorities and beliefs. Examinations of political partnerships or rivalries, in particular, can yield new understandings about their protagonists' motivations and fears. It takes a remarkable political relationship to reveal all that and just as much about a moment in history.

This book is not a comprehensive retelling of the Obama administration's years in power, nor is it a chronological reconstruction of each of the president's and vice president's decisions or disagreements. It does not aim to cover everything important that has happened to either or both of its subjects in the last twenty years, and it is not a pair of profiles of two men who have been profiled plenty. Neither is it the jolly ballad of a straightforward friendship nor a blow-by-blow chronicle of relentless and intricate political maneuvering, just as it is not some sort of sordid tale of a secret rivalry.

Instead, these pages aim to tell the true, winding story of a nearly two-decade relationship that has a claim to being the most consequential of any in twenty-first-century politics, having shaped—both actively and indirectly—not just four presidential campaigns and two different political parties, but also wars, the recovery from a devastating near-depression, movements for social equality, the fight for the future of American democracy, and now, depending on how you're counting, three presidencies. The story is both longer and far more complicated than widely appreciated, starting in 2003 with a pair of men in a hurry who at first could hardly have seemed more different and continuing deep into 2022, with the former partners considering their joint place in history and their individual positions on either side of an antidemocratic abyss. It covers a bond that has at times been tense, affectionate, nonexistent, and ironclad. And it has nearly always been surprising once the public-facing veneer is stripped away, revealing the presidents' degrees of willingness to learn from, disagree with, convince, ignore, tolerate, and embrace one another.

There is both short-term and longitudinal value in studying the dynamic. Appreciating its shifting contours can help us reconsider the modern presidency and vice presidency, especially their limits and opportunities at a time when the executive office is undergoing one of its most radical transformations in decades as its occupants explore its constitutional and practical boundaries. More immediately, the two overanalyzed but insufficiently understood politicians deserve a serious exploration of the consequential events that molded each of them around the other. The popular notion that they share some sort of uncomplicated bromance (to take a word from a never-ending reel of gauzy photo montages, listicles, and memes) sprouted from the truth of a genuinely warm friendship between two men who came from different generations and cultures. But if we want to truly understand the men or their moment, uncritically subscribing to that neat narrative—which ignores real unease and outright tension—benefits neither the public nor the presidents. That their relationship has been complex, and sometimes fraught, and that it is still evolving from a distance does nothing to detract from its extraordinary profundity compared to two and a half centuries' worth of strained ties between presidents and their deputies, and between many presidents and the others who have held the role.

* * *

Biden had said too much, and he knew it. He was in Milwaukee, just shy of a month into his tenure as president, gazing out at Anderson Cooper and a phalanx of CNN cameras. He was trying to promote his pandemic relief legislation, but the host wanted to know about his life in the White House, too, and Biden told the truth.

It was taking the seventy-eight-year-old some time to get used to his new home, even though he'd spent years working in the building. "I get up in the morning and look at Jill and say, 'Where the hell are we?'" he joked. This part wasn't surprising, of course: everyone knew he'd been there for eight years with Obama, but no one expected the transition to be easy now, considering not just that the White House would be an intimidating place for anyone to live, but also taking into account the monumental challenges that Biden had to face after Trump's rampage of a term. "I have only been president for four weeks, and, sometimes, because things are moving so fast—not because of a burden—it feels like four years," he continued. "There's so much happening that you focus on, you're constantly focusing on one problem or opportunity, one right after—*ad seriatim*."

So far, no surprises. But as Biden kept going, Cooper seemed to recognize that the new president was on the cusp of inadvertently dropping a surprising insight into the shape of his interactions with his former boss.

By this point in Biden's life and career, public cracks in the joint image he had built with Obama—shaped over their weekly lunches and their almost daily morning sessions in the Oval Office to receive regular briefs of the world's horrors together—were largely a thing of the past. Now, though, Biden was feeling reflective about his job and the weight of history, and he admitted that he'd only recently realized that he'd never before actually been inside the White House residence—where presidents and their families live, and where they tend to keep their personal lives.

This surprising revelation might have said a lot about his relationship with Obama—How was it possible he had never been inside his friend's home, just feet from their offices?—and the host tried to follow up. But Biden caught himself, and quickly, clumsily pivoted away from it.

This wasn't the time to get into all that.

The legacy of the partnership between Biden and Obama will undoubtedly be a subject for debate by partisans and historians for many decades to come, but no credible analysis will be able to deny that it is genuinely historic—not because of its governing and political substance during the 2008-to-2017 crucible but more concretely because of its sheer longevity and its participants' prolonged, if inconsistent, interdependence. As unlikely as the relationship may have been at its outset, its survival has often been even less likely. Biden is only the ninth person to have served as vice president for two full terms, and he is the only one who then went on to win the top job with such an open reliance on his association with his old boss—let alone a mostly continued affinity, a largely intact joint political project, and an ongoing give-and-take.

Yet the truth is that for all that's known about the political side of their relationship, glimpses into the personal side have been relatively fleeting. As a matter of policy, neither Obama nor Biden speaks about their one-on-one conversations with each other to almost anyone, with only exceedingly rare exceptions. This yearning for privacy reflects an allyship that took years to solidify, and which matured over repeated political travails that forged a mutual understanding—and personal anguish that fueled an implicit trust. As multiple friends of both men said in a series of interviews for this book, it is impossible to understand their bond without internalizing that even at their lowest moments, no one seriously questioned Biden's loyalty to Obama, a rarity for the White House in modern American history.

Nonetheless, the story of the pair is also a tale of an often-unbalanced partnership. Over time, their respective levels of dedication to the alliance have been uneven, usually because Biden thought more about it, a dynamic that persists to this day. This reality is inextricable from the facts that, for all the twists and turns of his distinguished career, Biden had never truly been the protagonist in Washington's collective story for more than a few hours at a time until 2021, and that he remade his public profile and largely reconceived of his own self-image while he was at Obama's side. Obama made no such modifications in Biden's shadow. But, with Biden replacing Donald Trump in the White House, Obama found that his legacy may still be defined largely in terms set by the Biden years.

It is also the story of two political trajectories that are undoubtedly linked but which, in fact, have fluctuated often, and not always together. An uncomfortable but clarifying fact of the time since their paths began converging is that when one was riding high politically, the other was often on a downswing, even if it was temporary or concealed from the public. At various critical moments, too, their analyses of the landscape were less harmonious than outwardly appreciated. While Obama clearly read the country's mood, fears, and hopes far better than the comparatively irrelevant Biden in the lead-up to 2008's election, it was Biden who identified trouble that Obama struggled to acknowledge ahead of 2016, though both were shocked by Trump's victory. In 2020, their separate diagnoses of voters' wishes each ricocheted between accuracy and misguidance until a deadly pandemic scrambled Americans' expectations and their own.

Their years of back-and-forth, too, lend themselves to the conclusion that while Obama's skill as an orator and inspirer was often necessary to his successes, it was also usually insufficient by itself. And while Biden's much-vaunted role as chief operator, especially with respect to Capitol Hill, has often also been insufficient to effect change alone, it has sometimes been necessary. The pair didn't articulate these roles as such to one another, but they only once succeeded in encroaching on each other's political comfort zone. Even then, late in 2020, this role reversal wasn't a conscious choice so much as the product of urgent circumstance.

A reasonable verdict of their joint experience, then, is that the modern presidency requires a mix of some inspirational qualities often styled maddeningly vaguely in the political press as "leadership" and unsentimental execution and realism in the face of ever-mounting structural barriers. Though the perfect balance is perhaps not achievable, as the Obama-Biden duo often painfully demonstrated, it is sometimes approachable, as they have at times also shown. Still, it is little surprise that it took a dozen years of semiformalized partnership for Biden to viscerally understand one view of Obama's. Only as president did Biden absorb, in full, that the twenty-first-century presidency is definitionally a job under siege.

Now, that siege is only accelerating at what Obama and Biden agree is a likely hinge point for the American experiment. And their relationship is one key to interpreting either the heart or the conclusion of a momentous political era. Which it is has yet to be determined.

THE LONG ALLIANCE

PART I

2003—2012

CHAPTER 1

2003–2004

J oe Biden knew better, but he couldn't help himself. It was a warm, sunny day early in 2003, and once again he was thinking about running for president.

Something like this happened more or less every four years since he'd first arrived in the Senate three decades earlier. The conversation would, invariably, start as a low whisper somewhere in his head, or in some aide's notes, or some party boss's late-night bullshitting sessions: *Should Biden run for president this time?* Then he'd let his mind wander.

He rarely let the talk get this far, though, usually because his family would intervene before he turned his Delaware parlor into a proto-campaign war room. His adult children, Beau, Hunter, and Ashley, were encouraging more often than not, but they'd want him to get the timing right. His sister, Val, would almost certainly be his campaign manager, officially or effectively, if he pulled the trigger—she'd run every one of his races since he first ran for class president at Archmere Academy—but she was a realist. His wife, Jill, an English teacher, was the straight-up skeptic. She was wary of a repeat of 1987's disaster, and, well, Joe didn't like to talk about what had happened then. None of them did. They were all right, of course, so Biden tended to come back with the same answer: *No, probably not. Not this year.*

Except sometimes he'd still agree to hear the argument through. (*Can't hurt!*) Then the messaging guru or pollster with the bright idea would get to talking, and Joe would get to thinking about what a campaign would sound like, what his presidential cabinet might look like, what his first bill might be . . . and he'd have to be reeled back in. That was usually Jill's job. This time, though, the family had already had its discussion, and they'd agreed pretty easily that the moment wasn't right for him to try to unseat George W. Bush, a wartime president.

So Biden knew he shouldn't have let this latest small group of strategists into his home to pitch him anyway. It was just that they had some good points. *Didn't they?* He was sixty now and a senior senator, a heavy hitter in Washington. He was years separated from both his last embarrassing campaign and the Clarence Thomas mess, the two big dark marks on his record. He had the foreign policy chops and blue-collar cred to make Bush sweat, and he was no liberal compared to the other potential candidates, a fact that would probably help him in swing-state Ohio, say, or Virginia. Hell, maybe he was the only one who *could* beat Bush. It all sounded pretty good when you put it like that. No one here thought he was past his prime, or repeated the usual Washington insider "joke" that "nobody likes to hear Senator Biden speak more than Senator Biden himself." So Joe, uncharacteristically, kept quiet and kept listening.

So did Jill, who fumed as she sat out by the pool. The family had already decided this didn't make sense. This had to stop before they all got hurt again. She got up and found a Sharpie in the kitchen, and made a decision she and other Biden inner circlers would later recount with reverence. (Jill even wrote about it years later in a memoir.) In big, unmistakable letters, she wrote *NO* on her stomach and, in her bikini, walked into the living room. And that was that.

One year later, Biden had another job in mind. This was typical for a man who had a way of convincing himself that *this* moment—really any moment—was right for him to make *his move*—any move—even though he'd then probably spend months wondering how, exactly, to make it.

It wasn't that he was tired of the Senate. He loved it, and had for basically all his thirty-one years there. He'd put the latest presidential talk behind him and thrown his support behind his friend John Kerry, a colleague he'd first met when they shared a political consultant in 1972. But thirty-one years *was* a long time. He'd already been the top Democrat on two of the chamber's most important committees, first judiciary then foreign relations. And Secretary of State Joe Biden? Now, that sounded pretty good.

Biden knew Kerry was considering giving him the job. They sat together on the Senate's foreign relations panel and they talked about it sometimes when Kerry stole moments away from the campaign trail. So Biden started thinking about how he'd reroute the American wars in Afghanistan and Iraq away from Bush's path (which Biden had once backed enthusiastically), and he tried coming up with a list of Republican senators he might be able to enlist for help on the course-correction, since it would almost certainly be a politically delicate proposition. He leaned into Kerry's campaign, too. On conference calls he offered Kerry, a Vietnam vet, advice on talking about Iraq—a war Biden had voted for and championed, but only after his plan to disarm Saddam Hussein had been squashed by political gamesmanship. He drafted his top foreign policy aide Antony Blinken to generate ideas for Kerry's speeches on international affairs, too, and he even sometimes chimed in with strategies for winning Pennsylvania, where he grew up. And sure, he told Kerry's aides that spring, he'd be happy to speak at the Democratic convention in Boston that July.

In truth, this arrangement was basically an afterthought. Biden understood how these conventions worked by now—this would be his eighth. No one *really* cared what most of the speakers had to say, he knew, and certainly any undecided voter who tuned in would just be interested in hearing from Kerry or some celebrity he'd lined up for an endorsement. Those regular people weren't paying attention to Senate committees or Biden's recent work to avoid a debacle in Iraq. But Biden was all-in on supporting his old friend, and if he was being honest, he really liked the quadrennial schmoozefest. So of course he'd go. He always did. Boston was a quick flight away, and it was an easy favor to John.

He just wouldn't be a headliner, so would only have a few minutes to talk. Fine, he wasn't in the cabinet yet. If nothing else, it would be good for a twelve-second clip on the six o'clock news back home. Something fun to remember when he was secretary.

* * *

Joe Biden was a political world away after midnight on the morning of Saturday, May 8, 2004, when Hillary Clinton got in the backseat of her car in Chicago and reached for her phone. The former first lady, now nearly halfway through her fourth year in the Senate, still had a few hours before she could sleep at home in northwest Washington. She was on her way back to the airport after a long, tiring evening of shaking hands and taking pictures.

Ahead of her still was a flight back to Martin State Airport, north of Baltimore, with Democratic National Committee chair Terry McAuliffe—a dear friend but also the possessor of a motormouth powerful enough that Clinton obviously wouldn't be sleeping much on the flight. It was late and she'd see her husband in the morning, but she knew Bill would want to hear about the night before she took off.

The entire evening almost hadn't happened. Thunderstorms in the Midwest that afternoon had threatened to cancel her trip before she'd even left for Chicago, but she was curious enough about the man who was expecting her in Illinois that she'd told the two aides on the Maryland tarmac with her and her Secret Service duo that she wanted to wait out the weather. It would be worth it, she figured, because of a project she and Bill had been working on for a few months. Ever since she'd decided not to run for president that year, they'd been trying to cultivate and elevate a group of promising pols a generation younger than them. Best-case scenario they'd become useful allies, worst they'd be grateful duds. The informal roster was coming along nicely. Anthony Weiner was a thirty-nine-year-old loudmouth Brooklynite making waves in the House of Representatives, and Harold Ford Jr. was a younger, smoother congressman from Memphis with big ambitions for the Senate and beyond. The Clintons were also watching John Edwards, a helmet-haired North Carolina senator who'd just ended his presidential campaign but looked like a good bet to join Kerry on the national ticket that summer.

For a few weeks now, Clinton had been hearing murmurs about this Senate candidate in Illinois, too. His buzz sounded different, somehow more electric than the usual pundit-class rumors she was used to hearing. Dick Durbin, the state's usually dry sitting Democratic senator, swore by him, and Jon Corzine, the Goldman Sachs exec turned New Jersey senator now in charge of the Democrats' Senate fundraising operation, gushed about him, too. There was plenty of reason to be skeptical, and that was putting it nicely: This guy was just a state senator, and how could you get past his name? When Clinton's aide Huma Abedin had first heard it, she'd written it down for her boss as "Barak Obama," missing the c. Was his charisma really so overwhelming?

Still, it looked like he'd be a US senator in a few months, and now he was in search of some campaign cash. And, it turned out, he wanted to use Clinton's star power for a night. So sure, she was happy to fly out and headline a fundraiser with him at a private club, then another at a fancy hotel. She'd have to meet him eventually.

A few hours later, she waited for the former president to pick up the phone as she sped through pitch-black Illinois. "Bill," she said when his Arkansas drawl came on the line, "I just met our first African American president."

Clinton was, if anything, atypically late to Barack Obama's unlikely whisper network of DC insiders. Similar scenes of awe had quietly been popping up around town throughout the first half of the year. In February, liberal Chicago congresswoman Jan Schakowsky had tagged along with the Congressional Black Caucus on a trip to the White House to discuss the coup in Haiti. After the meeting, she went to shake Bush's hand and saw him draw back in apparent shock, his eyes fixed on the OBAMA campaign button on her lapel. Figuring he thought it said OSAMA, Schakowsky assured him: "Mr. President, it's *Obama*. Barack *Obama*, he's running for United States Senate." Bush, carefully, replied, "I never heard of him." Schakowsky assured him, "You will, Mr. President."

In the House gym on Capitol Hill that spring, a former congressman approached Senator Harry Reid and told him, "I got somebody you should take a look at, a state senator from Illinois." Reid, a quiet former boxer who brooked no bullshit and who was rising in the Senate—and who was therefore a useful man to know if you wanted a future there yourself— asked for this star's name. Hearing it, he paused with a thought similar to Bush's. "You gotta be kidding me," he frowned.

This was all, more or less, part of the plan. Obama and his campaign team back in Chicago's Loop could deal with the disbelief about his name. It was the word-of-mouth they were interested in carefully nurturing.

To some extent, they'd known it was coming. Obama himself had never exactly been short on confidence—no one who writes a memoir in his thirties is. He saw how people looked at him, talked about him ever since he'd been profiled in the *New York Times* as the first Black editor of the *Harvard Law Review*. He knew his academic brilliance was obvious, that, under the right circumstances, he could deliver a knockout speech, and that his personal story—Kansan mother, absent Kenyan father—was not just objectively interesting but clearly different. In 2002, at forty, and just two years after getting crushed in a congressional primary, he'd gathered about a dozen close allies and family members at his friend Valerie Jarrett's Hyde Park condo to pitch them on a run for the Senate. It'd be a big step up, but he was getting painfully bored in the legislature, and he thought he'd have a decent shot at beating the Republican incumbent, Peter Fitzgerald, if he could raise the cash to do it. No one thought it was a great idea at first—his political advisor Dan Shomon refused to run a Senate campaign, and another political consultant, David Axelrod, urged him to think about waiting for Chicago's mayoral race to open up instead—not least because he'd probably be entering a crowded field of famous locals in the Senate race and barely anyone had any clue who he was, even in Chicago. But Obama's wife, Michelle, a rising lawyer in the city, OK'd it, and the candidate-to-be went ahead with the planning.

He'd faced a crossroads almost immediately in the form of an invitation from his longtime supporter Bettylu Saltzman, an important activist, to an antiwar rally that October. The politics of the moment weren't obvious for a young Democrat looking for a future beyond Springfield, Illinois. Bush was marching toward war in Iraq, and plenty of liberals were furious, but it wasn't easy for national-level Democrats to oppose Bush openly without furious blowback and declarations of their lack of patriotism. On the other hand, the crowd would be made up of lefties, not triangulating senators. Obama told Axelrod, who spurned the advances of high-paying former Wall Street trader Blair Hull to join Obama's campaign after recognizing his potential, that he wanted to use the opportunity to make the case for international alliances and against flimsy justifications for war. He'd be introducing himself as the left-leaning ex-organizer that many expected him to be, but also, he hoped, a pragmatist willing to buck political convenience.

He set off to write the speech longhand—a sure sign that he was taking it seriously, since he usually spoke off the cuff or relied on staff to write his remarks if he didn't much care about the speech of the day. Axelrod, who rarely escaped comparisons to a walrus because of his distinctive mustache, called fellow consultant Pete Giangreco to gauge the wisdom of the approach. Giangreco, who'd also turned down other candidates to join Obama, summed it up: The candidate would get points for honesty, but would he look too weak? Obama needed not just Black voters in Chicago and activist-adjacent liberals but cautious white suburbanites, too, and this was a national issue they were all watching closely.

Obama opened the speech by insisting, three times, "I don't oppose all wars," before making the turn: "What I am opposed to is a dumb war. What I am opposed to is a rash war." In the moment, it wasn't clear that he was onto something. "Did he really have to call it 'dumb'?" Giangreco asked Axelrod. "We have people going over there and dying." Obama, though, struck a nerve. A few months later, a focus group of white women in Northbrook, outside Chicago, effused over him, comparing him to liberal heroes Paul Simon, the former Illinois senator, and Bobby Kennedy. Obama's support was growing, but he was still running behind both Hull and another better-known candidate, state comptroller Dan Hynes, with just months until the March 2004 Democratic primary.

This didn't stop Obama and his team from starting to think a bit bigger. For one thing, he stood a decent chance of becoming just the third Black senator since Reconstruction, and he obviously deserved a platform. Both Axelrod and Giangreco were working on John Edwards's presidential campaign at the time, too, and Axelrod used that perch to talk up his Senate prospect to national reporters eager for tips outside the cynical DC bubble. Obama's name started appearing in articles as a potential long-term prospect for *something*.

Yet back in Illinois his team held off on spending too much cash to promote him, on the candidate's orders. Obama had told his campaign manager, Jimmy Cauley, an irreverent Kentuckian, that he'd run up his credit card debt in his failed 2000 race and that Michelle had promised to kill him if he did it again. So it was only as the closing stretch approached that they started spending money on TV ads that portrayed Obama as both an aspirational changemaker and a regular guy. The first one featured a slogan that Obama found trite but Axelrod wanted to use to appeal to Black voters in Chicago. Obama only relented to "Yes We Can" when Michelle agreed that it would resonate. Another showed Obama with a farmer talking about working with Republicans; a third was about union jobs. The final ad, which Obama at first considered cheesy and slightly unseemly, featured Paul Simon's daughter comparing the candidate to her father, who had just died, shortly before the ex-senator was supposed to endorse Obama.

The spots did half the work. "I've been going around this race for two years, going to every Rotary supper, and only now do people go up to me in the grocery store," he told Cauley after they started airing. Meanwhile, news broke that Hull's second ex-wife had, at one point, been granted an order of protection against him. The revelation spurred a drip-drip of brutal reporting that culminated in the revelation that Hull was accused of being violent and verbally abusive, and had once allegedly threatened to kill her.

Hull's support collapsed just as Obama's rose: in the final weeks before the election, Obama's polling jumped from the midteens into the forties. "You believe this shit?" he asked his consultants, who barely did. None knew how to react when, on March 16, he won the primary by nearly thirty points, demolishing their projections with just about every group of Illinoisans, not just in Chicago and its suburbs but also including the group they'd been most worried about: less educated white voters outside the city. Even Obama had—atypically—underestimated his appeal. It didn't take a once-in-a-generation talent or a fully funded consultant budget to recognize that maybe Obama was onto something no other Democrat had quite figured out. These were the exact kinds of voters Kerry was starting to struggle with ahead of November, and that Democrats more broadly had been having trouble with since the Bill Clinton–era 1990s.

* * *

Bush was still reasonably popular in the spring of 2004, and his war in Iraq—all anyone could talk about, at least aside from the final *The Lord of the Rings* movie and wardrobe malfunctions—wasn't far behind. Both the president and the war, however, had started their long-term decline, and the populace had begun to retreat into the partisan corners it tended to frequent in the months before a presidential election ever since Kerry had effectively become the Democrats' nominee in March. Still, Kerry's party was grappling for coherence in opposition to the Republican administration, unsure of where to find hope or inspiration in the post-Clinton years and unclear on how to galvanize its half of a country that was still getting used to its new wartime reality and the attendant culture.

It would have been ridiculous to suggest that the senior senator from Delaware—three decades into his career as a DC fixture and convinced that he was finally about to take the next step he'd been trying to figure out for years, even if it was contingent on someone else's success—and the up-and-coming Senate nominee from Illinois—semianonymous but clearly inspiring and bursting with self-confidence—were on anything resembling a collision course, or even set for an encounter anyone should care about.

If they had a common project, it was considering the dawn of a country and world reordered by 9/11 and America's subsequent military excursions. But then, that's what everyone was trying to figure out. For now, they were essentially operating in different political galaxies. A lot would have to change for both of them, and fast, for their trajectories to bend toward each other.

* * *

The people who made up Obama's inner circle—friends like Jarrett, a shrewd and influential local operative and businesswoman, but also Axelrod, a well-known and thoughtful reporter turned consultant who was becoming a confidant—had been around politics long enough to recognize an opportunity when it presented itself. Not only had Obama unexpectedly crushed his primary opposition, but he also suddenly looked likely to be a senator. Peter Fitzgerald, the Republican incumbent, had decided not to run for reelection, so Obama now faced unknown former investment banker Jack Ryan, and was clearly favored. That meant he had a bit more time on his hands than he'd expected, which he could use to position himself for a splashy entry to DC. He was already turning into a minor political celebrity, welcomed for meet and greets and fundraisers after the primary by East Coasters who fancied themselves savvy donors. The Clintons hosted one, financier George Soros another.

It was a lot to take in, even for someone constitutionally allergic to second-guessing himself, and Obama withdrew slightly in private, growing more contemplative and talking less, but asking more pointed questions about the campaign plan in strategy meetings. It would soon be clear to those outside his immediate inner orbit that he was planning for the long term.

After the primary, Axelrod and his business partner David Plouffe set out a plan that was a long shot but that could cement Obama as a star: they wanted to convince Kerry to offer Obama the keynote address slot at July's convention in Boston. Their pitch was simple. Here was a young, dynamic speaker—a rare bright spot down the ballot in a challenging environment for Democrats nationwide—who could draw attention away from Bush and onto the theoretical vibrancy of Kerry's party. The two Davids and a DC-experienced communications staffer named Robert Gibbs, who joined Obama from Kerry's campaign, tried to schedule Obama and Kerry to be in the room together. They succeeded first at a Chicago fundraiser, and the reviews came back positive; Kerry was impressed. He was doubly so after they appeared together again at a public roundtable discussion on health care and trade. Meanwhile, the trio of strategists started mentioning Obama more in conversations with friends in the nominee's orbit, which didn't go unnoticed back in his Boston headquarters.

Kerry's team didn't mind the not-terribly-subtle effort. His campaign manager, Mary Beth Cahill, had been trying to convince the TV networks to cover more of the convention live than they usually did, and Obama was becoming the kind of sizzling draw that might entice them to consider it. Kerry—a party stalwart but hardly anyone's idea of a political dynamo after two decades in the Senate despite his entrée to national politics as a famous antiwar Vietnam hero—needed the political help, too. Polling showed him within striking distance of Bush throughout the spring, but seldom in the lead. Bob Shrum, Kerry's strategist, brought the idea of elevating Obama to the nominee. "This guy has an unlimited future, and if we give him this opportunity that'll really help him," he said. Kerry shrugged. "That's fine with me," he replied. "My future is now."

Cahill called Obama directly to deliver the news. Obama, riding between events, thanked her and turned to Axelrod. "I know what I want to say," he told his strategist, who looked back, curious. It was immediately obvious Obama had been ruminating on this in his typical grand terms, and he told Axelrod he wanted to tell his own story as part of America's, as the strategist later recalled in his memoir. It would certainly be different from the speeches that every other Democratic politician would be delivering.

* * *

About two hours before John Kerry was due to speak on the final night of his July convention in Boston, Biden half-jogged to the lectern. He hadn't thought as much about this speech as some others he'd given in his career, mostly because he'd been saying all this stuff in public for months. But it was still the national stage, a juicy chance to set out a new center-left vision for American engagement in the world, maybe, or at least to send the message that he was worthy of the country's attention again.

He was introduced as the Senate foreign relations committee's ranking member, a formal title that would have read as inscrutable jargon to casual viewers if there were any, but which, to the crowd of professional partisans inside the FleetCenter, was meant to convey his gravitas—*here's the top Democrat working on international policy.* Almost immediately, he got to the point. "Tonight, our country stands at the hinge of history, and America's destiny is literally at stake," he said to the quiet arena, which just seconds earlier had been grooving to Mavis Staples's soulful belting of "America the Beautiful." The next president's "overwhelming obligation," he continued, "is clear: make America stronger, make America safer, and win the death struggle between freedom and radical fundamentalism."

The C-SPAN cameras panned out as Biden kept going with his grim warning, and they revealed an audience only half-engaged as he insisted an opportunity lay ahead. They caught a bored-looking Hillary Clinton, who'd spoken from that stage with much more fanfare on Monday, adjusting her hair. Biden, though, plowed on, starting to shout a bit, as he always did when he was tired or frustrated—or when he could tell he wasn't connecting, or when he wanted to make sure you couldn't miss that *this* point was important. This had been his style for years, since before he was first elected as a twenty-nine-year-old over three decades earlier, back when his childhood stutter and tough upbringing—child of a man who moved the family to find work and then reinvented himself as a used car salesman, an adventurous but self-conscious golden son in an Irish Catholic family raised on tales of seeking fairness and the importance of maintaining the honor of the family name—were a more recent memory. Back long before his beautiful young family was destroyed, and before he'd become the Democratic Party's rising star, then flamed out, and then clawed his way back to genuine—if self-serious—importance, never letting himself forget the nadirs but also refusing to wallow.

"We were told by this administration we would pay no price for going it alone! But that is obviously wrong," he continued, to patchy applause. "Because we waged a war in Iraq virtually alone, we are responsible for the aftermath virtually alone."

It was all straightforward Democratic fare, the kind of argument the nominee had been making all year, too: Bush had lost the world's trust. This audience of political pros and hobbyists not only knew it by heart but also knew the real headliner—the presidential candidate—was still a few hours away. When Biden turned to the matter of Kerry for the first time, he followed the campaign's instructions to project martial strength to counter Republicans' accusations of wimpiness. "John Kerry, when he is commander in chief, will not hesitate to unleash the awesome power of our military on any nation or group that does us harm, and without asking anyone's permission," he said. But you could trust his judgment, Biden added. He slipped briefly, calling Kerry "John Kennedy," but rolled forward without acknowledging the mistake (or wishful thinking), instead precisely hitting his lines about Kerry's preparedness. "It's time to recapture the totality of America's strength, it's time to restore our nation to the respect it once had." Biden closed after ten uneventful minutes with the kind of lofty line he loved, even if it could mean whatever you wanted it to: "It's time to reclaim America's soul."

The cameras, looking for something vaguely interesting to broadcast, panned out and found Clinton again, this time zooming in on the back of her head as she talked to a reporter, facing away from the stage. They returned to the set only when the next speaker strolled on. Here was retired general Wesley Clark, a failed presidential candidate, reporting to the mic to insist on a lot of the same stuff Biden just had, only with more reminders that he'd actually served in wars. Biden's time on-screen was done; he hadn't so much as cracked a smile.

No one in the crowd was likely to disagree much with what Biden had said, nor were they likely to remember it. He was background noise, even though he was speaking in what should have been the buildup to the convention's highest-profile evening. It was already obvious that all anyone would remember from Boston had already happened two days earlier.

Obama had been prone to thinking expansively about his place in the world since long before that summer, and he'd long harbored the conviction— rarely expressed, but deeply embedded—that his unique personal story, oratorical skills, and belief in consensus-driven liberal-flecked politics that transcended partisan bickering would, eventually, inspire a lot of people as long as he introduced himself the right way. A convention wasn't necessarily the intuitive place for him to do it: he'd had a bad experience at Al Gore's confab four years earlier, buying a cheap last-second Southwest ticket to Los Angeles only to be turned away from the rental car desk when his credit card was declined. Confined to the outer rungs of the Staples Center because he wasn't important enough to get anywhere near the stage after losing his congressional primary that spring, he ran into Raja Krishnamoorthi, a fellow young Chicagoan who'd worked on Obama's 1998 state senate campaign, and sighed at his circumstances. Keynote addresses could be fraught, too: Obama had seen Harold Ford Jr. flop that year, and he kept that uncomfortable memory in mind as he sat down to write.

From the start, Obama told Axelrod and Robert Gibbs he would write this speech himself. They knew he was a talented writer but agreed partly because he was proposing to write something personal and partly because he sometimes came off as flat when he delivered someone else's words, even if they were a professional speechwriter's. Gibbs replied by sending Obama copies of keynote speeches that had worked out well, including an especially galvanizing trio: Mario Cuomo's legendary 1984 address, Ann Richards's from 1988, and Barbara Jordan's from 1976.

As the summer aged, Obama took to his yellow legal pads between spurts of work at the state senate in Springfield—sometimes he wrote in the bathroom at the capitol—and on his long car rides back home to Chicago. After midnight one evening in July, he felt like he finally had a satisfactory draft and sent it to Axelrod, who was vacationing in Florence. By this point, Axelrod's work for Edwards was done and he was fully bought into the Obama project—that spring he'd recruited Democrats' leading speech coach Michael Sheehan to help Obama by telling Sheehan that this candidate was "the one," and that they had to take this speech seriously, since Obama could "go all the way." He read the speech as it printed off the fax machine, handing pages off to his wife, Susan, as he finished them. By the third one, he turned to her and predicted the speech might go down in history.

It still needed work—it was at least two times too long, for one thing—and Obama's inner circle was still nervous about how Kerry would present him in Boston. So as another consultant dove in on the first of more than a dozen rounds of drafts with Obama, the rest of the team worked its connections to make sure Obama would get sufficient promotion from the nominee and a spot safely in the prime-time lineup.

The whispers built in Boston even as Obama was stuck in Springfield for budget votes that inconveniently dragged on, forcing Jimmy Cauley, Obama's campaign manager, to reserve a private plane to shuttle them and Michelle to Massachusetts whenever Obama was finally free to go. Obama wasn't slated to speak until the final Tuesday of the month, but the team's real deadline for getting there was the preceding Sunday morning, when he was booked for *Meet the Press*.

They got in with only a few hours to spare and little time to prep. Obama wasn't quite nervous, but he was extraconscious that he was walking into a defining moment for his career, no matter how it went. Almost immediately, *Meet the Press* host Tim Russert caught Obama off guard by asking him to answer for a quote he'd given *The Atlantic* that would be published the next day. Obama had been critical of Kerry (he "just doesn't have that oomph") but now explained that he'd spoken to the magazine months earlier, when Kerry was still developing as a candidate. Russert brought up Obama's 2002 Chicago speech opposing the Iraq war, which had helped put him on the map, and asked if Kerry had been wrong to vote for invasion. Obama had at least prepared for this question, and parried it by noting the senator had access to information he didn't, then pivoting: what he was concerned about now was the path ahead.

The rest of the weekend's media blitz was only slightly less perilous. For the first time in front of a national audience, he got—and dodged—ridiculous-sounding questions about whether he'd run for president one day. Still, Obama tried keeping his mind on his speech and, when he had time, on meeting the kinds of people who he hoped could help him in Washington. He recognized Bill Clinton's former chief of staff and budget director Leon Panetta walking into the arena, introduced himself, and asked if they could meet about budget policy after the convention.

Mostly, though, he holed up at his hotel and his practice room under the stage. The Kerry campaign had already thrown Obama two significant bones that no one else got. First, they'd originally offered him an eight-minute speaking slot but conceded seventeen minutes after Axelrod's haggling wore them down. (Obama's first drafts clocked in at more like twenty-seven.) Second, they granted him far more leeway than typical to share his own words, rather than the nominee's preferred message of military strength and international responsibility. They'd agreed to this when it became clear he wanted to intertwine his own history with talk about values that all Americans shared, which was consistent with a vague unity theme Kerry was also pushing. Their condition was that Obama refrain from ripping into Bush—they were desperate to keep things mostly positive that night—which suited his personal political interest in positioning himself above the fray of workaday politics.

The real trouble began when Kerry's top staffers reviewed what should have been a nearly final draft. Obama had written an emotional arc that would crescendo with a riff about transcending political divides, referring to "red" and "blue" states in a nod to the trendy way of analyzing politics ever since TV networks used those colors to identify Republicans and Democrats in their 2000 election broadcasts. This was too close to Kerry's script, and a young speechwriter named Jon Favreau came down to talk to Gibbs. Gibbs knew how Obama felt about the line and replied: *you tell him*. When Obama heard the request to cut the line, which was really a demand, he was furious and refused to budge, creating an awkward stand-off in the bowels of the stadium.

Obama often got quiet and stewed when he was angry, and after some choice words he stalked back to the hotel in search of a resolution, Axelrod in tow. The strategist tried reasoning with the candidate. The way he figured it, Obama just had to give up a line and Kerry would give him the chance to speak to twenty million people. That was a pretty good bargain, and he should just forget about the line.

Obama reluctantly relented but promised he wouldn't forget about it. Axelrod and Gibbs, who was on his way to earning Obama's trust with his quick attitude and DC chops, had a bigger concern, anyway. It took real work to get Obama used to speaking into a microphone for an arena-size crowd, and it was still a work in progress in Boston. Months before, Axelrod had explained to Sheehan that Obama was comfortable speaking to a church-style audience, but that not only had he never used a teleprompter before, he also had a hard time stopping himself from yelling. Sheehan walked him through the mechanics of talking to an audience split between a loud convention hall and the produced broadcast that most people would be watching on TV—a dynamic that was old hat to almost every other speaker in Boston. To make it look on-air like the crowd was booming, Obama should talk—but not scream—over the applause, assuming there was any.

Obama walked into the FleetCenter the afternoon of his speech after days of run-throughs, and turned to David Mendell, a *Chicago Tribune* reporter he knew. As Mendell later recounted, Obama, alluding to the NBA's new teen superstar, said, "I'm LeBron, baby, I can play on this level. I got some game." It was self-consciously arrogant, enough to be disarming, but also true, and thus classic Obama. It was also a vivid reflection of how his confidence—or at least his unwillingness to let himself get inside his own head—persisted even though he also knew he only got one chance to introduce himself to the country. Inside, he took Gibbs's tie because they determined it looked better than his own. When his speaking slot approached, Axelrod walked him up to the edge of the stage, visibly nervous. Obama put an arm on his shoulder and coolly reassured him that he knew what he was doing.

His team did, too. Obama's emergence hadn't all been inspiration and lucky timing. They already knew that the moment had to be nurtured, and then carefully designed, before Obama could seize it. A few weeks earlier, Cauley had gotten a call from Tom Lindenfeld, a former Axelrod business partner who'd helped Obama in the primary and who was now running the party's delegate floor operations at the convention. They needed to pay for signs to distribute in the audience for Obama's speech, Lindenfeld told him. Cauley hesitated—it would cost around $20,000—but Lindenfeld insisted it would be an important part of the visual on TV. He had advice for the design, too: make the signs blue with white lettering—keep it clean, just Obama's name—on noncoated paper so the arena lights didn't reflect off them and render them unreadable. He also advised Cauley to make the sign order bigger than the standard one, since they wanted to create the impression that the arena was extrapacked and extraenthusiastic about Obama when he spoke. Cauley relented, but Lindenfeld still had to convince the Teamsters on-site to help him shepherd in the signs after the truck delivering them broke down in Ohio and delayed their arrival past the Secret Service's deadline for bringing material into the arena. With just hours to go, he distributed the placards not just on the convention floor and around the lower bowl, as was standard for every speaker not named Kerry, but also up and down the FleetCenter's tiers.

The effect, at first, was underwhelming in the room. Only the delegates directly in front of Obama and in the Illinois section held the signs aloft when he walked onstage and struggled to modulate his voice's volume for the TV audience's benefit. Axelrod and Gibbs slipped out from backstage to watch from the arena, and found themselves standing behind George Stephanopoulos, the former Bill Clinton advisor turned ABC host, and Jeff Greenfield, a journalist who'd come up as a speechwriter for Bobby Kennedy.

It didn't take long, however, for a murmur to break out across the convention floor alongside the rustle of signs being picked up from row to row. Obama, in a voice that seemed an octave too low for his body—but quickly adjusted to the arena's volume—started by talking about his father, who was "born and raised in a small village in Kenya. He grew up herding goats, went to school in a tin-roof shack." He talked about his veteran maternal grandfather, who enlisted after Pearl Harbor, and spoke about what it took for him to make it to this stage: "That is the true genius of America, a faith in simple dreams, an insistence on small miracles. That we can tuck in our children at night and know that they are fed and clothed and safe from harm. That we can say what we think, write what we think, without hearing a sudden knock on the door."

It was unlike any other speech the crowd had heard or would hear in Boston—more ambitious and more hopeful, and for long stretches not obviously about Kerry vs. Bush at all—and Obama was getting into a groove. He spoke about struggling Illinoisans he'd met and then, occasionally, about Kerry.

And then he hit his stride, building up to the carefully workshopped lines Kerry and Favreau had forced him to alter. He discussed collective responsibility, community connection, and a fierce yearning for fairness among neighbors as fundamentally American values.

It is that fundamental belief—I am my brother's keeper, I am my sister's keeper—that makes this country work. It's what allows us to pursue our individual dreams, and yet still come together as one single American family. E pluribus unum. Out of many, one.

Now even as we speak, there are those who are prepared to divide us. The spin masters, the negative ad peddlers who embrace the politics of "anything goes." Well, I say to them tonight: there is not a liberal America and a conservative America—there's the United States of America. There is not a Black America and a white America and Latino America and Asian America, there is the United States of America. The pundits like to slice and dice our country into red states and blue states: red states for Republicans, blue states for Democrats. But I've got news for them, too. We worship an awesome God in the blue states, and we don't like federal agents poking around our libraries in the red states. We coach Little League in the blue states, and yes, we've got some gay friends in the red states. There are patriots who opposed the war in Iraq and there are patriots who supported the war in Iraq. We are one people, all of us pledging allegiance to the stars and stripes, all of us defending the United States of America.

Well-designed conventions have a way of overwhelming their crowds, between the dramatic lighting and booming acoustics and inspirational music and videos. But now the effect wasn't limited to the delegates, who had in many cases flown across the country specifically because they wanted to be bowled over by Kerry and his lineup. As Axelrod later recalled, he saw Greenfield lean over to Stephanopoulos and say, "This is a great fucking speech."

Obama's life just changed, Axelrod told Gibbs as the applause continued. The memory of Cuomo's 1984 appearance was inescapable. Until that moment, it had been history's most famous convention address. That speech, everyone knew, had made Cuomo a national celebrity. It had also almost immediately started a round of earnest whispers: *that guy should really run for president in four years.* The camera panned, repeatedly, to a smiling and applauding Reverend Jesse Jackson, and to an obviously impressed Hillary Clinton, who nodded slightly.

* * *

The Friday after the convention, Obama was ticketed for a budget flight back to the Midwest with the rest of the Illinois delegation. This amused him more than anything—"Jimmy, you flew me down here on a G5 and you're taking me back in a cattle car?" he ribbed Cauley—but the arrangement devolved into chaos almost as soon as they got to Boston's Logan International Airport.

Obama was mobbed when he stepped inside, surrounded by Democrats traveling home from the convention carrying leftover signs and asking for autographs. Once he waded through the crowd, he was pulled aside for an extra screening. Cauley let his frustration bubble over. "You don't know who this is?!" he asked the TSA agent. Obama looked back, annoyed, if unsurprised, by the security check. "Jimmy, my name is *Barack Obama*, I know what my life is," he said.

He no longer did. The rest of the airport, which was starting to look unnavigable as word spread that Obama was in the terminal, was now a problem, too. Fearing for his candidate's safety and patience, Cauley convinced an American Airlines representative to let Obama wait in the lounge before his flight, and after retrieving him from the TSA, they slipped inside.

They'd barely been able to catch their breath when Cauley's phone started ringing with an unknown number. He picked up, only to find former Soviet president Mikhail Gorbachev on the other line, wishing to congratulate Obama for his speech. After determining that this wasn't a joke, he handed the phone off to Obama and stepped outside to let them talk.

It was, finally, a good chance for Cauley to catch his breath, and to think about what on Earth was happening. Clearly, whatever it was, it was bigger than he'd signed up for. Outside the lounge the crowds had subsided, and the operative looked around for something to do.

Joe and Jill Biden quietly sat alone and unnoticed by the window, waiting for their own flight out of town, when Cauley approached. The Bidens were gracious when he introduced himself—Obama's speech had obviously been great, Biden thought, though he was more taken by its focus on everyday Americans than by his unity talk. He told Cauley that his young candidate had plenty of potential.

But Biden had been around long enough—had gone to enough conventions, had seen enough keynote addresses—to know better than to fall for the celebrity aura that was already settling around Obama. Biden hadn't really spent much time thinking about Obama at all that week—Kerry's campaign was the real story, as far as he was concerned. Still, since he had some time, he might as well make sure Cauley understood that it wouldn't necessarily be smooth sailing from here.

Listen, Biden said, unprompted. There's a right way and a wrong way to do what you're about to do.

Obama would be erring gravely if he tried to spin this one speech into political superstardom right away, Biden suggested. He had to prove himself still, to demonstrate he was as substantive as he was stylish. Biden could still remember how John Glenn, the world-famous astronaut, had settled into the Senate, but there was a more recent example, too. Look at how Hillary Clinton had done it in her first few years in the Senate, he told Cauley. Instead of bursting onto the Capitol Hill scene in 2001 on the strength of her fame, she'd kept her head down, worked on unsexy issues, and made some important, policy-minded friends. Biden then looked at Cauley like he was sharing something momentous, wisdom that could only come from a three-decade veteran of the world's greatest deliberative body. Make sure, he said seriously, that he's a workhorse, and not a show horse.

Obama sat inside the lounge about forty feet away, oblivious of the conversation, let alone the advice, which was really the conventional wisdom.

It was the first time, but far from the last, that Obama's and Biden's political trajectories were crossing as they headed in opposite directions, their reads of the political environment subtly clashing months before anyone could realize it.

* * *

Obama wasn't exactly surprised to find himself here, on the precipice of power, just four years after getting stomped in a little-noticed House primary, which itself was just four years after he'd been elected to the state senate. It was already one of the quickest, least likely rises anyone in politics could remember, but, well, in his own mind he *was* LeBron, baby. Still, he could not possibly have predicted the circumstances. His good fortune was compounded a few weeks before the convention when his Republican opponent, Ryan, imploded amid news that his ex-wife had accused him of taking her to sex clubs and trying to coerce her into having sex in front of people. The state GOP settled on replacing him with Alan Keyes—a Black far-right perennial candidate who stood no shot of winning but who, party bosses figured, might be able to scuff Obama's image. The result was that, yet again, Obama found himself under far less immediate political pressure than most candidates would be a few months before election day.

He was looking forward to returning to some version of normalcy back in Chicago. He'd enjoyed campaigning mostly under the radar early in the primary—he only agreed to pay for a campaign SUV when reporters started tailing his car as he drove it to events—but bristled at the inconveniences of even the local spotlight. He went to great lengths to hide his smoking habit, which embarrassed him, and hoped to use the postconvention respite to spend some time with Michelle and his two young daughters, Sasha and Malia, whom he hadn't seen enough of in recent weeks.

He knew, of course, that he'd picked up some buzz. Viewing it all with the detachment of a man who read the world in terms of story lines, he found the resulting spectacle vaguely amusing rather than exciting. The night of his convention speech, Cauley and another aide had to bear-hug Obama just to get him inside the room where they'd planned an after-party, it was suddenly so packed with well-wishers. Michelle had refused to go inside, even when informed that a celebrity—Steve Buscemi—was there. But, Obama figured, this kind of attention was probably mostly confined to a crowd that went out of its way to attend conventions in the first place: political operatives and obsessives.

A few days later, however, reality started to set in. For one thing, Random House was going to reprint *Dreams from My Father*. He'd initially pitched the book as being about his time at Harvard Law School, but he submitted it as a memoir and exploration of his identity. It sold OK when it came out in 1995 but then quickly settled into obscurity. Now, though, Obama would be making real money off his writing for the first time. Then there was his new normal at home. Walking back to his car from campaign headquarters after a planning retreat, Obama was inundated with honks of greeting from the street; one man even stopped his cab and got out to say hi.

Still, maybe this was Chicago-specific? He agreed to take the family on a "summer vacation tour" of the state, during which he'd hit thirty-nine counties and thirty-nine cities in five days, and they were looking forward to the getaway from the city and spotlight. Almost immediately, though, he had to abandon the RV. Hundreds, and sometimes thousands, of people were unexpectedly showing up to these suddenly rocking small-town events, slowing him down and turning the tour into a no-sleep week of glad-handing and highway sprints that Obama privately started calling "the Bataan Death March" while he rode in an SUV apart from his family.

OK, Obama thought, *fine*. Clearly he'd broken through. He was surprised, but gratified, by the reception. Surely, though, it was limited to Illinois? This illusion, too, was shattered a few weeks later, when he went on a run in Martha's Vineyard—where the family was vacationing—and noticed people taking pictures of him jogging. Michelle, for one, lightened the mood in moments like this. "Must've been a pretty good speech," she'd say, in what soon became a private refrain. But the RV tour changed her thinking. Barack needed better security, she thought, and she told his aides as much. She was right, they admitted—her husband was now receiving threats. They hired private security and started screening the packages that arrived unbidden to the office.

That tour also delivered Obama a positive development: a burgeoning relationship with Dick Durbin, the Democratic senator from Illinois, who appeared with him in public and started counseling him more seriously in private. This was useful for Obama and Axelrod's next project, which was to use this newfound celebrity—Charles Barkley swung through Chicago to see him one day, Harry Belafonte came calling another—not just to pad his lead but also to start making friends in DC.

First, though, he needed to learn the ropes. In the constellation of Democratic senators who could be useful to Obama when he eventually got to town, South Dakota's Tom Daschle, who led the Democrats in the Senate, was on top. Daschle was eager to help Obama, who peppered him with questions about how DC worked. But Daschle's main concern was, first, winning Senate seats, and he enlisted Obama to raise and send campaign cash to fellow candidates more in need of the funds. This opened Obama's eyes to one ugly aspect of Washington he hadn't had to worry about so much up to that point: the unrelenting cash dash. On one call, a fellow Senate candidate asked Obama for a six-figure donation. Obama shook his head after hanging up. "What the fuck? I'm a state senator!" Daschle, however, was in a tough reelection fight of his own, and as Daschle's standing looked more precarious with election day approaching, Obama started spending more time talking to Reid, who dispatched him to visit with other candidates in person.

Obama trod carefully into the fall. His plan to prove he could be a team player for Democrats had to be balanced with a studied avoidance of any possible whiff of controversy, or any suggestion that he was actually more liberal than he was. That image would not only dent the above-it-all reputation he was trying to cultivate but also potentially damage the party overall, now that he was becoming one of its faces while Kerry focused on winning over so-called security moms in the political middle. When Obama visited San Francisco to raise money, he insisted he not be photographed anywhere near the mayor, a fellow Democrat named Gavin Newsom, who had started a national firestorm by sensationally authorizing same-sex marriages that weren't legal.

Obama followed the cautious plan, and deep into the fall, he mulled over his loose expectations for his first few months in Washington with a rotating cast of advisors including Axelrod, Gibbs, and Jarrett, but also Durbin, Daschle, and the South Dakotan's chief of staff, Pete Rouse, a friendly but nonetheless imposing fixer and strategist who'd been around so long he was known in town as "the 101st senator." There'd be some interest when Obama got there, of course, but he was sure it would wear off quickly. President Kerry would be the real story in January. And that was fine: Obama was confident he wouldn't be just another boring senator

mired in constant debate about budget provisions or procedural responsibilities, but he was still working out what, exactly, he wanted to focus on
when he did arrive.

Seven hundred miles to Obama's southeast, Biden was just counting down
the hours to Kerry's inauguration. By late October he was pretty sure he
knew what his future held, and on election day positive reports rushed
into Kerry HQ from the swing states.

Bush's demise looked certain as the afternoon of November 2 progressed, and at around 4:00 p.m. eastern time, Biden connected with Kerry,
who suggested he'd have a formal offer for Biden the next day, once Kerry
became just the second candidate to unseat an incumbent president in a
quarter century. It sure looked like Senator Biden was about to become
Secretary Biden.

Three hours later, in Chicago, Axelrod told Obama it looked cooked—
Kerry was going to win. His own margin of victory, meanwhile, was
quickly becoming a chasm.

While he waited for the result to be formalized, Obama's staff was
downstairs at the Hyatt Regency finishing the setup for his victory party.
No result was in doubt at that point, but Obama knew his words might be
watched closely that night, and it was important to get the visual right—to
Axelrod's specifications, which he'd calculated with Obama's political
future in mind.

As a result, this wouldn't be the usual setup for a victory party in Chicago. None of the baggage-laden aldermen or state assemblymen, union
chiefs, or hangers-on who usually lined up onstage behind a victor would
be allowed up that night. The campaign team only wanted to see one shot
in the coverage: Obama, alone with his family, smiling and waving as blue
and white confetti rained down. Staffers were stationed at each of the
stage's four corners to stop anyone else from approaching.

CHAPTER 2

2004–2006

The Bidens sat at home as the maps turned red on election night. Jill, growing upset, went to bed first, but Joe kept his eyes on the TV as Kerry's chances—and his own big plans—disappeared. Jill woke up the next morning in an even worse mood. She knew her husband. Of course he was already planning his 2008 campaign. And could you blame him? Sure, Kerry might run again and Al Gore wasn't out of the picture. But why shouldn't Joe try? He'd been a senator far longer than Hillary Clinton or John Edwards, and wasn't he more charismatic than the other Democrats who were probably also already thinking about it? *Of course.*

Biden held off on saying anything about this out loud out of respect for Kerry, but Jill was actually a quick convert to the idea—she couldn't believe Bush had been reelected, for one thing, and figured that if they started seriously considering it now maybe that'd give them enough time to plan properly. It didn't take much work to convince his tight inner circle of advisors, either. The notion of running became the frame for a series of conversations about Biden's return to the Senate, which were led by not only Biden and his friend and counselor Ted Kaufman but also included staffers like Antony Blinken and a cast of allies who'd worked for the senator over the years—veterans of Democratic politics like lawyers Ron Klain and Mark Gitenstein, and his strategists the Donilon brothers, Mike and Tom.

As Biden saw it, he was coming back in a position of power thanks to his seniority and popularity. Biden opened Senate Democrats' January retreat at the Kennedy Center by grinning to Reid, the new top Democrat: "Harry, I could've been leader, but the free car wasn't worth it." Biden never had much interest in the Senate leadership track, though, and if there was going to be a tug-of-war over the future of the Democratic Party, he determined he should focus on promoting himself as a tough-minded moderate whose heart was with the working-class folks he'd grown up with in Scranton.

The truth was that Biden had a knack for landing squarely in the center of his party's internal ideological spectrum on issue after issue. Though he never let himself see it this way, it was very much an open question whether that was at all what the country—let alone Democrats who just backed another longtime senator widely associated with the 1970s and 1980s—would be even remotely interested in now, with the national mood souring on Washington's wars.

But this image—his "brand," he called it—was a sensitive topic for Biden, stemming as it did from his genuinely middle-class and blue-collar upbringing, even though he'd spent more than half his life in the rarefied halls of the Senate. As strong as he believed the brand to be after years of cultivation, it was far from the consensus view of him on Capitol Hill. Plenty of his younger colleagues either considered him a blowhard who was years past his peak—a classic in the genre of veteran senators overly reliant on staff, whose ideas of persuasion were just yelling on the Senate floor—or barely thought of him at all. Yet inertia wasn't the only reason he kept getting reelected and elevated on important committees. He mattered. Even foreign leaders picked up his calls, recognizing his exuberant handshakes and acknowledging that his name carried real heft around the world after so many years in the Senate.

As Washington and the shell-shocked Democrats began addressing Bush's second-term agenda, he sought a new aide to get his domestic policy operation in order. But he almost didn't hire Klain and Tom Donilon's recommended candidate, Terrell McSweeny, after her interview with Ted Kaufman, perhaps Biden's closest advisor. She was the obvious choice, yet while describing her perception of Biden's economic posture she called him a "populist," to which Kaufman, startled, objected. Afterward Klain had to call to explain what she meant—not that the famously warm senator was a William Jennings Bryan–style fire-breather, but that he was a prounion defender of the middle class.

Biden had little doubt, however, that his true opportunity was global. Over the years he'd come to believe that the executive branch of government had immense power, maybe too much, over foreign affairs, and he'd soured on Bush's judgment after initially holding out hope that the president's more competent hires would steer him away from disaster. Now, as the top Democrat on the foreign relations committee, he saw himself as the single most critical counterweight to the White House while the war in Iraq spiraled out of Bush's control. He could, he figured, hold Bush and his administration to account, or at least articulate an alternative vision for the wars. The committee would be his source of real influence in DC, and therefore his true focus.

His perch there also empowered him to evaluate the Senate's newer faces, since seats on the prominent panel were in high demand. One young senator in particular stuck out.

Biden was fairly sure he understood Obama long before they actually met: in many ways he'd been in a similar position when he first arrived in town. Obama was one of just two new Democrats who'd been elected that November as a GOP president reviled by liberals won reelection. Biden, too, had been a rare Democratic bright spot when he won the same night that Richard Nixon cruised to a second term.

That experience, though, also left Biden—who was enrolled at the University of Delaware when Obama was born—wary of fresh faces promising big things. He'd known basically nothing when he first got to the Senate after a stint on the New Castle County council; he needed years to learn his way around the place, let alone to become a policy expert. But Biden had been forced to grow up, immeasurably and wrenchingly, when just after his election his wife and daughter were killed in a car accident that also sent his sons to the hospital. He tried quitting the Senate before he was even sworn in, but Mike Mansfield, the Democratic leader from Montana, prevailed on him to stay and came up with an arrangement to help the devastated thirty-year-old fulfill his duties as a senator while raising his shattered young family—letting him work from the hospital and then making it easy for him to commute between DC and Wilmington regularly.

Biden was, of course, impressed by Obama's convention performance, and he recognized the symbolic importance of his position as the only Black senator. But he simultaneously found it hard not to be at least slightly annoyed by the headlines that seemed to follow this new guy everywhere, as if he was a fully formed supernova and not a rookie. On Obama's first day in the Senate, a reporter asked him about his place in history. And then there was Iraq. Biden resented how dismissively liberals were talking about the Senate's vote to authorize Bush's invasion, sure that they didn't understand the full context that went into the decision. He was aware of Obama's 2002 speech on the matter, and didn't quite think it fair that he and others could now weigh in on the war without having had to record a vote themselves.

And yet the two were still hardly on track for any sort of confrontation. There was no reason their careers had to intersect at all at this point; the Senate could be a big place if you wanted it to be. And though they didn't disagree a ton on domestic policy, there was no denying that their backgrounds and trajectories, feelings about and understandings of DC, and conceptions of political power more broadly made them seem as close to opposites as was possible for two senators within the same party.

But Biden was curious, so when the Senate's new star asked to meet early in 2005, he quickly said yes and invited Obama to his office in Capitol Hill's Russell Building for a sit-down. The conversation was easy and low stakes: Biden knew Obama wanted to join his committee, and he determined he'd be happy to have Obama as long as he was serious about it. If nothing else, he might get the committee some headlines. They only had time to speak briefly, and Biden told Obama he'd make sure he got the assignment. He then suggested they meet again sometime for a longer, more substantive discussion where they could get to know each other a bit better. Biden was on to something: if there was going to be anything approximating a working relationship here—let alone a partnership—it would take real, iterative work from the two almost diametrically different men.

They'd just have to find some time they were both in town, since Biden took the train home to Wilmington every night and Obama was trying to spend as much time as possible back in Chicago, where Michelle and the girls had remained. Obama was impressed Biden still kept up this commute; Biden liked that Obama was a family man, too.

They could get a simple Italian dinner on Capitol Hill, Biden offered, hoping to put the younger man at ease but also being realistic, since—as he often reminded people—he'd been elected at twenty-nine and hadn't made money independently, so he usually ranked as the poorest senator. "Nothing fancy," he said.

Obama, however, drew back. "Oh," said the forty-three-year-old, "we can go to a nice place. I can afford it." Biden, surprised, detected more than a hint of arrogance and a hefty serving of presumptuousness. The meeting ended on a sour, and uncomfortable, note, with no dinner scheduled.

At least that's how Biden saw it.

Obama wasn't quite sure what to expect from the senior senator the first time they sat down in DC; he had too much going on inside his own head to think about Biden much at all. It wasn't just cockiness, though his immense confidence was evident to anyone who interacted with him. His own life was changing dramatically by the hour. Obama had spent his first few days in Washington dodging a swarm of reporters and trying to work out how he'd balance his responsibilities there with family time in Chicago and constituent time in the rest of his state. He also scheduled a requisite round of suck-up meetings with older members—the kind of glad-handing he hated deep in his core and suspected to be near the center of modern politics' rot, but also, he acknowledged, probably the kind of thing that was necessary if he wanted to achieve anything of consequence in the Senate. Closer to home, not only was he now a bona fide famous person, but real money was also starting to fill his bank account for the first time as a result of the arrangement to reprint *Dreams from My Father* and publish a second book soon.

So when this old-school senator who'd first been elected when Obama was an eleven-year-old going by "Barry" offered up a cheap dinner, it was hard not to take it at least somewhat personally. The gesture struck him as condescending at best, borderline offensive at worst. His reply was as much a rejoinder that Biden needn't treat him any differently from any other senator as it was an impatient reflection of his new truth. He *could* afford it now. He wasn't upset to walk away from the meeting without scheduling the dinner.

Obama didn't think he needed much more veteran guidance on the Hill, anyway. By January he'd already spent weeks talking to an ideal Sherpa. After Obama met Pete Rouse, Tom Daschle's chief of staff, at the convention, they chatted on occasion about what Obama could expect when he got to the Senate. Obama was pretty sure he knew how to legislate, thanks to his time in Springfield, but recognized he had little clue about how to navigate the specific egos and traditions of the Hill, especially as his notoriety and expectations rose in tandem. So when Daschle lost his seat Obama tried convincing Rouse not to retire after thirty-odd years in the Capitol and to instead take a massive status cut and join Obama's office despite his ninety-ninth position in the Senate's seniority ranks. He had to ask twice before Rouse relented, won over by Obama's pitch: he needed to learn the personalities and the quirks of the chamber, and wasn't looking for more national fame or higher office. Someone had to help him understand what pitfalls to dodge and what toes to avoid stepping on, and after developing and following a strategic plan for a year and a half or so, Rouse would be free to finally retire.

The first parts of the project were simple. Obama needed to establish his areas of focus, so needed committee assignments. Most of his campaign team the previous summer had been unaware that Obama had convened a series of late-night, hours-long calls organized by aides and allies including his longtime staffer Raja Krishnamoorthi and University of Chicago economist Austan Goolsbee with subject-matter experts to get him up to speed on federal issues. This gave him some guidance as he tried figuring out how to use his newfound public profile to the greatest policy effect. Determined to prove his seriousness, he was at first worried that Harry Reid would ask him to head up Senate Democrats' campaign wing, so he made his interest known instead in a wide range of prestige committees, including Health, Education, Labor, and Pensions, the commerce committee, and both the finance and agriculture panels. Obama had a mind for policy specifics but hadn't picked a lane yet. His concern for now was more about getting a good assignment than the details of what it was.

A big part of his plan also involved ducking away from the spotlight for at least a few months lest Illinoisans start to get the impression they'd elected someone with more interest in his own political future than in legislating for them. Rouse, Axelrod, and Gibbs took Obama off the national TV circuit, sensing little upside when he got questions about a possible presidential campaign the day after he won his seat in November. He denied interest, but it was a fair topic to discuss, and he'd had to convince Rouse he had no intention of running when he was recruiting him to run the Senate office. In fact, he had started informally and secretly discussing the possibility of pursuing national office with Valerie Jarrett almost immediately after winning his spot in the Senate. But for now it was "categorically untrue," he'd told Rouse: his children were too young, Michelle would be against it, and he still wanted to get established in DC. The line of inquiry flattered but also annoyed Obama.

Still, it clearly wasn't going anywhere—after he took the oath of office, reporters overheard his daughter Malia, then six years old, asking the question, too. It wasn't crazy, but he couldn't possibly say so out loud. It would be committing an unforgivable Washington faux pas to admit even fleeting interest in higher office, let alone so early in his Senate career, and it would likely tank his relationship with his suspicious older colleagues who liked to see new senators pay their dues.

Perhaps the most delicate piece of Obama's entry to DC was his introduction to a group of senators who, a generation or two ahead of him, had seen their fair share of hotshots come and go. Biden was one of many. He was on the list because of his spot on the foreign relations committee, but plenty of others, like Reid, were higher priority. Others still had simply seen enough to warrant an in-person meeting, for which Obama would trek from his new seventh-floor office in the Hart Building. When Obama was assigned Connecticut Democrat Joe Lieberman and Ohio Republican George Voinovich to be his formal mentors, he spent their lunch in the Senate dining room flattering their experience by asking them for details on life as a senator. "I don't think Senator Obama needs much mentoring," Lieberman told Voinovich after.

Never particularly adept at feigning interest, though, Obama for the most part found these meetings a slog. He was happy to make time for older senators from whom he thought he could learn, and he only slowly found them. One was Ted Kennedy, who had near-legendary status within the Democratic caucus thanks to his family and his liberal record, and the larger-than-life aura he actively cultivated in official Washington.

They met soon after the election, and Kennedy was still so personally affected by Bush's reelection that he wouldn't discuss it directly. If anyone knew about promising young liberal senators, though, it was Kennedy. Not only was he himself a former great hope and brother to John and Bobby, but he'd also seen decades worth of Democrats try to emulate his family or soak in its atmosphere. Biden, a fellow Irish Catholic whose initial 1972 Senate campaign positioned him as a kind of working-class Kennedy, was one, and Teddy had joined him that year in Wilmington for a campaign stop. That was fifteen years before Biden ran for president with even more explicit attempts to mimic the Kennedy appeal—he tried to be the fresh-faced energizer reinvigorating America—before his plagiarism of Bobby helped bring him down. Obama, meanwhile, was less open about his sentimental feelings for the family but privately loved finding out that the desk he'd been assigned on the Senate floor was RFK's old one. In person, Obama said little to this effect to the seventy-two-year-old. But Kennedy was charmed, not offended, by Obama's confidence and his questions about the photographs of Cape Cod on display in the office. Soon after, he sent Obama one of them.

Still, Obama's North Star was Hillary Clinton. Four years earlier she'd arrived as the Senate's biggest celebrity in ages, but she'd since kept her head down and forged enough internal relationships to build a reputation as a respected senator. As early as October, before the election, Gibbs had emailed Philippe Reines, a top Clinton aide, for advice on setting up Obama's press shop, and once the Obama team arrived in Washington most of the new senator's other aides sought wisdom from ClintonWorld counterparts, too. Rouse and Clinton's chief of staff met, and Obama's body man, Reggie Love, sat with Clinton aides at the Senate café Cups to talk about staffing a famous senator. Another senior Clinton advisor walked Obama's new legislative director, Chris Lu—the senator's ex–law school classmate and himself an accomplished Democratic lawyer—through how Clinton's team had balanced her time in New York City with her upstate responsibilities, an equation Obama was now considering about Chicago and rural Illinois.

At the beginning of February, Obama and Clinton met at her office in Russell. Her advice was straightforward—talk to people ahead of you in seniority to show respect and try to work on some serious legislation soon—and they hit it off more than Obama had with almost any other colleague. They soon found themselves gravitating to each other on the Senate floor in the downtime between votes. Obama didn't know it, but he was doing a pretty good job of following the *keep your head down* advice Biden had given Jimmy Cauley in Boston half a year earlier.

* * *

Washington was a discouraging place to be a Democrat in the opening months of 2005. Biden's situation was typical: plenty of the party had been confident Kerry would win not only on a wave of anti-Bush sentiment but also because of his basic competence, and had been planning their next steps accordingly. Obama was no exception; to the degree they'd thought about it, his advisors assumed he'd be able to grow close to the Kerry administration and avoid having to worry about his own national profile for a while. As a result, no one with much influence had given a lot of thought to what, exactly, the party should stand for in a second Bush term other than opposition to his ill-fated plan to privatize Social Security, a vacuum that bore grief and then fury after the campaign ended in volleys of rancorous attack ads. The party, really, had been struggling with its direction ever since Bush won election with the help of a Supreme Court decision in 2000, though increasing skepticism about the war in Iraq was, at least, offering it an organizing principle that it might still choose to embrace even more fully after Bush's reelection.

This all made for a foreign environment for Obama, in particular, fresh as he was off coasting to victory. He was taken aback when, on one of his first days in Washington, some Democrats tried objecting to the certification of Ohio's electoral votes—a move he found so provocatively undemocratic that he ditched a set of scheduled interviews with prospective staff members to make an impromptu maiden speech on the Senate floor, which is usually a momentous and meticulously planned rite of passage for first-year legislators a few months, not days, into their tenure.

"I am absolutely convinced that the president of the United States, George Bush, won this election. I also believe that he got more votes in Ohio," Obama said, trying to tamp down the left-wing protest while acknowledging concerns about disenfranchisement. "This is not an issue in which we are challenging the outcome of the election. And I think it's important for us to separate out the issue of the election outcome with the election process." He'd come to Washington at least somewhat hopeful he could transcend the day-to-day political scrum, but his honeymoon ended abruptly when influential liberals who'd expected him to be a savior after his convention speech now complained about him on their blogs.

Obama quickly concluded he'd been right about DC when he inveighed on the campaign trail against its unproductive culture. It didn't help that he'd grown close with Daschle, who became embittered about the Senate after being booted from it, or that he hadn't spent much time thinking about the day-to-day aspects of the job. He was dismayed by how busy he suddenly was, his days packed with endless meetings about nothing. He developed a practice of carving out time on his schedule for one-on-ones with aides during which he'd ask them to walk alongside him as he worked through ideas, but also, sometimes, where he just had them stroll along to maintain the appearance of being busy. He would listen to music on his headphones and decompress before going home to watch *SportsCenter* in his small rented apartment—after which he'd resume writing his book, only to wake up, go to the gym, and do it all again.

It was a solitary way to be a senator, made all the lonelier by his family being in Chicago, and he was extrasensitive about being present for his daughters, given his own father's absence when he was a child. He worked out a plan to arrive in Washington on Mondays or Tuesdays whenever possible, to return to Chicago on Thursdays or Fridays, and to reserve Sundays for the family. This left Saturdays for his travel around the state for town halls, a central component of the more formal strategic plan Rouse drew up with input from Axelrod and Gibbs, which also included finishing his second book and launching a political action committee to help other Democrats.

The idea was to set Obama's Senate career on a promising track. But already there was a national-level subtext. Obama would be on any nominee's short list for the vice presidency in three years' time whether he liked it or not, they figured, so he might as well position himself. He chuckled dismissively whenever this prospect was brought up—he'd be a terrible Number Two, he'd always say. His aides, who had incentive to see him rise to national office as soon as possible, by and large agreed given his impatience with Washington. But this was also because he was considering another possibility: returning to Illinois to run for governor if the race opened up in 2010, a concept that appealed to him because he was already starting to get the sense he'd be a better executive than a one-in-a-hundred legislator, let alone anyone's second-in-command.

* * *

Biden was just back from his fifth trip to Iraq when he sat down with Bob Schieffer on set at CBS in mid-June 2005. He was there to talk about the state of the war, as he so often had on the Sunday morning shows. He exhibited little restraint in informing the *Face the Nation* audience that the Bush administration was "not telling the truth" about the circumstances on the ground or Iraq's capacity to stand up a democratic government anytime soon. He was preaching to a divided congregation: though the war had plummeted in popularity since 2003 and this downward trajectory seemed obvious, national polling showed that the nation was still roughly split on whether the decision to invade was a good one, whether the war effort was moving in the right direction, and whether troops should stay in Iraq until it stabilized or return home sooner. So Schieffer kept at that topic and held off until the final moments of Biden's two segments on air to try another question. He surely figured it wouldn't make real news, but that he had a journalistic duty to ask it: "How far along are you on this idea of running for president? Is that a real possibility, or—"

Biden couldn't help himself: "It's a real possibility. My intention, as I sit here now—I've proceeded since last November as if I were going to run," he said, revealing a process no other pol would ever publicly expose so long before election season. He was trying to gauge support, he continued, but "I'm acting now, in terms of finding that out, as if I'm running. My intention now is to seek the nomination." He conceded he could still change his mind, but Schieffer, surprised, tried to get him to repeat his announcement. "My intention is to seek the nomination," Biden repeated. "I mean, I know I'm supposed to be more coy with you, I know I'm supposed to tell you, you know, that I'm not sure."

This was not exactly shocking to Biden's colleagues, not least the ones he worked with most on the foreign relations committee. They'd watched as he relished becoming Bush's Democratic foil in the Senate as far as the nation's foreign entanglements went; his glee in questioning Republican officials for the camera was evident. His inability to resist making news about himself was even less surprising.

It was all happening just as Obama arrived at the committee, looking to expand his international chops and eager to stack his days with its hearings and reports rather than the busywork required by another, less exciting assignment, Environment and Public Works. At first, though, he had little reason to interact directly with Biden at much length, at least not one-on-one. The senior-most Democrat only convened his colleagues occasionally to make sure they were on the same page ahead of controversial hearings featuring Bush administration officials, and since Obama was so junior, he had no role in setting tactics. Obama did, however, spend plenty of time watching Biden after he grudgingly agreed to follow Lu's suggestion that he get in older senators' good graces by sitting through every committee hearing from start to finish, even when they took all day.

They tended to take longer, Obama quickly realized, when Biden was speaking. His role as the newest member of the panel meant Obama always spoke last, after every other senator took their turn. Biden usually spoke at the top of hearings, and he tended to ramble, clearly loving every minute of it. "Joe Biden is a decent guy, but man, that guy can just talk and talk. It's an incredible thing to see," Obama told Axelrod, a nice version of his growing feeling that Biden represented a generation of senators who'd overseen Washington's decline into impracticality, even if he was perfectly friendly and obviously knew his stuff. (This wasn't exactly self-aware analysis: Obama also had a penchant for talking at extreme length when he felt like it, but at least he spoke in neatly diagrammable paragraphs, not epic-length run-on sentences.) Obama usually kept this sentiment between him and his closest aides—once, as Biden held court during confirmation hearings for Bush's secretary of state nominee Condoleezza Rice, Obama handed a staffer a note reading, "Shoot. Me. Now." He didn't see much improvement in committee hearings. Later, he looked at Samantha Power, one of his foreign policy aides and a former star journalist, and said, "Here we go again" as Biden resumed speaking. He leaned back toward her, as if he was going to ask for advice, and whispered, "I'm sorry you have to witness this."

He wasn't always so discreet, especially when his frustration boiled over. Late in 2005, when a prospective donor asked him about Biden, Obama replied with a story encapsulating his exasperation: once, when a Republican official was coming to the committee to testify, Biden gathered the Democratic members and told them he wanted the witness to feel like he was in the hot seat, on the record, for the meeting's scheduled one and a half hours. The official's answers had to be the story of the day. Biden then proceeded to open the hearing with a fifty-five-minute monologue, Obama said.

Even this extreme loquaciousness still didn't really distinguish Biden from a lot of the rest of the Senate in Obama's eyes. Within weeks of his arrival, Obama was complaining to advisors that there was no strategy to be found there and that—as he once vented while bursting out of the chamber while flapping his hand open and shut—"Blah, blah, blah! That's all we do here, is talk." Even in the minority in Springfield he'd helped craft legislation and deals—he'd built ties with Democrats and Republicans alike over poker games—but here the older, slower members showed little interest in this kind of work. And when he did get to vote on things, he griped, it was often on bullshit measures that could come back to bite him politically down the road.

One saving grace and source of education was Obama's unlikely relationship with Richard Lugar, the understated top Republican on the foreign relations committee. The pair connected in 2004 when, as a candidate, Obama took to citing Lugar's initiative to reduce risks posed by old Soviet nuclear weapons as the kind of thing he'd be interested in working on, too. Lugar wrote to Obama that he would be happy to help him join the committee, and Obama adopted the quiet older Hoosier as an informal mentor. When Lugar invited him on his annual summer trip to the former Soviet Union in 2005, Obama jumped at the opportunity to tour old weapons facilities. His admiration for Lugar peaked when, in Siberia, the pair was detained on a runway. Obama tried to find a way out, and fast. Lugar, who'd seen it all before, knew the saga would be over soon and replied that it was a great time to take a nap. To close readers of the Senate, it was easy to interpret their friendly dynamic as an implicit rejection of Biden's style. Obama had nowhere near this level of relationship with the committee's top Democrat.

Obama was on his way back from Siberia when he caught footage of New Orleans underwater on an airport TV. He was on the phone with his office back in Washington, and his top aides said he should really head to Louisiana to survey the damage from Hurricane Katrina. Obama hesitated, since it wasn't his state. But the images stuck with him: Black Louisianans, in particular, had disproportionately just seen their lives destroyed, and he was the lone Black senator. He hesitated to talk about racism immediately—he would talk about it on his own terms, when the time came, he figured—but he agreed to fly down and appear with Bill Clinton and George H. W. Bush, and then to lift his self-imposed national media ban to talk about what he'd seen and what the Bush administration should be doing.

The positive reaction to his media blitz fed a flood of new invitations to speak to local and state-level Democratic events. Obama had refused most such asks since arriving to the Senate, but he now caught his advisors by surprise when he wondered if they could arrange a plane to let him attend one of Malia's dance recitals in Chicago and the Florida Democrats' state convention on the same night. Perhaps he wanted to step further into the national spotlight after all. So, as Obama kept saying yes and 2006 neared, Rouse asked if he should draw up a plan to consider how to use the coming midterm season to increase his visibility further, just in case a "perfect storm" appeared for him in 2007 and 2008. His proposal—to build the reach of Obama's personal PAC, raise cash for colleagues and candidates, and promote the forthcoming book—sounded good to Obama, who signed off in January.

Still, more of Obama's attention was on making sure he was correctly articulating his worldview in his first few months in office. He'd been bristling at the assumption that he was some sort of party-line liberal or even especially progressive, and after lefty activists protested his choice to defend some Democrats who supported Bush's nomination of John Roberts to the Supreme Court, he saw a chance to define himself as a different kind of Democrat. He wrote in the popular *Daily Kos* blog, which had been lighting him up for his apostasy, that the notion that Democrats simply needed to show more backbone was naive and divorced from the reality of everyday Americans, who had no interest in demonization or purity tests. As Obama saw it, this way of viewing the world invited permanent minority status for his party.

He was also invited to deliver the commencement speech at Knox College in Galesburg, Illinois—once an Underground Railroad hub, host of a Lincoln-Douglas debate, and home to a closed Maytag factory—which he used to lay out his economic priorities with some historical sweep. With the help of policy advisor Karen Kornbluh and speechwriter Jon Favreau, Kerry's old aide, Obama framed the modern American economic challenge and opportunity as being of a piece with the labor and antitrust movements after the Civil War and the push to open college for veterans after World War Two. "I saw it during the campaign when I met union guys who worked at the plant for twenty, thirty years and now wonder what they're gonna do at the age of fifty-five without a pension or health care, when I met the man whose son needed a new liver but, because he'd been laid off, didn't know if he could afford to provide his child the care that he needed," he said. "It's as if someone changed the rules in the middle of the game and no one bothered to tell these folks." He identified automation and outsourcing, the rise of China and India, and conservatives' belief in the "Ownership Society," which he likened to "social Darwinism," as factors to reckon with. The latter "is especially tempting because each of us believes we will always be the winner in life's lottery, that we're the one who will be the next Donald Trump, or at least we won't be the chump who Donald Trump says: 'You're fired!'" he said. Instead, he argued, Americans needed to insist on affordable college and job retraining, reliable health-care coverage and pensions, and more funding for research. The speech was light on specific proposals but, by the standards of Democrats talking about globalization and the transforming economy, notably forward-looking.

This was just as well, since Obama was at the same time trying to avoid saying too much about the actual topic du jour. Obama had told Rouse upon arriving in the Senate that he didn't want to involve himself too deeply in the Iraq debate yet, since his views about the invasion had been well known since 2002 and he saw little upside in the back-and-forth that was unfolding in hearings and private meetings between the administration and lawmakers like Biden. Even when he wanted to reconsider tenets of his own stance opposing the war, he didn't consult other senators but arranged private debates among aides including Gibbs, Rouse, Power, and her fellow foreign policy advisor Mark Lippert.

Obama's sessions were more or less irrelevant to the policy debate consuming Pennsylvania Avenue. Biden's views weren't. In 2005, Biden was still steaming over the way his joint proposal with Lugar to circumvent a full invasion had been squashed two years earlier when fellow Democrat Dick Gephardt made an end around and publicly, surprisingly, backed Bush's plan to invade. Biden joined the supportive group, but he and Lugar and a handful of others including Nebraska Republican Chuck Hagel still thought the course of the war would be dramatically different if these guidelines had been ratified. They had wanted invasion only to rid Saddam Hussein of weapons of mass destruction, not for regime change, and only with United Nations or congressional approval—which would be contingent on Bush proving the need for military force. The disappointment of this plan's failure continued to paint Biden's interactions with the White House until he turned to a new idea in mid-2006, when he ran into foreign policy grandee Les Gelb on a delayed flight. They should wind down the war by splitting Iraq into autonomous Kurdish, Sunni, and Shiite regions, they wrote in a *New York Times* Op-Ed that Biden had Blinken—by then already one of Biden's closest aides, who was basically family and certainly capable of inhabiting his voice—pull together after the flight.

This proposal had the added benefit of being a useful talking point ahead of Biden's probable campaign, which was by this point growing real enough that he, Kaufman, Blinken, and McSweeny were pinning down its core policy proposals. Biden was on board with promoting new ways to make college more affordable, especially community college—a topic that interested him in particular as Jill, a community college instructor, was then on her way to receiving her doctor of education degree, after which she would primarily be known in Biden's circles as Dr. B. On most issues, though, he had weeks' worth of questions for McSweeny and the experts she brought in for him—"I don't just understand, I overstand!" he liked to smile and say, by way of shrugging apology. This diligence would come in handy, he was convinced, on the eventual campaign trail.

Why, he debated for hours, was a single-payer health-care system preferable to a Medicare buy-in for fifty-five-year-olds? (He worried that other popular proposals were too complicated: we're going to tell everyone they need to have health care but then they have to go buy it?) Why, he asked, were medical leave and equal pay policies so difficult to implement? And what, he kept wondering, was happening to the middle class? Why couldn't you support a family on one income? If he was going to run for president, he figured, he better have some answers. If he was going to be a leading contender, he'd surely be pressed for specifics.

Obama only moved closer to the national spotlight as he accepted more invitations and raced to finish his book at night, hoping to deliver the manuscript in time to combine the publicity tour with his high-profile travel for midterm candidates. Curiosity spiked when he traveled to Africa that summer with massive international fanfare and a local reception that reminded old hands of Bobby Kennedy's trip to the continent in 1966. To his aides, it was an eye-opening display of his power to attract media and maybe to turn around international sentiment about the country after Bush's two terms—even if back in Washington some of his older colleagues, like Biden, saw the coverage and found it all a tad messianic.

Still, though, he hesitated to talk about the elephant crowding the door-way. Early in 2006 his senior Illinois colleague Dick Durbin—hardly known for overexuberance himself—started arguing to Obama that he should run for president, insisting the lesson to learn from Kerry's loss was that spending more time in the Senate and building a record doesn't make for a better presidential candidate. The moment picks the candidate, he said. Soon after, Jan Schakowsky, the liberal Chicago congresswoman, told Obama to take Durbin's words seriously. He was noncommittal until a few months later, when Axelrod weighed in: "We haven't had a true summons to hope and change like the Kennedy campaign in forty years," he told Obama, urging him to consider the opportunity. They agreed to defer any serious discussion until after the midterms but didn't yet tell anyone that conversation was coming.

Of course, it was obvious to anyone paying attention. Rouse's latest memo spelled out how Obama was now the most requested surrogate for Democratic campaign events, and that if there was even a 10 to 15 percent chance he might run, then he should spend two to three hours at a time doing these events, meeting local pols and press around the country. As his team tried building enough buzz online to get his email list to a hundred thousand subscribers, Obama finished his book in time to make it on Oprah Winfrey's show before his final campaign blitz. The combination of stumping and book sales paid off immediately: ahead of one event in Minneapolis for Senate hopeful Amy Klobuchar, Obama aide Alyssa Mastromonaco had to convince the candidate's team they needed a bigger room than the three-hundred-capacity space they had reserved. They simply didn't get big crowds here, Klobuchar's aides assured her, to which Mastromonaco insisted they didn't understand what was about to happen. Over three thousand locals showed up.

Obama grew more comfortable with the speculation about his future as the political momentum grew impossible to ignore, and he accepted an invitation to Senator Tom Harkin's Steak Fry, the late-summer fundraiser in Iowa that doubled as a launching pad for presidential hopefuls. Steve Hildebrand, a prominent local strategist, volunteered to show Obama around, while Axelrod quietly ordered up polling in the first-to-vote state to gauge Obama's potential support. Obama still wasn't even admitting that he was considering running, but his appearance there was enough to dissuade one likely 2008 candidate—former Virginia governor Mark Warner, who was in the audience—from a campaign of his own. Soon thereafter, a similar appearance at a New Hampshire Democratic Party fundraiser helped convince Indiana senator Evan Bayh, another probable contender watching from the sidelines, not to run, either.

* * *

In the fall of 2006, John Kerry was finding that once you get close to the presidency, it's nearly impossible to give up the dream. His remaining advisors didn't see any path back to the nomination, let alone the White House. That didn't stop him from asking some of the top donors from his last campaign to meet, just in case. At one lunch, Kerry grew frustrated as the mogul across the table told him he wasn't buying his pitch, informing him that the last thing people wanted right now, after eight years of Bush, was a retread. Kerry replied, *Fine, but aside from Hillary Clinton, who might the nominee even be?* When the donor replied that he wouldn't rule Obama out, Kerry was incredulous. This was too much for an old-school rules-follower who believed in climbing the dues ladder rung by rung. He muttered that he'd quit politics if Obama became the Democrats' nominee.

Kerry—whose spokesman denied this encounter years later, and who soon became encouraging of Obama's presidential aspirations—wasn't alone. Gore was also skeptical about Obama at first—to plenty of DC veterans the very idea that he'd be ready for the presidency was almost offensive—as were a range of governors who hadn't met the man in person, but who figured they'd been around long enough to know he had no shot.

As the spring had progressed, Obama hadn't exactly been inclined to agree—he was sure he *could* run, and certainly that he could do the job—but he remained skeptical that the timing made sense for him. He was forty-five, which put him in the same age range as Bill Clinton when he'd become president, but before that you had to go all the way back to JFK to find a winning candidate younger than his fifties. Then again, the same history showed that Democrats really only won with youthful outsiders. Still, though, he'd spent less than two years in the Senate. Bill Clinton had at least been a governor for over a decade. And the others who might run? Hillary had been first lady and a senator, Edwards had been a senator and Kerry's running mate, and Bayh, who was still publicly considering a campaign, had been a governor and a senator, and he was the son of another famous senator, too. Hell, Bill Richardson had been a congressman, a cabinet member, and a governor. Connecticut's Chris Dodd had been in DC for three decades—come to think of it, his dad was a well-known senator, too—and Biden even longer.

Harry Reid, however, disagreed that any of this mattered. Obama didn't know what to expect when the leader summoned him to his office, thinking that perhaps he'd done something wrong. They'd developed a good working relationship—Obama appreciated the way Reid protected Democrats from tough votes when Republicans tried pinning them down on topics like abortion and the estate tax. Reid, meanwhile, had been convinced of Obama's potential and impressed by his self-awareness ever since the young senator's first floor speech about Iraq. Reid had congratulated Obama on the persuasive address as soon as it was over, and Obama replied soberly: "I have a gift, Harry," which stuck with the Nevadan.

Now, seemingly out of nowhere, Reid told Obama he should think about running. It was obvious that Obama hated this job, he said, and "ten more years in the Senate won't make you a better president." He'd motivate young people, minorities, and moderate white voters, Reid said, and Chuck Schumer, another Senate operator, agreed. "If you want to be president, you can be president now," Reid said. In the moment, Obama replied, "I don't know, Harry, I don't think so," but his calculus instantly shifted—he knew something important was happening, and he'd later frequently think back on the conversation, and eventually write about it momentously. He'd assumed Reid would be with Clinton and that her fellow New Yorker Schumer would too, but now Reid told him that while he'd have to remain neutral publicly, they were worried about her baggage. None of the other potential candidates sitting in the Senate came up at all—not Dodd nor Bayh, and not Biden, either.

Still, between trips to flog the book and campaign for midterm candidates, Obama kept trying to plan for his next few years in the Senate. When he met with Montana senator Max Baucus, the top Democrat on the finance committee, about joining his panel after the midterms, Baucus replied that he wasn't sure, since Obama might want to run for president and wouldn't be around much in 2007. Obama laughed and agreed, but said he might also run for governor in 2010. Baucus counseled him to run for president, since opportunities to do so tend to be fleeting. Obama started hearing this argument a lot. Daschle, for one, said something similar when they talked about it, adding that staying in DC too long often just makes one cynical. Ted Kennedy's words, in particular, stuck with Obama, who later wrote about them, too. He said that while he wouldn't endorse anyone because he had too many friends in the race, "The power to inspire is rare. Moments like this are rare." Kennedy said Obama didn't have the luxury of choosing when to run, but as Durbin had argued, sometimes the moment chooses you. And if you don't run, he said, you have to be OK with knowing the chance passed you by. Kennedy didn't say it out loud, but Biden was an obvious counterexample—someone who'd run twenty years earlier and was still chasing the dream.

Of course, not everyone was encouraging, even among the crowd Obama handpicked to ask for advice—the types least likely to share the obvious conventional wisdom that Clinton and the Democratic establishment would steamroll him. When Obama asked to see Harold Schaitberger, the head of the international firefighters' union, which had helped fuel Kerry's campaign, the labor chief said over breakfast on Capitol Hill that he wasn't sure Obama was ready. Lieberman, too, was careful, if slightly more encouraging. He'd been Gore's running mate only to drift right and lose a primary for his own Senate seat, which he then won back by running as an independent that fall. He told Obama his own standards for considering new campaigns: make sure you know why you're running and that you're confident you can do a better job than the other candidates, and don't do it if you think you can't succeed. He paused and told Obama that unless he really screwed it up, it couldn't hurt to run, since he'd increase his visibility and stature in the Senate. Obama asked what Lieberman would do in his position, at which point the elder senator paused for about ten seconds before replying, "If I were you, I would run."

All this advice was on Obama's mind when, at a book event in Philadelphia in late October, just about every person in line urged him to run. On the car ride back to Washington afterward, Axelrod and Gibbs brought up Obama's appearance the next morning on *Meet the Press*. Host Tim Russert would surely now roll out the tape from January 2006, when Obama had denied any interest in 2008, Axelrod said. Obama agreed it was inevitable, then surprised his advisors. Tomorrow, he said, he'd tell Russert he was seriously looking at running. Gibbs and Axelrod looked at each other before Gibbs turned back to Obama and asked if he'd mentioned this to his wife. Obama paused, and looked back blankly, then said Gibbs had a good point and that he'd call her when they got back to DC.

Obama called Michelle, Russert played the tape, and Obama made the news—"After November seventh, I'll sit down and consider. And if at some point I change my mind, I will make a public announcement and everybody will be able to go at me." But, he said, "it's fair, yes," to say that he was now considering running for president. He'd seen enough of DC to know what the capital now needed.

Democrats won back the House and the Senate on November 7. On November 8, a group including the Obamas, David Plouffe, Pete Rouse, Valerie Jarrett, Alyssa Mastromonaco, consultant John Kupper, and strategist Steve Hildebrand, plus Obama's close friend Marty Nesbitt, piled into Axelrod's office in Chicago. They were there to finally, really, start the conversation by considering the fundamental questions. Should Obama run, and why? And, more to the point, could he win?

Nearly five hundred days had passed since Biden's announcement. It never occurred to either senator to discuss the coming campaign with the other.

CHAPTER 3

2007–2008

Bill Clinton had a word of warning for Biden. The senator was about to officially launch his campaign in January 2007, and the ex-president's wife looked poised to dominate the field. This didn't stop the two world-class chatters from catching up, though, and Clinton—four years younger than Biden but living the comfortable life of a retired pol with less time-consuming pursuits—laid out a problem he predicted Biden would soon encounter. When long-serving senators ran for president, he warned, they tended to deploy "Beltway Speak"—talking about laws and government programs in too much technical detail without tying them back to voters' lives.

Clinton had a point, but not about Biden. For one, he'd been a senator forever but had always gone to some explicit, self-conscious lengths not to act like one. He still went home almost every night to his family in Wilmington, so he didn't hang out socially with his colleagues as much as one might expect, and had thus avoided picking up their worst insidery habits. Plus, he was notorious among those in the know on Capitol Hill for demanding, sometimes cuttingly, that his aides talk like real people when briefing him, nixing jargon and abbreviations specifically to avoid the problem Clinton was talking about. Then there was Biden's well-earned reputation for simply talking far too much, and far too loosely.

He didn't make it past his first half-day as a candidate before this once again became his problem. He had choreographed a launch to establish himself as a serious contender for both votes and donor dollars. The idea was to start by talking about moving toward a resolution in Iraq, which he and his inner circle thought might propel him toward the informal top tier of candidates then occupied by Hillary, Edwards, and Obama—who each looked like they stood a real chance at the presidency given Bush's terrible image and Republicans' consequent unpopularity.

Instead, Biden was greeted with a wave of outrage when the *New York Observer* published an interview in which he described Obama as "the first mainstream African-American who is articulate and bright and clean and a nice-looking guy." At first, Biden didn't see the issue—*Wasn't it obvious he was complimenting Obama?*—but supporters immediately inundated him with dismayed calls.

It took a few hours for him to acknowledge the misstep in a private phone conversation. Obama was unamused but replied that he didn't think Biden was racist and also knew he didn't mean offense. It was a delicate moment for Obama, too. He knew he would speak about race as the campaign continued, but thought this was too early in the election season to make a major statement, since he was trying to introduce himself to as wide an audience as possible and didn't want voters to think his campaign was predicated on the fact of his race. Anyway, his overall campaign message was supposed to be about overcoming differences, and this was hardly the kind of comment he wanted to respond to at length.

Biden also apologized to the Reverend Al Sharpton, the civil rights activist who'd run in 2004, and said he hadn't meant to insult him, Jesse Jackson, Shirley Chisholm, or Carol Moseley Braun, all Black Democrats who'd campaigned for president before. Soon after, on a call with reporters, Biden tried to clean his message up further, calling Obama "probably the most exciting candidate that the Democratic or Republican party has produced at least since I've been around."

Obama was eager to move on. So were some of Biden's prospective donors and endorsers, who stopped answering his calls less than twenty-four hours into his campaign—they saw what he refused to: this obviously wasn't his moment. That Biden couldn't or wouldn't see this was indicative of his broader inability at this point, so many years into his comfortable Senate perch, to read national politics as he once had and would again years later. It was Obama, not him, who seemed to have a finely tuned divining rod for the unsettled country's mood.

A few days later, the senators saw each other at a committee meeting. Staffers watched from afar as they approached each other and, just out of earshot, started talking, then quietly laughing. It was cordial, even friendly, but quick—an acknowledgment that both of them wanted to move on, and that neither had much else to discuss with the other. While Biden's aides sighed with relief—their boss's reputation was mostly intact, even if his presidential ambitions had been mortally dented—not all of Obama's staffers were over Biden's comment, and thought their boss still might confront him in person. But he was much more sanguine about Biden than they were. *What*, they asked each other, *the fuck?*

* * *

Here, again, was the mismatch. If Obama seemed perfectly built for modern campaign trail politics, Biden was immediately exposed as out of sync with the times. Biden, as a result, was simply not the point for Obama. From the start there was a categorical difference in their candidacies. If Obama caught on, as he looked likely to do, he could be a historic world figure, and as his campaign matured his transformational promise turned him into an international phenomenon. Even in his best moments, Biden never looked like more than a talented senator, and he wasn't out there promising a new political culture, let alone an era of unity. You could read the difference as a matter of naivete versus realism born of experience—plenty in DC, and certainly in Biden's orbit, did—or as a gulf in aspirations and hope sprouting from differing understandings of what the country was looking for after eight years of Bush. But Obama vs. Biden was not even a comparison most would think to make.

It would later come to feel inevitable that the race became a legendarily brutal war of attrition between Obama and Clinton, but in the opening months they circled each other more carefully. Clinton, who'd hung a picture of Obama in her office after meeting him, didn't even think her younger colleague would actually get in the campaign at all until it suddenly felt like a fait accompli at the end of 2006. Obama, too, started out with no personal animosity for Clinton, though he and Rouse dispatched a team of senior aides led by Lu to monitor every statement and move coming from her office, just to make sure they were cosponsoring the same bills and being careful about their points of departure on policy.

That the story of the primary did almost immediately become "Obama vs. Clinton" suited him well, though, especially as he got off to a shaky start. Obama had decided to run late in 2006 after lengthy conversations with Michelle and his inner circle and a ruminative trip to Hawaii. He had an OK chance of winning, he figured, and he was convinced he had a unique opportunity to change the culture in Washington, to represent a much bigger change in the country and its politics overall, and to inspire a generation of Americans, including Black children who would grow up with the first Black president. But it wasn't all blind hope and anti–status quo talking points. Axelrod, Plouffe, and co had carefully planned out his path to the nomination—focusing at first on pockets of young liberals and undertargeted minority communities, and planning a robust online organizing presence unlike anything the 2004 race had seen, especially in states with caucus contests where they could pick up delegates in unexpected ways. They combed through results from focus groups that pollster David Binder stealthily ran with caucus-goers in Des Moines and Cedar Rapids, too, to gauge how he was resonating. But despite the excitement surrounding Obama's launch in January, Clinton still looked formidable, if not nearly impossible to beat, with most of the party establishment in her corner and filling her campaign's bank accounts. Obama was never far from her in polling or national media attention, but her mastery of policy and support from the party's longtime leaders were staggering. Plus, at some important early moments Obama fell dispiritingly flat, like when, at a Service Employees International Union forum on health care, he struggled to articulate the details of his plan despite promising it would be an important piece of his presidency. The disappointing performance led some pundits to question his preparedness and some policy wonks to doubt his seriousness.

Still, he was drawing crowds and leaning into the distance between him and his leading opponents on the issue of the day. Every time he retreated into moody silence off the trail, second-guessing the wisdom of his campaign or its tactics and agreeing with his critics, Axelrod would remind him, "The same people who are saying this are the people who thought invading Iraq was a good idea," which would again crystallize for him the promise of change central to his bid and his opposition not just to Clinton but most of the rest of the field, too, including Biden. The truth was that there was some nuance to the difference between his position on Iraq and most of his opponents'—many had backed the war, but few of them had actually been as gung ho about invasion as campaign trail rhetoric made it seem. Yet voters by and large read the matter as a binary between him and

Clinton, an impression Obama's team leaned into by handing out copies of the text of his 2002 speech opposing the war.

Obama was, at the time, becoming comfortable with the idea that his job as a campaigner and politician was to tell voters stories about who they were as a collective, a far more expansive view of the role than many longtime pols were willing to take. (Ask Biden, who tried winning votes by reciting his résumé, and who seemed to view the domestic job of the president at least through a Hill angle: passing legislation, first and foremost.) Obama wasn't dismissive of legislative nitty-gritty—far from it—but, in his typical unemotional and slightly detached way, he saw it as a tool in his more sweeping mission, rather than an end itself. When, during the primary, he said that Ronald Reagan had been more transformative as a president than Bill Clinton, the resulting reaction and commentary illustrated the stark divides in the party: Obama's point was that Reagan had shifted the culture. But to a taken-aback Clinton, his wife, and her supporters, it was an affront that maligned the effectiveness of the forty-second president's governance.

Biden watched these scraps with both interest and significant annoyance to be left out of them. He seldom disagreed with Obama's policy priorities in the main, even if he had marginal nitpicks, and he remained impressed with his chops as a campaigner. But he tended to agree more with Clinton's view of the world than with Obama's. Clinton and Biden held more faith in institutions than in people to change Washington. Stylistically, too, Biden and Obama couldn't have been more different, a fact that played out daily on the trail. Biden could be overwhelmingly tactile and affectionate with voters, even when he wasn't catching on. Obama was good at retail politics, too—he liked talking to real people—but he always held himself back from fully engaging with every last voter's life story, drawing less energy from the exchanges than Biden and remaining, at his core, distant with everyone except family and longtime advisors, self-consciously cool in both senses of the word. This only added to his reputation, which he built up with his big, inspirational speeches. When Biden and Obama saw each other on the trail, their own interactions could be markedly friendly, almost clubby, compared to the somewhat icy relationships both started to form with some of the other candidates like Edwards. But it was always Biden who approached Obama backstage at debates and forums—he could see that Obama was catching fire, and he was impressed. Always eager to be near the center of the action, he sidled up to the younger man and did his usually chummy bit, and felt the aura, though he still struggled to fully understand it. Their backstage conversations were seldom longer than a few minutes, and never particularly interesting.

Still, to the degree that Obama thought about Biden as an opponent, it was often with eye rolls. When Obama was scheduled to speak after his older, still notoriously talkative colleague at multicandidate events, Obama would turn to his traveling campaign team and ask, lightly but pointedly, how far behind schedule they thought he'd be this time.

Biden, though, thought about Obama plenty. But no matter how impressed he was, he started throwing elbows when it became clear that his young colleague wasn't fading away and thus stood in his way. The Iowa Democratic Party's Jefferson-Jackson Dinner is remembered for Obama's holy-shit breakout speech among the state's voters and for Clinton's jab at him ("*Change* is just a word if you don't have the strength and experience to make it happen"), but Biden, too, got in on the Obama ribbing, remarking on the audience's heavily Obama slant by walking onstage and pronouncing, "Hello, Chicago!" which some in Obama's orbit read as a clumsily veiled accusation they'd packed the crowd with out-of-staters.

Most of Biden's idea, though, was to highlight his own experience in contrast to his opponents'. In *Promises to Keep*, the book he published before the campaign, he tartly wrote that the Jimmy Carter years made him understand "that on-the-job training for a president can be a danger-ous thing," and he made the argument even more explicitly in the cam-paign itself. In August in Iowa, George Stephanopoulos opened the first debate by bringing up a recent statement Biden made to *Newsweek* that Obama was "not yet ready" to be president.

Biden started by softening the blow now that he was on the same stage as Obama, but only on the surface: "Look, I think he's a wonderful guy, to start off, number one," he said. The *Newsweek* quote, he continued, was specifically about Obama's preparedness with respect to Pakistan policy and the threat of jihadists with nuclear weapons. Biden tried pivoting to his proposal to establish "a long-term relationship with Pakistan and sta-bility." Stephanopoulos, though, didn't let Biden off the hook. "You did go beyond talking about Pakistan. You were asked, Is he ready? You said, 'I think he can be ready, but right now I don't believe he is. The presidency is not something that lends itself to on-the-job training.'" Biden replied, "I think I stand by the statement." He had to. All his ads and speeches were about his steady hand after three decades in DC.

No one in Obama's orbit was happy with this line of discussion, naturally, but they weren't terribly upset by it, either. He had been clear with his contention—arguably the whole point of his campaign—that Washington experience wasn't necessarily equating to good results, and that a new perspective was needed. Left unsaid, but never far from the surface, were the questions: *How had things gone over the fifteen years since the Clintons arrived in Washington, anyway? Let alone the thirty-five years Biden had been around?* When Obama finally got to defend himself from Biden and Clinton, who was making a similar case, he shrugged it off. "I don't actually see that much difference, or people criticizing me on the substance of my positions," he said onstage in Des Moines. It didn't escape him that the debate had opened with the recitation of poll results showing him effectively tied for the lead in Iowa with Clinton and Edwards, with the levels of support for all three in the mid-20 percentages. Biden, Stephanopoulos revealed, was at just 2 percent.

* * *

At least as far as politics goes, Biden's story is often told through the lens of his presidential campaigns, so it often begins in 1987. In truth, he started feeling out the edges of national politics, yearning for something more than his beloved Capitol Hill, even earlier. Biden spent his first restless years in the Senate trying to establish himself as a sensible moderate who could chart a path forward for his aging party, dismissing Washington liberals and admitting as early as 1974, at thirty-one years old and just two years since his family tragedy, that he'd likely consider running for the White House.

There was an impossibly grand sense of destiny involved. When Biden first arrived in DC, he'd temporarily been given a seat on the Senate floor between colleagues from the North and the South, and he somehow convinced himself he was sitting between John Calhoun's old desk and Daniel Webster's, a convenient "fact" that he insisted helped remind him to try bridging ideological divides. In 1976 he dipped his toe in national waters by backing a political ally, Pennsylvania governor Milton Shapp, for president before Shapp quickly flamed out. Unchastened, Biden turned to Jimmy Carter, another outsider, and became the first elected official outside Georgia to back him. Finding himself frustratingly outside the new president's inner circle when he got to Washington, however, Biden entertained serious pitches from party operatives to challenge Carter in 1980, and then to try to oust Ronald Reagan in 1984. Their arguments never clicked, though, until Reagan was reelected, and by his third term, Biden could fully envision a 1987 campaign.

That year profoundly reshaped his view of the world and of Washington, and also of himself. The moment appeared to make sense for him. Newly elevated to the chairmanship of the Senate's judiciary committee, Biden stormed into Iowa, the first state to caucus in the Democratic primary, to present himself as a charismatic, handsome, serious-minded change-maker here to usher in a new era of post-Reagan politics. His appeal was Kennedyesque, at least according to him: he could *move* people, and could pick up where Bobby left off.

His first problem, though, was that he was needed back in DC—Supreme Court Justice Lewis Powell's retirement meant he had to run the hearings for a replacement, and thus had to split his attention, sometimes shirking debate and speech prep. His bigger issue was that one reason he sounded so much like a Kennedy was he was quoting one, and not always telling crowds that's what he was doing. Late in the summer, as his private polling showed him climbing in Iowa, the campaign manager for Michael Dukakis, his rival, secretly shared evidence with reporters that Biden had plagiarized parts of an important speech from Neil Kinnock, a Welsh politician. Revelations that he'd also been using RFK's lines soon followed.

The senator maintained that this was clearly a mistake. He'd quoted these lines with appropriate attributions in other speeches. But the firestorm derailed him just as Supreme Court nominee Robert Bork's hearings intensified, and Biden dropped out, fuming to reporters, "I'm angry with myself for having been put in the position—put myself in the position—of having to make this choice. And I am no less frustrated at the environment of presidential politics that makes it so difficult to let the American people measure the whole Joe Biden and not just misstatements that I have made."

Still furious back in Wilmington, he met with his family and closest advisors to figure out his next steps. Kaufman compared Biden's position to Winston Churchill's after he resigned following the disaster at the Dardanelles, only to return as prime minister—Biden still had the presidency in his future. Mike Donilon, too, had an optimistic spin. He'd surveyed Delaware voters and found that three-quarters of them thought he should run again. Still, Biden's year kept spiraling even after he defeated Bork's nomination. Early in 1988, he collapsed with the first of two brain aneurysms that nearly killed him—at one point, Jill walked in on a priest delivering last rites at her husband's hospital bedside before shooing him away. His recovery represented his first long stretch away from the Senate since he was first elected, and it forced the middle-aged man in a hurry into a bout of uncharacteristic self-reflection.

One result was a retreat from the campaign lifestyle. He remained an important figure in official DC thanks to his seniority and committee roles, and he occasionally stepped into its central, controversial sagas. In 1991, while still running the Senate's judiciary committee, he oversaw the Supreme Court confirmation process of judge Clarence Thomas, which included allegations from lawyer Anita Hill that Thomas had sexually harassed her, only for Biden's committee members to harshly grill her on the matter. Three years later, he helped write and shepherd Bill Clinton's crime bill to law, another move he would later both tout— for its tough-on-crime measures and inclusion of the Violence Against Women Act—and then eventually have to answer for politically, for a resulting regime of overincarceration, especially of Black Americans.

But he wouldn't even hear arguments about running again until 2000, and even then he eventually dismissed the idea. Still, though, he stewed. It wasn't until 2007, facing an entirely new and unflinching media environment two decades after the fact, that he owned up to 1987's reality: "I made a mistake, and it was born out of my arrogance," he said. "I didn't deserve to be president."

In *What It Takes*, the landmark book about the 1988 race that Biden considered to be something like an X-ray of his soul, Richard Ben Cramer wrote about the "connect," or the "Biden Rush," a nearly palpable *thing* that would happen when Biden was really grooving and his crowds were really locked in, and it was obvious to everyone that something special was happening between this charming pol saturated with emotion and an auditorium of Iowans or New Hampshirites. Two decades later, Biden still had access to this magic—that much was obvious to the aides and family members who'd stuck with him. He could rip out one-liners like nobody's business when he was on his game—"Rudy Giuliani, there's only three things he mentions in a sentence: a noun and a verb and 9/11," he said of the Republican candidate at one debate in October 2007, after practicing the line with speech coach Michael Sheehan (the same sought-after coach who'd helped Obama hone his convention performance three years earlier). And when he was feeling it, Biden could bowl anyone over with his in-person knack for just totally enveloping you emotionally, internalizing your story, telling you his own. His own staffers held back tears when, in July, he stayed in Iowa City for hours to answer questions from gay voters about their rights and sat with his arm around one young man as the sky grew pitch-dark. He could have irresistible fun, too. When moderator Brian Williams took a few sentences to ask in a debate in South Carolina if he'd be able to control himself as president given his reputation for rambling and putting his foot in his mouth, Biden simply smiled, leaned into the microphone, and said, "Yes."

What he couldn't do was get the magic to stick with any consistency, or get anyone to care. Voters, not just in Iowa and New Hampshire but everywhere, were hungry for change, and not just the kind of partisan switch from Bush that Biden was promising. His pitch—experience, moderation, responsibility—was fine, but it paled in comparison to the hopeful message offered by the man who might be the first Black president and was promising a new dawn in DC or the strength-and-solutions-oriented line offered by the candidate who would be the first woman commander in chief. Biden had entered the race expecting a serious look from caucusgoers, donors, and the press, and he suspected Obama and Clinton would blow each other up and clear his path, in a repeat of 2004's sequence, when Kerry rose after Howard Dean and Dick Gephardt effectively torpedoed each other's candidacies. Instead, from Day One, Biden was taken aback to find that his junior colleagues weren't being asked to answer to his proposals. Like any political also-ran, he was instead being mined for sound bites in response to *their* latest ideas and controversies.

This dynamic only grew more pronounced, especially after Obama and Clinton blew the rest of the field out of the water with their first blockbuster quarterly fundraising hauls. Biden, always a mediocre raiser because he hated sucking up to rich guys and simply hadn't had to do it much to get reelected in a small blue state, struggled to keep his campaign afloat. When staffers blocked off an hour for him to call donors, he sometimes only spoke to two people instead of the dozen they'd scheduled because of his aversion to the task and because he preferred extending the few conversations he was comfortable with—asking random financiers for their thoughts on his strategy for half an hour at a time. He was plainly miserable doing even that. Once, when a young staffer handed him a list of names and numbers to call for dough, he replied, "Get the fuck out of the car," another aide later recalled—the kind of prickly impatience he seldom displayed in public but flashed to advisors who asked him to do things he found distasteful or annoying, even if they were necessary.

Mostly, though, Biden's mood swung as the year progressed. He'd kicked off the cycle by dismissing Obama even before the "articulate" mess, predicting to the New England Cable Network that he'd "be a little surprised if [Obama] actually does run," suggesting that instead, the Illinoisan would make a dynamic running mate for someone. Obama was, Biden had said, on "everyone's Number Two list." Yet the younger man's appeal was obvious and unavoidable. He and Clinton outdrew Biden at every multicandidate event, sometimes by thousands of voters. Approaching one early Iowa "cattle call," a loyal Biden friend drove past miles of buses decorated to support the two front-runners, and asked the senator's traveling aide where Biden's supporters were. She shrugged, "We're hoping for a snowball effect." Biden couldn't decide how he felt about one particular parallel that kept being drawn. "I was the Barack Obama!" he sighed to the *Boston Globe*, referring to his '88-vintage buzz, suggesting that he understood the Obama appeal. But he also bristled when this idea was brought up by others, since Obama had been in the Senate for just three years. In 1987, Biden would point out, he was in his fifteenth year in the chamber, so the comparison was slightly insulting to that campaign's memory.

One consolation, at least, was that he was far from alone. At times during debates when Obama was being treated by moderators like the front-runner, Biden caught Clinton's eye, as if to say, *What is happening? Where is this coming from?* Then they'd pull one another aside in the wings to shake their heads, unable to wrap their minds around how Obama had risen, or why Americans were going in for his brand of inspiration when he had no experience.

One of Biden's closest friends in DC, Chris Dodd, was there for the ride as a candidate, too. The Connecticut senator had even enrolled his kids at school in Iowa in a bid to win over undecided caucus-goers. The pair went back to the 1970s, hung out backstage at debates, and once split the cost of a private jet from Washington to New Hampshire. But the very fact that they needed to save like that hinted at a bigger, unspoken problem: they were canceling each other out with their similar but not very scintillating pitches and reputations as old-school East Coast Senate moderates. That fact sometimes left Biden stewing and pissed at his old buddy when he was searching for explanations for his own lack of traction as Obama crisscrossed the country in comfort and Clinton chartered a helicopter to take her around Iowa.

Mostly, though, Biden privately observed the unfairness of it all as if from afar, only occasionally breaking through his funk to put on a big grin in public or to step back and laugh to an aide while packing a prop plane with his luggage in the middle of the night that *running for president is a hell of a thing, isn't it?* After events throughout the fall, Biden would return to his SUV and fume to his traveling retinue that he wasn't catching on because the journalists covering him were too young to understand him, or how impressive his career had already been. The bigfoots were out chasing Obama or Clinton. *Did these kids even know who Bork was?* By the winter, this complaint had trailed off. He no longer had any reporters regularly trailing him at all, and he mused aloud about how to catch people's attention. Maybe he should just announce a running mate now, or roll out a slate of cabinet picks?

He took to rambling about his résumé and his plans, waiting for *something*, anything, he said to light up an audience, or at least an audience member. When it wasn't working, which was most of the time, he just kept going as crowds thinned. By the end of the year, his brother Jimmy was a regular presence, standing at the back of rooms and waving his hands at Joe to get him to stop talking when he'd gone on too long.

Still, deep into December, mired in the low single digits in polling, Biden still thought he had a shot. If he got third in Iowa, he figured, he'd have good reason to continue his campaign into New Hampshire, right? All he needed was for voters to be annoyed with how negative things were getting between Obama and Clinton and to stay away from the caucuses. Weird things could happen if there was a low turnout. *Right?*

* * *

Ever since the 1987 debacle, when he felt taken advantage of by Democratic strategists he didn't know too well, Biden had kept his inner circle tight. In his distinctly open-armed style, he built layers upon layers of outer orbits of advisors. He listened to them on occasion, but he mostly just pinged those guys when he felt like it. At the toughest moments, he relied only on the core group, which by that January included stalwarts like Ted Kaufman, Mark Gitenstein, Ron Klain, Tony Blinken, and Mike and Tom Donilon, who had cumulatively spent over a century by his side. They were joined, as always, by family members like Jill, his sister Val, and his sons Hunter and Beau—the latter, at that point Delaware's attorney general, was often the final voice in his dad's ear before debates or big decision moments. A handful of other aides, including Larry Rasky, who'd helped guide his campaign communications, and longtime consultant John Marttila, were there, too. As the caucuses closed late on January 3, 2008, it was this group that had to talk him through reality.

There had been a surprise in Iowa, after all. Voters were far more energized by the campaign than the Wilmington brain trust had projected. Turnout was not low. Instead, it was the highest it had ever been, the race having captivated and energized the state. Obama had surged to first and Edwards to second, with Clinton coming in a shocking third. Biden, though, hadn't even gotten close to Bill Richardson. He finished with less than 1 percent of the vote. It was over, his advisors told him. At least he'd beaten Dodd.

Back in Washington, Biden did his best to move on. A few days after returning from the trail, he ran into Bayh in the Senate gym and shook his head: "Boy, you had that thing figured out better than I did." He grinned at his colleague, who'd chosen not to run after thinking about it. "Neither of us had a chance!" He dove back into his committee work, too. In February, he flew to India and then Pakistan with Kerry and Hagel.

Still, even across the world, he couldn't fully shake Iowa and found himself fully wired, pacing the hallways of the top floor of the Islamabad Marriott before the three senators were due to fly to Afghanistan. By chance, he ran into a group of fellow Americans who were in town to monitor Pakistan's parliamentary elections, and he recognized the former congressman Jim Moody among them. "Hey man, you wanna get a milk-shake?" Biden asked. He proceeded to regale Moody, liberal foreign policy thinker Brian Katulis, and a third colleague with his thoughts on the possibilities for American foreign policy after the Bush years.

He would spend the rest of the year planning his party's new vision for the new era as the committee's chair, he explained. Biden's companions already knew that he was an expert, but now he made clear just how well he personally knew a huge range of world leaders, and how thoroughly he'd planned to use his Senate perch to influence the new administration, whether it was Republican John McCain's, Clinton's, or Obama's. As it got late, it also became clear that he wasn't over what had just happened. The campaign between Obama and Clinton was still raging, and, sitting in the lobby restaurant eight thousand miles away, Biden returned to it. *I knew more than anyone else in the race about foreign policy*, he said.

CHAPTER 4

2008

The months after Iowa would go down in history for the sheer animosity of the showdown between Obama and Clinton. Clinton was guilty of old thinking, borderline corruption, and complicity in the devolving Iraq war, if you believed Obama fans. Clinton's followers accused Obama, meanwhile, of unacceptable naivete, false promises, and even, in one case, continued drug use. Biden was determined to stay away from it all. He took semiregular calls from both candidates as they courted his endorsement and foreign policy advice, but he refused to take sides, watching from a distance as his Senate colleague Dianne Feinstein eventually hosted the pair to broker the final peace once Obama won.

So it would have been understandable if Biden were still far from Obama's mind as the de facto nominee touched back down in the United States late that July. Obama had been on a whirlwind tour of Afghanistan, Iraq, Israel, Jordan, the United Kingdom, France, and Germany that was designed to highlight his comfort on the world stage but which—after he spoke to over two hundred thousand German fans in Berlin and drew full-court coverage of his trip's Middle Eastern leg—also served to highlight his star power. He was greeted, upon landing, with an ad paid for by his Republican opponent John McCain that painted it all as a bit frivolous. "He's the biggest celebrity in the world. But is he ready to lead?" asked the dramatic spot, which alternated shots of Obama with pictures of singer Britney Spears and socialite Paris Hilton. In public, Obama's publicity team dismissed the effort, and in private his research aides quickly found that the clip backfired and offended the women voters they were targeting. But the candidate himself was disproportionately sensitive to the implication that he was all flash and little substance—a sore point that dated back to his earliest days in the Senate—and he told his top aides that he knew he needed to fix the impression before it settled in voters' brains. The most effective way to do that was with a decision he'd been considering on and off since late January: his running-mate pick.

The topic had been vaguely on his mind ever since the aftermath of the South Carolina primary, which he'd won commandingly with overwhelming support from Black voters. John Edwards's representatives had quietly approached Obama's to gauge his interest in a deal. The North Carolinian would endorse him if he named Edwards as his Number Two, a move that might help hasten the end of the primary against Clinton. Obama, though, brushed the idea aside, since he considered the vice presidential pick the most important political and governing decision he'd have to make on the campaign trail, and he had no interest in being locked into Edwards already. This was just as well—it turned out Edwards, whose personal life would soon explode in sordid scandal, had made the same offer to Clinton, who also turned him down. Obama, however, thought occasionally of the matter as his chances of winning the primary improved throughout the winter and spring, by which point he was pretty sure he'd win the presidency, too, thanks to Bush's plummeting ratings and Americans' traditional hesitance to keep one party in presidential power for three straight terms. Obama confidentially asked his aide Chris Lu to start planning his presidential transition in May.

This had all happened fairly quickly, considering that about half a year earlier he appeared to be souring on the whole process, if not the presidency itself. Obama never wavered from his campaign, but in quiet moments his aides found him grousing about the bitterness, repetition, and warped priorities of the stump. This disappointment was a product of the idealism that inspired crowds and volunteers, though it was sometimes a bit much for the people closest to him. (They nonetheless recognized the power of this idealism with voters.)

The flip side was an unbudging self-assuredness that Obama insisted was realism. In private, this could express itself as impatience or dismissiveness of the realities of the job, especially the day-to-day aspects of it that Obama regarded as grimy. At times, he mused that the presidency wasn't the best job in the world, but the ex-presidency was. This was a grim joke for some of his confidants who still darkly remembered him saying, late at night during one of their first January 2007 strategy sessions at a law firm conference room in Washington, that even if he did win, he knew a president could only control about 15 percent of his agenda. As late as that December, when he sat privately with New York City mayor Michael Bloomberg, he spent part of the meeting asking Bloomberg about the mayoralty, confiding that if he didn't win the presidency he might still return to Chicago to run for governor or maybe even mayor.

Now, though, he'd clearly given thought to what kind of sidekick he'd want in the Oval Office. In separate private chats with Jarrett and Axelrod, one name kept surfacing. On the flight back to Chicago from early May's North Carolina primary, a victory that had finally convinced even the cynics in Obama's orbits that he would really beat Clinton to the nomination, he listened as Axelrod said they should be thinking seriously about how to tackle the running-mate question. *I think Joe Biden might be the right guy*, Obama replied, and rattled off his reasoning. He'd been pragmatic, not emotional, when thinking it all through: Obama and Biden may not have been close at all, but he didn't know many of the possible picks all that well. Biden had been good and disciplined—if not a headline grabber—in the primary debates, but he also had decades of Washington experience that Obama lacked and could use at his side as he dealt with Capitol Hill, in particular. Plus he seemed to appeal to white ethnic voters who'd so far been wary of Obama. This was all why purveyors of conventional wisdom thought he'd make a good Number Two, and for once Obama agreed with the DC chattering class. "I think he could be the one," Obama said—a much more considered answer than Axelrod had been expecting before they'd started any formal process.

But Obama also insisted that he hadn't made up his mind, that the Delawarean was simply high on his mental list, and that he wanted a real, rigorous procedure to make the decision. Plus, he started grumbling half-jokingly, he wasn't even all that enamored with the idea of having a running mate in the first place, since he was pretty sure he was on track to win and didn't much like the idea of being bogged down with someone else's baggage. Why would he want his legacy intertwined with someone else's for all of history? "Did you find our magic bullet candidate yet?" he sometimes said with a smirk to Plouffe, as the campaign manager later remembered. "Can we get a constitutional exception, and not pick anyone?"

The core campaign team met in Chicago in June to seriously consider their options for the first time. There, they discussed pros and cons of every Democratic governor and senator, a handful of House members, business and military leaders, and some mayors, identifying an initial list of twenty possibilities that soon ballooned to thirty. Yet few of these were realistic options, since the criteria for selection were already clear: first, they must do no harm to a ticket that looked well positioned to win. Axelrod also reminded the group of his maxim that a politician's greatest strength was his greatest weakness, as well, and that Obama's youth and promise of change meant he would be wise to choose someone who could balance those qualities, which meant someone with literal gray hair and experience in both Washington and abroad. These suppositions were backed up by findings from hush-hush focus groups of high-value voters in top-tier battleground states like Ohio, and even-more-secret polls that ran potential VP pick names by swing voters.

The early stages of the process were made especially fraught by the question of how to handle Clinton, some of whose more upset voters were still threatening to withhold their vote in November. When the candidates met at Feinstein's, Obama had told Clinton he wouldn't make her go through the unpleasant vetting process unless he decided she had a serious chance at the job. Back in Chicago the idea of including her on the ticket as a unity gesture was a nonstarter to many aides who would take years to get over the primary. The Obama team settled on keeping Clinton's name in the mix as they leaked and floated options, but she wasn't taken seriously as a possibility, a fact that political insiders decoded when Chicago announced that Patti Solis Doyle, whom Clinton had acrimoniously fired as her campaign manager a few months earlier, would run the eventual running mate's operation, no matter whom Obama chose.

It didn't take long for the campaign team to settle on a shortish-list of six after ignoring some suggestions—Harry Reid floated Bush defense secretary Robert Gates and Ted Kennedy urged Obama to consider Kerry—and ruling out Dodd when he started facing uncomfortable questions about whether he'd received preferential treatment on personal loans from mortgage lender Countrywide Financial. (He denied it, but Obama didn't want to take the risk and also removed longtime DC insider James Johnson from his VP selection committee for his more serious ties to the scandal.) Clinton remained, at least in theory, alongside Biden, Bayh, Richardson, Virginia governor Tim Kaine, and Kansas governor Kathleen Sebelius.

Still, even early in the summer, this group was really much smaller. This was clear even to its members. When Obama called Richardson to ask if he'd agree to be vetted for further consideration, the New Mexican replied, "Come on, you're going to pick Biden. Why are you going through this?"

Biden, though, was also skeptical. He was in an Amtrak car on his way from Washington to Wilmington in June the first time Obama called to ask if he wanted to be considered. Biden wasn't surprised by the call, and he turned Obama down. No, he said, he was sure he could do more good by running the foreign relations committee. He believed it, but he was also—understandably—tired of the national political circus after two failed campaigns that had ended in embarrassment. Plus, he'd been around DC long enough to know the vice presidency could be a thankless job unless its holder was careful and the president cooperated. He didn't know Obama well enough to have a sense of how it would go, and he at least knew what he would be getting back in the Senate. Obama, though, countered that he was serious about Biden, and that he needed an answer. He urged him to think about it. When Biden again refused, Obama asked him to at least talk to his family first, knowing nothing big happened in BidenWorld without Jill's and Beau's input anyway.

To the people who'd spent the most time with Obama in recent years, his persistence with Biden was perplexing. Obama still sometimes worried aloud about Biden's loquaciousness and ego. *Was this guy really the right person to consistently represent me and my winning brand of smart, cool change?* And to the aides who'd spent two years with Obama in the Senate, it was as if he'd forgotten all the condescension and dismissiveness he'd once detected from Biden, too.

As DC embraced the guessing and tea leaf reading about the VP selection, its favorite quadrennial parlor game, Rouse asked Obama outright about his apparent about-face on Biden. Obama replied that they'd gotten to know one another on the campaign trail, mostly on the sidelines of multicandidate events, and that he'd enjoyed talking to Biden casually behind the scenes. Mostly, though, he was impressed by Biden's performance in the debates, in which his seriousness and lack of interest in flash stuck out from his unremarkable presence in the rest of the campaign. Obama thought Biden had been winning the debates repeatedly, even if few people noticed, because he obviously only defended positions he felt strongly about and, unlike Obama himself, didn't feel the need to clear his throat with context and caveats for a minute before launching into his answers. Biden was also clearly genuine in his affection for real people like the Scrantonians he'd grown up with, Obama thought, after witnessing him talk about economic policy. This meshed well with his preexisting conviction that Biden's insistence on going home every evening out of dedication to his family was a redeeming quality no matter how long he droned on in committee meetings.

Obama was banking on the family to turn Biden around. A few hours after his call with Obama, Biden gathered them to discuss whether he should reconsider and agree to be vetted. To his surprise, Jill and his children thought he should take it seriously—he might be able to help Obama in important swing states, and as VP he could do a lot abroad while still traveling less than if he were secretary of state, a possibility that had been worrying Jill in particular. But it wasn't until he spoke with his ninety-year-old mother, Jean, that he was jarred out of his ambivalence. *Let me get this straight*, she said. *This man has the chance to become the first African American president, he wants your help, and you're going to turn him down?* she asked, incredulously. Jill chimed in, urging him to grow up. Still, he couldn't decide, and he kept calling individual family members to talk it all through. They back-channeled on a strategy to convince him, carefully sequencing their arguments and their conversations with him. They were relieved when he finally consented to be vetted. Still, some family members harbored suspicions that he was being overly emotional and sabotaging his own chances.

Biden did have real doubts, but not about himself. Self-assurance had never been a problem for him, though it came from a different place than Obama's own prodigious confidence. They hadn't discussed this, but the pair had in common a set of semiembarrassing stories in which they both, as young men, told their would-be in-laws about their presidential ambitions only to be greeted with disbelief. Yet if Obama's self-belief came from his vague sense of destiny and hope in the American people, Biden's bluster was borne of repeated insistence in his childhood and early adulthood that he was good enough, and smart enough, despite his blue-collar background, his somewhat debilitating stutter, and, especially, his lack of an Ivy League education. He often told the story of when he told his mother he was going to meet the Queen of England and Jean replied, "Don't you bow down to her," just like she told him, "Don't you kiss his ring," when he was set to meet the pope. "You're a Biden. Nobody is better than you. You're not better than anybody else, but *nobody* is better than you."

And even though he'd entered 2007 musing about how attractive Obama would be as a vice presidential possibility, he knew it was a realistic option for himself, too. The thing was, he'd seen seven presidents and eight veeps come and go since he got to DC, and he knew how hard it was to be an effective or memorable VP given that the role's power relies entirely on the president's conception of it. *Does anyone even remember who Lincoln's vice president was?* Biden liked to ask, rhetorically. So as he'd made the rounds talking to allies and friends about his 2008 campaign before announcing it, he shut the line of conversation down quickly when Bill Bradley, the former senator and presidential candidate, predicted Biden would end up as the next Number Two.

Instead, some members of Biden's staff came to believe he was really running to be the next secretary of state after getting close to the job in 2004. That gig was more autonomous, he would remind aides during their interminable internal debates over which position was more powerful. This posture peeked out in public, too, sometimes in eyebrow-raising ways: just before the caucuses in Iowa, he urged voters to consider whether their preferred candidate would be "smarter than their secretary of state," which seemed to imply that he thought he'd be that top diplomat, since he probably wasn't going to win the presidency. But mostly, he wavered—in part out of a calculation that he would be wise not to be seen openly angling for the job, and in part out of his remaining thought that he would, in fact, be better off back in the Senate. "Absolutely, positively, inequitably, Shermanesquely, no," he told a Wilmington reporter. "I will not be anybody's secretary of state in any circumstance I can think of. And I absolutely can say with certainty I would not be anybody's vice president, period. End of story. I guarantee I will not do it." After dropping out, he insisted yet again that he'd have more influence on his committee than as VP.

Yet in private, he couldn't stop himself from holding out some hope. At one Washington fundraiser to pay off remaining debt from his campaign in March 2008, a donor asked if he'd be willing to be considered as secretary of state for either Obama or Clinton. "I don't want to be considered," he replied, "I want to be called." His pride wouldn't allow him to grovel for the job, but he was pretty sure he was in position for it anyway. In one sense, he was lucky, and never found out: Clinton's campaign, which was notorious for measuring drapes it had no business even thinking about, had secretly put together short lists for both the vice presidency and Foggy Bottom, and Biden wasn't on either.

Still, the VP question lingered, and as he kept getting mentioned in the loose speculation, his major concern with the job became more relevant. He hadn't worked for anyone since just after he left Syracuse's law school. It seemed crazy to start now, after four decades as his own boss, especially since he'd have to answer not only to a candidate nineteen years younger than him, but also to a coterie of strategists and number crunchers who fancied themselves brilliant world-changers after beating Clinton. His suspicions of the people around Obama only increased when, deep into the vetting process, the lawyers in charge started asking about his son Hunter's business entanglements, which Biden found invasive and overly personal, and also a sign that he wouldn't be fully trusted.

But the process continued, and Biden's competitive interest increased. At his final meeting with the vetting lawyer in his Senate office, Biden paused at the final question: Why did he want to be the vice president? Biden, half-truthfully and half-strategically, replied that he didn't. Greeted with surprised silence, he continued, with a verbal shrug. He didn't, he said, but if it was what Obama thought was needed, he'd do what was best.

Obama had, in recent months, been growing on him, too. Biden had been impressed by the way Obama's campaign had inspired and marshaled an army of young volunteers and then swamped Clinton and the party machinery. But he was especially taken with Obama's dexterity as a campaigner. Still, it was only in March 2008—more than three years after they'd met—that he fully bought in.

Biden watched from afar as Obama delivered a speech in Philadelphia about race in America within the context of his candidacy after news outlets revealed inflammatory statements made by his Chicago pastor, the Reverend Jeremiah Wright. (Most infamously, Wright had said "God damn America" for "killing innocent people" and argued "America's chickens are coming home to roost" after the 9/11 attacks.) The address was universally treated as a major moment in the campaign, grappling as it did with the legacy of slavery, racism, faith, and systemic inequality in thirty-eight gripping and aspirational minutes. "Race is an issue that I believe this nation cannot afford to ignore right now. We would be making the same mistake that Reverend Wright made in his offending sermons about America—to simplify and stereotype and amplify the negative to the point that it distorts reality," Obama said. "Contrary to the claims of some of my critics, Black and white, I have never been so naive as to believe that we can get beyond our racial divisions in a single election cycle, or with a single candidacy—particularly a candidacy as imperfect as my own. But I have asserted a firm conviction—a conviction rooted in my faith in God and my faith in the American people—that, working together, we can move beyond some of our old racial wounds, and that in fact we have no choice if we are to continue on the path of a more perfect union."

Once it was over and he got his hands on a transcript, Biden sent it to his closest aides, remarking that the content was beautiful, that it was obvious Obama had written it himself—high praise coming from Biden, who'd grown extra-attuned to the authenticity of campaign speeches since 1987—and that his delivery had been "incredibly" impressive. On the phone with one longtime advisor, he tried describing it, but words failed him. "Boy, this guy is . . ." he started, but his voice—saturated with admiration—trailed off.

By early August, Obama had narrowed down his list to Biden, Bayh, and Kaine, with Sebelius's name still floating on the outskirts of the conversation, and he scheduled secret one-on-one interviews with the trio of finalists.

Bayh went first. The Hoosier first met Obama back in 2004, when a mutual friend in Chicago had set the pair up so Bayh and his wife, also a lawyer, could talk to Barack and Michelle about balancing family and Senate life. But plenty of people around Obama saw Bayh as, first and foremost, a Clinton person, since he'd been close with Bill when they were both young governors and he had endorsed Hillary in 2007, then rebuffed Obama's advances late in the primary. He was, though, at fifty-three a relatively youthful, square-jawed legislator with unquestioned experience and a home address in competitive Indiana, and he'd been through the VP process before. In 2000, he was vetted by Gore, who told him—correctly—that even if he wasn't selected, his profile would rise. In the eight intervening years, the process had gotten significantly more complicated, and Bayh expressed surprise to Obama's team when he got the forty-page document to fill out, considering that 2000's version was one-fifth the length. He called the lawyer assigned to his candidacy when he read the final question, which appeared to be asking if there was anything out there, true or false, that could damage him or Obama. "What?" Bayh asked the vetter. "You want to know scurrilous rumors?" Yes, came the response, we want to know those, too. "I don't keep track of those!" Bayh replied.

In person, hidden away from the press in St. Louis, Obama was more relaxed, and it was obvious he wanted to suss out their personal chemistry. When Bayh walked in for his interview, Obama gestured to a stack of papers about three feet high on the table—the senator's completed vetting documents—then, for three and a half hours over cheeseburgers, they spoke about other things: how they would interact in the White House, and about their personal styles of governing and legislating under stress. Bayh left the meeting under the impression that he had a real shot at the job, and he canceled his family's planned vacation to the Grand Canyon so he could meet with Plouffe and Axelrod in West Virginia instead for a follow-up about more specifics. What he didn't know, though, was that Reid was lobbying against him. The Senate leader hadn't been impressed with him in the chamber, suspecting him of just wanting to be president. More importantly still, he recognized that Bayh represented a state with a Republican governor, and so would likely be replaced by a GOP senator if Obama picked him.

Obama was more interested in Kaine, a warm but serious figure with whom he'd felt a personal connection ever since they'd met in 2005 and realized their mothers had grown up in the same small town in Kansas. Kaine encouraged Obama to run a few years later, arguing that people liked him and he shouldn't wait until people found reason to dislike him. He kept in touch with Plouffe and Axelrod, and even invited Obama to Richmond, the old capital of the Confederacy, for one of the first symbolically potent events of his campaign after he launched it in Lincoln's Springfield. Kaine, fifty, had been skeptical that Obama was serious about picking him, but he agreed to be vetted for Obama's initial long list after the candidate called him while Kaine was on the way to his oldest son's high school graduation. As the process progressed, Obama insisted that Kaine stay on the list even when advisors questioned the wisdom of his inclusion. Sure, you could argue that he'd be a pick like Gore was for Clinton, reinforcing the nominee's political strengths, but more realistically they were too similar: they were a pair of young, hopeful, relatively inexperienced and fairly liberal Harvard Law grads, no matter how practical and effective either was as a politician.

Still, when they met surreptitiously in Indiana, Obama took the prospect of their partnership seriously, as did Kaine, to the point where they got to talking about legislative priorities and political trade-offs. When Kaine asked about Obama's appetite to pursue difficult choices like health-care reform even if his standing suffered, Obama replied that there was no point in being president if you don't do the hard things, and he admitted that if he passed real health legislation his first midterm elections would likely be especially tough thanks to GOP backlash. As the meeting continued, Obama admitted to Kaine that he was the choice of his heart, and Biden the choice of his head. But he was torn. Sometimes, he said, he went with his heart, and sometimes with his head.

Biden, meanwhile, had been making calls. Once it was clear he was a serious contender, he reconnected with Walter Mondale, Jimmy Carter's vice president and his former Senate colleague. It was little known, but the two had actually first discussed the vice presidency in 1976, when Mondale was auditioning for the role and he wanted advice from Biden, the only person in Washington without a Georgia connection who actually knew Carter. Now Biden had given some thought to different models of the vice presidency—he couldn't stand what Dick Cheney had done, wasn't sure Gore had been as effective as he could have been with his discrete assigned projects, and wondered about Lyndon B. Johnson until he read Robert A. Caro's *The Passage of Power* and understood that Johnson had been miserable in his role as JFK's Senate liaison. Mondale's version of the job, Biden concluded, was the best, and he now studied the memo that Mondale and his advisor Dick Moe had written for Carter proposing a then-unusual general-advisor arrangement rather than a more circumscribed but vague second-fiddle understanding.

Biden and Ted Kaufman, perhaps his closest confidant, met with Mondale and Moe to ask for specifics, and for guidance on what to ask of Obama. Mondale had gotten Carter to understand that the vice president was the only one who could give him unfettered advice, and had told him he could be an effective advisor only if he saw every piece of material, no matter how classified, that crossed the president's desk. He could play an important role for Carter on Capitol Hill and in selling his agenda around the country, he said, and in Washington's corridors of power, given the new president's relative lack of familiarity with them and his own considerable experience. That had all worked—Mondale succeeded in turning the job into a good one, and he wasn't a glorified assistant or has-been, as he'd feared. The potential parallels to Obama and Biden were clear. But, Mondale told Biden, the most important thing was that he secured a firm agreement to be the last person in the room whenever the president was making a decision.

By the time Obama and Biden were scheduled to meet surreptitiously at the Graves 601 Hotel in Minneapolis in early August, speculation over the pick had reached new, untenable heights. Obama had asked Mastromonaco—who'd helped run Kerry's selection procedure—to keep the process as quiet as possible. She gave the three finalists internal code names—C1, C2, and C3—and flew them to their meeting destinations on chartered jets from nonobvious private airports. When his turn came, Biden arrived wearing a bomber jacket, aviator sunglasses, and a baseball hat to disguise himself, but he immediately waved to a neighboring plane upon disembarking in Minnesota. The aide traveling with him called Mastromonaco, concerned: he was way too recognizable.

Still, Biden got to the hotel undetected and kicked off the meeting by counterintuitively explaining why the vice presidency might actually be a step down from his current perch, but why Obama should choose him anyway. The pair went back and forth about the results of Biden's vetting—he really didn't have any money, Obama joked, unwittingly calling back to their uncomfortable first meeting in the Senate—and asked whether Biden actually wanted this job versus the secretary of state role. Biden replied that this one made more sense if he could truly be the final person in the room with Obama for his decisions, if he could attend his intelligence briefings, if he could maintain a serious, wide-ranging portfolio as opposed to accepting specific small tasks, and if Obama would commit to having a weekly, agenda-free lunch with him whenever they were both in Washington. To Biden's surprise, Obama was comfortable with each condition and replied that he'd need to be candid right back to Biden in order for it all to work. Biden agreed with that, too, and promised to stay completely loyal to Obama's decisions, even when he disagreed with them.

This all sounded good, Obama said, but he wanted to make sure of one more thing. It wouldn't work unless Biden viewed the vice presidency as the capstone of his career. Biden joked back: "Not the tombstone?" He got the hint, he assured Obama: he was sixty-five, and Obama wouldn't have to worry about him jockeying for a future presidential run.

They spoke for around two hours. Pretty businesslike, by their standards.

A few days later, Axelrod and Plouffe set off to meet with each candidate one last time. Biden was their first stop, and they arranged to meet with him at his sister Val's house across the border in Pennsylvania to avoid the reporters who were starting to watch for movements outside Biden's family home in Delaware. Jill and Beau picked the Davids up at the airport in an effort to demonstrate that all things Biden were a family affair and drove them to Val's, where they met Joe next to the pool. Biden was acutely aware that the main thing standing between him and the job was his inability to stop himself from talking at length, and he nevertheless amazingly kicked off the meeting with a twenty-minute monologue about not only that fact but also about how even though he'd thought he would've been the best president, and even though he didn't particularly want to be the vice president, he would do everything he could to help Obama. The rambling was a sight to behold—he still wouldn't consider subsuming himself into the Obama orbit or style—but Axelrod and Plouffe later agreed that over their two hours at Val's Biden had convinced them of his authenticity, and they were reassured by his promise to take Obama's position on matters where they disagreed. He also reminded them that he knew the Republican nominee McCain extremely well, and that his insights on their opponent would be useful.

The performance was particularly interesting to Plouffe, one of the rare professional Democrats from Delaware who'd never worked for Biden, and who'd had an unpleasant first real experience with him in 1994, when Plouffe coordinated campaign events between Biden and a Senate candidate. Biden wasn't terribly useful for Plouffe's candidate, Delaware Democrat Charles Oberly, since he figured (correctly) that Oberly would lose and Biden didn't want to alienate his colleague, incumbent Republican Bill Roth.

Now, though, Plouffe thought Biden could do well in the vice presidential debate—the running mate's major test—and he could see the broader political argument for choosing him. It helped Biden that he had a handful of important surrogates in his corner: on the campaign side, ad maker Larry Grisolano advocated for picking Biden because of his skill with middle-class messaging, and Chicago-area congressman Rahm Emanuel, a profane and strategic knife fighter who was now advising Obama, sensed the nominee's interest in Biden and told him they'd worked well together on the assault weapons ban when Emanuel was a White House advisor to Bill Clinton. Reid, meanwhile, agreed that Biden made sense—it would help to have someone in the White House who understood Capitol Hill and wouldn't cost him a Senate seat, since Delaware's governor, who'd appoint his replacement, was a fellow Democrat.

This still wasn't consensus, though. While Bayh's meeting with the Davids was uneventful, he had quiet supporters, too. Anita Dunn, for one, was a senior advisor to Obama who'd formerly worked for Bayh, but while she wanted to see him in the role, she didn't push hard for him. The same went for Dan Pfeiffer, another Delaware Democrat who'd never worked for Biden but had spent time on Bayh's payroll before joining Obama's comms organization.

All the while, public attention to the search was reaching levels that Obama's brain trust considered absurd, with reporters camping outside contenders' homes and pinging them with constant questions despite everyone in the know being sworn to secrecy. To throw the press pack off the scent in the final days, Obama's aides leaked that Chet Edwards, a Texas congressman, had been vetted, but they omitted the fact that he'd been ruled out long before then. It gave them a few days to breathe while media attention briefly shifted to Waco.

Back in Chicago, Obama's team pulled video clips of the three final contenders to slot into ads featuring the eventual ticket, while Plouffe ordered up bumper stickers and buttons featuring three different logos. The speechwriting team set out to write acceptance addresses.

From Pennsylvania, Axelrod and Plouffe flew to West Virginia to see Bayh, and then to Virginia to meet with Kaine, who had a better chance. But Kaine disarmed them from the start: *If I were Barack, I wouldn't choose me*, he told the Davids. *We're too much alike.*

Flying home from their visit with Kaine, Axelrod and Plouffe agreed to reaffirm to Obama that the choice was obviously up to him, but that in their estimation Biden was, barely, ahead of the others. Bayh was probably the safest pick, they agreed, and Kaine felt like family, but the politics favored Biden. Obama agreed. He was embarking on a quick vacation to Hawaii, during which he'd make a final decision. He watched, satisfied, as Biden then left for Georgia on a Senate mission after Russia invaded South Ossetia, a perfectly public illustration of the experience and competence on the world stage he'd get with Biden. Obama called to offer the job when he returned from Hawaii, and Biden picked up while in a dentist's waiting room as Jill underwent a root canal. He agreed to take the job and to follow Obama's wishes as long as it didn't tarnish his beloved brand (he wouldn't, for example, wear any funny hats—a solid rule of campaigning ever since an unfortunate photo of a helmeted Michael Dukakis and a tank had backfired three decades earlier). He was, of course, excited, but still reminded himself to remain responsibly wary. When he returned home and told his family, his daughter Ashley cited one of the Irish poems he was always quoting, Seamus Heaney's "The Cure at Troy." (The relevant lines: "History says, Don't hope / On this side of the grave. / But then, once in a lifetime / The longed-for tidal wave / Of justice can rise up / And hope and history rhyme.")

"Dad, this is hope and history," she said. "Oh great," Biden replied, at least according to his own later recollection. "He's hope, and I'm history."

CHAPTER 5

2008

"**W**ho'da fuckin' thunk it?!"

Biden was ebullient when he first met Solis Doyle, his newly assigned campaign chief of staff, ahead of his unveiling in Springfield as Obama's running mate. She'd also gotten beaten by Obama as Hillary Clinton's first campaign manager, and he figured she'd share his slightly bashful awe of the Obama political operation. Viewed from an operational angle, the new partnership appeared to have the makings of a promising marriage from its first week. The day after Obama offered Biden the job, his transition chief John Podesta summoned Kaufman and Gitenstein to a law office in Washington, where he unveiled a team of roughly three dozen Democratic pros working secretly to set up the prospective Obama administration, and introduced them to the transition's head of personnel. Obama wanted Biden's longtime DC fixtures plugged into the planning.

Biden himself, meanwhile, hardly had time to breathe before the Democrats' convention in Denver, which began three days after he joined the ticket. So when, in Colorado, Obama's senior team asked to meet to bring him up to speed on the campaign, he sought to send a message of cooperation. The Obama team was surprised, however, when Biden showed up to their small room with not just his core aides but also his entire family. The space quickly became too crowded for comfort, and the Chicago team, stymied, delayed its plan to walk Biden through the strategy and policy books. Biden, though, didn't see the problem. Once he and the relevant political staffers were finally settled around the table, he laid out the situation from his perspective: this is what the Obama folks had signed up for. But he was the new guy, he said, and he recognized that they'd been working on the campaign for a year, so he'd do what they asked as long as they were direct with him.

It was all a planned shtick, but, for the moment, it worked, and his sense of glee intensified as he watched Obama's nomination acceptance speech later that week—he turned to Solis Doyle and, genuinely inspired, whispered, "Oh my God, no wonder he won." It helped that his family and Obama's got off to a good start, too. Jill and Michelle had already found common cause in their wish to help military families, and Biden's boisterous swarm of grandkids took the Obama daughters into their adventurous fold as they explored the convention grounds and held a sleepover.

This was the rosy view of Week One—the one both sides were eager to talk and leak about. As would quickly become a pattern, the truth was more complicated. It would take Biden some time to realize it, but he was suddenly facing a test of just how much his older, Senate-centric style of politics made sense in the Obama-era party. As he came to see it, not only did he make sense, but his legislative chops and realism were also downright necessary for a hope merchant to succeed. It's not clear that the considerably busier Obama ever stopped to consider the question once he picked Biden. It would arguably be one of the enduring ones of the entire Obama-Biden era.

The complications started shortly before Biden was unveiled as Obama's running mate. Biden leveled with Solis Doyle. Yes, he said, he was in awe of what these guys had done. He hadn't seen it coming, and he'd do what they wanted him to do. However, he said, when they won in November, he really did expect to be a fully empowered partner with a seat at the table and an understanding that he'd be the last guy in the room with Obama every day. This, he reminded her, was the promise.

Biden's maiden speech proved an eye-opening first challenge: It had been written in Chicago to the Obama campaign's specifications, but the running mate insisted on making it sound more like himself. What exactly this meant was, by and large, inscrutable to his new minders. Axelrod and Plouffe had wanted him to just read the text, but when he first got the copy he stared at it, took out a red pen, and, for several hours, rearranged paragraphs. He reminded the unsettled Obama team that he needed to be comfortable with the speech if they wanted him to read it. They had no choice but to agree, even though they thought he was just trying to prove his independence.

A more significant disagreement still was brewing with Biden's first solo campaign trips approaching. He understood that Obama's team had assigned him a new set of aides—fine, that's how this worked—but after being surrounded constantly by a reassuring combination of Kaufman, Val, Beau, Larry Rasky, Mike Donilon, and strategist David Wilhelm throughout the primary, he stopped short when he heard he'd now be barred from bringing any of his own staff on his trips. Obama's campaign leadership figured that they'd picked Biden for his personal qualities but not his unimpressive campaign trappings—as they saw it, this was a marriage of convenience, and nothing about it should be allowed to distract from The Barack Show. This, Biden told Solis Doyle, was unacceptable. Chicago had to allow him the comfort of having his own people with him. He wouldn't let his plane take off without either Kaufman or Donilon on board, he said, and she ran this demand up the flagpole to the campaign's unimpressed leadership. She eventually came up with an informal list of aides who could join him—but never all together—which included Kaufman, Donilon, Blinken, and Evan Ryan, another Biden aide who happened to be married to Blinken.

The air of mutual but still subterranean suspicion only deepened as he was asked to defend Obama's policy proposals on TV and in person. For months before joining the ticket he'd griped to his aides that the nominee's positions on some priorities were too complex for voters to understand, even when Obama said that this was because of the costs and that there wasn't always some tax loophole to exploit to make the numbers work easily. Now, Biden summoned McSweeny from Washington to help him understand Obama's plans and to find ways to reconcile them with his own. On some issues, like health care, they determined, he could just say that they were all trying to reach a goal of universal coverage, they'd just been in favor of different mechanisms to get there. Now he backed Obama's plan. On bankruptcy policy, where Obama stood to Biden's left in proposing new reforms to help seniors and disaster survivors against the wishes of the financial institutions that had considered Biden an ally, Biden agreed to support the nominee's plan, and also to back his more skeptical position on Iraq—where Obama wanted to withdraw troops and

Biden wanted to split the country up into federations to reform it. In the broadest ideological terms, at least, they saw eye to eye, even if they didn't always agree on methods.

Still, it took repeated meetings with Obama's policy team leaders to drill home the message that they would just have to disagree about some matters of principle—like the Catholic Biden's more conservative approach to abortion rights—and for Chicago to get Biden to stop reminding them of his own campaign's economic proposals.

None of this back-and-forth was visible in public, and it was largely par for the course with running mates. So only when some tension threatened to peek out did Obama's staff show real concern.

Shortly after Biden joined the ticket, Obama's brain trust got wind that he had been chatting off the record with the reporters traveling in the back of his plane and had suggested he'd have made the best president of all the primary candidates. A conference call with Solis Doyle was hastily arranged. Axelrod, Plouffe, Rahm Emanuel, and co were making too big a deal of this, she said. *Of course he thought that. He ran against Obama!* But Biden's lack of message discipline was already becoming a pattern that Obama's strategists—who sometimes saw his job as simply not creating inconvenient headlines—felt they had to deal with. He'd conceded that Clinton would've made a great president at one event, and had spent way too much time answering voter questions at others. So, after sending Solis Doyle a series of "what happened?!" memos that didn't change anything—including after Biden publicly objected to an Obama campaign ad that suggested McCain was old and out of touch because he didn't know how to use a computer—they curtailed his responsibilities. (It didn't help that the McCain camp also created an ad of its own recounting Biden's praise of the Republican and his primary-season criticism of Obama.) Biden wouldn't take any more reporter questions and could greet voters only on his rope lines, they decreed. Worse, from Biden's perspective: they gave him a teleprompter to read off at his events, ensuring they'd be highly scripted and minimally interesting. It was all offensive, so Biden wasn't surprised when he heard through the grapevine that Obama had joked to his campaign team that he'd told Biden, "I want your advice, Joe, I just want it in ten-minute, not sixty-minute, increments."

The biggest insult in Biden's view was how little his input appeared to matter to Obama's inner circle. Even as he happily agreed to campaign for the ticket in unglamorous secondary and tertiary markets across states like Florida, Colorado, and Ohio, he sat for a morning call every day with Solis Doyle, his Obama-assigned press person, and sometimes a speechwriter, during which they'd hear from Plouffe and Axelrod about the daily message and instructions, with little opportunity for suggestions. He knew there was a more consequential evening strategy call every day with Obama, but that he wasn't invited to that one.

At times, he found the heavy-handedness amusing in its preciousness, especially since it came against the backdrop of a campaign that looked increasingly certain to win, with Obama's star still rising and McCain flailing for attention. Plus, no one doubted that Biden *was* helping—especially in the upper Midwest, where he was tasked with implicitly reassuring more conservative voters that Obama was no radical—or that Obama himself openly appreciated it.

Ahead of one stop in Green Bay, Biden was handed a memo drafted by the campaign's Wisconsin leadership instructing him not to mention Brett Favre, the Packers hero who'd recently left for the New York Jets, and who was therefore polling terribly in the state. On the ground, Biden did what he did best, schmoozing effortlessly with cooks and patrons at an iconic diner across from the football stadium. He got perilously close to the danger zone, almost like he was mocking Chicago as he brought up rooting for Bart Starr's Packers as a child, since the nuns at his schools were fans. When he went to leave, having charmed the crowd and avoided any mention of Favre, he chuckled to the local campaign leader that his warning was the best political memo Biden had ever gotten.

The racial element of Biden's place on the ticket was no small matter either. Throughout the summer and fall, the Democrats retained some uncertainty that voters would actually support a Black candidate when November came around. Biden was never explicitly deployed to calm race-based fears among white voters, but there was never any doubt that his presence on the ticket was partially intended to send that message.

But with victory in sight, Biden could hardly shake the suspicion that Obama's eggheads back at headquarters didn't sufficiently appreciate his campaign skills or insights, and that some saw him as a foolish distraction they couldn't fully trust. He came to see Solis Doyle—who was usually tasked with enforcing their restrictions—as part of the problem, and he mostly stopped speaking to her, preferring to have instructions relayed through Kaufman. He took, too, to asking campaign aides he met in swing states whether they'd ever worked at Obama's HQ. If they weren't "a Chicago guy," he'd invite them to ride with him in his bus or motorcade for the day, just to prove a point.

Nonetheless, none of it soured Biden on Obama himself. The two barely spoke, Biden remained impressed with Obama's political skill, and it wasn't obvious that Obama was even aware of the drama. And as their chances improved by the day as summer turned to fall, Biden took solace in the fact that no one outside the campaign could see what he was dealing with. It wouldn't hamper his popularity or his public role as VP.

It also helped that he performed perfectly when called upon.

In late 2006, when Obama was still considering whether to run at all, he'd confided in Axelrod that he was more worried about McCain—the heterodox Republican war hero known for his straight talk and popularity with the press after his failed 2000 campaign—than Clinton. Axelrod typed out a response in one of his memos. That relatively moderate version of McCain, he wrote, couldn't win the primary in 2008's Republican Party. Axelrod was correct: to win the nomination, McCain had to tack far further to his right than Obama had expected, since the GOP's newly emboldened activist wing demanded a brand of uncompromising and brash conservatism fueled by grievance politics that would have seemed entirely foreign at this level even four years earlier.

And now, soon after Obama hired Biden, McCain shook the race by selecting as his running mate Sarah Palin, the young hard-core "conservative" Alaska governor who was so new to the scene that Biden had no clue who she was when Axelrod told him the news. The more Biden learned, the more surprised he was. He thought McCain knew better— he'd expected him to pick Joe Lieberman, a longtime Democrat who was now supporting the Republican, to send a message about cross-party appeal. Obama was surprised, too. *What was the GOP thinking? Why hadn't its adults intervened? This was the vice presidency!* Palin had been on the initial expansive list of potential Republican running mates that Obama's team had once compiled so they could prepare opposition research, but her choice was so unexpected that Chicago hadn't actually prepped for her at all beyond adding her name to the initial, long forgotten list. Obama, though, immediately suspected that the untested

Palin wasn't up to the national task and he urged his newly worried supporters—including, at one Los Angeles fundraiser, Tom Hanks—not to be concerned just because he was, for once, not the story of the day. Still, he recognized that he had a narrative problem now, since so much of his appeal was based on promising change, which Palin could presumably do, too, albeit from a very different direction. At the very least, she could certainly sap him of buzz, with the global media scrambling to figure out who she was.

All of which meant extra pressure fell on Biden, whose showdown with Palin at their debate in early October would now be one of the campaign's marquee moments. Biden embraced the opportunity to prove himself and to return to the spotlight as Palin's foil, not least because while he'd been effective in skewering McCain as a Bush retread during his campaign stops, his family had been growing increasingly uncomfortable with this attack-dog assignment, considering it out of character for him—to the point where they tried calling some Obama aides to urge a new emphasis for Biden.

When Michigan governor Jennifer Granholm first arrived in Wilmington to play the role of Palin in Biden's debate prep, Biden struggled to stop himself from attacking her performed naivete. If he went on offense at the real debate he'd come across as condescending, mean, and possibly sexist, his advisors and Granholm told him, and he agreed that debating Palin was an underrated challenge. This point became undeniable to Biden when Republicans accused Obama of sexism early in September for referring to Palin's promise of "change" by saying, "You can put lipstick on a pig, but it's still a pig." (He was, in fact, referring to McCain's policies.) It only got harder when Palin exposed her intellectual vacancy in a pair of staggeringly uncomfortable interviews with Katie Couric at the end of September. (What periodicals did Palin read? "Um, all of 'em, any of 'em that, um, have been in front of me over all these years.")

In practice sessions, Sheehan encouraged Biden to think of the debate as an episode of *Meet the Press*—he should just answer the moderator, and ignore the other guest, who would implode on her own. Granholm tried baiting Biden by upping the outrage in her mock answers—at one point, she quoted My Little Pony—and Biden's eyes bulged, but he restrained himself and ignored it. The tack worked onstage in St. Louis, the most widely watched VP debate in history, and the Palin threat was defused without incident. That the evening itself was mostly devoid of fireworks—perhaps the spiciest moment was when Biden called McCain "out of touch," and Palin tried to defend and deflect, and later to ignore the moderator—was a major internal victory for Biden, a powerful reminder to voters enamored with Obama that they were voting for him, too. It was a huge sigh of relief for Democrats who'd been spooked by the briefly all-too-real threat of a McCain-Palin White House, but who now remembered their confidence that Obama would win, along with his trusty sidekick Biden.

It didn't, however, entirely fix Biden's strained relationship with some members of the Obama inner orbit. Later in October, at the end of a long campaign swing, Biden let loose slightly at a fundraiser in Seattle and assured the crowd that his experience would be a useful backstop for Obama. What he said, though, sounded a lot like McCain's standard line of attack. Within six months, he predicted, the world would challenge Obama. "We're gonna have an international crisis, a generated crisis, to test the mettle of this guy." This time, when Obama heard about it, he decided he'd had enough. "Why the hell would Joe say that? It plays right into their argument. It was sloppy," he told Axelrod, who was also furious, having already spoken sternly—alongside Plouffe—with Biden about staying on message. Obama then called Biden himself. Their conversation was testy this time. Obama told Biden he didn't need this from his running mate, while Biden refused to back down and thought Obama was overreacting to his truth-telling. Obama had a point; Biden had again misread the political moment. McCain's campaign quickly started running an ad that quoted him ominously.

But as the dust settled, Biden and his advisors still thought Obama had missed the mark. Biden wasn't *wrong*, they maintained, even if what he'd said, and how he'd said it, wasn't necessarily politically useful. Whenever reporters or pundits surfaced the idea that Biden couldn't control himself, or that he was especially gaffe-prone, Kaufman would remind them that Biden had been on the Senate's intelligence committee for a decade and had never let any sensitive material slip.

Mostly, though, the world moved on, and Biden faded further into the background as Obama approached the presidency. Fair enough: he wasn't the main story, and neither were the voters he was charged with courting, since they seemed to be drifting toward Obama in sufficient numbers. It was friendly when Biden and Obama did speak, but it was rare, and Biden scarcely even made it onto national TV as the newspapers and networks assigned their youngest reporters to follow him, the least newsworthy of the principals on the two tickets. Even Clinton, who'd agreed to campaign for Obama, sometimes got more coverage, an especially annoying dynamic to Biden, who caught wind of the fact that the Obama team had tried initially to get her, not him, to respond to Palin's GOP convention speech. She'd turned them down, and Biden got the assignment. If you wanted to read it pessimistically, it was starting to look a lot like a redux of the old DC saying that "Mondale's plane took off when he became vice president and disappeared from the radar." Still, Biden knew this was inevitable to some extent, and he was blown away by the energetic crowds and the campaign's event production chops when he did appear with Obama every few weeks.

Plus, whenever he would get frustrated with his teleprompter mandate or his interview schedule or the calls from Chicago, Kaufman would turn to him and, quietly, give him a reminder that it was all worth it—even if his dedication to maintaining the relationship was, necessarily, more persistent and intentional than Obama's. "Three words," Kaufman would say to Biden. "Air Force Two."

* * *

Obama found himself in a curious situation in the late summer and early fall: he'd been more stung by the cantankerous senator McCain's accusation that he was a hollow "celebrity" than most people appreciated, and his campaign had responded by shifting its focus away from large rallies and toward more intimate events, which McCain then started dwarfing once Palin joined his ticket. On the surface, this made it seem like McCain had political momentum, and it was matched by the traditional polling bump candidates tended to get after their convention. Briefly, the race appeared to be neck and neck. So on Sunday, September 14, Axelrod called a meeting of the campaign's highest-ranking officials to consider their path forward. Usually, Obama skipped these kinds of calls and asked for a readout later. This time he asked to join.

They spoke for a while about which battlegrounds to target and what messages to send as they tried ramping excitement back up ahead of the debates. As he typically did in big meetings, Obama sat back and listened and absorbed the nuances, chiming in only occasionally with a clarifying question or comment that would redirect the conversation if he found a certain line of argument unproductive. As the session wound down, he spoke up. He told the team that, as they'd just been discussing, they needed to up their game in the homestretch. They were probably going to win, he assured them, but they'd let McCain define the last few weeks, and they did better when they were on offense, not chasing Palin. And "listen," he added, "I have something to share." Speaking within a circle of trust, Obama revealed that Hank Paulson, George W. Bush's Treasury secretary, had called him and told him "about something that's going to happen overnight that's going to have a profound impact on the markets. I can't tell you what, but it's going to be big." Obama explained that he'd told Paulson he'd be as helpful as he could, and he now instructed his aides to be careful to not get caught playing politics given the sensitivity of the moment that was coming.

Lehman Brothers collapsed the next day. The race, and Obama's prospective presidency, shifted on their axes.

Politically, the biggest short-term change was McCain's plummeting standing, especially after he inexplicably insisted "the fundamentals of our economy are strong" that Monday and soon after tried suspending his campaign in a gambit to appear serious, despite having no obvious role to play in stopping the unfolding financial and economic crises. Debates and interviews that had once looked likely to focus on foreign policy now became economy-centric, and Obama started talking more with Harry Reid about what was needed from him back in DC with the Hill rushing to slam together a plan to rescue the banking system. He had to think as a senator and the de facto head of the party, but also as the likely next president, who'd probably have to keep legislative momentum going for further relief for homeowners and citizens who were starting to lose their jobs by the hundreds of thousands.

It was like a switch flipped. Obama had been speaking occasionally about structural economic risk issues with Robert Wolf, a UBS executive and donor who'd become a close ally and friend, but now he also convened a weekly briefing call on the specifics of what was happening and how best to respond once he got to Washington—convinced as he was that he had little time to spare in bolstering the teetering economy, let alone to step back and consider how to make sure he was implementing a long-term fix.

On the calls, which University of Chicago economist Austan Goolsbee helped coordinate and Wolf joined to give a perspective about market dynamics, Obama usually started by turning to Larry Summers, the former Treasury secretary who'd recently left his post as Harvard's president for a hedge fund, for a broad perspective on the latest developments. He'd then bring in Warren Buffett, the legendary investor who invariably brought the conversation around to his interactions with regular people struggling in Omaha. Robert Rubin, Summers's predecessor at the Treasury and a long-time banker, would hold forth about his old department's responsibilities and capabilities, and Paul Volcker, the former Federal Reserve chairman, would speak about the Fed. Obama viewed the calls as a rapid-fire education from the people he trusted most to shape his economic thinking—for the most part a finance-friendly group, but also one that was well within the Democratic mainstream of the day, so not one he considered disrupting by bringing in more progressive perspectives. Biden wasn't invited.

As Obama bounced between the campaign trail and Washington, where he tried to be helpful in rallying support for the Troubled Asset Relief Program (TARP) to help bail out financial institutions, he reconsidered the task ahead of him. Whereas he'd once envisioned his presidency as a chance to try to heal domestic divides, like some sort of secular minister of morality and shared values while he also tried reengineering America's reputation abroad, he now also saw what was likely to be a historically brutal recession unfolding and recognized that minimizing its harm and rescuing the faltering housing market, as well as the auto and financial industries, would be his first orders of business no matter what he'd been campaigning on. This would almost certainly be a largely legislative endeavor.

Still, he was confident that, as he liked to say, for all the noise, politics was played between the forty-yard lines—that bipartisan compromise was possible on most big issues, and that partisan divides were largely exacerbated by pundits and activists. Especially when it came to the issues he'd been campaigning on, where his positions were popular, adults in DC could find agreement. If longer-term structural reforms to American society would be on his docket, they could wait slightly while he wrestled through a technical fix to this immediate disaster. (He didn't always ask Biden, but he seldom had reason to believe his compromise-first running mate would disagree.)

To those around him, meanwhile, it was almost like Obama started acting as if he were already the president. He was spending more time on calls with his policy advisors and fellow senators, and, while plainly happy to be approaching the Oval Office, he was also talking less during his downtime, clearly working through the severity of the moment instead of joking around. Once, in the fall, an aide observed that Obama sure seemed to be spending a lot of time talking to Republicans working to pass TARP. He wasn't sure if, were the parties flipped, they'd be working so hard with Obama, the aide said. Wasn't Obama even more likely to actually win the election if nothing got resolved yet and Americans kept blaming the tanking economy on Republicans in power? the aide asked.

Obama was unimpressed with the question or its implied argument, which he'd previously heard from fellow Democrats who thought he was bending over too far backward to help Bush, and that his naive idealism was getting in his own way. *Yeah, probably*, he said, but the whole reason he wanted to be president was to solve problems, and if he could get in front of the recession even a little and circumvent some pain for some people, it was worth it. He was sermonizing now in the way that induced eye rolls among even some of his most loyal allies. They feared his sanctimony would get in the way of real progress once he won, even if this idealism did endear him to millions of Americans who treated him like a once-in-a-lifetime savior. But, nearly two years into his campaign, he'd been thinking plenty about this point, and he wanted to make it no matter how moralistic it seemed. If the work decreased his likelihood of winning slightly, he said, it was worth the risk because it was the right thing to do.

Still, the intel he was getting on his weekly calls kept darkening deep into October. As the campaign lurched to a close that fall, he paused, pulling up to one of his hundred-thousand-person-strong closing rallies. Gazing out on the scene, he repeated a thought he'd been considering. He sighed: "You know, we're not going to be able to satisfy their expectations even under the best of circumstances. And this isn't the best."

Years later, Biden liked to tell the story of how, after he and Obama climbed down from the stage in Chicago's Grant Park on election night, where the new president-elect had just addressed a quarter of a million people in person and innumerable others watching around the world, Biden's mother,

Jean, took both of their hands in hers. "Honey, come here, it's going to be OK," she said to Obama, in Biden's retelling. "Joey, he's going to be your friend," she told the skeptical vice president–elect.

Biden had spent the early part of the evening apart from Obama, in his own Hyatt suite with his family. When the race was called the Bidens joined up with Obama; Michelle; her mother, Marian Robinson; and Jarrett and headed over to the park. There, consumed by the moment, Joe and Jill held a laptop up to the crowd and patched in Beau, who'd deployed to Baghdad and was watching the election results with his unit. Though Biden had known this night was coming, heavy emotions overcame him as he soaked in the adulation and the realization he'd finally made it.

Obama, meanwhile, was quieter than usual. When Axelrod, Plouffe, and Gibbs walked into his hotel room once the race was called, they immediately saw that he looked different, as if some invisible weight had settled on his shoulders and deepened the lines on his face, just like all the clichés warned would happen.

A few hours later, deep in the night, once he'd addressed the teary crowd and he and Michelle had made the rounds of his biggest supporters, Obama found his way to a tent where some of his longest-serving aides were gathered, exhilarated. One recalled a conversation from when he was deciding whether to run. They'd spoken about how people would feel the morning after he won, the first Black president offering them real hope after eight wretched years, sending a signal across generations that the world had really changed. Obama looked back, hopeful but more somber than anyone could reasonably expect given the circumstances. Even in moments of extreme accomplishment, the presidency is ultimately a solitary job. He replied: "We have a lot of work to do."

CHAPTER 6

2008–2009

Three days after the election, Biden brought a small group of his closest advisors together and told them he'd been thinking about his job. Obama's presidency would obviously be historic, and he'd been impressed with what he'd seen from the man himself as the economy fell apart around them. But, Biden said, he still needed to figure out how to earn Obama's trust if he wanted to make any mark as VP. Biden took solace in the fact that Obama had promised him something like a full partnership when he'd interviewed for the job in Minneapolis the previous summer, but he also knew that Obama was wary of Biden's tendency to talk at length, and that many of the same campaign advisors who'd tried to minimize Biden that fall would be joining Obama in the White House. In Biden's view, as later memorialized in the memoirs of one aide in the room, it was still a very live possibility that he could get stuck "attending state funerals" or being put "in a closet for four years."

This wasn't theoretical to Biden. He'd seen plenty of president-VP duos up close since he was first elected to the Senate, and those relationships had spanned a spectrum from productive to toxic. More to the point, he had no problem remembering the details of the earlier partnership to which his and Obama's was now most obviously compared: that of John F. Kennedy, a young liberal hero, and Lyndon B. Johnson, an older maestro of Capitol Hill. That dynamic had been marked by suspicion and perhaps the most pungent psychodrama-slash-rivalry of any in the White House's history. The task now for Biden's inner orbit was to work out how, exactly, to optimize his vice presidency and ensure he'd made the right choice to leave the Senate—and how to make clear he would be deferential without debasing himself. "I'm not going to grovel to this guy," Biden said, according to his aide's written recollection. "My manhood is not negotiable."

Biden kept Walter Mondale in mind—he'd gotten as much out of the job as anyone by serving as a reliable advisor to Carter. Now Biden was sure that he could be genuinely useful to Obama in negotiating with the Hill, appointing judges, and helping rebuild the country's reputation abroad. Yet the vice presidency was one of American history's wicked problems, and no one needed to remind the people in that room of the long procession of famous warnings about the job Biden was now assuming. John Adams, the first vice president, had said of the gig, "I am nothing, but I may be everything," which roughly matched the apparent expectation of the nation's founders, who enumerated no responsibilities for the second-in-command except overseeing the Senate. In theory, this provided an opportunity for each holder of the job to mold it to their wishes, but the reality was that the role was in the president's hands. Johnson's deputy, Hubert Humphrey, whom Biden knew from the Senate, had hated it and wrote that the vice president could either choose "acquiescence" or "hostility" to the president, which was actually a nice thought, considering that he also compared the job to "being naked in the middle of a blizzard with no one to even offer you a match to keep you warm." It was all slightly daunting. Biden told both his friends and potential hires that he probably had just six to nine months to solidify his working rhythm with Obama. Plus, he conceded, he knew he had to do so while changing the long-held DC perception of him as loose-lipped and personally ambitious. He was going to be loyal and an asset, and he never wanted that questioned. He had no inkling yet of just how deeply he'd wind up reinventing himself around Obama.

What he also didn't know yet were the details of the job. He surprised his closest associates by revealing that he'd only ever been to the Naval Observatory—the vice president's residence—twice: once to visit George H. W. Bush, and once to see Gore. But Biden had a solution for this gap in his experience. In one early transition meeting in Chicago with Obama, the incoming chief of staff Rahm Emanuel unveiled a draft organizational chart of the White House. As Biden and a handful of his top advisors studied it, they noticed that Emanuel had penciled in Klain—who, along with Tom Donilon, had helped run Obama's general election debate prep—as the administration's communications director. Biden spoke up: *I'd been thinking of Ron as my chief of staff*, he told Obama. Klain, a consummate DC insider, hadn't just been the judiciary committee's chief counsel when Biden was running it, but he'd also spent four years as Al Gore's top aide when he was VP. Obama agreed after thinking it through for a day, and Klain sketched out a memo for Biden about how to approach the job, using the lessons he'd learned from his time at Gore's side.

The broadest principles were cautionary: Biden should avoid just choosing a limited number of big-picture issues to take charge of, to make sure his relationship with Obama didn't deteriorate over time as those issues lost salience, like Gore and Bill Clinton's had—and so that Obama wouldn't forget that he needed Biden, much like Carter needed Mondale. Biden shouldn't hesitate to take on difficult tasks Obama didn't want to deal with, and he should insist that Obama's team have full visibility into everything he was doing to avoid suspicions that he was creating an independent fiefdom.

This part was especially important, since Biden and Obama still didn't have the trust that, say, Clinton and Gore had built up over two extra months together on their ticket in 1992. To make it work, Biden's aides gingerly told him, he had to stop talking about how much better qualified for the top job he'd been—he'd lost the primary nearly a full year earlier—and Klain suggested that they insist on the weekly lunch between the president and vice president that Biden had already floated to Obama. Combined with the hour-plus they'd soon spend together every morning getting the President's Daily Brief—an often terrifying, always sobering rundown of intelligence from around the world—they'd make up for their lack of campaign trail face time quickly. This would also let Biden get more comfortable stirring up debate and challenging the president's assumptions in meetings, another important part of Klain's suggestions.

There was one more factor Biden wanted to consider as he and Klain mapped out his office: he wanted to be as little like Dick Cheney as possible. Biden hated how Cheney had all but created an unaccountable shadow presidency for long stretches of Bush's tenure, having convinced Bush to maximize his stature from the start and then gathering a slew of powerful allies across the administration while building his own, independent pockets of influence to set against Bush's loyal staff. He appreciated that Cheney had made the office especially relevant to the daily functioning of the White House but partially blamed him for the way Bush's presidency had spiraled out of control, especially abroad. He saw no upside—especially not as his standing with the Obama team went—to continuing the perception that the president and vice president could represent competing power centers.

As far as Biden was concerned, there was little room for subtlety in making this clear to anyone Obama-adjacent who'd listen. Just hours after Obama was sworn into office in January, a group of incoming aides arrived at the White House to scope out the place. As they roamed the empty offices, a commotion interrupted them. Biden was arriving to inspect his own new digs. The Obamans watched from the hallway as the new VP looked around the room approvingly. Then he paused and pointed to drill holes in the floor where Cheney had installed a safe, which had since been removed. He grinned, shook his head, and looked up at the assembled young Democrats. "It's weird, man," Biden said. It was like Biden was trying to send the Obama aides a message: he knew his way around here, and they wouldn't have to worry about him.

In some important ways, Biden needn't have been concerned. It had been obvious to Obama even before he'd won that his wouldn't just be a crisis presidency but also an administration born into a series of cascading economic disasters unlike any the country had seen in at least seven or eight decades. Within the company of trusted aides he was open about not being an expert on Washington's inner workings after spending so little time in the Senate—he had never even been inside the Oval Office until he met with Bush there that fall. He said he would take all the reliable help he could get. On the hungover morning of Wednesday, November 5, Obama, Emanuel, and John Podesta summoned Biden, Ted Kaufman, and Mark Gitenstein to help the new president begin selecting his top cabinet officials, starting with his attorney general and secretary of state. It was arguably the most important set of decisions Obama would make, and Biden was in on them from Day One, as he would be for the rest of the cabinet deliberations throughout the transition. While Biden had been out campaigning, Kaufman and Gitenstein had remained close with Podesta and the transition operation as they set up the new administration.

For the most part, Biden took pains to defer to Obama and to stop himself from talking for too long about potential hires whom he'd known for years, but at least once he helped Obama navigate a potential political minefield. As eager as Obama was to make Hillary Clinton his top diplomat—presenting a radically new post-Bush face to the world—some of his allies were desperate to dissuade him after the acrimonious primary, not least because about half of Democrats still harbored some resentment over that race and there was little upside for Obama in resurfacing those tensions and thus risking kneecapping his own popularity. Their resistance was almost as urgent as Clinton's, as her own loyalists recoiled from the idea, too, though in their case it was because they still regarded the Obama forces with residual bitterness. (Two people who remained particularly stung by the Obama vs. Clinton contest were Michelle Obama and Bill Clinton, who both took longer to get over it than their spouses. Both still thought Hillary made perfect sense for secretary of state.) The task of secretly convincing her without any of the mistrust spilling back into public view and splitting the party, therefore, was perilously delicate. Obama called both Clintons repeatedly to ask her to consider it, and then dodged her calls when she tried turning him down.

Not even some of Obama's top aides realized how important Biden was in wooing her behind the scenes. Less than two weeks after the election he spent forty minutes on the phone with her, and then with the ex-president, making the case that she should accept the job for the good of the country. He then played along with sympathetic Clinton aides who were trying to work an inside gambit: Reines told her to call Biden to wish him a happy birthday, even though his actual sixty-sixth birthday wasn't until the next day. Biden was ready for the call. Reines was just trying to get Clinton on the phone with him so he could again press her to accept the offer.

The Clinton hire, coming after Biden's own selection, was widely read by the political press as evidence that Obama was assembling a so-called team of rivals to address the world's various catastrophes, and Obama leaned into this notion by speaking often of his genuinely held belief that his aspirational politics could unify Americans, and reasonable Washington pols, in a time of crisis. Not only did he ask Bush's defense secretary Robert Gates to stay in his job, but he also tapped two more Republicans, Congressman Ray LaHood and Senator Judd Gregg, for other cabinet posts. Among friends, he insisted that his expectations weren't narrowing as the economy staggered, but rather that he'd been reading about Franklin D. Roosevelt's legendary first hundred days. It helped, of course, that an unheard of two-thirds of Americans approved of him, according to Gallup, and that he'd have a whopping fifty-eight-seat majority in the Senate on top of a huge advantage in the House. Major legislation seemed reasonably within reach once he plugged the economic holes.

Things still didn't feel quite rosy in Chicago. Obama was introduced to the presidency's 24/7 all-crisis-all-the-time nature just days into his transition when Illinois governor Rod Blagojevich was arrested for trying to sell Obama's newly vacated Senate seat. Within weeks, news broke that Tom Daschle, whom Obama had asked to lead his health-care reform effort, hadn't reported his taxes correctly, and that Tim Geithner, Obama's Treasury nominee, had tax issues of his own. Rumors swirled, meanwhile, that Gregg was now wavering over whether to back out of his nomination as commerce secretary. All of it paled compared to the storm dominating the daily news. The morning after Biden summoned his inner circle—four days after Obama's win—the front page of the *New York Times* looked almost apocalyptic: U.S. JOBLESS RATE HITS 14-YEAR HIGH; G.M. SEEKS BAILOUT. One refrain could occasionally be heard in the office halls, coming from Jim Messina, a senior political aide. As he later remembered in an oral history of the administration, he had a question. "Where the fuck," he took to loudly asking, "is our honeymoon?"

* * *

Chicago's dreary winter was getting to Obama, as it always had, and Biden was finding it tough to get a handle on the rhythm of things at Transition HQ in the Kluczynski Federal Building as he shuttled back and forth between Illinois, Wilmington, and Washington, dodging snowstorms when he could. Neither was in a great mood when they gathered the White House's senior staff-to-be in a conference room on Tuesday, December 16, for a frank session with their economic advisors.

Obama knew that the news would be grim, and that the crisis would define the early days of his tenure, though he didn't yet understand the full extent of the coming devastation—or that it would set the tone for his entire first term. Obama had dispatched his legislative affairs director Phil Schiliro to work with Reid and Speaker Nancy Pelosi to start drawing up an initial economic response bill back in October, and they'd pieced the basics together by the time Obama was elected. Schiliro then made sure his counterparts on Capitol Hill kept the lead on ironing out the specifics. This wasn't how Obama was hoping to spend his entire transition. Obama's team, meanwhile, was studying the numbers. Rahm Emanuel and Larry Summers warned Reid on December 10 that they would be facing a deep recession with a massive shortfall in demand. Still, they'd told the majority leader at Obama's request, they wanted the legislation to include some measures mandating fiscal discipline, since they didn't want to signal to the country that they would be indiscriminately pumping cash into the cratering economy.

Though crafting the bill was an urgent task, they could argue it was a longer-term concern than the immediate question of how their administration would warn Americans about just how bad things would soon get, since the mainstream press, at least, still insisted on seeing the meltdown as a Wall Street problem, and not yet a concern for normal people's wallets—even though 2008 ended as the worst year for job loss since the end of World War Two, with over eleven million people unemployed. So when Summers and Christina Romer, the incoming Council of Economic Advisers chair, prepped their first big briefing for Obama, Biden, and co, they made sure to start with a bang that would clarify the stakes.

"Mr. President-elect, this is your holy shit moment," Romer said, effectively kicking off a meeting that would go down in ObamaWorld lore. The specifics weren't much sunnier. Obama listened quietly as Austan Goolsbee unspooled the situation in the housing market, Geithner warned that with the banks no longer lending it was possible half the nation's financial institutions could be insolvent and they might need another bank bailout, and budget director Peter Orszag said the ordeal would add trillions to the debt. Biden, who'd brought Klain and his top economic advisor, Jared Bernstein, to the meeting, sat at Obama's side, trying to soak it all in. Romer, an expert on the Great Depression, summed up the danger: they could be facing the worst economic downturn since then. Summers added that he saw a one-in-three chance at another depression. "Jesus," Biden replied, not quite under his breath. Obama, feeling no better, offered the latest version of his go-to joke—"It's too late to ask for a recount." He sighed, then pivoted the conversation to the response.

The economists had already been debating the size of the relief package among themselves: Romer had originally argued for legislation that would cost as much as $1.8 trillion, but Summers rejected that idea out of hand, so she came back with a set of proposals: investments of roughly $600 billion, over $800 billion, and $1.2 trillion. Summers had replied that the $1.2 trillion option was still "nonplanetary," and put the first two options into the memo he then distributed to the room. Obama now asked what was achievable in Congress, and Emanuel replied that they could talk about something in the $750 to $850 billion range, but that a full trillion was simply not realistic from a political perspective; they shouldn't even try selling it to the public, let alone the moderate Democrats they'd need on their side before they even thought about winning over any Republicans. This assertion was backed by focus groups that pollster David Binder had stealthily been conducting, and polling that Obama's campaign strategist Joel Benenson had run, which both showed that voters recoiled at the idea of spending a trillion dollars simply because it just seemed like a huge number. Obama turned to Biden to see what he thought, and—sensing that moments like this were exactly why he'd been picked for the job, and thinking of his former colleagues in the Senate—Biden nodded in agreement with Emanuel. Obama sided with his VP, figuring that if more stimulus was needed down the line, then they could return to this discussion after the first wave became law. At the time, this seemed like a sensible conclusion to Biden. The weight was on both of their shoulders now. As they later left the room, Goolsbee approached Obama and told him that may have been the worst briefing for any incoming president since Franklin Roosevelt in 1932, maybe since Abraham Lincoln in 1860. Obama looked back at the economist, who'd been advising him since 2004, and, thinking of the mountain of horrifying meetings he'd been having about the state of the world, replied that he'd had worse briefings that week. (When he later recalled the moment in his own memoir, Obama left out Lincoln.)

The next day, it was up to Schiliro, administration economist Jason Furman, and budget official Rob Nabors, not Obama or Biden, to lay it all out for Reid, explaining that they hoped to implement the package quickly and sell it to the public as both necessary, given the crisis, and responsible, given the budgetary restraints they wanted to include and promote. Obama himself sat privately with the congressional leaders a few weeks later, confident that he could get them all on the same page even if he hadn't known them long. Though this crowd had known Biden for decades in some cases, Obama thought it was important that he personally now underscore the urgency of the matter by revealing that his economic team was working around the clock to figure out a way out of the chasm, but that without the legislative plan up to three or four million more jobs could soon be lost. He preemptively acknowledged that the level of spending he was asking for was shocking but said he was trying to avoid political gamesmanship, and hoped the Republican leaders in the room could agree. Mitch McConnell, the dour and uncompromising GOP Senate leader, replied that he wanted to be part of the process of crafting the bill and that he thought Republicans could get behind a tax relief measure. Obama, unwilling to make any promises but eager to keep Republicans engaged, said there was no monopoly on good ideas, and that the only test he would apply was: Would it work? John Boehner, McConnell's outwardly warmer but politically guarded and wary counterpart on the House side, weighed in to agree that they were in unprecedented times, but he warned that his caucus had been uncomfortable with how quickly TARP had passed, and that they wanted the chance to offer amendments on this legislation. Obama again cautiously agreed that he wanted transparency—the public needed to know where the money was going, and accountability was key—but he cautioned that this was no time to score political points: he wanted the law signed by Congress's Presidents' Day recess in February.

It was only when Jon Kyl, the right-wing Number Three in the Senate GOP, spoke up to suggest that Obama was floating an arbitrary dollar figure and that they should consider making it all a tax cut, that the president-elect felt the heat rise in the room. Obama had initially thought this would take just $400 to $500 billion, he said, but that number had grown by necessity, as dictated by his economists. He'd met with all fifty governors, he continued, and forty-eight of them were desperate for help (only South Carolina's Mark Sanford and Texas's Rick Perry, both Republicans with their eyes on the White House down the line, held out). He repeated himself, appealing to his GOP interlocutors. On this one, let's not try to score cheap points, he said, certain they'd see the light and never fully considering the possibility they'd see his insistence as condescending. If this turns partisan, we all look terrible. However you've been doing things, he continued, is no longer acceptable.

It would be too neat by half to say that either Obama or Biden was hopelessly naive about the GOP, that they expected full cooperation and good faith only to be blindsided by reality. The truth is that both of them knew, and Emanuel reinforced, that most Republicans would almost certainly oppose their stimulus and try to paint it as an unaffordable and irresponsible opening gambit from an inexperienced new president. Biden, in particular, started hearing early in the transition from a handful of his former Republican Senate colleagues—with whom he was still plenty friendly—that McConnell was already urging them to be disciplined against Obama in order to claw back ground for 2010's midterm elections. Still, amid all their optimism and hope for a new era, neither let himself see reason to worry that McConnell's or Boehner's ground troops would demand total ironbound unity against the popular new administration in the face of such a crisis.

Because, well, why wouldn't some reasonable Republicans consider going along with the plan? In the moment, this hardly even felt like a question. McConnell had just called the bank bailout "one of the finest moments in the history of the Senate." During the transition, Obama also told Democratic senators that he expected to easily strike a deal with the Kentuckian to quickly confirm a big array of his nominated judges. Emanuel, meanwhile, had heard from some of his former GOP House colleagues that they were interested in supporting Obama's opening economic bill if it included money for high-speed rail and similar infrastructure investments.

Obama projected his lack of interest in partisan warfare and his wish for a new era of comity by telling Reid, who was skeptical of all the happy talk, that he didn't want to see Joe Lieberman punished and stripped of his seniority in the Democratic caucus—as some of his colleagues wanted— just because he'd supported McCain in the presidential race. And when it came to the recovery act itself, Obama figured he was preempting a lot of GOP concerns by instructing his cabinet to find $100 million in cost savings in 2009 to signal seriousness about their spending levels, an effort internally nicknamed "Project Dave" after a 1993 movie about a regular guy standing in for the president, which included a scene where Dave consults his accountant. To criticize their profligacy after that, to cynically let voters believe the stimulus and bank bailout were the same thing, to accuse the administration of corruption in doling out the stimulus money, and to cheer as it plummeted in popularity after a party-line vote . . . Well, that kind of partisanship would be beyond the pale. *Wouldn't it?*

It wasn't until Obama soon marched up to Capitol Hill to meet with the Republican lawmakers about the stimulus, only to be greeted with news that their House leaders were mandating total unity against the measure, that he turned to Axelrod and said, disbelievingly, "This shit's not on the level." That injury was sprinkled with insult when, early in February,

Gregg—the Republican New Hampshire senator who'd already recused himself from the stimulus vote—decided against taking the commerce secretary gig after all, calling himself a "fiscal conservative, as everybody knows, a fairly strong one" and citing "irresolvable conflicts" with Obama over the legislation.

* * *

The role of Senate whisperer was a mostly natural fit for Biden, at least when viewed from the outside. He'd spent thirty-six years there and knew its personalities as well as anyone. If there was any asterisk, it was that he'd been more of a committee man—focused on vetting judges and then on setting foreign policy—than a legislative wheeler-dealer, but he'd been around long enough and passed enough bills that this was hardly a concern to Obama, let alone to Biden himself as he surveyed the stimulus push and tried to work out his place in it all.

He was eager for some responsibilities, as he'd spent the first days of the transition saying yes to any ask that came his way, yet still not directly tackling the crises that were consuming Obama's days. (Early on, when his old rival Bill Richardson called to see about getting a midlevel staffer a relatively obscure job in the Agriculture Department, Biden got it done so quickly that Richardson, taken aback, replied: "Jesus, I never thought I'd hear back from you!") But Biden's exact job with respect to the Senate still wasn't so intuitive to the people who mattered most, starting with Harry Reid.

In January, the leader went out of his way to publicly remind reporters—and the administration—of his independence by underscoring that "I do not work for Barack Obama, I work with him," and he banned Biden from Senate Democrats' weekly members-only caucus lunches unless he was invited, worried that his ex-colleague would try to gather undue sway and allies. (Reid's private inspiration was Robert A. Caro's multivolume biography of Lyndon Johnson, which he read partly as a warning about the senator turned VP's over-the-top influence.) Still, he knew Biden remained in close touch with his friends like Dodd and Kerry, and of course Kaufman, who replaced him in the chamber, and that he still used the Senate gym. Emanuel, meanwhile, saw himself, not necessarily Biden, as the administration's primary go-between with Reid, Pelosi, and the Hill after his own six years in the House, a point he liked to underscore internally by noting that his office was bigger than Biden's.

Still, the recovery was obviously a chance for Biden to assert his influence, and from the earliest meetings about what the legislation should actually contain, he caught Obama's attention by proposing individual projects while the president preferred to think about the big picture. At their first session, Biden grew agitated that Obama and his team weren't thinking enough about how they'd explain their investments and mobilize Americans around them, and he started making the case for putting the country on an energy-efficient "smart grid." Carol Browner, Obama's top climate advisor, replied that it would take a decade to get the permits for something like that, to which an energized Biden replied, "No!" that they simply needed to get the right people in the room and it would be approved immediately. Obama talked him down but recognized that Biden was onto something: it would be a grave missed opportunity if Americans couldn't see concrete changes from all this proposed spending, and didn't end up making the connection that his stimulus had created that change.

As Republicans lined up to oppose the measure and sought to portray it as reckless spending, however, its popularity dropped precipitously, and Obama, uninterested in seeing his own standing droop accordingly so early and with so much on his plate, grew progressively more hesitant to fight back by promoting the package as the massive investment in transportation infrastructure, education, and clean energy it was, to the point where his aides authorized to speak on the record were instructed to refute the (true) idea that they were talking about some of the most significant advances on long-standing liberal priorities in years. But to Biden, the widening chasm between the bill's substance and its public perception couldn't be chalked up to just Republican obstreperousness; it was reflective of the divide between Obama's economists, focused on Wall Street's macro perspective, and, as he started fuming in private, the laborers in places like Scranton.

In later years, commentators would struggle to pigeonhole Biden's ideology at this time. He was far from tuned in to the full economic detachment that many were starting to feel, and his regular invocations of Scranton quickly became the stuff of caricature within the West Wing, especially with the entire financial system appearing to be on the verge of collapse and Obama focused on keeping it intact. But as Wall Street wobbled, Biden's long-standing distance from its leading lights gave him some perspective that he felt the finance-friendly staffers surrounding Obama sorely lacked, not that he'd yet say anything like that out loud. The transition's personnel operation was run by a Citi alum; if Biden himself was tied to the financial industry, it was primarily through Delaware's credit card corporations, not the Goldman Sachses of the world. It was one reason he soon proposed to Obama a middle-class task force, a group he would lead to keep himself in the economic discussions and to try ensuring all the administration's focus wasn't on high finance.

It was not, therefore, inevitable that the bill's passage would come down to Biden's ability to win over a handful of his former Senate colleagues. For the moment Obama's role as chief inspirer and galvanizer was seen as the game changer, and though Biden's operator position possibly might be necessary at some point, it was not yet obviously needed here. Yet he unambiguously saw the recovery as a chance to prove himself and carve out space for himself within the administration. While the actual package writing and dealmaking was handled primarily by a combination of Emanuel, Schiliro, Reid, Pelosi, and their elected confidants, Biden was brought into the strategy sessions when it came time to figure out how to woo the two necessary GOP senators to reach sixty votes overall for the roughly $800 billion package. Reid had been working on Susan Collins, of Maine, and Obama, too, had tried winning over her colleague Olympia Snowe. But Biden, like Reid, knew that no Republican would agree to break with their party and effectively be the politically toxic "sixtieth vote," so they needed to find a sixty-first and, if possible, sixty-second and sixty-third to dilute the blame from conservatives.

Biden considered a list of relative moderates he'd served with and approached them to gauge their openness to compromise: beyond the Mainers, he talked to his frequent Amtrak travel companion Arlen Specter of Pennsylvania, Alaska's Lisa Murkowski, Ohio's George Voinovich, and Florida's Mel Martinez, and he thought about trying Richard Lugar and Utah's Bob Bennett. Each warned him that a vote for the bill would probably be a step too far for them, since they'd likely be ensuring themselves primary challenges from hard-core right-wingers if they sided with Obama. Biden couldn't believe that they actually believed this and narrowed his focus to just Collins—he called her constantly, even when she was at home in remote rural Maine with bad cell service—and his old friend Specter. (Snowe already appeared to be on board.)

It was, he thought, a matter of persistence. It worked, especially once Reid secured a massive funding bump for the National Institutes of Health that Specter requested. The bill passed with sixty-one votes.

It was a triumphant moment for Biden, if not for the administration as a whole, which by this point was so mired in economic bad news that Obama held the bill signing in Colorado, far from the glare of Washington's cameras and the bulk of the political press corps. Still, the effort had made clear that Biden could deliver for Obama when it was most needed. The vice president heard only later that Collins, Snowe, and Specter were immediately treated like outcasts by their fellow Republicans, who scarcely even spoke to them for six weeks after the vote. It got so bad that Biden in April succeeded in convincing Specter to become a Democrat, bolstering Obama's majority. Murkowski, Lugar, and Bennett all got, and later lost, the primary challenges they warned about; Voinovich, Martinez, and Snowe retired rather than continue in this environment.

Obama himself was conflicted as he signed the bill. It was one of history's largest investments in hugely important fields. Some of his aides occasionally reminded him that some whole presidencies passed without accomplishing anything of that scale, let alone during a crisis like the one still playing out around the country. But Obama knew it was already unpopular and he was furious with the near-unanimously negative GOP response—not one House Republican voted for it. An old warning by former Bill Clinton advisor James Carville became a mantra in the West Wing when Obama's top aides discussed how to turn its image around: "You can't get caught whistling past the graveyard," he'd said repeatedly. As they saw it, too many people were in economic pain for them to start cheering their legislative victory or insisting things were getting better.

So Obama was skeptical when, a few days later, Biden proposed what he called a "recovery summer" (after focus grouping the terminology, Obama's aides had decided "recovery" was preferable to "stimulus"). He wanted to take charge, he said, and not just to ensure that the money was spent correctly on efficient and helpful projects but also to pitch the investments to voters by focusing on individual stories of Americans helped by the measure, even as the rest of the administration struggled to convince an increasingly disillusioned electorate that they were doing their best to create jobs. Obama agreed to Biden's proposal, opening a new door for him. Almost immediately, the vice president began convening and running regular cabinet meetings to talk about implementing the law through the federal agencies, calling mayors, governors, and local officials to gauge their needs, and traveling around the country to try to draw positive headlines for the administration.

It was frustrating work at its best, but Biden insisted to Emanuel that it was necessary if they wanted people to understand the legislation—Clinton had failed to do that with the crime bill in 1994, he said, and he'd never forgotten that lesson. The unemployment rate was still hovering around 10 percent into the summer, and even Biden's former colleagues in the Senate regarded him quizzically when he visited their caucus lunch and encouraged them to get their chins up: there was massive political opportunity in the bill, he said, if they focused on promoting its construction or education projects in their states. He didn't get much buy-in. They looked on, unimpressed, as he insisted, "There's gold in them thar hills!" He didn't get far with the outside game—that, perhaps, was better left to Obama, and the rest of the world's disasters soon took precedence for the president. But the relationships Biden started to build within the government with the push would prove invaluable over time.

* * *

This became obvious within the White House almost immediately: Obama's aides were, by and large, far more interested in him than most staffers are with their bosses, some bordering on obsessive. On the outer edges of the administration, this dynamic surfaced in cringeworthy ways. Around Washington, it was common to see young Democrats carrying marked-up copies of *Dreams from My Father*, which they tore through, considering it a key to the new president's thoughts. But closer to the Oval Office, this dynamic had the effect of tightening the circle of confidence around the president, the staffers with direct access to him guarding it closely and effectively shutting out advice and chatter from outsiders, no matter how well meaning they were. Depending on whom in this orbit you asked, various members of the Biden team were on the bubble between confidant and interloper. Some Obamans had read *Angler*, a searing new book about Cheney's vice presidency written by the journalist Barton Gellman, during the transition, and they entered the administration on the lookout for warning signs of encroaching Cheneyism. When Biden floated the notion of giving Blinken—his longtime aide and now his national security advisor—the designation of assistant to the president, too, Emanuel rejected it out of hand, fearing a situation like the one Cheney had engineered with some of his advisors, granting them disproportionate access to, and sway over, the president.

More potentially troubling, though, was the accumulation of eyebrows slightly raised by Obamans at BidenWorld's suggestions. Once, when a senior staffer in the VP's office suggested that the White House consider establishing outreach offices for specific constituencies within the Office of Public Engagement, he was dismissed with a sigh in front of a packed room of his new colleagues: *You clearly don't understand the people's mandate. Obama has unified our country.* (The offices were greenlit a year and a half later.)

Still, at the highest levels this precise attitude was rare. Klain was regularly present at the daily 7:00 a.m. senior staff meeting from the start, and Mike Donilon was quickly integrated into the political planning meetings initiated by Emanuel. Tom Donilon became Obama's deputy national security advisor. The first and second families, too, were starting to spend more time together. Not everyone bought in—Biden's son Hunter was especially wary of the Obama loyalists after what he saw as nonstop condescension from them on the campaign—but Hunter's daughter Maisy was fast friends with Sasha, the younger Obama daughter, and they soon became basketball teammates. This, in turn, drew Michelle and Hunter's wife, Kathleen, close.

All the while, though, Obama and Biden themselves were still figuring each other out, sometimes disjointedly—Biden still rolled his eyes behind Obama's back at his aloofness and discomfort in glad-handing with fellow pols, while Obama still sighed when Biden went on for too long in meetings, occasionally tapping him on the arm to shut him up—and sometimes in public.

One day after the inauguration, they met with a large group of incoming senior aides in the auditorium of the office building across the street from the West Wing. Traditionally, the president would address them and then the vice president would swear them in, but Biden had been told by the advance team that there'd been a change of plans and that they'd do that part later, in private. After Obama spoke, however, he turned to Biden and asked him to swear them in. Biden was surprised and froze for a second. The day before, Chief Justice John Roberts had fumbled as he delivered the oath of office to Obama, forcing the pair to redo it in private after the formal inauguration, just to make sure there was no question about the legality of Obama's presidency. "Am I doing this again?" Biden now asked, hesitantly inching toward the lectern. Told yes, he tried killing time before he got a copy of the oath to read out and joked, "My memory is not as good as Justice Roberts's." The room laughed, but Obama, in full view of the cameras, grimaced and lightly pushed Biden toward the microphone to get down to business. It was a light, throwaway moment to Biden. To Obama, it was a needless jab at Roberts, someone he didn't want to antagonize. He told Biden as much once they left the room.

Biden, who'd come around to the idea that his boss was a prodigiously smart and complex thinker with a finely tuned political acumen, was surprised by Obama's humorlessness. He was baffled when something similar happened again a few weeks later. Addressing House Democrats just as Washington was focused on the stimulus package, Biden admitted: "If we do everything right, if we do it with absolute certainty, if we stand up there and we really make the tough decisions, there's still a thirty percent chance we're going to get it wrong." This notion wasn't controversial to the VP, it was just the basic deal with government programs. Klain, however, immediately started fielding calls from livid Obama aides who couldn't believe Biden was handing their opponents ammunition, just like he had while campaigning in Seattle a few months earlier. Asked about Biden's comments soon after, Obama forced a laugh. "I don't remember exactly what Joe was referring to—not surprisingly," he said, then went on to explain away Biden's comments as a meditation on how no single measure would solve the huge problems ahead of them. Biden thought this was uncalled for. Why would Obama make fun of him on TV instead of just talking to him in person? He said as much at their lunch soon after, arguing to Obama that while he had misspoken, statements like Obama's would undermine Biden's ability to contribute to the administration. Obama apologized and agreed that their disagreements shouldn't play out in public.

Obama kept his promise. When Biden's tongue next got him in trouble—a few months later, amid a swine flu outbreak, he told interviewers he would advise family members not to travel, contra administration guidance that was designed to avoid a panic—Obama said nothing in public and shrugged behind the scenes. That's just Joe, he said. It was left to Robert Gibbs, now the White House press secretary, to clean up Biden's remarks after a tense back-and-forth with his apologetic press staff, who knew Biden was just being honest about protecting his family, even if he was wildly off message.

In typical Washington rumor mill style, this was all significantly more dramatic in the eyes of people two or three degrees of separation away from the conversations that Obama and Biden were having themselves than it was to the principals. Inside the building, Biden figured he'd know it if he ever truly fell out with Obama, and this wasn't that—especially not after he'd proven his worth on the recovery bill and they'd begun holding their lunches, which were already comfortable. On the contrary, he felt enough like a member of the team that he immediately preferred his West Wing office to the larger space he had across the street, not just because of its proximity to the Oval Office power center—just a matter of steps, he liked to show off—but because it was easy to catch Obama's attention from it.

The space itself wasn't very big, and Biden often winked to guests that his Senate office had been fancier. But he tried to cultivate a grand aura there. The walls were painted the kind of rich blue that accents the important rooms of official Washington. In meetings, Biden often made a show of gesturing toward the president down the hall, and of looking up and nodding at the portraits he'd hung of John Adams and Thomas Jefferson, the first and second vice presidents. It scarcely occurred to visitors to point out that they were the second and third presidents, too.

CHAPTER 7

2009

Six days before the inauguration, Biden's mood was grim. He'd just landed back stateside after a fact-finding trip to Kuwait, Pakistan, Iraq, and Afghanistan, and he had little good news for his new boss. He'd flown out with low expectations—he knew the territory as well as any elected US official and had even brought a Republican ally, South Carolina senator Lindsey Graham, because the debates over the wars' futures would undoubtedly be intensely political and he wanted to start off on a bipartisan footing. Biden also knew he'd probably play an especially large role in the knotty task of setting the countries' future paths since Obama was sure to be preoccupied with the economy for a while.

The Afghan leg of the trip was even more of a disaster than he'd anticipated, and, back in Washington, he told Obama as much. For months, he'd suspected military leaders were presenting an unrealistically rosy view of the state of play and he'd been getting fed up with the country's president, Hamid Karzai, who he didn't think was serious about fighting obvious corruption. Still, Biden had long said, at least it wasn't Iraq, where Bush had in 2007 multiplied the American military presence to quell the violence before ordering a withdrawal. The situation in Afghanistan may have been unacceptably disordered, but maybe that war effort was still salvageable, Biden thought. It's why Obama was arguing for a shift in attention and resources to Afghanistan, which had been getting short shrift, especially considering that 2008 was the deadliest year yet for American troops there.

Now, though, Biden said he was perplexed. They had been elected on a wave of antiwar sentiment and Obama would soon send more troops into Afghanistan—the "good war," some people around the president-elect called it, in contrast to Iraq—to right the campaign there. Yet in person, Biden saw no evidence of a long-term plan. Karzai once again proved impossible to pin down and unwilling to pledge full cooperation, so trusting his government to stabilize seemed naive. *Who knew when his country would have functioning and trustworthy leadership?* Biden now asked, forecasting minuscule political appetite in DC for a long, sustained commitment in Afghanistan. The takeaways from his meetings with Americans and allies on the ground were even worse, he revealed to Obama. Ask ten different people to describe the US goal in Afghanistan, he said, and you'll get ten different answers. They were better off focusing their efforts on targeted missions aimed at threats across the border in Pakistan, he suggested. It was time to ditch lofty ambitions of so-called nation-building, and to be realistic.

Years later, veterans of the administration would describe the ensuing months of debates over the future of American engagement in Afghanistan as the crucible that sealed the Obama-Biden bond and understanding. The saga forced each of them to repeatedly consider and reconsider the other's motivations, experiences, and influences. They were under intense sustained political and emotional pressure, with a constant, defining imbalance—Biden always having to, and more willing to, think more about Obama, the ultimate decision maker, than vice versa. Instead of wrenching them apart, this pushed them to forge a reliable working pattern. It revealed Biden to be more loyal than his skeptics feared and Obama to be more ideologically flexible than his fans wished. But the repetitive gauntlet of alternately methodical and slapdash disputes about troop levels also made one thing impossible to deny: both were discomfitingly unprepared for the churn of their own administration's internal politics, neither Obama's insistence on plowing through politics-as-usual nor Biden's expertise in Washington's halls of influence sufficient to break the restraints. This proved far more significant than either expected.

Biden entered 2009 clear about where Obama stood on Iraq and Afghanistan after debating against and then campaigning with him for nearly two years, but their personal dynamic on foreign affairs wasn't intuitive, since they'd had little one-on-one time on the Senate committee. It still wasn't obvious when the president-elect first dispatched his deputy to Central Asia and the Middle East that January, nor even when Biden returned and they showed private signs of a burgeoning friendship between discussions on the topic—like when they wandered the West Wing together the afternoon of their inauguration grinning at the over-size photos of them that the White House staff had hung along the halls that morning.

Biden frequently professed his admiration for Obama. After one early marathon, meeting-packed day, he marveled to aides about the president's seemingly natural and unbothered ability to lead three sessions in a row on three different issues with obvious mastery of the material. Biden, by contrast, demanded notoriously intensive briefings before every big meeting to make sure he understood every possible angle. (Obama was often well briefed, too, just not within earshot of Biden, and not so obses-sively.) Still, Biden also openly admitted that he was slow to understand how Obama operated, so he asked some of the president's confidants like Jarrett to come by his West Wing office for a series of weekly one-on-one breakfasts that he hoped might decode the president's decision-making processes and provide a key to his priorities. He was surprised after thirty-six years in Washington's byzantine murk to find that Obama had no code or style of subliminal messaging. If he said something, he meant it.

That still didn't mean Biden always understood the man, who some-times seemed to come from a separate political universe entirely. That's what the lunches were for. When Obama first agreed to Biden's proposal to set up a weekly lunch meeting, he envisioned them as time to privately strategize and discuss sensitive matters, but he also confided to advisors that he needed time to develop the relationship with Biden, so would probably talk about family and life in the White House, too. As such, it was important to keep the lunches informal, which Biden—who agreed that they still didn't know each other very well, even by Washington's super-ficial standards—also thought was wise, since it would be easier to earn Obama's trust in person than in the huge debate-style policy meetings the president liked to lead. In the earliest days Biden hung back in some of those large meetings, trying to suss out the positions, personalities, and argument styles of influential aides and cabinet members while Obama typically absorbed the debates silently. (Hanging back was a relative con-cept for Biden. He still spoke plenty, just less than he preferred.) Then, in their face-to-face setting, each could share his considered view. This would help Obama consider his options, and he found this useful almost immediately.

On policy matters he quickly took to asking Biden to stay behind after multiparty meetings so they could debrief. But the lunches were their privileged time, private enough that after a few months it wasn't rare for top aides to both Obama and Biden to have no idea what they were discussing inside, even if Biden brought in the index cards he sometimes prepared with specific topics to raise. He held them close. One of Klain's primary responsibilities as Gore's chief of staff had been to write the VP a regular memo for his structured weekly meeting with Clinton, which would include specific prioritized requests from White House and cabinet departments. Klain did the same for Biden, but after a few weeks Biden told him not to bother writing them for him anymore, since his lunches with Obama off the Oval Office were already freer flowing than Gore and Clinton's had ever been. They were real-life conversations about what each of them was thinking about. That Obama found them useful—he enjoyed just getting to engage with another human outside his family without immediate decision points on discussion—was a huge relief to Biden, who grew more comfortable around the Oval, and therefore less nervous about proving himself in others' eyes.

Around the same time, he and Obama independently instructed Klain to scrap another Clinton-era practice. For a few weeks, Biden introduced Obama nearly every time he was giving remarks, on nearly any topic, then stood behind him silently. Clinton loved when Gore performed as VP-cum-hype-man. Obama didn't think he needed the help. Biden thought he had better things to do. And they weren't quite buddies yet, but he no longer felt like he had to prove his worth to Obama.

* * *

What Biden read as Obama's lack of emotion or curious distance on the matter of the wars in Iraq and Afghanistan was really the outward manifestation of a silent, occasionally tortured internal debate Obama was having with himself and had been having for months. This was when Biden started to consider—if not always agree with—Obama's seldom-stated but clearly felt conception of the presidency as definitionally under siege. Obama had been trying to send the message that he was serious about reorienting focus from Iraq to Afghanistan ever since he'd visited Baghdad as a candidate the previous July, though the specifics had still needed ironing out. He'd hoped that trip would put to bed the punditry about McCain's relative advantage on foreign policy experience, but also that it would set the general tone for the eventual Obama administration's posture toward American military engagement. For months he'd criticized Bush's overreliance on the military and referred to the fight in Iraq as the "war of choice," compared to Afghanistan, the "war of necessity." Obama got one political boost shortly before he arrived when Nouri al-Maliki, Iraq's prime minister, embraced his proposal to withdraw US troops from Iraq within sixteen months of taking office—it made him look like a serious international player—and then another when cameras followed closely as he met with David Petraeus, the general in command of forces in Iraq.

The private portion of that encounter would prove more consequential. Petraeus and Ryan Crocker, the US ambassador to Iraq, spent an hour laying out the plan for the next stage of the troop surge, arguing that they'd been reducing violence dramatically, preparing to hand the next president an entirely transformed situation. They then took questions from Obama and his companions on the trip, Chuck Hagel and Senator Jack Reed of Rhode Island, at which point Obama pushed Petraeus to define when he would know it was time to leave the country. Petraeus refused to be pinned down on a timetable, and when they then spoke one-on-one after the bigger session, the general insisted that Obama be open-minded about his proposed timeline, lest the enemy just wait it out, to which Obama said that would always be a risk and that it shouldn't stop them from exiting.

But Obama did concede to Petraeus that he would be somewhat flexible, and he left feeling that he'd established some respect, even though the entire exchange had been uncomfortable, not least because some on Obama's team suspected Petraeus of being a Republican with the 2012 presidential race in mind for himself. As Petraeus and others in military leadership saw it, though, Obama was insisting on effectively pitting the efforts in Afghanistan and Iraq against each other for attention and resources even while he insisted on a wind-down in Iraq. This was reason for concern.

When Obama took office six months later, some of the decision work had been made for him—Bush had committed to withdraw from Iraq by the end of 2011—but he recruited Bush's defense secretary Gates to stay on in part by assuring him that he was not reflexively antiwar and was hoping for some continuity, but also that he was, in fact, serious about his promise to prioritize Afghanistan. It was a sign of significant trust when, five months into their term, Obama turned to Biden during a national security meeting in the Situation Room and said, "Joe, you do Iraq," entrusting him with shepherding the drawdown.

It was primarily intervention-first conservatives with little love for Obama's ultimate goals who saw the assignment as a pawning-off, more evidence that the inexperienced president himself was too focused on Afghanistan. Contrary to press coverage that made it seem like Obama handed Biden the portfolio on a whim, the pair had been discussing Iraq's future and Biden's role in it with Emanuel for two weeks. Biden was, in fact, surprised by the abrupt way Obama made the decision, but the trio had discussed the necessity of assigning Iraq to someone who could cut across agencies and represent Obama's interest rather than that of State, the Pentagon, or the intelligence community, and, Emanuel emphasized, someone who could deal with Iraqi politicians at the highest level. Biden started traveling to Iraq every few months, delighted and honored by the assignment but conscious of his increasing load. He was now in charge of not just overseeing the stimulus money's use, but also of winding down a brutal war, two unequivocally tricky tasks with little obvious political upside in the moment. This was the VP's trap, and Biden had to be careful not to be seen as only taking the toughest, grimiest jobs—the ones most likely to tank the administration's, and his own, popularity.

It was, though, still an opportunity. While Biden was happy with his reputation for international experience, for a man who reached the vice presidency on the strength of that record, his lack of an easily definable foreign ideology was striking, and it meant he could afford to be flexible for his new boss. Obama was promising a new day abroad, and Biden could be a face of it while trying to shape the new approach internally. Biden had never exactly been a hawk—he voted against the first Gulf War—but it took years of inconsistent questioning of, embrace of, and souring on US military intervention—in the Balkans and then Iraq—for him to arrive at his current downright skepticism. When he launched his presidential campaign in 2007, he was straightforward in his regret. "I made a mistake" in voting for the invasion of Iraq, he wrote. "I underestimated the influence of Vice President Cheney, Secretary of Defense Rumsfeld, and the rest of the neocons; I vastly underestimated their disingenuousness and incompetence." It took him longer to turn on the effort in Afghanistan, his disenchantment growing the more he met with Karzai and saw the futility of increasing international funding in the face of local corruption.

A few days before he left for Iraq and Afghanistan in January, Biden had pulled Gates aside after a meeting and asked for advice on how to define his role in the national security realm. Gates—who'd served under seven, now eight, presidents—had recommended replicating George H. W. Bush's model as vice president, where he picked his spots to weigh in and mostly kept quiet in Reagan's meetings so as to maintain his influence and not be seen as just another player in the overall security landscape. Biden thanked him, thought he couldn't have disagreed more, and resolved to do the opposite. As he and Obama saw it, Biden could be the White House's roving linebacker dispatched to handle individual problems but also to run point on large swaths of terrain delegated to him by a president who was notably unconcerned about diluting his power by handing off responsibilities to his trusted advisors, if not a wider circle. Biden was empowered almost immediately to be the face of the administration in outlining their new hope to reset relations with Russia at the first major western foreign policy conference of their tenure, in Munich in February.

If everything went according to the loose plan Biden and Obama envisioned, this kind of thing would be a big part of Biden's job. The arrangement would see Biden lean on his ties to global figures he'd gotten to know on the foreign relations committee—the *New York Times Magazine* that year gave him the nickname "He Who Knows All World Leaders"—and embrace his oft-stated belief that foreign relations is simply "a logical extension of personal relationships," just with higher stakes. Obama never saw the appeal of such an approach, but this, to Biden, was the fun part: on one early trip to Baghdad, when bad weather forced his team to drive to the Green Zone in what the troops called armored "ice cream trucks" rather than taking helicopters, Biden grinned and insisted they go through with the voyage despite the danger. They had to show local leaders the respect of making it in person, he said.

The personal touch also gave his approach to some countries an extra charge, considering how quick Biden could be to take things personally. He never forgot it when Russia declined the administration's early request to establish lines of contact between his office and Prime Minister Vladimir

Putin's while Obama spoke with President Dmitry Medvedev. And he rarely went a few days in the White House without reminding colleagues that he could really, truly no longer stand dealing with Karzai.

* * *

The internal meetings set to define the future of the war in Afghanistan began almost immediately, presenting a high-stakes playing field on which to define the Obama doctrine. At once, they put to the test Gates's warning that if Biden was an active daily participant in such discussions, he'd lower himself to the status of "just another advisor" as Obama tried mapping the path forward.

Obama entered office to an urgent request from General David McKiernan, the American commander in Afghanistan, for tens of thousands of new troops to combat the Taliban ahead of August's elections, which everyone involved hoped would change the course of the war. The National Security Council convened on Obama's second full day in the White House, Biden seated immediately to his right. The president opened the meeting by reminding the room that he'd campaigned on sending more troops but hadn't fully determined what that should look like, and wanted to reset the strategy more broadly from the Bush years. This was basic information to everyone there, and Petraeus, who was now in charge of Central Command, replied that to stop al-Qaeda from fully returning, Obama needed more troops—thirty thousand ideally—and what Petraeus called a counterinsurgency strategy to prop up the Afghan government and society, and to support its army and police while sweeping out enemy combatants by force, to which Michael Mullen, the chairman of the Joint Chiefs of Staff, agreed. Obama had started to ask whether in their estimation all this was necessary immediately when Biden jumped in for the first time. They were getting ahead of themselves, he said. They needed to come up with the new strategy, and to agree on their ultimate goal in Afghanistan, before they talked in such terms.

The debate lines were thus drawn only hours into the administration. Biden was desperate to stop Obama from being sucked into a never-ending war of his own, and another faction led by Petraeus, Gates, and soon often including Hillary Clinton, too, sought to convince Obama that this initial kind of increased engagement was merely the baseline for a responsible war effort. Obama asked counterterrorism expert Bruce Riedel, a former

CIA analyst, for a full-scale review of the country's Afghanistan and Pakistan strategies and policies, to be delivered within sixty days, before his first NATO meeting. On his flight back from Munich a few days later, Biden insisted to a group of reporters that he wouldn't let the military "bully" Obama into making a decision on troop deployments using "artificial timelines."

When the group met again a few days after that, Obama's national security advisor James Jones, a retired four-star general, gave the president four options. He could wait for Riedel's report before making any troop-level choices; send seventeen thousand in immediately; send seventeen thousand over two phases; or send twenty-seven thousand. In the room, the second option was a consensus choice for almost everyone but Biden, who argued that Obama should wait for the review's results. Riedel said that he would take that position, too, in a perfect world, but that, realistically speaking, sending in seventeen thousand now would give Obama more options during the summer, around the election. Obama agreed but was unnerved when that wasn't the end of his first engagement with the military as commander in chief. He had already signed the paperwork when his special assistant Doug Lute, an army lieutenant general who'd been Bush's former "war czar," and whom Obama had asked to stay on, told him that someone in the Pentagon had actually done their math wrong. They'd only counted combat forces, not support staff. The real number Obama needed to approve immediately was twenty-one thousand.

Thirty-eight years into his life in public service, Biden had never thought so hard about how to behave in meetings. Though plenty of his early behavior as Obama's running mate and VP was guided by Mondale's example, here he knew he couldn't just choose to be quiet in big internal debates. Mondale had a pattern of stepping back to protect Carter from having to side with either him or a cabinet member in front of others; Biden had no interest in that kind of effective recusal. Instead, he figured, he now had way more latitude to say whatever he wanted. Obama had promised to listen to him, and since Biden wasn't the one who had to make the final decision, he didn't have to worry as much about everyone in the room parsing his every last word. It was quickly clear that this would be useful as far as Afghanistan was concerned—Biden kept thinking back to Hubert Humphrey, who'd once told him that his greatest regret as vice president was not standing up to Johnson more on Vietnam. After decades of running hearings, Biden had no problem playing the role of boundary-pushing aggressive questioner, and he was thrilled when Obama soon sat him down to explicitly ask him to play bad cop during their debates with the generals and national security team. In order for Obama to make sure he understood every possible angle of every possible argument, he said, he needed Biden to pressure-test them: "Joe, I want you to say exactly what you think. I want every argument on every side to be poked hard."

As Biden saw it, he could do this best by not just agitating to pull troops out—the ultimate conclusion of his now fully baked skepticism—but also by probing every one of the military's assumptions no matter how annoying they found him, and intentionally making arguments that would stretch the terms of the debate. This would give him a runway to make his case, he hoped, and it would help Obama get some clarity to craft his own conclusions—which he would also discuss with Biden at length during their repeated one-on-one conferrals outside of these larger national security sessions. Biden embraced the plan, but Obama also made sure Biden assented never to second-guess or relitigate Obama's final decisions when they disagreed.

This arrangement was never explained to the military leaders in the room, and it took some getting used to, even for Obama, who soon saw Biden's interpretation of his marching orders on display. Riedel reported back with the review's recommendations in March, arguing that Obama should consider Afghanistan and Pakistan as one topic, that he should focus more on training Afghan troops, and should consider more economic support, on top of a counterinsurgency (COIN)-like approach to the southern part of Afghanistan, as Petraeus had advocated. Clinton and Gates seemed to agree when Riedel presented his findings to the group, but Biden again cut in to point out that historically interventions had failed in Afghanistan thanks to a combination of its history, culture, geography, and demographics. He asked the biggest-picture question possible: Since the government there wasn't reliable and now his colleagues were considering sending even more resources in, were they not just risking prolonging their failure? It was an argument he would return to repeatedly, and he proposed instead that they consider focusing on the threat of al-Qaeda in Pakistan, where its leaders were, rather than focusing on democracy-building in Afghanistan. They could consider sending small, targeted teams to conduct operations along the borders, couldn't they?

No one had yet spoken for this much time in any of these sessions, and the military leaders couldn't hide their annoyance. Obama was usually warm with Biden in meetings, but sometimes he impatiently put his hand on Biden's sleeve to stop him from rambling. This time, though, he let him keep talking. Mullen replied that this approach wouldn't solve the root problems ailing Afghanistan, and that they needed to send in more money to earn Afghans' trust and weaken al-Qaeda, to which Biden replied that sounded like a huge suck of financial resources and their limited political reserves, considering Americans—and lawmakers—had little patience for an extended investment.

Obama, however, was also talking plenty to Clinton and Gates, and at the end of March he announced his new strategy, which appeared to endorse a military buildup in parts of the country, a broader Petraeus-style COIN approach elsewhere (depending on how you parsed his careful language), and a goal "to disrupt, dismantle, and defeat al-Qaeda in Pakistan and Afghanistan, and to prevent their return to either country in the future." It took only a few more days for him to find that he was already running out of political capital, just as Biden had warned. At the NATO meeting in April, few allies were willing to hear out his pleas to increase their own troop levels.

The summer fighting season in Afghanistan went badly, and it was hard not to conclude that August's elections were a fraudulent disaster, marred by Taliban attacks across the country, widespread threats to cut the fingers off citizens who'd voted, circulated videos of pre-filled-out ballots for Karzai, and hundreds of thousands of nullified votes. These disqualifications left Karzai below the threshold for a win, but he declared himself the victor anyway, only for the second-place finisher to drop out of the mandated runoff because it was all a sham. It was an unambiguous blow to Obama, who'd invested so many troops and dollars in the effort just months earlier. He now put Doug Lute in charge of a deeper policy rethink. This was hardly underway, however, when the administration's internal politics exploded on him. Obama had replaced McKiernan with Stanley McChrystal at Gates's recommendation in May, and not long after the Afghan elections the *Washington Post* published details of McChrystal's private assessment of the war for Gates. The report was brutal, and Obama was blindsided by its publication. He had been privately considering the findings for weeks, but the *Post* headline itself was enough to significantly ramp up public pressure on him to multiply his investment in the war and send in more troops, as McChrystal said he desperately needed. "McChrystal: More Forces or 'Mission Failure,'" it read.

As Obama saw it, he'd spent his first months in office carefully making a set of sober choices that hadn't irresponsibly altered the course of the effort—he had launched an expert review, sent in more troops, explained his new strategy to the nation, and replaced both his commander and ambassador—but within the West Wing the leak was immediately read as a sign that Obama's military counterparts were getting restless and looking for leverage to box him into a spot where he had no choice but to hugely increase troop numbers. Obama's style was nothing like Bush's had been, the new president putting a premium on deliberation and repeatedly telling his briefers, "I can't defend it unless I understand it." He wanted to make sure he was getting the full information about every decision, and told Gates soon after taking over, "What I know concerns me. What I don't know concerns me even more. What people aren't telling me worries me the most." It stuck with Gates. At the same time, though, Obama was new to dealing with military leaders and contorted himself to make sure they knew they had his respect, even if he sometimes wanted to agree with Biden's more open skepticism. After all, he kept siding with them.

But leaks like this one were "fucking outrageous," in the VP's words. He again told Obama that he couldn't let the military leaders make final decisions, since they would never recommend withdrawal or even troop reductions. Obama pulled Gates and Mullen aside in the Oval after the Joint Chiefs chair testified on the Hill that a slimmed-down Afghanistan strategy wasn't possible. Did they not respect him? Obama asked. All this back-and-forth was distracting him from being able to get anything else done internationally, Obama thought, and it wasn't exactly making their war efforts more popular. As such, Biden felt that it was on him to provide an even more aggressive counterweight to the military representatives when they all got around the same table again, bringing with him years of reputational heft from the Senate, unlike the younger president who Biden thought might be susceptible to Pentagon pressure campaigns. "The military doesn't fuck around with me," he told his former Senate colleagues when they'd catch up. But they were obviously trying to jam Obama.

By the fall, Biden was convinced that the entire mission in Afghanistan had drifted irrevocably from its original purpose, and he told Obama that he was starting to risk taking political ownership of the war. Eight months into his presidency, Obama felt that he already owned it, and though his frustration with the lack of progress was now obvious to Biden, he still didn't agree that the answer was to effectively admit defeat. When McChrystal and Petraeus then gave Obama three options for the next phase of the fight, he resolved to take his time considering whether to send ten thousand troops to train the Afghan army, forty thousand to fight the Taliban, or more than eighty thousand to blanket the country, even though it was obvious from the way they presented it that the military expected him to choose the middle option.

Biden now tried a slightly different tack, recognizing that the generals, and even possibly Clinton, were in favor of a COIN-like approach that mirrored what they'd done in Iraq. He still argued that Afghanistan and Iraq were fundamentally different and thus required significantly separate approaches, and still argued for a more targeted counterterrorism effort focused on al-Qaeda, but when McChrystal presented his report, Biden stopped him on a slide that proclaimed the mission was to "defeat" the Taliban. What did "defeat" mean? he asked, not letting up until the military staff consulted the Pentagon's definition of terms and conceded that they would not be able to fully disable the Taliban so agreed to replace "defeat" with "degrade."

Despite such internal victories and his increasing facility with mind-melding with Obama on other topics, it wasn't surprising that Biden was starting to feel isolated in his position, sensing that the momentum was with the military arguments for another big troop increase. But in a series of subsequent meetings, he started leaning in on an argument that no one in the room was in a position to question, given his background: they would simply not be able to sustain congressional support for constant increases in investments, he insisted. The young administration had already hugely increased the number of troops and had been rewarded with a highly suspect Afghan election. They couldn't argue that the troops were obviously helping, so when Congress started asking, how could they defend the proposition that doubling down on the strategy would change anything?

In small meetings inside the Oval Office, Obama would exhale and flash his annoyance that the only conversation they were having was about troop levels, and not strategy, and that he felt hurried to make a decision before he had the answer to basic questions like whether the Afghan forces had the capacity to fulfill their side of the plan, which was to hold on to regions once the American-led forces cleared them of the Taliban. When he met with the principals in the Situation Room at the end of September, it was clear Biden had made some headway with Obama. The vice president riffed about how the intelligence reports they were getting had been overstating the ties between the Taliban and al-Qaeda, pointing out the low number of foreign fighters in Afghanistan. Obama listened closely. The next day, with more people around the table, the president insisted on distinguishing between the Taliban and al-Qaeda when they talked about threats, and watched as Biden pushed for evidence that the Afghan Taliban agitated for attacks outside Afghanistan. (There was none; they were only a threat within the country.) When, at the beginning of October, McChrystal appeared to brusquely dismiss Biden's preferred scaled-back approach during a public appearance, Obama told the general to cut out the open disagreements.

Biden was constantly in search of allies. Early in 2009, he started quietly inviting groups of officials and external experts over to the Naval Observatory. "We owe the president options, we owe him answers, we should take the time to get this right," he would say before talking through the internal state of play and workshopping possible arguments. The conversations could last all night—once, while Obama was considering the fall troop-level request, Biden hosted Lute, Hagel, and former Bush-era State Department official Richard Armitage for a three-and-a-half-hour dinner to discuss Biden's options—and he also made a point of pulling aside others who were in on the national security meetings who he thought might agree with him, conferring not only with Blinken but also Obama's Homeland Security advisor John Brennan and the National Security Council's chief of staff, Denis McDonough. The colleagues helped Biden refine his arguments, but it was still ultimately up to him to make his case to Obama.

There was still one argument Biden could make that he knew he shouldn't, even though it was hard to shake. That fall, he hosted a breakfast that included Richard Holbrooke, the special representative for Afghanistan and Pakistan. Holbrooke, who was roughly the same age as Biden, had a reputation for egocentrism, but he'd seen it all over a long diplomatic career and he was close to Clinton. Obama was skeptical of Holbrooke, at best—he'd bombed his secretary of state interview a few months earlier—and had lost patience with him almost immediately when Obama and Biden visited Foggy Bottom to swear him in, only for Holbrooke to compare Afghanistan to Vietnam in his remarks. Holbrooke kept at it often enough that once Obama interrupted his grandiose-sounding soliloquy on the parallels to ask, "Dick, do people really talk like that? And do people really think this is Vietnam?"

Obama knew there was something to the comparison—he sometimes asked presidential historians about LBJ's path—but he recoiled whenever he heard it because he took it as a sign that the speaker came from a different era and refused to learn anything new. "I am probably the first president who is young enough that the Vietnam War wasn't at the core of my development," he later told the author Bob Woodward, insisting he had no interest in perpetuating a civilian-versus-military dynamic like the one that bedeviled Johnson. "So I grew up with none of the baggage that arose out of the dispute of the Vietnam War." This was just as well to Biden, who always knew he had to tread carefully with those parallels, too, given his own history. He'd never been part of the protest movements as a young adult, had gotten a draft notice for the war but was disqualified because of his asthma, and then didn't make opposition to Vietnam a central part of his 1972 Senate campaign, though he said at the time he wasn't against it ideologically, he just didn't like how the government was handling it.

But he'd seen up close how the war and reaction to it had shaped both politics and the nation for over a decade—when she was in high school Jill Biden had even known one of the students later shot at Kent State—and used it as a warning in his private conversations. Leaving Afghanistan was a necessity no matter what Obama and Clinton thought, he once told Holbrooke, as the diplomat recounted in his diaries, which were later excavated by journalist George Packer. If they didn't exit like they had in Vietnam, Obama wouldn't win reelection, he continued—though it had been messy, Nixon had survived the withdrawal. Holbrooke seemed to agree, and Biden pushed him: Why hadn't he spoken up and said so to Obama? Holbrooke said he'd held back on this view because he had to maintain working relationships with a wide range of decision makers. Biden was annoyed. But then again, he never went quite that far, either.

Obama spent October 2009 considering his options, but he faced a country losing patience as support for the war shrank away. When he gathered advisors that month he tried leaning into Biden's position, toying with the idea of a new focus on al-Qaeda in Pakistan, but Clinton and Gates pushed back by arguing again that they couldn't unlink al-Qaeda from the Taliban in Afghanistan. Both Biden—who thought another troop increase would decimate Obama politically—and military-allied aides—who thought it was their only option—were cautiously confident they had Obama on their side ahead of his big decision. Still, the president withheld his true thoughts. Ahead of one important meeting with the generals, Biden asked Obama for five minutes of his time, during which he insisted: "You've gotta stand up to these guys, because if you don't, they're going to treat you like you're their puppy for the next three years." Obama stared back. "You know, Joe," he said, "it'd be fun to let you be president for just five minutes to see how you'd handle it."

Throughout the fall, Obama had been chairing a series of Situation Room meetings to consider his options. He had a lot on his mind and wasn't sure anyone else understood exactly what that meant. So the room fell silent when, at the opening of one such session, he pushed himself away from the table and sat back. "I'm not quite ready to start this meeting," he said. "I have a question," he continued. "How much is this going to cost? If I approve what we're considering, what you're asking me to consider, a forty thousand [troop] increase?" The answer was in his prep memo, which he'd read, as always. But he wanted someone to say it out loud.

No one in the room had experienced a silence quite so uncomfortable there before. Principals, including Gates and Clinton, flipped through their binders or turned around to whisper to their own aides. After a beat, Obama turned to Lute. "Doug, do we have an estimate?" Lute replied that yes, they projected an outlay of $120 billion if he approved the troop request, which would bring the total number of American troops in Afghanistan above a hundred thousand. Obama nodded and looked back around the table. "That's my point. I just came out of several hours of consultations searching for several billion a year on early childhood education and I was denied. We could not find it." He then pulled himself back toward the table. "OK," he said. "Now let's talk about spending $100 billion to send a hundred thousand troops to Afghanistan."

And then it was November, and still Biden didn't know what Obama was going to do. The pair had spent endless hours together discussing Afghanistan, and they'd started each day together for Obama's regular intel and economics briefings, as well as plenty of the national security–focused Principals Committee meetings. In group sessions, Biden had been advocating for the ten-thousand-troop option—the lowest-impact one on the table—but military leaders had only included that in their presentation to Obama as an unrealistic lower bound to force his hand toward the forty-thousand-troop option, since a counterterrorism-first operation like Biden wanted was out of the question in the minds of not just the generals, but Gates and Clinton, too.

By the week of Thanksgiving, it was decision time. That Wednesday, Obama told his advisors this was the hardest choice he'd yet made, but that he was inclined to call for a thirty-thousand-troop deployment as long as he could demand a focus on how they would get out of Afghanistan. Biden, however, was in Nantucket for his regular family Thanksgiving getaway, growing agitated that he was out of the loop but refusing to return to Washington even when Hunter and Beau urged him to. When he called Obama and heard that he was settling on roughly thirty thousand troops, Biden steamed and started handwriting, and then securely faxing, a series of half a dozen increasingly frustrated memos for Obama insisting that the president be clear about the overall strategy and not think only about the troop levels. He returned to the White House ahead of schedule that Sunday, aware that Obama would be surprised to see him, and insisted one last time that the president only make this decision if he was sure of it and would stick with it, to which Obama replied he was only committed to what worked. When Biden then again tried to catch Obama privately before one final large meeting about the strategy, Obama said it wasn't necessary for them to talk again, but Biden tagged along with him anyway, urging him to stand up to the generals. At this point he was fully aware that he was risking outright infuriating Obama.

Inside the Oval, Obama went around the room one last time. Biden wasn't alone in his skepticism. Lute argued that if Obama sent in so many troops there was still a good chance Afghanistan wouldn't look any different thanks to its unreliable government and security forces, while Pakistan couldn't be trusted and allies would wobble in their commitment, but Obama would have spent a massive amount of money on it all. Few other perspectives were surprising or new at this point.

Obama outlined his plan, which he would unveil that week in a speech at West Point. He'd call for thirty thousand new troops and ten thousand more in NATO ally forces and support staffers to pursue what was in essence a COIN operation within Afghanistan's cities and a counterterrorism effort outside them. This was all being done with the expectation that he would start withdrawing troops in July 2011, he said, to force urgent reform on the ground, and it would all be reviewed by the end of this year. It was close enough to the McChrystal request that generals like Petraeus said nothing, even though they didn't like the idea of articulating a withdrawal date.

Then Obama turned to Biden and asked, "Joe, you OK with that?"

Biden, sullen, looked back. "Well, I'm your loyal soldier," he said. They understood each other by now. "But you know my view, Mr. President."

CHAPTER 8

2009–2010

Obama had been getting used to the idea that his first midterm elections might be a ferocious expression of grievance against him ever since that first terrifying economic meeting in Chicago a month before his inauguration. After the session ended, Axelrod had approached the president-elect and told him they were already on course to get their asses kicked in two years. Emanuel agreed, revealing that he'd started getting panicked calls from his former House colleagues. At the time, Obama shrugged—plenty could change, and what could he do about it at that point?—then walked back into his office. There was some degree of "no shit" in his feelings on the matter. Biden had just warned them all about the difficult politics they were about to face on Capitol Hill in trying to get out of the economic hole, and the president's party almost always lost ground in its first referendum, even when it didn't have a once-in-a-generation recession to deal with. That fact was only compounding the problem of winning over politically vulnerable allies on economic matters, which, in turn, then further made the overall picture even more desperate. As if all that weren't enough, Obama was trying to do a lot more than most presidents off the bat, which would certainly spark extra recoil. Still, it wasn't until a few months in that he even began to grasp the true scale of the possible backlash.

After Obama had selected Biden the previous summer he had looked for ways to keep Tim Kaine close and, recognizing that they basically saw politics the same way, he'd made the Virginia governor the DNC chairman. Obama asked him to be "his eyes and ears around the country" and to tell him what no one else would about the national mood. Kaine took the assignment seriously and, as one of just about two dozen people with

Obama's personal contact information now that he was president, directly sent him a written report each month about what was working and what wasn't.

It didn't take long for the latter part of the memos to heavily outweigh the positives, even as the macroeconomic picture slowly stabilized. For months, the reports got progressively darker, revealing not only communities struggling with their finances but also Americans in a deepening malaise with increasingly entrenched skepticism about the opportunities for them in the postcrash economy and downright cynicism about Washington's willingness to do anything about it. Republican activists were plainly radicalizing, too, though it wasn't yet clear what the new Democratic president should—or even could—do about that, even with his personal approval rating remaining shockingly high, in the sixties, for his first half-year in office.

This was the landscape within which Obama sought to enact the most dramatic change to the American health-care system in history, an endeavor he knew wouldn't be simple but also one that he was convinced was necessary after hearing a parade of horror stories while campaigning—and after watching Democrats try to get it done his entire political life, continuing a push that was older than he was. He'd made the intention clear when recruiting his cabinet and senior team, insisting internally that he wanted to get millions of Americans without access to insurance covered, to hold insurers to account, and to mandate coverage for preexisting conditions. No other policy push could possibly help so many Americans all at once, he'd figured.

He shouldn't have been surprised when, as soon as January, even some of his own top advisors said he was being unrealistic about the political moment. It wouldn't be clear for months that they were the ones underestimating his persistence. Biden was first and loudest, building on the case he'd started making during the transition that, given the state of things, voters would give Obama "a pass on this one" if he focused only on the economy. Over a few weeks in Roosevelt Room meetings, he told Obama, with increasing agitation, that pushing a health-care overhaul would kneecap his presidency from the start. Insisting on this kind of historical political loser in Year One while facing an already unsettled public would swamp the rest of the agenda, he said, urging Obama and the rest of the administration to listen to his analysis, since he had by far more DC experience than the rest of them. Obama, however, was unimpressed by the next step of Biden's argument, which was that he had to focus on middle-class economics. Well, Obama asked more than once, what exactly would that look like? We're already doing everything we know how to do for the economy, so all you're proposing is giving up on health care. That was status quo DC thinking.

Biden, however, wasn't alone, and Emanuel was on his own mission to steer Obama to other priorities. He'd had a front-row seat for the failure of Bill and Hillary Clinton's universal health-care push, and he advised Obama to at least prepare a backup plan if his comprehensive one failed. First, though, he brought Chuck Schumer to the White House to advocate for a combination of family investments, jobs plans, and immigration overhauls instead of health care. If that wasn't to Obama's liking, the senator suggested, they could consider a manufacturing program being pushed by some midwestern Democrats. At the very least, they should wait on health care until Congress had more of an appetite for such a huge push, a suggestion that sounded good to the already overwhelmed economists in the room. Still, Obama was unmoved, refusing to budge in these large meetings and increasingly impatient with the arguments.

It wasn't until Obama had a series of smaller conversations with Axelrod that others in the administration started to sense the inevitability of the health-care effort. The strategist approached the matter with two competing mindsets. First, he was a father who had experienced the system's flaws while almost going bankrupt trying to get care for his daughter with epilepsy. Second, though, he was a political advisor who saw little but doom in the effort. He told Obama that the data showed Americans were vehemently opposed to government involvement in their care, and that while he agreed the system needed drastic changes, they could wait until the recession was under control. Obama had been internalizing all of Biden's and Emanuel's arguments, and understood Axelrod's concern. But, he said, "What are we supposed to do? Put our approval rating on the shelf and admire it for eight years? Or draw down on it and do things of lasting value?"

On this much Biden agreed; he just thought Obama should do it over more time, not all at once. Obama kept scheduling health-care reform planning meetings, so Biden could see where this was all headed, but he still tried arguing for a less dramatic first effort. At one session, the president and VP listened to a procession of policy experts' pitches before Biden tore into them for five excruciating minutes. *This will never pass, we'll get bogged down on it, and it will distract from everything else*, he said, amazed that the room still couldn't see this political certainty. Obama shifted in his chair, his discomfort and impatience more obvious by the moment as Biden's voice rose into a yell. The president had already made his decision, and this wasn't the cerebral, considered way he wanted to have his policies determined.

Both Obama and Biden recognized the precarity of the moment, but where one saw opportunity for dramatic change that might yet shift the cynical culture of Washington and, over the long run, help Americans who needed the support, the other feared his boss was missing a dire political reality. Nonetheless it would have made theoretical sense for the ensuing push for reform to deploy their complementary skills, Obama the inspirer trying to soothe and then galvanize a hurting nation while Biden worked the inside game in Congress to get the necessary House majority and sixty votes in the Senate. The VP did, after all, support the ultimate goal of revamping the insurance system. Instead Obama gave Biden no central strategic role on the initial push as they designed their policy. Biden was rather deployed for individual vote-winning missions on Capitol Hill over the course of the fight, an important but more targeted role that left him to focus happily on separate projects. In the White House others were entirely focused on the health-care effort, which Biden still suspected might be blowing the administration's political goodwill. Biden, thus, was as surprised as Obama was relieved when they ultimately pulled it off, setting up a lasting legacy less than two years into their administration. By then, though, both had little choice but to admit even amid their elation that they'd still been caught off guard by the size of the GOP-led wave of fury and the depth of the Democratic terror that had hit them.

For the moment, however, it was Obama's intense assurance about his political abilities and radar that won out. He repeated to Biden and his team that he'd promised a big-picture reform and that's what he'd deliver, even after the first few Friday senior staff meetings where Christina Romer gave them early looks at abysmal jobs numbers. See? Obama would ask after absorbing the reports of millions of Americans losing their jobs, and therefore their coverage. There was nothing financially sustainable about the health-care status quo. To the arguments that he'd be overwhelming the rest of his agenda by pushing on health care, he replied that they just had to get the legislation through before the midterms, at which point they'd lose political momentum and running room. Then, he'd say to immense skepticism—but with little doubt of his read on the public's pulse—if it all worked, they could stop worrying about political suicide, since voters would appreciate the reform's benefits.

This was only rational, he figured, and Obama's unemotional style, insisting on treating everyone as logical actors, ruled the day in his White House. So much so that when in February CNBC personality Rick Santelli went on a televised rant about a program aimed at helping homeowners avoid foreclosures, roaring that "the government is promoting bad behavior," that it was making successful Americans "subsidize the losers' mortgages," and "we're thinking about having a Chicago tea party in July," the administration figured they could reason with him to head him off. Obama dispatched advisor Stephanie Cutter to give Santelli a call, hoping that would be the end of that.

* * *

No one close to Obama thought there was anything preordained about his decision to prioritize health care until he was elected. He'd clearly cared about the topic for years, at least as far back as his time leading the health-care committee in the Illinois state senate, where he'd annually introduced a constitutional amendment to establish health care as a fundamental right. That experience had given him an education in the history of the matter, so he knew that DC had been discussing reform for nearly a century and that Democrats in particular had been pushing for some sort of single-payer program since the Truman administration. But despite his 2008 promise to enact universal health care by the end of his first term, neither his aides nor the public appeared to consistently consider it a top real-world priority. For many, it seemed just a campaign-season promise, especially after Obama bombed at the Service Employees International Union (SEIU) health-care forum in the primary—where he clearly wasn't yet up on the specifics of his own proposal—and then amid the primary-season debates over his decision not to include an individual mandate to buy insurance in his plan. Yet he'd taken seriously the constant tales of unaffordable care that he'd heard at town halls and on rope lines, and had no issue with the idea that this fight would be the first, and probably the most prominent, domestic test of his approach to the presidency.

Obama wanted to be intimately involved in setting the bill's text, but he almost immediately put its passage in Reid's and Pelosi's capable and immeasurably more experienced hands, which at first forced the Senate into the spotlight. Reid would have to find votes to pass it from skeptical moderates, and Pelosi had no such pressing requirement. Reid and Biden hadn't always seen eye to eye since they had different focuses as colleagues, but they both knew the Senate as well as anyone and therefore understood what a political lift this was going to be. The House had just passed a cap-and-trade scheme, but Reid decided to shelve the environmental plan in order to focus fully on the health-care side. Obama trusted his and Pelosi's judgment and bill-passing chops as long as they coordinated regularly with Emanuel; they could leave the policy to his team and the external political-slash-moral campaigning for the measure to him.

Obama continued to figure even after a few months of DC slog that he still had a decent legislative majority and a universally agreed-upon sense of purpose within his party with the economic recovery still in rough shape. So why should he spend all his time marching over to the Hill or inviting attention-seeking lawmakers to his home to hang out? When, in the health-care push's early days, he began understanding that some conservative Democrats were skeptical, he insisted on hanging back, sure they would come around for their party eventually at Reid's prodding. He was unwilling to be the one to woo or strong-arm them so early, figuring his political influence should be held in reserve until it was absolutely needed.

Biden, however, watched curiously. His style of negotiation was different, as they had already learned when discussing the stimulus bill. Not only did he want a lot more person-to-person face time with counterparties than Obama ever did, but he also tended to start at a point of basic agreement, then build on deals, adding pieces that each side wanted to make everyone happy. Obama, though, usually started from his ideal spot and negotiated down to a place of mutual acceptance, and he didn't much like doing it. Biden was starting to suspect that Obama didn't enjoy negotiating—or members of Congress—at all. He wasn't hanging around with guests at White House receptions after giving his welcome remarks, and he only rarely had even his former Senate colleagues over for strategy sessions. It was all stuff Biden would've loved to do as president but which Obama thought was superfluous and, often, bullshit—a long cry from his weekly bipartisan poker game in Springfield.

But Obama wasn't wrong, at least when it came to Washington's Republicans. He was aghast in May when GOP pollster Frank Luntz circulated a twenty-eight-page memo to his party's representatives on Capitol Hill instructing them on how to talk about the president's health-care plan. They should call it a "Washington takeover," Luntz had written, since "takeovers are like coups—they both lead to dictators and a loss of freedom. What Americans fear most is that Washington politicians will dictate what kind of care they can receive." They should avoid mentioning Obama directly, since he was still popular, the pollster had advised, and instead frame the fight against the bill as a war against "politicians" getting involved in health care.

It was an early piece of a broader reorientation of Republican Party strategy toward stopping Obama's presidency in its tracks. Around that time, Obama asked Biden in one of their lunches why he thought Republicans suddenly seemed to be in perfect lockstep against him, and why they were proving so difficult to even get to the negotiating table.

Biden had been considering this question and was glad Obama had asked. First, he told Obama, he had to consider that the culture change was a long time coming, dating back to the election of Newt Gingrich and the subsequent rise of his acolytes—conservatives who specifically ran against "business as usual" and "the establishment," and whose whole platform was shaking Washington up. Over time, that attitude had become a dominant ethos among the loudest Republicans, and one of its central tenets was never being perceived as cozy with any Democrats.

There were more factors to consider, like recent reforms in the earmarking process that made it harder to bring politicians to the table with one another with the promise of perks for their districts, Biden conceded. But the second major factor he blamed was the recent explosion of money in politics. It had given politicians extra reason to go home to their districts over the weekends, as so many of their races were hard fought and their opponents well funded, Biden explained. This meant the pols were spending less time together in DC, so fighting one another came a bit easier.

Obama, who'd barely spent any time at all with his colleagues during his brief stay in the Senate, listened and considered it all quietly. This was why he'd chosen Biden, and why he was still content with that choice whenever he thought about it.

They wanted the health-care bill done as quickly as possible, and as the summer of 2009 arrived the only approval it still needed before it went to a vote was from the Senate's finance committee. This effectively left the legislation in the hands of Max Baucus, the committee's Democratic chairman, and both Reid and Biden—who'd known the Montanan forever—counseled Obama to give him time to work through his issues and get the members of his panel on board. No one thought setting an artificial deadline was a good idea, though, and conservative groups used the delay as a chance to organize. Both Obama and Biden were thus blindsided when, in August, Democratic lawmakers were greeted back home by angry right-wing crowds branding the push as "Obama care" in an attempt to poison both the president's popularity and the image of a bill they likened to a Communist plot.

Within the West Wing this was viewed as little more than organized political violence—Gibbs compared the town hall disruptions to the 2000 "Brooks Brothers riot," where GOP staffers posed as Florida locals protesting the presidential recount—but they should have known something like this was coming when, in July, South Carolina senator Jim DeMint said on a call with an Indiana congressman named Mike Pence and a group of activists, "If we're able to stop Obama on this it will be his Waterloo. It will break him."

It was impossible to avoid the conclusion that neither Obama nor Biden, nor anyone else in the White House, knew quite how to deal with this new wave of organized conservative fury by the time Sarah Palin started claiming in August that the proposed law would include "death panels" to determine who deserved care. As the health-care plan's popularity sank and more congressional town halls were overwhelmed by protesters calling themselves members of the "Tea Party," their primary concern was still with making sure Baucus remained on track. They were convinced the disruptions were a sideshow, akin but not necessarily connected to the unhinged "birther" movement that had started bubbling back up to ludicrously claim Obama's presidency was illegitimate because he was supposedly really born in Kenya. No serious Republicans were talking about this stuff, they figured, so it felt distant and deserved little concerted pushback or consideration, even though Obama was unamused to find himself villainized and then attacked with a racist conspiracy that wouldn't go away. The health-care bill was the matter at hand to the president and chief of staff, and well into the summer Obama and Emanuel were still sure they could find enough Republicans to make a deal.

Reid had always trusted Obama's sense of national politics but he sometimes thought he had to remind the president of some truths about Capitol Hill. One was that with a caucus as ideologically diverse as his, they had to work even for the Democratic votes; he couldn't expect them all—from Vermont socialists to Nebraska conservatives—to simply fall in line just because they shared a party with the president. Baucus, an old-school pol who'd gotten to Washington only two years after Biden, was one such complicated case. He had made clear that his committee would take its time because he was eager to get bipartisan support, led by Maine Republican Olympia Snowe and, he hoped, Iowa's Chuck Grassley. Obama felt good about Snowe and was open to the idea that Baucus could win over Grassley, yet another long-serving senator but a staunch conservative. Reid remained uncertain, though convinced that he had to let Baucus try or else he might lose the Montanan's vote as well, which would likely doom the entire endeavor.

Obama resolved to apply a light touch as Baucus's negotiations with Grassley wore on through the summer, but he lost patience with each week of Baucus's insistence to Reid and Emanuel that he was making progress but wasn't quite there yet. Even when Obama hosted Baucus in the Oval Office in July to demand a vote soon, Baucus prevailed on him to give him just a bit more time, promising a full vote in September. Obama was frustrated, but Baucus, from his vantage point at the other end of Pennsylvania Avenue, couldn't understand why Obama wasn't putting more effective pressure on senators himself. From his perspective, the president's staff was hyperinvolved as Baucus and Grassley whittled down the bill to find something the Republicans and the conservative Democrats might be able to support, but Obama himself was sitting back except for occasional check-ins.

That only changed in August, when Ted Kennedy, a longtime champion of health reform, died of brain cancer, dealing a serious emotional blow to Senate Democrats. Obama brought Baucus and Grassley to the White

House soon after and listened as the Iowan held court about what he still wanted to see in the legislation, before Obama, exasperated, finally asked if there was anything they could do to get his support, to which the Republican said he guessed not. So when Baucus finally held a committee vote on a slimmed-down version of the bill—Snowe voted in favor, Grassley objected—and Pelosi's House passed a broader version that fall, it was clear the task was still far from done. They now had to convince a group of moderate-to-conservative Democrats like Lieberman, Louisiana's Mary Landrieu, and Nebraska's Ben Nelson to go along with it all, too, before they returned to the idea of winning GOP support.

Years later it would seem obvious that Republicans wouldn't have gone along with the bill no matter what any Democrat did to woo them. Biden, however, sometimes felt like he was just sitting there in the early stages of negotiations, waiting to be fully deployed to find a strategy for winning over the people he'd served alongside for decades if the president was unwilling to develop those relationships himself. Most of his frustration, though, was with the people surrounding Obama. There was no doubting Emanuel's Hill chops, for example, but Biden often regarded him as too quick to resort to partisan fights. This probably came from the chief of staff's past in the bare-knuckles House, which contrasted with Biden's preference for traditional senatorial conciliation. More often, though, the VP read Obama's negotiators and policy advisors as brilliant but impossibly distant from the political pressures lawmakers were facing, let alone their constituents' concerns. It wasn't uncommon to hear Biden, on the sidelines of some meetings, marvel at the economic team's detachment— comments he often cut with pointed humor by starting, "Well, I just went to the University of Delaware, but . . ." to implicitly accuse the Ivy Leaguers of elitism or out-of-touch thinking.

Education had, in fact, been a minor obsession of Biden's for decades, the product of massive self-consciousness he'd felt ever since getting a job at a law firm out of Syracuse Law even though he'd been competing with students "from Georgetown, Harvard, Yale," as he later wrote, still amazed nearly half a century later. He'd long been convinced such schools had almost magical influence to confer on their alumni—what he called the "river of power"—and when he joined the Senate he reveled in getting some control over some of them: "We had about thirty-five jobs to fill— and about 2,500 applicants, most of them from Harvard Law or the University of Chicago or Stanford. I couldn't even make a paper cut. Should I hire a Rhodes Scholar to be a receptionist?" he later remembered thinking. Now, as vice president, he was surrounded by these types.

From the perspective of some of Obama's top aides, however, these kinds of complaints from Biden were absurd and perhaps offensive. They thought little of his perspective that they should be schmoozing his former colleagues a bit more enthusiastically, so they were content to let Biden keep his focus on winding down the Iraq war and implementing the stimulus. As far as plenty of them were concerned, he was just another member of the team—there was no point in considering his relationship with Obama at all. Biden was hardly a main character in the national drama over health-care reform as the political tide turned against Democrats, and there was nothing strange about that. He had his own assignments. As for the prom-ise that he'd be the last guy in every room with Obama? Well, thought some of his internal skeptics, sorry, but Obama was in a lot of rooms.

Every day as Washington got colder and the negotiations dragged on, the senior White House staff gathered for strategy sessions and carefully went through a list of senators to make sure they knew where each one stood on the bill. Whenever they worried that one seemed to be wavering, they would turn to the front of the room and gauge Obama's interest in engag-ing him or her. Quickly, though, they figured out that this wasn't his pre-ferred way to spend his time, but that Biden was eager to be dispatched and that he and Reid could coordinate an effective approach for his ex-colleagues.

Biden had actually been talking with Baucus for months while Grass-ley's support was theoretically on the table, though this wasn't widely known even within the West Wing. Now, as the fall became winter, Reid handed Biden a list of Republicans to call to make sure they understood the leader was ironing out a provision to give states flexibility on covering abortions, and the VP also rang his own party's main holdout, the Nebras-kan Ben Nelson, too, to back Reid up on the matter. With a vote possibly approaching, Reid also asked Biden to keep tabs on Landrieu and Arkan-sas's Blanche Lincoln, two more centrist Senate Democrats who might be wobbling but at least respected Biden, and the VP started calling them regularly to remind them that he understood their political incentives and worries.

These were all steps in the right direction in Biden's eyes, though no one doubted that the health-care push was still Obama's baby, or that it was still only inching along. Still, by late 2009, Biden wasn't going to let that perception or the exact contours of the West Wing's divisions of labor get to him too much. He didn't much care for the headline ("After Cheney"), but he was proud when the *New York Times Magazine* explored in November whether "Joe Biden [could be] the Second-Most Powerful Vice President in History," pointing to his recovery work, his stewardship of Iraq, his role in the Afghanistan debates, and his privileged position in Obama's ring of advisors. Some of the president's quirks still baffled Biden, but he remained in awe of Obama himself even as they spent hours on end together each day, and the VP was starting to think that his boss wasn't getting the credit he deserved from fellow Democrats or the defense he needed in the face of unfair Republican assaults.

Obama largely agreed, and wasn't feeling quite so optimistic. The general sense of siege, the frozen economy, the apparent health-care gridlock, and, most frustratingly, the administration's inability to convey to the country just how much progress they'd already made combined to turn that fall and winter into an emotional low point for almost everyone in the president's orbit. Obama couldn't figure out how to make Americans appreciate that the economy was no longer in an absolute free fall, or how badly he wanted to see the health-care bill passed. Nearly a dozen times Reid privately told him he couldn't get to sixty votes, and almost every time Obama replied that passing the bill was more important to him than getting reelected.

He was also confounded by concern on the left that the negotiators might still remove the government-run insurance plan—the "public option"—from the bill. He conceded that was a possibility, but he didn't consider the option to be at the heart of the legislation, so he was sure it wasn't worthy of such intense consternation, considering how much reform would still be done without the option. He again hung back in November when Lieberman said on *Face the Nation* that he was against a public option. Obama, Biden, Emanuel, and Reid all felt blindsided by the announcement, and Reid summoned Lieberman to his office as soon as he got off the air. When Lieberman arrived at the Capitol, he was greeted by Reid, but also a frazzled Emanuel, Schumer, Durbin, and Dodd. Emanuel immediately asked if he should take Lieberman's statement to mean that he wouldn't vote for the bill if a public option was included, and when Lieberman assented, the chief of staff asked for a commitment that Lieberman would vote for the bill if it was removed. It spoke volumes that, when Lieberman agreed and Emanuel replied, "The public option is out of the bill," Lieberman still thought Biden—who wasn't in the room—deserved credit for imposing political practicality on Obama's operation instead of leaning into ideological war.

Still, it wasn't until January, after both the House and Senate passed versions of the measure and Obama then hosted a conference of both chambers' Democrats to negotiate between the two line-by-line, that the effort took on its final grim urgency. When Scott Brown, a GOP legislator, won Kennedy's old Senate seat in liberal Massachusetts it was an obvious portent of a forbiddingly dark political mood, a political earthquake that shook Washington and suggested a Republican tsunami was on its way later that year. More immediately, it forced Democrats to reshape the legislation into something more conservative and friendly to the insurance industry than the House liberals wanted. Their party no longer had sixty votes in the Senate and stood no chance of winning GOP votes at this point, so if they still wanted to make the bill happen after nearly a year of trying, they had to resort to a parliamentary tactic called reconciliation to massage together versions of the legislation that had already passed for a simple-majority approval of the final measure. The entire effort appeared on its deathbed; Schumer at this point again argued that they should back off the health-care push in favor of a middle-class economics emphasis. But Biden now joined Obama in putting his full faith in Pelosi to win over her terrified and furious members in support of a package that could pass both bodies.

Obama rarely drank in office and Biden didn't drink at all, but the president gathered his VP and a small group of senior aides who'd worked on the efforts to celebrate the final vote over martinis in late March 2010. Obama was exhausted and his outlook on the condition of Washington was calcifying, but that night his confidence was radiating and his glee was evident. Biden, who had recently returned from a politically tense Middle East trip that took place at the peak of the vote counting, was downright impressed it had actually worked. This was the massive overhaul for millions of Americans that Democrats had been chasing since he was a baby. Biden wasn't acting when, two days later, he introduced Obama at the Affordable Care Act's signing and whispered to him close enough to be caught on the mic, "This is a big fucking deal." After Obama spoke, the pair walked off side by side, clasping each other's backs, like nothing could separate them.

* * *

Late on Christmas Eve three months earlier, Dodd had left the Capitol after voting to pass the Senate's version of the bill and stopped by Ted Kennedy's grave at Arlington National Cemetery. It was freezing and he had a long drive back to Connecticut ahead of him, but the senator wanted to pause to take stock of what he'd just done. Standing there, Dodd resolved to retire after thirty-five years in DC rather than run for reelection in 2010. He was proud, but the political writing was already on the wall for his entire party and Capitol Hill was no longer the productive, convivial place he'd once considered it. Dodd was hardly alone. Shortly before the vote, Ben Nelson had approached Reid after months of negotiations. "My career is over, because I will not get reelected," the Nebraskan said. "But I'm going to vote with you."

No one knew what the new Washington would look like once the health-care fight was over, but the early signs weren't encouraging as Democrats reckoned with the possibility of losing their hold on the House to a GOP with no intention of cooperating with Obama on much of anything at all. To make matters worse, the Tea Party's rise was no longer deniable. Reid, for one, sat both Obama and Biden down in March to warn them not to underestimate the fury out there after returning from a campaign event in his hometown of Searchlight where his supporters and Tea Party activists exchanged volleys of eggs and his car had been pelted. Biden then zeroed in on the unbelievable fight for his old Senate seat, where Republican congressman and ex-governor Mike Castle looked like he had a shot at beating the Democratic candidate, New Castle County executive Chris Coons. Castle, however, was failing to fend off a shocking challenge from a far-right activist named Christine O'Donnell, who at one point ran an ad insisting she wasn't a witch.

This all left Obama in no position to take much of a victory lap for the ACA, and he instead retreated further into his self-contained version of the presidency, preferring to unwind after long days of work with friends from back in Chicago rather than Washingtonians and openly complaining about "the bubble" that surrounded him at all times—not just the entourage but also the hubbub, internal politics, leaks and finger-pointing, and detachment from the real world. At particularly difficult times, he turned to Emanuel and mused about what life would be like with no decisions to make at all, off on a beach in Hawaii.

Biden saw the impending doom, which was compounded by January's *Citizens United* Supreme Court decision opening the floodgates for even more money to pour into politics, and seized the chance to get back to the campaign trail. He began popping up around the country but found in district after district that the vulnerable Democrats were under assault from attacks funded by Kansas's libertarian Koch brothers, and that there was no equivalent big-money operation arriving to defend them.

Within the White House, the defense plan was scattered and constantly evolving, though Obama and Biden had no problem showing a united front now, having passed a massive stimulus and a once-in-a-century health-care plan, and having at least theoretically mapped out the end to two wars and rescued the country's automakers from collapse. They were also by now downright comfortable around each other, and their supporters loved seeing the occasional photos of them unwinding together, like when they watched Sasha Obama and Maisy Biden playing basketball and Pete Souza, the White House photographer, caught them delightedly high-fiving. Americans were far less triumphant as they experienced the painfully slow and unequal recovery. But if their constituents couldn't see their accomplishments, Obama and Biden figured, what could they do?

They struggled for coherence, and Obama cast about for answers and for something to blame. One Saturday in August 2010, the political team gathered in the Roosevelt Room for an expectations- and strategy-setting session to get everyone on the same page for the midterm campaign season. Axelrod kicked it off by explaining what Obama and Biden needed to do to support the congressional and senatorial campaign committees, which were in desperate need of money, before Emanuel turned the meeting over to Mike Donilon, who'd integrated himself into Obama's team seamlessly. Donilon proceeded to lay out their challenge in new terms: they—meaning Obama—couldn't just argue that these new conservative big-money groups with strange names were stealing democracy, since that was too abstract a point for voters to understand and their initial efforts to make that case had fallen short. "That doesn't mean anything to anyone," Donilon said. Instead, they had to actively make the case for the administration's accomplishments, which everyone in the room agreed were considerable, and to bet on them to carry Democrats to success.

With the meeting winding down after the presentations, Obama tried to buck everyone up. "Mitch McConnell is a jackass, he can't become majority leader, we can't have that!" he said, arguing to some knowing laughter that a lot was at stake here. "This is gonna be hard work," he said, "but we can enjoy it, having fun back on the trail."

He then stood up to leave and let his frustrations with quotidian Washington politics get the better of him, sending the meeting sideways. People kept trying to get him to "message" better, no one was acknowledging how much he'd accomplished, and reporters had been asking about administration intrigue too much for his liking. "We gotta stay on the same page, so you know, Rahm, if you're saying one thing to one reporter and another to someone else, we're gonna know about it," he said. He rapped his knuckles on the table twice and strode out, leaving the room in stunned silence as his aides looked around wide-eyed, wondering what had just happened. This was no way to approach a reckoning.

CHAPTER 9

2010–2011

Obama shared the politically acceptable half of his thoughts at a press conference the Wednesday after Republicans reclaimed the House by netting sixty-three seats, more than they had in decades. It was a "shellacking," he conceded, created by the "inherent danger in being in the White House and being in the bubble." Because he'd been too focused on the daily responsibilities of the job, he said, "sometimes we lose track of the ways that we connected with folks that got us here in the first place." In private he was less conciliatory. "Well, that was a disaster," he said to his senior staff that day inside the Roosevelt Room. But, he continued, he'd had political capital and he'd spent it. Now he had a list of things to get done in the next two months before John Boehner replaced Nancy Pelosi, and he wanted everyone around the table focused on them. Heads turned quizzically—*What doesn't he get about what just happened?*—before Biden spoke up.

The VP revealed that, in anticipation of losing the House and seeing it dominated by no-compromise wing nuts, he'd been in mostly secret discussions with Mitch McConnell about striking a deal to prolong Republican-favored George W. Bush–era tax cuts in exchange for an extension of aid to Americans who'd been unemployed over the long term. Obama, who was about to take off for a long and strategically important trip to Asia, knew plenty of liberals would be upset about this kind of deal, but his view of his job hadn't changed just because of the election results—they had to get as much done as they realistically could, within their political boundaries—it was that only now did he recognize, painfully, how serious those boundaries were. He turned to Biden and articulated his assignment for the next two months: get up to the Hill and see what other deals you can strike before the bad guys get to town.

The blustery confidence was only so convincing. Obama was still processing just how hard the wave of backlash had hit, making his first ever electoral loss in Washington an especially brutal one and leaving no doubt that he would have to try some new tactics if he wanted credit from anyone for all he'd done—or even an acknowledgment that he'd been dealing with an economic calamity and a recalcitrant GOP. But Biden saw in the West Wing's political recalibration and Obama's brief absence a chance to reassert himself. Plus, Rouse was temporarily stepping in as interim chief of staff following Emanuel's departure, and the ex-senator had always had a good relationship with the old Senate aide. The mandate wasn't to sell change to the public—that was Obama's thing, and he was struggling with it at the moment. It was to get votes even if the right thought they were overreaching and the left thought the proposed change wasn't aggressive enough. (Schumer, hardly a progressive, argued that the White House should refuse to compromise with McConnell and make Republicans pay the price for not renewing middle-class tax cuts.) Biden knew he could make a deal, and he wasn't about to let the midterm loss overwhelm him. He'd seen control of the Senate flip eight times during his many years there.

The resulting spree was more productive than either the president or VP anticipated, and it not only fed into the long-term optimism on which Obama stubbornly insisted even in the face of electoral wipeouts but also fueled his residual hope that he could get some reasonable Republicans to the table on issues that really mattered. Biden shepherded to a successful vote the repeal of the seventeen-year-old Don't Ask, Don't Tell rule barring gay, lesbian, and bisexual people from serving openly in the armed forces, and then, four days later, the New START arms control treaty with Russia. He, too, bought into the optimism, albeit with the caveat that some short-term tweaks to the White House's political approach were still badly needed.

You couldn't tell from outside the White House, but 2010's lame duck session was personally important for Biden, as well, giving him a chance to not only prove himself but also think more analytically about the partnership with his boss—but not quite close companion—after two draining years. They weren't golf buddies and rarely hung out socially. Biden wasn't always a fan of Obama's distant or sarcastic style, and he thought he was still too quick to overlook his allies in the legislative branch. But their working rhythm was as functional and drama-free as any president-VP partnership in recent history, and Biden had been given real trust, he concluded. He thought Obama was right: they still weren't getting the credit they deserved. So he saw an opportunity to make a statement two hours deep into a venting session with the beleaguered House Democrats. Anthony Weiner was complaining that Obama wasn't enough of a "leader" and that he was negotiating too much, and Biden cut in furiously. "There's no goddamned way I'm going to stand here and talk about the president like that!" he yelled back.

Obama heard a report of what had happened almost immediately, and instantly understood that he could rely on Biden for these kinds of over-the-top displays of fierce loyalty. A few months later, with their reelection campaign approaching, Obama ended a meeting with his political team by revealing that someone had leaked details of his personal reflections about the first term's strengths and failings. Sitting at the head of the table, he icily looked around the room and said, *You are my closest people, the ones who helped get me here, and you're going to be the ones to help me stay here. I've trusted you with everything I've ever done, yet one of you has decided to share what I've shared with you in confidence.* Obama said he couldn't believe it, stood up, asked the perpetrator to meet him in the Oval Office, and left the room.

After a terrifying still moment, Biden quietly chimed in. *This man has been with you at every single moment. He's trusted you,* he said, reddening. *You have no idea how glowingly he speaks of you and how proud he is of this team.* This was more than a betrayal, Biden said. It was inexcusable. *Every one of you owes him that loyalty and that confidence. You better get it together,* he concluded, and stormed out. The aides were stunned, but those who'd been watching Obama and Biden the longest were also, somewhere beneath their fear and personal political calculations, almost touched.

It would have been only rational to assume that by mid-2011 Biden's internal influence was on the upswing after his legislative maneuvering, with the Iraqi troop drawdown nearing a conclusion, and considering the wide acknowledgment that middle-class economics deserved more atten-tion. Yet when he'd taken the job with Obama he had effectively allowed his public profile to be redefined by the gig—never mind his long record—and his own view of himself had lagged that transformation. As such, to the degree that many people thought of him at all in the presidency's first two years, it was often as Obama's implementation man.

The administration's new recalculation of its priorities and approach, though, brought with it a staff reshuffle and thus some new thinking about how Biden could deploy himself. For one thing, in 2011 Biden inserted himself more into the running of the place by starting to attend the daily senior staff meeting regularly.

Biden had also been puzzling with his own staff about Obama's trouble explaining his accomplishments, and he latched on to the idea of using the VP's office as a lab for experimenting with new ways to get the word out. At first, this just meant getting him on Twitter before the rest of the administration to reach a new audience. (Not that he himself ever tweeted.) Before long, though, his team realized that rebranding Biden as more accessible would get him more attention.

He agreed to lean into a less known but potentially politically helpful view of his personality best typified by the satirical newspaper *The Onion's* depictions. (One popular 2009 headline probably crossed the line, but made the point succinctly: "Shirtless Biden Washes Trans Am in White House Driveway.") If his office could embrace the politically palatable parts of the caricature and position him as a lovable rogue, a friendly guy who talked too much but just loved muscle cars, ice cream, and his family by playing it up subtly in White House videos and in his own speeches, that would be hugely preferable to the "gasbag senator most comfortable on the set of a Sunday talk show" rep he'd been worried about falling back into. It also fed into the bromance narrative that was beginning to bubble up as the press noticed him and Obama starting to act a bit more chummy around each other. (Take the *PBS NewsHour* website's hard-hitting summary of an interview Biden did in January 2011: "Biden Enjoying Role as Vice President, Close Friendship with Obama.") Those stories—which often included quotes from the VP about how he and Obama liked each other, but few details—tended to get scores of clicks from liberals eager for a feel-good companionship tale. Obama and Biden both found it all mildly hilarious and true enough, if substantively slightly off the mark and beside the point of the work they were actually trying to do.

If Biden valued any part of his role above all, it was still his guaranteed position as "the last guy in the room" for Obama, even if he ended up disagreeing with the ultimate decision. Over the spring of 2011, this promise got its highest-stakes test yet, once the president was presented with a suite of options for action on a compound in Pakistan that the government had been secretly surveilling for nearly a year, believing it to be Osama bin Laden's.

Obama thought there was no clear best option between waiting for more information or ordering either a targeted drone assault, a more dramatic airstrike that would take out the entire complex, or an in-person raid. In mid-April Gates gave him reason for extra concern. Any kind of mission would undoubtedly harm the American relationship with Pakistan, he explained, and therefore imperil the remaining mission in Afghanistan. But he also went through some worst-case scenarios, including a possibility he considered based on his own tenure as assistant to the CIA director, when in 1980 an attempt to rescue hostages in Tehran had failed. It was possible that the Pakistani government could imprison American troops if they were caught, Gates said, though he still said he was most confident in the plan to send in a raid.

A week and a half later, Obama gathered the entire national security team for their recommendations, considering that the intelligence was only 50 percent certain that bin Laden was there, and no one knew if he had armed guards. Leon Panetta, the CIA director, was most in favor of a Navy SEAL–led raid, and the national security advisor, Tom Donilon, then backed him up. Gates now said he actually wanted to consider the drone option, even though this would make it harder, if not impossible, to identify the terrorist's body after the strike. Clinton weighed the options carefully out loud before saying she narrowly favored a raid, since this was their best shot at bin Laden in the decade since 9/11.

Biden, however, took his time in urging significantly more caution, making a case that sounded familiar to the veterans of the Afghanistan debates who sat around the room, outside of which no one knew what was being discussed. To start, the intel wasn't good enough to risk it, considering the massive political costs if they failed, Biden thought, and Obama wouldn't win a second term if this all fell apart. He then doubled down on the argument with Obama one-on-one after the meeting, continuing to urge him to wait for more information. Obama took it all in and, as usual, refused to tip his hand. He understood the calls for caution but worried that Biden and Gates were both too scarred by past failures, yet another mirror of the Afghanistan troop-level debates, when he effectively banned mention of Vietnam from his periphery. He was leaning toward a raid.

He brought the group together again on the last Thursday in April, with the SEALs all ready to go and in Afghanistan, awaiting orders for sometime that weekend. Obama opened the session by lowering expectations: he wasn't going to announce any decision there, but he wanted everyone's thoughts one last time. Gates now explicitly brought up the 1980 disaster and how it was widely thought to be the end of Jimmy Carter's presidency. Panetta, a former congressman and then chief of staff and budget director for Bill Clinton, said an average citizen would assess the intel and decide to go for it, and added that they would regret it if Obama passed now. Hillary Clinton, who'd often aligned with Gates over the previous years, again spoke at more length about the pros and cons but ultimately agreed with Panetta that they would regret it if they didn't go for it. After some more unsurprising offers of encouragement, it was Biden's turn.

As the vice president saw it, he hadn't yet completed his job of pressure-testing the decision, as he thought Obama would want him to do. So much could go wrong with the Pakistanis, he said, and they still weren't taking seriously enough the possibility that a botched raid could effectively end Obama's presidency then and there. After he finished going around the room, Obama stood up and said he'd make his final decision overnight.

Biden moved to catch up and walk out with Obama, ensuring he could get a final word, before pulling Ben Rhodes and deputy national security advisor Denis McDonough into a small conference room to debrief and to exhale. He was—as always—just trying to stretch Obama's options, giving him room to make a decision, he said to the pair of aides who had also grown close to Obama. Back in the residence, Obama couldn't shake Biden's and Gates's warnings. The prospect of a presidency-ending mistake based on bad intelligence haunted him, but, he determined, not enough to outweigh the possibility of finally catching bin Laden.

The famous picture taken by White House photographer Pete Souza captured the scene that Sunday: Obama, hunched over in his seat, listened as Panetta narrated the agonizing approach and Biden stuck to his right side as if glued there, silently gripping his rosary. When one helicopter crashed on-site, both asked first about the SEALs but then thought privately about Carter. They only felt like they could exhale hours later—once the mission was completed, bin Laden's body was identified, the SEALs were back in Afghanistan, and Obama was free to tell the world about it.

In the ensuing weeks Biden would, privately, whisper to his trusted aides that he'd actually been for the raid but had spoken up against it to make Obama seem braver, figuring that this made Biden seem like a good soldier. There was no evidence at the time that this was true, or that he'd actually voiced his support to Obama in private. (He was, for the moment, spared the embarrassment that would come a year later, when documents uncovered in the raid were published. In one letter bin Laden encouraged al-Qaeda fighters to kill Obama as "Biden is totally unprepared for that post, which will lead the US into a crisis.")

In any case, he had other reasons to feel confident these days. In recent months he'd resumed his campaign to push Obama toward a dramatic drawdown in the number of troops remaining in Afghanistan, arguing again that both Congress and the public were turning even harder against the war than before, while the military was trying harder to game Obama than it had previously. After a series of debates not unlike the 2009 ones, Obama ultimately decided to withdraw ten thousand troops by the end of 2011 and more by the following summer, effectively siding by that June with Biden by insisting that most of the remaining troops focus on the kind of counterterrorism the VP had been arguing for all along.

* * *

Plouffe put it this way: they could talk about improving macroeconomic numbers all they wanted, but if you're out of work, your unemployment rate is 100 percent, and if you live in a small town and walk down Main Street, you aren't going to ignore the shuttered stores. That, to you, is the economy, and that, to you, is what to think about Obama. By mid-2011, no one sitting in on the White House's senior staff meetings doubted that they would have plenty to run on the next year between the recovery (slow as it was), the ACA (politically ambiguous as it still was), bin Laden's death, and their auto rescue. But equally, no one could find much to argue with in what Plouffe was saying. Not when they knew Obama's ratings were still dipping as a sense of economic malaise burrowed deeper into the public, and as they could sense a bunker mentality taking hold of the West Wing in real time while pundits kept dinging the president for failing to forge more compromises with a GOP that was demonstrating zero willingness to find middle ground on anything. The summer's collapse of an attempted "Grand Bargain" with Boehner only made matters more wretched. Obama had proposed massive cuts to beloved social programs in exchange for tax increases amid the debt ceiling debacle, when Republicans threatened to push the country into an unfathomable default over deficit policy, only for it all to fall apart thanks to Boehner's weakness with his own charges. That left Congress likely having to impose spending caps that infuriated liberals.

So perhaps it wasn't surprising when both Obama and Biden expressed some limited sympathy with the Occupy Wall Street activists who began demonstrating that fall but displayed little evidence of fully empathizing with them. Biden argued that the "middle class has been screwed" and conceded that it was a "really fair question" when asked if the administration stood in solidarity with the protesters. "What is the core of that protest?" he asked. "The core is the American people do not think the system is fair or on the level." Obama was even more careful a few days later: "I understand the frustrations being expressed," he said, before pivoting. "In some ways, they're not that different from some of the protests that we saw coming from the Tea Party. Both on the left and the right, I think people feel separated from their government. They feel that their institutions aren't looking out for them." Both were unsettled by the scenes on the news each evening but were thinking ahead to 2012, confident that they would win the national conversation about economic fairness over the GOP in their reelection campaign.

Nonetheless, when Axelrod commissioned a set of broad-scope focus groups to reset the political operation's thinking for fear that it was too stuck in a myopic DC mindset, everyone was startled by the findings. Americans were, unsurprisingly, frustrated with the slow recovery and increasingly perceived that the economic system was fundamentally unfair, but this was translating to a diminishing faith in the American dream. This brought the Obamans back to their central problem, which they were forced to acknowledge was much more complicated than they'd anticipated. You can't tell people the economy is improving if they don't think they're feeling it themselves.

The immediate response was to try refocusing on the middle class, acknowledging that it had been hollowed out and needed support, and making the case that Democrats were more likely to provide that than

Republicans. Still, Obama and his lieutenants were getting glum enough that at one point Plouffe called Messina, the reelection campaign manager, for a gut-check: He still thought Obama could win, right?

Messina's answer—Yes, of course, things weren't that bad and were getting better, plus they had a great operation in Chicago and anyway Obama was a once-in-a-lifetime campaigner—was less intuitive than he made it seem, at least as far as the daily political chatter was concerned. Never was this truer than a year out from election day, when the *New York Times Magazine* published a cover story by data analyst Nate Silver asking, "So, Is Obama Toast?" The article itself wasn't so apocalyptic—it posited that Obama was a slight underdog, given the state of the economy, which was unusual for an incumbent. But the headline was sufficient to send the White House and the political aides in Chicago into a furious rebuttal binge, from Op-Ed pages to private meetings with cable TV producers and anchors in which staffers insisted the polling wasn't so bad, but that the relentlessly negative—and, Obama often griped, maddeningly vague—coverage was having a corrosive effect on the president's base support.

It was classic Obama, then, to decide that maybe he could start to turn this all around with a speech, since his administration's focus on executive orders that it could push through without GOP support wasn't cutting it politically. He selected Osawatomie, Kansas, where 101 years earlier Teddy Roosevelt had famously outlined his "new nationalism," to argue for the government's moral role in building a fair economy, which dovetailed with the findings of his political team's polling: Americans believed Democrats were more likely to "fight for people like you," and Obama needed to lean into that message.

The idea was to reset the terms of the burgeoning presidential race, and in liberal corners it was a welcomed effort, joined by a proposed jobs plan that was more messaging tool than real legislative proposal. "This is a make-or-break moment for the middle class, and for all those who are fighting to get into the middle class," Obama said. "I'm here in Kansas to reaffirm my deep conviction that we're greater together than we are on our own. I believe that this country succeeds when everyone gets a fair shot, when everyone does their fair share, when everyone plays by the same rules." The *New York Times'* editorial board called the speech "a relief. He made it clear that he was finally prepared to contest the election on the issues of income inequality and the obligation of both government and the private sector to enlarge the nation's shrinking middle class."

There was no palpable change in real world sentiment, however, and Obama started to think more deeply about his challenge as 2011 came to a close. The communications problem was real, but so were the facts of the unequal recovery. And so was the dynamic that Joe Rospars, Obama's digital advisor, liked to point out in strategy sessions: in 2008 the task had been to take this guy who was loved and admired and to make Americans picture him as president. Now the challenge was reversed. They had to take a distant figure whom voters had exclusively seen in a suit for two years amid complicated circumstances and make average people think about the way they had loved him four years earlier.

Obama flew with his family to Hawaii, as always, at the end of the year, but he couldn't shake some creeping worries about the campaign. It had been a long few months, and he was only feeling slightly better than the previous year when, during one walk, he turned to Messina and asked, "Do you think I can win?"

* * *

Donor outreach was never Biden's job. It had never been his forte, and no one in Chicago was under any illusions: the big donors wanted to talk to Obama, no one else. (One of the president's billionaires sometimes told a story about Biden trying to win him over at a reception in 2007 by answering his question in such rambling depth that the mogul's back started to seize up and he had to find a chair to avoid hospitalization.) So when, in late 2011, Plouffe and Messina noticed that Biden's deputy chief of staff Alan Hoffman had quietly added some dinners with fundraising types to the VP's itinerary for his January trip to Los Angeles and the Bay Area, they swiftly shut them down.

If you squinted, this was becoming a pattern. A year earlier, the Obamans had nixed Biden's attempt to hire Kevin Sheekey, a Michael Bloomberg political aide, for fear that his ties to the aggressive New York press would prove a headache and that he was insufficiently loyal to the Obama cause. Stymied and perturbed, Biden had come back with a plan to hire Steve Ricchetti, a longtime Democratic operator and Bill Clinton aide once nicknamed "Steve Rodham Ricchetti" because of his close work with Hillary Clinton in the early 1990s. This, too, was a no-go for Plouffe and his team, partly because Ricchetti had been a lobbyist but also because he wasn't an Obama guy, either. Biden, however, was getting fed up and escalated the matter to Obama himself. The president relented, but only after a delay that Biden couldn't help but notice.

No one wanted to speak the issue aloud, but by early 2012 it was an undercurrent to much of Biden's interactions with Obama's political team: was he, after implicitly promising not to in 2008, preparing to run for president in 2016? They watched askance as he lined his schedule and stages with politically influential locals in battleground states, and they kept track of his staff's nondenial denials on the rare occasions they were asked about it through his opening years as VP.

The truth wasn't so devious, but there was something to the whispers. Biden had been upset as early as 2009 to find that his political future was being written off entirely by the DC press. He didn't know if he'd be in any position to run after two terms at Obama's side, but for his entire career he'd believed, and repeated out loud, various versions of the maxims "You're always on the ballot," "If you're not on the ballot you're dead," "You're either on your way up or your way down," or, most to the point, "If I'm walking, I'm running." Actively ruling out a presidential future would mean winding down a career that had started in the Nixon era, which might also reduce his leverage as VP, and he and Klain agreed early on to stick to a standard line: *I never said I wasn't going to run again. I would never close that door.* If skeptics saw that as a reversal, well, let them. Anyway, Biden himself *wasn't* thinking about 2016 in any active way, he was just interested in keeping his name in the conversation in case he did decide to run. Did he know that Ricchetti, Hoffman, Klain, Gitenstein, and Kaufman had secretly started drawing up the outlines of a possible path toward a Biden 2016 campaign earlier in 2011? Yes, he just didn't know any of the details, and he didn't want to yet, maybe ever. But that still didn't mean he wouldn't take it personally when some ObamaWorld staffer tried nipping it all in the bud.

At any rate, he was pretty sure their most recent piece of evidence that he was freelancing for his own political gain was a misunderstanding. Biden had long been a close ally of his fellow Catholic Bill Daley, the White House chief of staff in 2011. Both had opposed an administration proposal that would have required church-run hospitals and universities to cover contraception for their employees, though Daley was louder about it internally while Biden sought to make the case to Obama that he was risking his support with voters in politically split states like Pennsylvania. The problem, though, came in November when Obama found himself in a semiexcruciating Oval Office sitdown with Biden and Timothy Dolan, the archbishop of New York, for which he felt insufficiently prepared and inappropriately pressured, considering that he hadn't made up his mind on the plan. Obama vented about the meeting after the fact, and his aides rushed to piece together how it had happened outside the usual processes for setting up and preparing for such visits. Daley denied being behind the meeting, and Biden was clearly uncomfortable with the fallout.

The White House divided into camps, half pointing fingers at the chief of staff—who was already on his way out by then, his style a bad match for the president—and the other half suspicious of the VP. Biden, however, thought any blame on him was unfair, since he said he hadn't arranged the meeting and thought Daley had. He had no incentive to put Obama in a corner, he figured. And he at least thought that he and Daley saw eye to eye.

Biden's touchiness was justified. He'd been unsettled, at best, since the summer of 2010, when *Washington Post* columnist Sally Quinn had exploded a political bomb in DC by writing a column titled "Hillary Clinton Should Be Obama's Vice President," which argued that Clinton deserved the promotion as a reward for her service and Biden should be happy as secretary of state. This appeared to be coming from nowhere except summer boredom and—some people close to Biden suspected—perhaps a whisper network around Clinton that enjoyed stoking the baseless but nonetheless quadrennial rumors of a running-mate switch to burnish Clinton's reputation, no matter if they muddied Biden in the process. But it did get some people thinking, and it did get Biden sweating, if less in fear for his job than for his rep. These thoughts remained mostly internal throughout the summer until Bob Woodward said on CNN in October that such a switch was indeed on the table, prompting another explosion of speculative commentary that the White House could not ignore.

Obama shut the topic down soon after by telling an interviewer the rumors were "completely unfounded, completely unfounded, completely unfounded," which matched up with many White House aides' insistences that the entire line of inquiry was insane and a sign of the deterioration of

standards in the Washington press corps. Even some of the original Obamans who'd clashed with Biden a bit in the early days—Axelrod and Plouffe,
for example—had come around to him in the intervening years, so the
idea that there was some real anti-Biden movement in the administration
made little sense, not least to Obama himself. The president often insisted
to Biden skeptics that his positives as a partner far outweighed his gaffes,
and he regularly said when asked that choosing Biden as his deputy had
been his best decision ever. This was some relief to Biden and his closest
advisors, who nonetheless couldn't believe Obama had let the supposedly
unfounded rumors survive for so long under the apparent belief that they
were, on their face, too ridiculous to address.

The thing is: they weren't unfounded. Ever since Messina had taken
charge of the reelection campaign with Obama's political standing in trouble, he'd led a sub-rosa effort to reevaluate everything about the White
House with closely guarded research that no one knew about outside of a
group that included Obama, Daley, Axelrod, and Plouffe. Though none of
them approached this exercise expecting to recommend replacing Biden
with Clinton, they did, in fact, run and discuss polls and focus groups testing the proposition and gauging both Democrats' positives and negatives.
In the interest of finding the best possible solution for Obama's reelection
there were few boundaries on their research, except a hard-and-fast commitment that its details would never leak, especially not to the Biden team.
Worried that pieces would still trickle out, they rarely asked the question
about a ticket switch directly, instead testing Biden's and Clinton's names
out amid longer lists of campaign supporters and surrogates.

The public buzz a few months later was especially frustrating to this
group, then, since the VP question was only a small part of their project
and they'd quickly found that there would be zero political upside to such
a switch, not just because of the pair's relative images but also because it
would be perceived as disloyal and feeble. And Obama still wasn't actually
trailing any of his possible GOP opponents in the early head-to-head polling, so why would he need to do it in the first place? They were just being
responsible, they figured—it was "political hygiene," never anything close
to an actual proposal. Nonetheless, the fact remained that Obama had let
this research continue, even if he never weighed in on it directly.

And that's what stuck with Biden. He had briefly grown distraught as the chatter became a roar in October, but he refused to blame Obama directly, instead asking aloud why Plouffe, for one, hadn't knocked the reports down more forcefully. When he raised this internally, however, no one talked him down. The switch wasn't happening, he was told. But that didn't mean this was coming from nowhere.

CHAPTER 10

2012

Every Friday in Chicago before Axelrod, Messina, and deputy campaign manager Stephanie Cutter flew east for their Saturday White House check-in with Obama, the lead officials on the reelect team gathered in a conference room or called in over the phone to rank the Republican candidates in order of how likely they were to win that party's nomination and face Obama in the fall. Obama had been thinking about the possibilities on and off for four years, ever since he asked Axelrod when he was first elected whom he thought the GOP would choose the next time. The strategist had said that Mitt Romney, the former private equity executive turned governor of Massachusetts, made sense for 2012 after finishing second to McCain in 2008, and there was now no doubt that he was, indeed, the front-runner.

This was clearly unacceptable to the rest of the Republican Party, though, which spent 2011 and early 2012 promoting a series of extreme right-wing candidates instead. Tea Party congresswoman Michele Bachmann, who flirted with birtherism, was the first to have a moment in the spotlight, but the first to overtake the relatively stiff Romney in national polling was Texas governor Rick Perry, who was known for his secession fantasies long before he forgot the name of a cabinet agency he planned on eliminating as president on the debate stage. ("Oops.") Next came Herman Cain, a pizza chain executive with a gimmicky tax plan and, it turned out, a raft of sexual harassment accusations. Newt Gingrich, the conservative who'd helped transform Washington's culture into a partisan bullfighting ring as speaker of the House in the 1990s, briefly jumped into the lead, only to be replaced by hard-right social conservative Rick Santorum, an ex–Pennsylvania senator who was known as much for his draconian opposition to gay rights and abortion as for his sweater-vests.

Obama and his inner circle watched this all with detached amusement, figuring voters would never go for this clown show, only pausing to worry briefly when ex–Utah governor Jon Huntsman Jr., Obama's own ambassador to China, resigned to launch a campaign as a distinctly centrist candidate. But Huntsman's pitch promptly fell flat with the GOP's activist primary electorate, and even when Perry was the beneficiary of credulous coverage that painted him as a generationally talented campaigner, Axelrod urged calm—he'd worked against Perry on a race for lieutenant governor in 1998 and hadn't been impressed.

Still, the contours of the primary weren't actually all that friendly to Obama. Since the Republicans' preferred method of lurching right for their voters' entertainment was flexing their escalating opposition to Obama, daily political news coverage was overwhelmed with negativity toward the president, forcing Chicago to start airing ads defending him earlier than it had expected. And though Obama and his team remained confident that Romney wouldn't be able to run as the relatively moderate and business-friendly governor he'd been if he wanted to appeal to Republicans' ravenous electorate, his polling was far more consistent than anyone else's. Each week before they flew to DC, Messina closed the meeting having landed on the same conclusion atop the ranking. Romney was still—always—Number One.

Back in Washington, Obama was still more than happy for this all to play out slowly and luridly while he presented himself as "presidential," which was another way of saying he just wanted to do the job of president and didn't particularly relish returning to the campaign trail at all until the spring of 2012. He even refused to appear in the campaign's two-minute launch video in April. In the meantime, his advisors considered just letting the GOP continue to shoot itself in the foot by exposing views that would surely be broadly unacceptable to everyday voters. They barred anyone from the Obama administration down to the cabinet level from campaigning at all while the Republican primary dragged on into May. But Biden was getting restless, amused as anyone by the madness across the aisle ("This is not your father's Republican Party!" he took to marveling in meetings) yet eager to start making the case for Obama and against Romney.

Even when Obama did eventually join Biden in actively campaigning, though, attention was relatively hard to come by. His first kickoff rallies in Columbus and Richmond were large, but they surprised the president, the first lady, and their aides by not filling to the rafters, an uncomfortable eye-opener that immediately led to an edict to pause the schedule so they could all reconsider what, exactly, it would take to reclaim the 2008 buzz and beat Romney. If the answer had to do with putting more faith in Biden in a race about the middle class, though—a choice that would seem obvious given his political emphases—that trust was less straightforward than it might have been after four years of close partnership.

* * *

Obama had been convinced for well over a year: he was in favor of same-sex marriage—he had "evolved," as he put it—and he wanted to tell the world. Obama's personal politics were occasionally slightly more conservative than many liberals', but by early 2012 this was no longer one of those cases; he just wanted to get the timing right. His current public position against it was glaring, considering the disappointment some progressives were expressing with his first term and given the swift movement of the rest of his party on the matter. Pelosi, for example, had announced in February that she was in favor of Democrats' official platform supporting marriage equality. Still, every time Obama or one of his advisors brought it up, they found reasons to hold off, most of them straightforwardly political. They were worried about a backlash from swing voters.

In late 2011 Obama tasked a small group of trusted aides with helping him come up with a solution. He warned them that if some reporter asked him, he'd just be honest and say that he'd vote to legalize same-sex marriage were he a state legislator somewhere where it was up for debate, so it would make sense to either roll it out on their own terms or have a better plan than "hope no one asks."

His advisors were still wary. Messina at one point sat him down for a presentation revealing that they probably wouldn't have to worry about a negative reaction in midwestern swing states, since most independents and plenty of Republicans were OK with marriage equality. But he warned that with North Carolina set to vote in May on a state constitutional amendment to prohibit same-sex marriage, weighing in could be toxic in that battleground state, which might make the issue newly polarizing elsewhere. Others, still, were skeptical that Black evangelicals and working-class voters in Ohio and Michigan would be as accepting as they told pollsters, and Biden, arguing that they needed to worry about Catholics, advocated for waiting until their second term before Obama announced anything. This was the hot take of the hour in Washington—many self-appointed savvy pundits assumed the president would announce his support as soon as he was reinaugurated and clear of direct political danger—but Obama thought this was, to put it mildly, a stupid idea.

He was antsy because he didn't have a good explanation for why he'd waited this long, or for some of his past statements. He'd campaigned in 2008 in opposition of the Defense of Marriage Act, which since the Clinton administration had prohibited the federal government from recognizing same-sex unions, and then in 2011 ordered his administration to stop defending it in court. But when he spoke privately about these moves there was always a sense of lingering sheepishness about his contortions since his 2004 Senate campaign.

After answering the question a few different ways as a local candidate in the 1990s and early 2000s, in 2003 he'd backpedaled slightly on his earlier embrace of a registry of same-sex domestic partnerships and said in a questionnaire that gay couples should be allowed to have domestic partnerships recognized, but that the benefits they got should be examined for their fiscal ramifications. He was leaning not only into his ties to the fairly socially conservative local Black church at the time, but also trying to stay in line with Democrats' presidential candidates, who were largely in favor of civil unions. Privately he said this was all about trying to be practical, but then he'd appeared to backtrack even further in the 2004 general election, saying he believed marriage to be definitionally between a man and a woman before God.

Obama knew how baldly political this all looked in hindsight. As the reelection campaign launch neared in spring 2012, he determined that all the waiting and calculating was no longer tenable, and he signed off on a tightly held plan to make the announcement in either an interview with Robin Roberts on *Good Morning America* or on *The View* to get liberal voters engaged a few weeks after he got back on the trail.

Biden was happy to be a team player. He'd spent the last few months basking in the new, friendlier perception of him that voters seemed to have ever since he'd stopped trying to act like a self-serious senator most com-

fortable on the stodgy Sunday shows, but the Obama people had nonetheless asked him to do *Meet the Press* to help kick off the reelect in May.
He'd agreed out of a sense of cooperation, knowing full well that he'd have
to submit to five days of "murder-board" prep with staffers who ended up
drilling him on basic campaign messaging and talking through precisely
nothing of any news value.

Even once that was done the interview was still a day away, though,
and his mind was elsewhere as he sat, tired and dissatisfied, on Air Force
Two heading toward LA for a quick fundraising stop for the campaign.
He'd just asked his traveling staff for a copy of the remarks he was going to
give at this LGBTQ issues–focused event hosted by a gay couple in their
home, but had blown up when he saw that it was just the same old talking
points and then learned that there was nothing new for him to share as far
as the administration's positioning on gay rights went. He hated feeling
unprepared and he steamed as the plane landed, sketching out some quick
lines on a note card while his staff stared on in silence.

At the donor's home, he chatted with the hosts' kids on a staircase while
his aides set up. Concerned about what he would say, they determined
they'd have to have someone lying down in front of him holding up a boom
mic to record his remarks. It was a ridiculous arrangement, but Biden was
in no mood to fix it, and when the time came, he let loose. Why should
those children's parents be treated any differently from how his own children's were? he asked, though he never brought up marriage explicitly. He
launched into his standard praise of Obama—it's his administration, not
mine, he said—and then brought up how careful the president had been in
making sure the Don't Ask, Don't Tell repeal had been handled correctly
with respect to the skeptical Pentagon over time, seeming to imply that the
audience just had to trust Obama's processes, that he was headed in the
right direction on the equality issues that mattered most to them.

No one had much to say as Biden flew back east, and no one could tell
he was still thinking about that fundraiser when he sat down for one last
round of uneventful prep ahead of *Meet the Press*.

The interview itself started without much spark, as host David Gregory
teed Biden up to share the administration's economic talking points before
pivoting to Chinese human rights and briefly trying and failing to get
Biden to engage on the ticket-switch rumors. It was only on his thirteenth
question that Gregory asked the VP where he stood on same-sex marriage,

and Biden parried it. "Look, I just think that—that the good news is that as more and more Americans come to understand what this is all about, it is a simple proposition. Who do you love? Who do you love?" he said. "And will you be loyal to the person you love? And that's what people are finding out, is what—what all marriages, at their root, are about, whether they're marriages of lesbians or gay men or heterosexuals."

Biden hadn't really answered the question, but Gregory seemed to sense that he wanted to, and tried again. "Is that what you believe now?" he asked, and Biden quickly shot back: "That's what I believe." Gregory tried one more time, directly: "And you're comfortable with same-sex marriage now?" Biden gave in. "Look, I am vice president of the United States of America, the president sets the policy," he said, thinking back to Los Angeles. But "I am absolutely comfortable with the fact that men marrying men, women marrying women, and heterosexual men and women marrying another are entitled to the same exact rights, all the civil rights, all the civil liberties. And quite frankly, I don't see much of a distinction, beyond that."

Neither of them seemed to recognize the monumental scale of the reveal in the moment, and Gregory plowed along, asking if the administration would formally back same-sex marriage in its second term. Biden again hesitated before Gregory said it sure seemed like that's what Biden wanted. The VP now tried widening the lens, pointing out Obama's Don't Ask Don't Tell repeal and his moves to ensure equal treatment for gay couples through executive orders. And—*Why not?*—he went for a broader cultural point, too. "When things really begin to change is when the social culture changes," Biden said. "I think *Will and Grace* probably did more to educate the American public than almost anything anybody's ever done so far," he continued, referring to a TV show featuring gay characters that had been off the air for six years. He then told the host about the kids at the fundraiser, at which point they moved on to other matters.

Walking away from the cameras a while later, Biden turned to an aide and revealed that one thing from the interview was bothering him. "Did I get the jobs numbers right?" he asked. He had, he was assured. His staff sent the transcript over to the West Wing without warning or comment, as always.

Plouffe was the first to internalize the transcript, and he called over Jack Lew, the chief of staff, to take a look, too. The West Wing fell silent as staffers double- and triple-checked Biden's words before a shout rang out from Dan Pfeiffer's office: "*Will and Grace?!*" The quiet broken, a disbelieving fury took its place, wedged in by Obama loyalists who suddenly let loose every last frustration they'd had with Biden: *We can't trust him to say his lines and he's out of practice anyway*, went the nice version. *He's ruined what should have been Obama's historic moment because he can't control his loud mouth*, went the other. Both started and ended with *What the fuck?*

The elation that some staffers felt—the vice president had just endorsed marriage equality, which itself was a massive step—was drowned out in the moment by the political team's anxiety. If the immediate frustration was with Biden's freelancing, a secondary political concern soon stepped in. No one knew how this would play, and they hadn't prepared to defend it or to back Biden up. A few people close to Obama himself and the heart of the political operation thought it was tantamount to a betrayal, an example of Biden trying to position himself in front of the president, and Plouffe started calling Obama staffers who'd worked closely with Biden to ask how they could have let *their guy* ruin the careful plan. This was the biggest concern. What was Obama supposed to do now? If he went along with his initial idea and held off for a few more weeks, he'd look like he was just following Biden.

Obama himself was never one for the drama in which some of his staffers seemed to revel. When Plouffe and Lew told him what had happened, he stayed calm: surely Biden just didn't know about the rollout, he said. To Axelrod, he also urged that they all take a breath. "I'll talk to Joe," he said. "It was sloppy, but I can't get mad at the guy for saying what he believes, and what's in his heart. I'm not going to yell at him." To everyone he repeated, with a shrug, "That's Joe being Joe"—Obama had known what he'd signed up for four years earlier.

This was all fine to say out loud. It was probably the only thing he *could* say out loud. But Obama was, in fact, pissed that his planning had gone up in smoke, and then that Biden hadn't even given him a heads-up after the interview, or called him once it was clear they had a problem. Biden, meanwhile, basked in the positive headlines but bridled when, within a few hours, he started to read reports that included blind quotes accusing him of making Obama look bad on purpose. When he next saw him in person, he apologized to Obama for putting him in that situation but asked what on earth was going on with all this knifing in the press? Obama acknowledged that his team was forced to do quite a bit of cleanup but said, "Well, Joe, you told me you weren't going to wear any funny hats or change your brand." All that mattered was that their relationship stayed intact, Obama said.

This much Obama and Biden both later told staffers, creating a public perception that their meeting was easy. But Obama had actually kept going. He knew Biden had been in the room for the meeting in which Obama had revealed to his team that he was going to announce his change of heart but insisted that they needed a careful plan, and he now told Biden he couldn't believe the VP had put himself in front of their joint project. He had long since decided not to scold Biden every time he stepped out of line, so he left it there. But neither had much doubt after that lunch that this had been a serious bump in the road for them. Equally, though, neither had any doubt that Biden had been right.

That resolution only went so far. Obama still needed to figure out his own announcement, an imperative that grew more urgent in the ensuing days. Biden's initial follow-up statement minimizing the differences between them—put out under pressure from the Obama side—did little to calm anyone down, and on the following Monday Arne Duncan, their education secretary, said during an interview that he, too, was for marriage equality, which in turn led to a barrage of questions about Obama's stance for his press secretary, Jay Carney, at that day's White House briefing. Carney, who'd prepared for the question, said he'd leave it to Obama to discuss his personal views. (This was all uncomfortable for Carney, too; he'd been Biden's comms director first.)

Plenty of Obamans were annoyed with the pileup of negative coverage about the president—*What was taking him so long?*—and the next day North Carolinians voted by a wide margin to ban same-sex marriage in the state. At that point, Obama's silence was becoming one of the biggest political stories in the country, a fairly excruciating diversion from his campaign's brand-new relaunch. Pfeiffer and Plouffe set up the interview with Robin Roberts for that Wednesday.

The staff exhaled only when Obama got to the immediately televised point: "I had hesitated on gay marriage in part because I thought civil unions would be sufficient. That was something that would give people hospital visitation rights and other elements that we take for granted. And

I was sensitive to the fact that for a lot of people, you know, the word 'marriage' was something that evokes very powerful traditions, religious beliefs, and so forth," he said. But, he continued, having gotten to know so many same-sex couples who still felt constrained, "I've just concluded that for me personally, it is important for me to go ahead and affirm that I think same-sex couples should be able to get married." He immediately cautioned that he'd been hesitant to weigh in because he thought adding his voice often made issues hyperpolitical—as if this one wasn't already—and that he thought it appropriate that the matter be resolved at the state level. Yet as far as his political team was concerned, the saga was over. In Chicago, his fundraising staff soon reported its best day for online dona- tions of the entire year. The campaign's leadership had banned them from raising money off Biden's announcement.

In Washington, though, a new coolness set in between some of Obama's loyalists and Biden's aides, some of them no longer getting invites to regular White House staff meetings. Even the VP himself noticed when, despite being under the impression that he was supposed to be a leading voice on the reelection campaign as an attack dog against Romney, his public schedule was cut back for a few weeks.

From then on, he rarely brought any of this up with colleagues. But in private, in his innermost inner circle, he was still proud, no matter how uncomfortable he'd made Obama. Once some of the dust had settled, he and Beau sat down in front of a TV and together rewatched the interview over and over, to marvel at what he'd done.

* * *

Biden wasn't exactly worried about repeating 2008, but by the time he and Obama were both campaigning regularly for reelection that summer, he knew enough about the president to know that his own influence—internally, with negotiating partners, and as far as the public was concerned—was depen- dent on the health of their relationship. And he knew enough about that relationship to know that meant he needed face time. Their lunches were where they'd become friends, their daily hours of briefings where they'd become partners. So no one on his senior team was surprised when Biden pulled them aside soon after Romney finally won the GOP nomination and gave them a set of specific instructions. *Make sure you know exactly what Obama's schedule looks like*, he said. *If he's out campaigning three days a week and back in DC for the other four, I want to do the same—I want to be in town whenever he is.* Biden knew he couldn't be the last guy in the room for the president if he was always calling in from Orlando or Reno, and he knew it was on him to make sure he kept that status.

Biden was less worried about the campaign's big-picture strategy sessions, which were held monthly first in Chicago and then, after a while, in the White House. For one thing, those were often just used to share operational updates. For another, Mike Donilon was now a fully equal member of the team, giving Biden an important in for this go-round. What he didn't know for a while was that plenty of the real strategic discussions were happening on Saturdays, when Messina, Axelrod, and Cutter would fly to DC to meet privately with Obama. The very existence of the meetings was news to him when he read about them in the press one day over the summer, at which point he asked Obama what was going on. Obama, who had little patience for this kind of insecurity, brushed him off: *Jim just comes by, it's not formal,* he said. This wasn't totally true, which Biden quickly figured out, and he started joining, too.

No one thought twice about this, though, since it actually did make sense to have him there. If 2008 had been a campaign largely about Obama, the intervening years of economic trouble had made politics in 2012 an exercise in demonstrating understanding to struggling voters, and the Democratic brain trust, led by the president, now saw Biden as at least a stylistic match, especially for white voters in the upper Midwest and transplants to Florida who'd soured a bit on Obama and his perceived elitism, or at least distance, but couldn't bring themselves to vote for a Republican. In practice, that meant Biden would be deployed to do local interviews and intimate events in parts of those states where Obama would likely lose, but where the idea was keeping the margin of loss small while the president tried running up the score with bigger rallies in the more liberal and diverse population centers. No one was talking about voter microtargeting on Facebook here—they were speaking Biden's language. As Biden's team came to think of it, Obama would take Cleveland, and they'd take Chillicothe, a small city in south-central Ohio.

Another aspect of the functional division of labor was that Biden would do the stuff Obama didn't want to, even when it meant the VP would go deep on matters he hadn't actually had a direct hand in to make the case for his boss. He loved using a statistic that their Ohio state director Greg

Schultz had puzzled together, pointing out on the trail that one in eight jobs in the state existed because of the auto industry—which the administration had saved. His favorite line on the stump was made famous at the convention in Charlotte in September, when with obvious devotion he spoke at length about Obama's leadership: "Because of all the actions he took, because of the calls he made, because of the determination of American workers and the unparalleled bravery of our special forces, we can now proudly say what you've heard me say the last six months: Osama bin Laden is dead, and General Motors is alive!" Rarely did anyone stop to point out that Biden had been the strongest voice urging caution about the bin Laden raid and that he hadn't exactly been the face of the auto rescue.

This all worked because Obama implicitly trusted Biden while he himself was so focused on Romney. As he read more about the man, he grew to seriously dislike Romney and came to consider him a wooden version of Ronald Reagan reincarnate. As such, Obama had little interest in the minor parade of gaffes Biden began dropping as the campaign grew repetitive in the late summer, only letting himself become mildly exasperated— not outright frustrated—with the reports, which felt like they came in once a week. For one thing, Romney was proving plenty adept at sticking his own foot in his mouth, usually making himself look forehead-slappingly out of touch. (At one stop in economically struggling Detroit in February, he'd first bizarrely said he liked being in Michigan because "the trees are the right height," and then, in the same paragraph, revealed that his wife "drives a couple of Cadillacs, actually.") The Bidenisms only caused real headaches, anyway, when Romney and the Republicans tried using them to drive wedges between Obama and his core groups of voters, and they only came close to succeeding in doing so once, when the VP told a largely Black crowd in Danville, Virginia, that Romney's deregulatory agenda would "let the big banks once again write their own rules—unchain Wall Street." With those policies, he added, "they're going to put you all back in chains." Still, even with such an egregious misstep—an apparent invocation of slavery—there was little the Obama team could do but ride out the negative press and not schedule events for Biden in Virginia for a while. No one was going to force him back on a teleprompter at this point.

The whole ball game at that point was keeping the focus on their opponent. Messina had entered 2011 promising Obama he would win if it was a straight choice between the two candidates, but that it would be less of a sure thing if the contest was instead a more straightforward Democrat-versus-Republican fight over the economy, so his team had spent most of that year testing messages on Romney, starting with "Which Mitt?," an attempt to paint him as a spineless flip-flopper. The answer became clear, however, when they tested the argument that the private equity model Romney had helped pioneer was bad for employees, and that his tycoon's vision of the economy would be harmful for the country. They were worried at first that it would look like they were attacking Romney's personal success, but battleground-state focus groups quickly showed them that an old image of Romney and his colleagues holding wads of cash was a killer that would feed into their contention that he was more interested in enriching his friends than supporting workers.

The mechanics of making the case were of less concern to the campaign team than ever before, too, because of Obama's eventual willingness to embrace a super PAC for the first time. The vehicle, run by a pair of his ex-aides, got off the ground after its founders met in LA with Hollywood titans Steven Spielberg and Jeffrey Katzenberg, who immediately committed $4 million to the anti-Romney ad effort, opening a new cash spigot that rarely stopped gushing. And when, in September, Chicago caught wind of a secretly recorded video that appeared to expose Romney as a heartless capitalist looking out for his buddies, their messaging task appeared to be completed for them.

The tape, published by *Mother Jones*, showed Romney telling donors at a high-dollar fundraiser that "there are forty-seven percent of the people who will vote for the president no matter what, alright? There are forty-seven percent who are with him, who are dependent upon government, who believe that they are victims, who believe the government has a responsibility to care for them, who believe that they are entitled to health care, to food, to housing, to you-name-it." It couldn't have fed more perfectly into the central Obama-Biden argument about Republicans, and after a few days the Democrats spun it into an ad of their own, amplifying the damning clip for the middle-class audiences Romney talked about in it. Republicans tried downplaying it, but there was little denying Obama's momentum heading into debate season. Not even another all-time classic Biden gaffe the night before the first Obama-Romney debate—"the middle class," he said, had "been buried the last four years"—could dull the apparent high.

* * *

Biden was all set up in his upstairs living room at the Naval Observatory for a straightforward evening. The plan was to sit through Obama's first debate against Romney and then, once it was over, to go live on TV and praise his boss for an inspiring job well done against an out-of-touch vulture capitalist. Mike Donilon was there, as usual, and a speechwriter joined so he could tweak Biden's remarks in case anything interesting happened during the debate that warranted mentioning. The three chatted casually as the networks built up to the showdown, then fell silent when Obama and Romney walked onstage. No one could think of much to say as the next hour and a half unfolded.

It was clear inside the campaign's "boiler room" at the University of Denver that something was wrong almost immediately. Maybe the public couldn't see it, but this group of his top aides could tell Obama was thrown by the way Romney had ably joked about the date—it was the Obamas' anniversary—the first time he opened his mouth, showing much more comfort onstage than the president had expected.

Things didn't get much better from there. Obama rambled defensively, getting into the weeds of his economic record, while Romney, on an even footing with the incumbent for the first time, naturally looked more commanding than he had at any point in the campaign. The commentary on Twitter was turning against Obama, and his team was unsure what to do about such an unfamiliar dynamic. Some turned away from their computers within the first ten minutes. Some held out hope a bit longer but despaired as they watched real-time focus groups reveal that people were finding Obama to be flat and Romney to be pleasingly aggressive. Most of the rest threw up their hands when, about a third of the way into the debate, *BuzzFeed News* declared Romney the winner.

With five minutes left, Axelrod convened a conference call with the campaign's deflated brain trust and suggested some policy arguments they could try making to distract from the president's grim performance. A voice on the line tried cutting him off.

"Axe—"

Axelrod kept going on.

"Axe, Axe, Axe—"

He kept trying to talk, and Dan Pfeiffer butted in to say that wouldn't cut it. The line fell silent with the rare interruption. Advisors were devouring the coverage, and lingered especially on the live blog posted by commentator Andrew Sullivan, often an ardent Obama backer. "How is Obama's closing statement so fucking sad, confused and lame?" Sullivan wrote. "He choked. He lost. He may even have lost the election tonight."

Plouffe and Messina took over. Their live focus groups had shown Obama had won just one exchange—when Romney had belittled public funding for PBS by scoffing, "I love Big Bird"—and Plouffe ordered the staff to get someone in a Big Bird suit to every Romney event starting the next day. It would, he figured, distract a bit from the debate. At least it was something.

Truth be told, none of Obama's closest aides were really all that surprised. Prep had gone poorly from the start. Back in May, Axelrod and Klain, who was in charge of the debate program, had met with the president in the White House's Roosevelt Room and handed him a briefing document explaining that incumbent presidents always lost the first debate because they were often judged based on optics and it was always the first time the challenger got to stand next to them, on their level. But, they'd insisted in writing to an unimpressed Obama, they wouldn't let it happen to him, even though they were pretty sure Romney would be a better debater than John McCain was.

Obama proceeded to tear through the briefing books on Romney, his disdain for the businessman blooming for weeks as he came to consider him a retrograde faux-technocrat hardly worthy of his attention. This was fine as a general attitude, but it didn't help when it came time to practice actual debating. Obama would have no problem explaining his own record at length but then would get defensive and uncomfortable making a partisan argument. He was also far too aggressive when it came time to talk about Romney, especially his pregovernment time in the business world. Obama was punchy and distracted enough in his first practice sessions that the aides decided he'd better stick to explaining rather than attacking, and to do it quickly. (They shared a study that showed his average press conference answer was a full eight minutes long, which would never fly on the debate stage.)

Obama didn't take the feedback well, figuring he had more important things to do—like being president—and that he knew what he was doing, a mirror of how he'd treated the prep for other traditional, and somewhat rote, tentpole occasions like his annual State of the Union addresses. "I got this part," he often said during practice run-throughs, insisting that they skip ahead when they got to a section of a speech or, now, a topic for debate, that he didn't feel like revisiting. When he then flew west for a series of full mock debates outside Las Vegas with John Kerry standing in as his fellow Massachusetts patrician Romney, Obama was obviously annoyed by the setting—signs of the housing crisis were inescapable around the resort—and bored by the prep. He was even unable to land a convincing blow in practice on the topic of the 47 percent tape, leading his team to advise him to avoid it altogether, since everyone already knew about it and he wasn't helping. The final advice, then, was to "just stay above the fray" and, though he couldn't see why he shouldn't boast about his record, not to try to unpack every last piece of his first term. It would come off as defensive and pedantic.

Obama didn't think it had gone that badly when he first walked off the stage. Sure, maybe Romney had bested him here and there, but not in any way that deserved the kind of shock he detected on Plouffe's face. Plouffe, however, disagreed, and Obama then checked with Klain, who told him over the phone that it really was a whiff, and that the coverage was making it worse. Only when Obama got back to his hotel and absorbed some of the online commentary did he concede that he'd fallen short, but even then he latched on to an analysis that he just wasn't as desperate as other politicians for approval, which hindered his debating.

The rest of the coverage, however, riled him up—*How could he have let Mitt Romney of all people do that to him?*—and he brushed aside Klain's offer to resign from the debate team the next morning. He soon flew west for a series of major fundraisers and, on the motorcade ride to his hotel, told one of his largest donation bundlers, an executive he'd rewarded with a plush ambassadorship in the first term, "I promise you I'm not going to fuck up the second and third ones like I did the first. I promise you. I understand that this was not my best hour."

His people were happy to hear this attitude, but they needed more reassurance than that. Messina flew back to Chicago after the debate and landed at 3:00 a.m. to voicemails from Pete Rouse, Harry Reid, and Nancy Pelosi, all separately summoning him to Washington to calm everyone down. He stayed at the airport and got on the next flight east in time to meet with both the House and Senate Democrats, who were almost uniformly in a panic, insisting to the campaign manager that the president was arrogant and unfocused, and that he was going to cost them their jobs, too. Messina wasn't exactly calm himself, but he came armed with new polling numbers he had gotten overnight from Benenson.

It was true that Obama had lost ground, he revealed, but the race had just tightened because previously skeptical Republicans and some independents had returned to Romney. Obama was still leading, even if there was no arguing that the race was now too close for comfort.

Biden and Donilon sat there in silence when the debate ended. The vice president broke in after a beat. "Jesus," he said. "That was terrible."

He stood to get ready for his smiley video about how great Obama had done, which was suddenly a daunting task. He had to start thinking, too, about what he'd say in the morning, when he was booked for all sorts of morning shows to keep the narrative going.

He wasn't feeling much better when, a while later, Messina called to talk about the vice presidential debate, which was set for eight days later, in Kentucky.

"Hey, you know this, but we really need you to fight," the campaign manager said.

Biden did already know it.

Team Biden, led by chief of staff Bruce Reed and policy director Sarah Bianchi, had started getting Joe ready six months ahead of time. The prep was slow at first, mostly focused on getting him brushed up on policy. They knew he'd had a lot of pressure on his shoulders when he'd had to debate Palin in 2008 and that he'd done well. This time they figured he'd probably have to give the campaign a shot in the arm after the first presidential debate—which everyone knew was always a bit rough for the incumbent—but that he might not have a ton of time to get ready for his turn in the spotlight once the campaign season was in full swing.

Biden assented to the brushing-up sessions, but he only fully engaged when Romney chose Paul Ryan, a young Wisconsin congressman who styled himself as a policy wonk but who was at heart a spartan conservative crusader, as his running mate in August. The VP was polite about Ryan in public at first, but behind the scenes he was brutal, pegging him as the kind of Catholic who uses his religion for the wrong kind of politics, whose heralded budget proposal was dangerous and who only got a pass because he presented himself as such a golden boy of the GOP. Biden doubled down on his policy homework and instructed his preppers to hold off on bringing him Chris Van Hollen, the Democratic congressman from Maryland they'd lined up to play Ryan in mock debate sessions, until he felt 100 percent confident about every nook and cranny of the administration's record and Romney and Ryan's plans.

In the meantime, he debated Bianchi for hours on end and devoted himself to studying Ryan, recognizing that he might be a formidable opponent because they had complementary strengths—Ryan knew nothing of foreign policy, Biden hated talking about budgets—but that he was also predictable, always reeling off the same anecdotes about his hometown of Janesville. For weeks Biden and Bianchi sparred, and whenever Biden tore off a good line, a speechwriter would type up what he'd just said, print it out, and hand it to him to memorize. Recitation was how he'd gotten over his debilitating stutter as a child, and it was how he got comfortable in preparation for big moments six decades later.

He was confident by the time he summoned Van Hollen, who had used the time to fully embody Ryan, and he wasted no time in ripping into the congressman. The idea was less to engage Van Hollen-as-Ryan in an intellectual or ideological battle than to steamroll him with almost cartoonish charm, interjections, and warnings about the GOP ticket's extremism.

This was visceral, but it was also strategy. Biden had been hearing from dejected aides for weeks that Obama was blowing off his own prep. He had a feeling he'd need to step up for his boss.

The Biden debate team started the first day after Obama bombed in Denver with a white lie. They knew the Chicago brain trust was descending on Wilmington to monitor, and maybe take over, Biden's preparation after the president's disaster, and they wanted to make sure everyone knew that the VP understood the massive pressure now on his shoulders to stop the bleeding rather than compound it. He had this under control, thank you very much.

Reed and the staff had no doubt Biden was sure of himself, but they wanted him as comfortable as possible for the first mock session in front of Obama's team, lest the Chicago group feel the need to step in too aggressively and get in his head. So they said Van Hollen had a scheduling conflict, and that Bianchi would play Ryan that day. The congressman was free, but no one needed to know that. Playing the role of moderator was Shailagh Murray, Biden's trusted advisor who knew exactly what questions he had been knocking out of the park. Biden was, as they hoped, on his relentless A-game in such a familiar environment, completely rolling over Bianchi to such an aggressive and comical degree that, at one point, Plouffe turned to Klain on the sideline and asked, approvingly, "Is he really going to do that in the debate?!"

The next session, with Van Hollen, was even better, and Plouffe, Klain, and a handful of other Obamans urged him to keep going with the bulldozer act—the fewer full lines Ryan could get in edgewise and the more scathing critiques of Romney's austere conservatism Biden could pack in, the better. The risk of looking like a buffoonish cartoon character wasn't even worth thinking about, they thought. His goal had to be to excite Democrats who'd been freaked out by Obama's performance, and not to worry about Republicans. As soon as Obama's debate had ended the team had tried keeping supporters engaged by playing up the importance of Biden's showdown, and now they went into overdrive, encouraging extra attention on the matchup between the sixty-nine-year-old veep and the forty-two-year-old upstart. Biden was encouraged by their tone but wanted to be sure they were all on the same page. He'd followed instructions to be lukewarm against Palin, he told the combined prep squad, and he could approach Ryan either hot, lukewarm, or cold. They were telling him to go in hot, right? That's right, they said. Keep doing what you're doing.

Biden had seen enough of these debates to know that he wasn't going to be the story for more than a few days, and that his job was just to get the narrative back on Obama's side—to stop the slide that had started in Colorado. Still, he figured, he might as well try to get the pendulum swinging all the way back.

Obama called Biden on the day of the debate to give him an extra dose of encouragement, but Biden hardly needed it by then. He wasn't like his boss—no one would have to ask him the question Messina had posed to Obama regarding the first debate: "Why would your supporters fight for you if you won't fight for them?"

Their instructions couldn't have been any more different, either. The debate team's final advice for Obama had been to avoid any contentious back-and-forth. Biden had sat for one final review of his mock debate tape with Klain and debate coach Michael Sheehan in Wilmington before flying to Kentucky. At the end of the session, as he was preparing to leave, Biden asked: "Any last comments?"

Anticipating a fiery evening, Sheehan replied, "You really have to set in your head: Where's the line you really don't want to go over?"

Klain cut in before Biden could respond. "I'll make it easy," he told the vice president. "There is no line."

This kind of macho bluster might have been mildly embarrassing for a different kind of pol—for Obama, say. But Biden loved it and had been feeding off it for weeks. When he got onstage with Ryan, who'd been getting coverage for his obsessive workouts, Biden's first thought was, *I could physically take this guy.* And once the debate began, he followed the plan precisely, not necessarily scoring every possible point in favor of the Democratic administration but disrupting Ryan so readily and grinning so widely that he made his opponent look frustrated and overwhelmed off the bat.

Republicans couldn't believe what they were seeing—Biden was acting like a clown, wasn't he? It wasn't abundantly obvious that voters much liked it, either, though they certainly had no reason to fall for Ryan in his grand introduction to the national stage after Biden dismissed him as ridiculous for an hour and a half, on everything from Iran sanctions policy to his deployment of unemployment statistics.

The reaction in Chicago was almost unanimous delight, and Obama, who watched on Air Force One on the way back to DC after a day of campaigning in Florida, exhaled. None of them thought their campaign had stumbled irredeemably off track in Denver, but they all knew Obama had fallen down on the job and that the national story had needed to change, ASAP, to cut Romney's momentum off at its ankles.

Obama picked up his phone after Biden left the stage.

He felt a new kind of gratitude for his partner, like Biden had stepped up to fix his mistake. He told him that, thanked him, and revealed that Biden had given him some things to consider that night. Biden had reset Obama's way of thinking about the rest of his showdowns with Romney, the president said. He now saw that he could stop treating this all like a legal proceeding, and more like a campaign. And he knew how to campaign.

PART II

2012–2021

CHAPTER 11

2012–2013

The reelection, Obama suspected, had finally done it. Fresh off a victory that plenty of people around him believed was more consequential than his first for arguing—*proving*—that the election of the first Black commander in chief amid an economic catastrophe was no fluke, Obama called a cabinet meeting. He put aside the printed script he was handed and, looking out at his team, he riffed, predicting that they were entering a new era. If 2012 had shown anything it was that the politics of obstruction had failed, he said, and that there was little market for pure partisanship out in the real world, where Americans wanted to see Washington tackle big issues. He continued: as the appetite for gridlock was now on the wane, it was time for his cabinet to seize the opportunity to think big. The election was a referendum on thinking big, wasn't it?

Obama knew this was easier said than done, of course, especially since Republicans still controlled the House. But he thought there was reason to believe they might be open to new compromise on immigration policy, for one thing. Romney's loss had appeared to expose them as an aging party of white men in desperate need of change to stop a full-on descent into outright xenophobia and therefore permanent minority status in a quickly diversifying country. He knew that plenty of his advisors were skeptical of the GOP's ability or willingness to budge, but even hyperconservative screamers like Fox News host Sean Hannity had exited the Romney experience telling their radio audiences they'd "evolved" on immigration, arguing for a "pathway to citizenship" for undocumented migrants to "get rid of the immigration issue altogether" for their party.

Obama thought John Boehner, the leader of the Republican-majority

House, who reminded him a bit of the kind of transactional old-school GOP pols he knew back in Springfield, could wrangle his more obstructionist members—who'd presumably been chastened by Obama's reelection—into a more collaborative posture. At least he could shut them up while more reasonable moderates and conservatives retook control on the important stuff. Earlier that year Obama had told donors in Minneapolis that he thought "if we're successful in this election—when we're successful in this election—that the fever may break, because there's a tradition in the Republican Party of more common sense than that. My hope, my expectation, is that after the election, now that it turns out that the goal of beating Obama doesn't make much sense because I'm not running again, that we can start getting some cooperation again."

First things first, though. He couldn't look ahead to his second term until they finally resolved the so-called fiscal cliff, an ugly combination of painful slashes to government programs and tax increases that would automatically go into effect at the end of the year in just a few weeks without an agreement on Capitol Hill over spending and taxation policy. No one was particularly optimistic that it would be an easy negotiation after years of depressing budgetary brinkmanship, but perhaps they could wrap it up in time to have a normal holiday season, maybe even showcasing early signs of a healing working relationship among party leaders. It would be a good chance, too, for Obama to demonstrate that he was still willing to hit the negotiating table—a role at this point more widely associated with Biden, who was always sure he could find common ground with GOP leaders he'd known for years. Obama preferred to articulate broad values than to talk numbers with Boehner or Mitch McConnell, but he wasn't willing to step back entirely and let Biden take the lead now, especially with the memory of the previous summer's debt ceiling debacle—the low point of the Obama-Biden first term, if you asked the president—still sharp. Maybe things really were different now.

At least that was the hope before mid-December, before the period everyone in the White House would come to remember as the nadir of their entire eight years in office. The time when there was no longer any doubting that while Obama's capacity to ignite public passion and Biden's dexterity within Washington could combine to great effect, they were not always enough to overcome the capital's structural impediments—especially against an opposition party with no political incentive to budge.

* * *

The first reports were so horrific on that quiet, gray Friday that the White House staff waited for a minute, hoping the Associated Press would issue a correction—say it wasn't true—before someone had to inform Obama of what was happening in Connecticut. When he did learn from his counterterrorism advisor John Brennan about the monstrous school shooting that had killed over two dozen people, including twenty six- and seven-year-olds, he went dark and looked like he'd been sucker-punched in the stomach, thinking, as he said later that day through tears, trying not to let his voice break, "not as a president but as anybody else would, as a parent." It was the only time he ever requested that Michelle join him in the Oval in the middle of a workday, and even when she got there, there wasn't much to do but hug silently.

Biden usually handled tragedy differently, always immediately asking who he could talk to, who he could connect with, when he could go to the scene to help. This time he watched, feeling just as helpless as everyone else, as Obama briefly addressed the nation and offered little solace but, they both hoped, a reminder of shared humanity. He also made clear that he wanted to be involved in the broader, more lasting response, and within the week Obama tasked him with quickly compiling a roster of concrete proposals for reducing gun violence, an assignment both of them considered to be significant.

It was a good fit for Biden, who not only had a profound understanding of what parts of the government could do what, but who had also himself contributed to the formulation of the assault weapons ban in 1994, and whose chief of staff Bruce Reed had been working on suing gun manufacturers in various capacities since the Columbine shooting in 1999. The work would, necessarily, be split in two: as they considered how to expand universal background checks, create national databases for firearms, and implement mental health checks for gun buyers, they would both outline an aggressive suite of executive actions the administration could undertake immediately and identify legislative proposals to champion. Within Biden's office there were few illusions that the latter part of the task would be easy, since they would need sixty Senate votes to pass anything, which meant winning over some Republicans who saw gun control as anathema to their political identities and had little interest in crossing the firearms lobby. And that was before you even considered the GOP-led House. But, Biden advisors were often quick to point out internally, polling unanimously showed that the country had been moving in their direction dramatically on gun matters, no matter what the National Rifle Association said. There was obvious momentum for pushing the boundaries out on background checks, they believed, and previous country-rattling school shootings like Columbine and at Virginia Tech in 2007 had both given way to some policy changes.

There was, in fact, even more appetite within Obama's government for aggressive action than the president appreciated. Shortly after Obama asked Biden to take the lead, Education secretary Arne Duncan, Attorney General Eric Holder, and Homeland Security secretary Janet Napolitano quietly approached the VP to encourage him to propose aggressive, quick action through the agencies, since they were getting frustrated with the administration's lack of progress. Biden didn't need the push from the cabinet—he couldn't stop thinking about his wrenching conversations with families whose children had been killed, and he saw the executive actions side of his mandate as paramount. This was where he could make sure the existing background check system was hardened, for one thing.

Still, he resolved to be methodical about his approach, and he sat for meetings with not just victims of gun violence, their families, and progun control groups, but also the NRA and police chiefs, aiming to find loopholes to exploit and points of agreement to rely on. And then, when it came time to start selling the country on the plans he handed Obama in January, he returned to that territory, not just sitting for friendly glossy magazine interviews but also with sportsman publications where he could argue for the proposals to skeptical audiences. The administration, however, was mostly moving alone at that point. Obama announced that he would back legislation to implement universal background checks for purchasers, to ban assault weapons again, to prohibit high-capacity magazines, and to further restrict arms trafficking, but Harry Reid had already told him that while he wouldn't stand in the White House's way, he wanted Obama and Biden to push quickly, since he knew from previous experience that the NRA's grip over Republicans was ironclad. He would help try to win over some Democratic skeptics but he wouldn't use all of his own political capital or time on this effort, fearing it wouldn't go anywhere.

It didn't take long for everyone involved to conclude that the only conceivable path in the Senate was through Joe Manchin, the self-serious conservative West Virginia Democrat who liked shooting things in his campaign ads back home and working with Republicans in DC. He stood the only chance of possibly winning some GOP votes for a handful of reforms, even if that meant starting from a considerably less aggressive place than Obama or Biden preferred. Manchin was open to regulating military-style weapons, though, and it helped that though Manchin and Biden didn't always see eye to eye, they liked each other. In fact, Biden was the only person in the White House Manchin would even talk to, considering his cold relationship with Obama, whom he saw as too liberal on energy issues—years later the coal-state senator still wouldn't reveal who he voted for in 2012's presidential race—and early in 2013 Manchin told Biden that he'd be putting out a framework for legislation to impose background checks on purchases at gun shows and online, soon to be joined by Pennsylvania Republican Pat Toomey. In order for it to have any hope of passing with some GOP votes, Manchin told Biden, the VP couldn't let the White House endorse it.

If ever there was a chance for Biden to concentrate on wielding his Senate skills for the administration's benefit, this was it, he figured—an opportunity to shepherd something big into reality in front of a country paying close attention. He agreed with Manchin and persuaded Obama to step back, and then got to work trying to soothe the considerable fears of red-state Democrats like Baucus, North Dakota's Heidi Heitkamp, Alaska's Mark Begich, and Arkansas's Mark Pryor, at Manchin's request. He talked Manchin down, too, at one point convincing him to keep the provision mandating background checks for online sales in the bill despite Republican resistance, explaining that he still regretted leaving gun shows out of the 1994 crime bill's background checks section and didn't want to repeat the mistake.

But still, signs of genuine GOP openness to Manchin's framework were few and far between, and Washington was getting antsy. Biden's proposed executive orders were on their way to implementation, but January, February, and March slunk by without clarity on when Manchin-Toomey might get near the sixty supporters it needed to pass, each day making the political limbo even more untenable for conservative Democrats who were under mounting pressure back home to drop the reforms altogether.

Then, in mid-April, Reid drew the line. The Boston Marathon had been bombed two days earlier and the perpetrators were still at large, so attention was far from the Capitol. There appeared to be no end in sight for the gun debate after one Republican holdout, New Hampshire senator Kelly Ayotte, said she would join her party in rejecting the proposal, after all. Reid called over to the White House and said the debate had gone long enough—his caucus's moderates were bleeding politically and he intended to put the measure on the Senate floor for a vote in a matter of days. Obama and Biden quickly convened their senior staff to work through any possible plan to get to sixty votes by then, before Reid called back. Actually, he said, the vote would be the next day. He'd had enough and couldn't believe the White House couldn't see that Republicans weren't going along with them—on this, or on anything big.

Biden felt like the rug had been pulled out from under him—he was sure he just needed more time to win over his old colleagues. Obama went quiet, and then, within hours, as cynical as anyone could remember. Usually the president hid his anger or expressed it in sarcasm. Now, though, he seethed. Not at Reid, but at the political reality he could no longer avoid.

If a heart-shredding national tragedy—twenty little kids *murdered*—wasn't going to jar the GOP into cooperation, they were never going to get serious and work with him on anything, were they? No, he concluded, in a wake-up call of his own. Nothing had changed, after all.

* * *

There had still been some hope back in December, especially since no one considered the fiscal cliff situation extraordinary at all after the preceding years' series of budget-focused economic showdowns. Those felt more like dutiful drudgery than anything else, each party playing a predetermined role before an inevitable and painful last-second compromise. At 11:00 a.m. the morning after the reelect, then–White House chief of staff Jack Lew scheduled a conference call for the hungover senior staff: the president would be engaging with Boehner to find a solution to the impending cuts and tax increases, which would hopefully include sufficient spending reductions to mollify conservatives and robust enough extensions on middle-class tax relief paired with higher rates for the wealthy to keep liberals satisfied.

It didn't yet feel terribly relevant that Reid was determined to play hardball and expose Republicans' years of economic hostage-taking—

they'd been forcing Obama's Democrats into unfair compromises because of conservative hard-liners' outsize influence on weak GOP leadership, and he wanted an end to the austerity regime—or that McConnell was unlikely to agree to higher taxes for high earners. And no one thought to dwell on the demands of Boehner's loudest internal critics, right-wingers in his caucus who could tank any compromise he struck if they didn't think it was harsh enough.

It wasn't until ten days before the deadline that Boehner backed away from the negotiations, succumbing to the reality that his Tea Partiers would refuse to vote for any tax increase, even one only for people who made $1 million or more—as their speaker had proposed in hopes of forcing an agreement with Obama, who'd backed a $250,000 threshold. That left the situation up to Reid to resolve, and in the Oval a week later Obama, unamused and tired of it all, said he'd rather walk away with no deal than sign a bad one.

It was hard to blame him for the impatience. In the first half of 2011 there'd been talk of a "Grand Bargain" between the parties ahead of a deadline to raise the government's debt limit, and Plouffe had argued to everyone in the president's orbit that reaching a bipartisan agreement could be a serious boon to their reelection campaign. But weeks of Biden-led behind-closed-doors talks with Republicans had soured, the White House increasingly certain the GOP negotiators were insisting on an unreasonable budget that, for example, went after Medicare too intensely. Obama's own secret attempt to strike a deal with Boehner didn't go much better. The debt ceiling—the limit for the Treasury's borrowing—drew closer and Republicans started to make noise about threatening to let the government hit it if they didn't agree on spending cuts. That would mean the first-ever US default on its debts, which was universally regarded as a calamitous outcome that could forever tarnish America's place in the international economic system. So the outcry was significant when Boehner determined he couldn't get his most militant members to go along with any tax increases at all, even though Obama kept tentatively agreeing to spending slashes that his own supporters would hate. The president had little choice but to kick most of these matters down the road and focus simply on trying to avoid default.

Biden felt betrayed by the Republicans and Obama was furious they were willing to gamble with the world economy for narrow partisan gain.

Even after Democrats forced an agreement to raise the debt ceiling for a bit longer in exchange for serious spending cuts and the promise of more in the future if Congress didn't come up with a deficit reduction plan, the feeling around Obama was that the GOP had crossed a dangerous line.

That just wasn't how Biden thought. He was different from his boss. He was always looking for a deal, and he loved the muck of it all. This didn't always make him popular among Democrats—some of whom suspected he was more interested in the process than in the substance—even when Obama appreciated it.

Take his negotiation with McConnell immediately after the 2010 midterms. Biden sought to find common ground on a tax deal quickly, and when he reported the deal to Obama and his top economic and political advisors in the Oval on a Saturday morning, he presented it as a great compromise. The economists, however, objected to his agreement to extend one tax credit, since he'd allowed McConnell to strip out help for low-income families who actually needed it, and they thought he'd also given away too much on the matter of the estate tax, thereby benefiting the rich. Obama asked Biden to at least go back to McConnell with a payroll tax cut proposal. The Republican agreed to it, but only alongside the conservative estate tax plan and a low capital gains rate. Reid and Pelosi thought it was an awful deal, but Biden told Obama he was happy to take their flak since he'd gotten it done and the president was, at the end of the day, OK with it. Still, Reid—thinking of the upset liberals in his caucus and his own preference for pushing McConnell further—warned that they shouldn't blame him if the deal didn't pass. After it did, Reid told Obama that he, himself, would take the lead on the next round of negotiations. Not Biden.

Now, four years into their administration, the president's and vice president's respective relationships with Reid and McConnell were sometimes as revealing as their interactions with each other.

To Reid, the idea that Biden was ever Obama's Senate guru was overblown, though he was willing to let his ex-colleague say it out loud if it made him more confident as VP. The pair had been friendly but never especially close, and Reid considered Biden both overly loquacious and overly self-assured—Reid sometimes told confidants that they'd once faced each other on a chartered flight from Dallas to DC and he, looking at a clock above Biden's head, timed Biden speaking for three hours and eighteen minutes of the three-hour, twenty-minute flight. But they got along and, as longtime senators, did have a solid shared understanding of the way Washington works. And for a while at least, until Reid drifted left, they were fellow moderates. Still, Reid was far closer with Obama than with Biden, and Obama was open in his uncommon affection for Reid, seeing him as an underappreciated warrior for justice. He once gave Reid a signed copy of a famous photo of a five-year-old Black boy feeling Obama's hair in the Oval Office with a note reading, "This is the change you helped make happen," and Reid displayed it right outside his office.

But the president also appreciated the leader because Reid understood that Obama hated doing the relationship work, shying from being transactional even with his fellow Democratic lawmakers. Many liberal senators gave up on trying to be friendly with Obama early in his term, when he wouldn't even stick around for long at White House receptions—this was the part of politics for which he had no patience, and instead harbored considerable distaste—and among some of the longer-tenured Hill denizens, it was common for years to marvel at his lack of interest in engaging. "Chuck, you're the greatest politician I've ever met," Obama once told the notoriously schmoozy Schumer, who always retold the story with the important kicker: "He didn't mean it as a compliment." The "fact" that Obama had never called Blanche Lincoln, the conservative Arkansas Democrat and a swing vote on the ACA, to woo her for that bill was a rumor of special fascination in DC, though it wasn't true.

McConnell, meanwhile, disdained Obama, describing his negotiation sessions with the president as visits to the principal where he'd get a condescending lecture about how wrong he was before he could say a word. Obama, though, had detected early on that McConnell wouldn't be a cooperative partner, and he was right—the senator was convinced Obama wanted to turn the US into Europe and believed himself to be above Congress. So McConnell dedicated himself to stopping the new president as soon as he was elected. As a result, there was little Obama hated more than the common DC insider crowd insistence that he'd get more done if only he'd socialize more in town. Obama put it blithely at 2013's White House Correspondents' Association dinner: "Some folks still don't think I spend enough time with Congress. 'Why don't you get a drink with

Mitch McConnell?' they ask. Really? Why don't *you* get a drink with Mitch McConnell?"

Biden, though, didn't like that joke or what it represented. In the long list of Bidenisms, one of his favorites was his promise never to question his colleagues' motives, a principle instilled in him early in his career by legendary Democratic leader Mike Mansfield. Biden had considered maintaining a good working relationship with McConnell an important part of his job since he first became VP. They disagreed on almost everything and had seldom worked together in their shared quarter century in the Senate, but they both thought they understood each other's politics, even if Biden thought McConnell was overhyped as a tactician and McConnell thought Biden could be a bit buffoonish. (He had a story about Biden's nonstop talking eerily similar to Reid's, but the version he told was about two legs of a chartered flight, not one, and their destination was Raleigh, not DC.) McConnell often compared negotiating with Biden favorably to dealing with his boss, since Biden never opened their sessions by trying to prove McConnell wrong and instead tried quickly to find points of agreement.

Biden's willingness to engage with McConnell earned him the nickname the "McConnell whisperer" in the Obama White House's early days, and McConnell reciprocated at first because he figured he needed an in with the White House but couldn't openly negotiate with the comparably polarizing Obama if he wanted to keep the Tea Party off his back. The relationship rarely bore productive fruit, but it suited Biden and McConnell both, and in February 2011 Biden even visited the McConnell Center at the University of Louisville to give a speech about bipartisanship.

To some in Obama's inner circle, though, that was the whole problem. Biden fashioned himself too much of a conciliator, they thought—he liked to show off a huge table in his office that he'd gotten from segregationist senator John Stennis, who'd gotten it from Senator Richard Russell, a civil rights opponent who'd gotten it from President Truman, who'd gotten it from the government of the Philippines, as a sign of his statesmanship and commitment to bridging ideological divides. And McConnell—the same man who in 2010 told *National Journal* "the single most important thing we want to achieve is for President Obama to be a one-term president" in arguing he wanted Obama to change—was playing him, they believed. This conviction was hardly diluted by Biden's repeated internal insistence that the White House was always one deal away from breaking the GOP's policy of obstruction.

Yet in those negotiations with his GOP interlocutors, Biden was in fact always clear that he wasn't the final decision maker—Obama was, and the VP's job was to get him as much information as possible. That's why he, too, was often frustrated: it was common to hear Biden griping to his long-time aides that Obama was missing opportunities to engage on the Hill by refusing to talk to his former colleagues. Biden had a metaphor for his boss's style. "It's like Obama is at a dinner table he's never been at before and doesn't know it's appropriate to ask them to pass the salt," he'd say in moments of candor. "There are just things he could do that he isn't doing that are offending people. Obama's view is they're never going to move. But they're people! They can be influenced!"

Biden read Obama correctly: the president did, at times, feel powerless to change a thing when his partners down Pennsylvania Avenue wouldn't even begin to engage. This sometimes left him musing for days at a time about the limitations of the presidency that real people didn't seem to understand, though he always landed on the conclusion that his words still mattered, even when it felt like he was just the national narrator.

Obama, though, didn't always see it when Biden got discouraged. This happened more often than anyone outside his inner circle appreciated, usually when he couldn't envision his political future or his immediate use to the president. Those around him started to detect some of this toward the end of the reelection campaign, using his trips to Iowa—the first state to weigh in on presidential primaries, and thus usually the focus of fawning attention—as a proxy for Biden's view of his own post-Obama path. He hadn't talked very openly about running for president again, but all his friends knew it was always a possibility and so were surprised when he barely visited Iowa at all in 2012, even though it was one of the states he was supposed to be focusing on. In October, when he did stop by, he was in a bad mood, annoyed that not enough people had shown up to his rally in Grinnell. He'd had far more in other states recently, he fumed backstage. "And here we are doing these events with a few hundred, this just shows Iowans are spoiled!" he said, letting his past frustrations about the state that had harshly rejected him in 2008 spill out. "They don't deserve it!" When an aide asked shortly before the end of the campaign whether he was nervous, he shrugged. *Not really*, he said, deep in one of his moods. *I don't really like this job.*

But then, always, he snapped back. He was thrilled the next month when *National Journal* asked, "Joe Biden: The Most Influential Vice President in History?" a step up from 2009's *New York Times Magazine* report putting him in second place after Cheney. If you asked him at the right time, he would acknowledge that he'd grown as a politician during his years with Obama, the product of some weird chemistry that was almost like what happened when you play tennis with someone better than you. He'd upped his game, and he knew it.

That was one reason he fell further for the proliferating memes about him and Obama and their bromance as the second term dawned. He also recognized before Obama did that this stuff had some political power among Democrats. There was a clear yearning out there for an uplifting story about their interracial, intergenerational companionship. But it was also a new expression of politician hero worship, giving the Obama fans who treated him more as a celebrity than as a commander in chief a new dimension and a sidekick character in their fantasy. Aides in the White House loved circulating shots of the two laughing uproariously while reclining courtside at a Team USA basketball game ahead of the 2012 Olympics, looking like they had not a care in the world.

And it was true, they did really like each other by then, having spent so much time together. (A few years later, Michelle likened Biden to a "big brother" her husband had never had.) The arrangement Biden had negotiated and Obama had embraced back in 2008 meant they were spending many more hours per day in each other's company than average presidents and vice presidents, and certainly more than either of them had expected. That's what made it all work, even if the public perception among some overly romantic liberals was still unrealistically chummy considering the daily weight of their responsibilities running the country. They weren't exactly sharing ice-cream cones every afternoon.

It was also around then that Biden started to need Obama the most.

Beau Biden had first fallen ill in 2010, a year after he returned from Iraq. He was complaining of headaches and numbness, and his doctors said he'd had a stroke. When Joe Biden returned to the White House after rushing to see his son, Obama had bounded down the hallway to give him a huge hug, which meant the world to the shaken VP. He'd always thought of Beau—Joseph Robinette Biden III—as an upgraded version of himself and didn't know how to handle this.

But something was still wrong—Beau was saying he could hear music when none was playing, and in August 2013 he suffered a grand mal seizure during a trip to Lake Michigan. The doctor in Chicago saw a tumor, and the family descended on Thomas Jefferson University Hospital in Philadelphia, and then MD Anderson Cancer Center in Houston. There, he had the first operation on his brain mass. He had glioblastoma multiforme, a diagnosis his brother characterized as "a death sentence."

Biden did everything in his power not to shut down. He didn't want anyone to know. But he told Obama.

* * *

Reid didn't think it would be unreasonable to just go over the cliff at the end of December 2012. Boehner and Obama didn't appear to be any closer to solving the fiscal crisis with January approaching, and the Senate leader thought it was time to expose the Republican pattern of intransigence, especially McConnell's, to the American people right after they'd chosen to reelect Obama. Then the Democrats could do something like create a huge, popular child tax credit and gain the upper hand. Obama, though, had softened on his insistence on not striking a bad deal. He was growing concerned again about the shock to the economy if they didn't find some compromise, and he summoned the congressional leaders to the White House on December 28, three days before the deadline. He reiterated his priorities and questioned the GOP's willingness to compromise, but McConnell was having none of it, later writing, "Those two hours would have been more productive had I spent them napping." The Republican leader dug in even further when Reid rejected a near-agreement two days later, and McConnell took to the Senate floor to demand a change in the negotiating paradigm: he needed "a dance partner," he said. He needed Biden.

The VP was thrilled to oblige at this late hour, and after a day or so came up with a plan with McConnell to keep the Bush-era tax cuts in place for people earning under $400,000 and to impose a small tax hike on the wealthiest Americans. Not everyone around Obama was happy, though, once again viewing the result as a giveaway to the rich just when Democrats finally had some leverage. Obama called Reid to run it by him and the Nevadan fell silent. "You said you'd rather have no deal than a bad deal," he replied. "I don't think it's a good deal. I'll vote for it, but I'm not going to sell it. Either you or your VP comes up here to sell it."

Biden thought he was going to see his friends when he headed up to the Hill, and he prepared for the reception of a conquering hero when he encountered his former colleagues that evening. But the caucus's liberals were incensed, and even some of its supposed moderates were struggling to understand why they shouldn't hold out, expose Republicans' unreasonable stance, and then use the resulting outcry to cut taxes for working people. What was Obama thinking? some asked each other. How could Democrats now distinguish themselves from Republicans on economic policy? And how had McConnell rolled Biden like this? Reid heard the complaints and warned the caucus to treat Biden with respect, but then added that he wasn't going to pressure them to go along with the administration. No one confronted Biden in person—if they had, he would have defended the deal and insisted he was carrying out Obama's wishes to avert an immediate catastrophe—and they passed the measure after midnight on New Year's Day, almost all the Democrats willing to go along with the administration over their objections to the details. But the takeaway was stark for a growing group of Biden's onetime friends, Reid included, who couldn't get around the conclusion that the administration had sacrificed long-term gain for middle-class Americans and, presumably, the Democratic Party, for short-term political expediency.

Obama and Biden moved on, trying to steer the government's focus back to gun control before the spring. But the experience stuck with Reid, and early the next fall he decided to act on it. Obama had gathered Biden and both Reid and McConnell in the Oval for yet another round of negotiations, this time to try to avert a government shutdown created by a lack of funding and a looming demand from attention-hungry Tea Party senator Ted Cruz of Texas and some right-wing House members that Obama defund his signature health-care law if he wanted the government to stay open. Reid saw the situation as fairly simple—Republicans were splintering, and panicking—but sat aghast when Biden, whose main principle there was to ensure continuity, told McConnell, "We don't want you to lose, we want you to win." The VP meant he wanted to get this all resolved in a way that was acceptable to the part of the GOP he could still negotiate with.

Reid called Obama after the session for some blunt talk. He still liked Biden, he said, but Obama needed to bar him from this negotiation, no matter what. Republicans would try to say Democrats were holding government funding hostage, but Reid knew he could call their bluff and force them to cave after a few days of a shutdown that would be far more politically painful for them than it was for Obama. The president listened as Reid hammered it home: we can't have Biden swooping in to make some deal with McConnell to reopen the government and let Republicans declare victory.

Obama agreed, but stayed antsy, since he trusted Biden. He had Denis McDonough, his new chief of staff, call Reid repeatedly over the course of the shutdown to make sure the leader still knew what he was doing, that his endgame was still in sight. Biden sat tight, watching uncomfortably. "Ted Cruz has led them into a box canyon and they can't get out," Reid would reply. "I don't know how long it's going to take, but we're not going to give them an inch." It took sixteen days for the right-wingers to cave. Reid was winning Obama over to his style of confrontation. It was about time, the leader figured. He never let any of his aides disparage Biden in front of Obama. But the message he gave the president was the polite version of a popular refrain among some advisors in his office, and some of the VP's critics within the White House, too: "Biden's too horny for a deal."

CHAPTER 12

2013–2015

Two months into Obama's second term, he and Michelle hosted a pair of first-time guests for a private dinner in the White House residence. Their previous social interactions with Bill and Hillary Clinton were brief and relatively public at summer parties on Martha's Vineyard, but now their invitation for the former president and newly ex–secretary of state was purposely quiet and agenda free. The air was casual, and the four found themselves enjoying the evening more than they had expected as they reminisced about their travails as only first couples could. They talked about the future, too—the Obamas were weighing how impractical a post–White House move to New York City might be. The Clintons stayed past midnight.

They didn't discuss the one thing on everyone's mind. They didn't have to. Hillary Clinton was trying to relax, just weeks removed from Foggy Bottom. She'd said no when Obama tried to keep her in the administration by offering her the Treasury secretary job, and she was now insisting to friends and aides that she needed time away from government. But the topic of the 2016 presidential race, and whether she should enter it as the world's most admired woman for eleven years running (and seventeen of the last twenty)—and as Obama's enemy turned ally—was already following her everywhere. A few days earlier, it hung over every question as Obama and Clinton sat together for a chummy *60 Minutes* interview that Obama set up "to publicly say thank you, because I think Hillary will go down as one of the finest secretary of states we've had." Interviewer Steve Kroft introduced the "very improbable" segment by describing the two as onetime "bitter opponents" with a "rivalry that is one of the richest in

American history." He almost immediately asked whether he should be reading into any "political tea leaves" in the joint appearance. Clinton's on-camera deflection aside, the answer was clearly yes.

This went unspoken in their inner circles until May, when Clinton's longtime aide Huma Abedin visited the White House for a lunch and ran into Plouffe. When he asked Abedin how Clinton was doing, the aide wondered aloud if Obama's former campaign manager had time to sit down with the former secretary to discuss her future. Abedin was surprised when he agreed, and so was Clinton—her focus was mostly on writing a new book and figuring out a role for herself at her family's foundation. Everyone knew the presidential question was inescapable, though, and Obama urged Plouffe to be forward but encouraging with Clinton. The operative secretly visited her to start the conversation about what she should do to put herself in position to run in three years. When Clinton then visited Obama for jambalaya on the terrace outside the Oval Office, he did little to dispel the notion Plouffe had started to convey: the president believed Clinton represented the Democrats' best shot at keeping the White House after he left. She could reenergize his coalition of voters, he thought, and the country was ready to break another barrier and elect its first woman president. Still, he wouldn't say anything to that effect out loud, partially because he didn't want to sacrifice his neutrality already, in case he needed it down the line, and partly out of respect for Biden, who he was pretty sure wouldn't run, but who hadn't yet said so.

Plouffe soon visited Clinton again, this time with a memo he pulled together with the help of a few other former Obama campaign officials from the digital and data side. It was meant to lay out both how she should build an operation and what sort of big-picture questions she needed to answer about her rationale for running and her message. When the conversation then slowed for a few months as Clinton considered her options, Obama called again. In the fall of 2014, he told her more directly that it was time to get serious, that he still thought she was the Democrats' best bet to keep the White House, and that she had to tell him ASAP if this wasn't happening.

If this all felt rather fast, well, that was modern politics. And, to Obama's thinking, you could hardly blame him for trying to do some long-term planning. By the first summer of his second term, with scant Republican interest in cooperating on any of his priorities, he'd pivoted his domestic agenda almost entirely toward issuing executive orders that were binding but that could presumably be reversed by the next GOP president even before he or she went after Obama's harder-to-dislodge legislative achievements. (No right-wing rallying cry was more popular among Republicans than the promise to repeal and replace Obamacare.) It was also understandable that he was thinking about what came next, considering the daily drudgery of Washington. With his job approval numbers mired in the low forties and Republicans about to sweep the midterm elections for the second time in Obama's presidency, the outlook for his final two years in office looked uninspiring, at best. At one cabinet meeting late that year, he looked around the table at his administration's top officials and sighed, saying that during his campaigns they'd done such a good job of creating a brand—"like Coke"—and that it had faded.

Still, he figured that the country was diversifying and liberalizing, and that as long as the next Democratic presidential nominee mirrored his "change" appeal and engaged his particular mix of voters, his accomplishments would be safe. He preferred to think of political change in generational terms, but the elevation of the older Clinton—who'd proven herself a worthy competitor and then a powerful ally for whom he now had genuine respect—would represent a historic shift, too.

It also helped that she appeared to have basically no competition. A typical CNN poll that November pegged her at 65 percent support among possible Democratic primary voters, a good 55 points ahead of her next possible competitor, the progressive Massachusetts senator Elizabeth Warren. Biden's support was in the single digits.

Biden did his best to disguise his annoyance in early 2014, but to the people close to him, his blink-quickly-then-stare-into-the-distance-then-smile-tightly move hid nothing. The VP was standing next to Obama with a CBS camera pointing up at his face, having just insisted that he hadn't made a decision about running, but that Obama would be the first person he talked to about it. Obama, in turn, heaped praise on Biden as a partner, but then pivoted. "I suspect that there may be other potential candidates for 2016 who have been great friends and allies." Biden looked at Obama and then away as the president paused, then spelled it out: "I know that we've got an extraordinary secretary of state, who did great service for us and worked with me and Joe to help make the country safer." Biden had seen the earlier *60 Minutes* interview and had been unamused, though he wasn't about to tell Obama that he felt slightly betrayed. Direct confrontation with the boss wasn't his style. Now though, here was Obama again going out of his way to talk up Clinton, who hadn't announced her political plans any more than he had. It *had* to be intentional.

When Biden thought about it, so did the drip-drip of rumors that senior Obama aides, starting with his counselor John Podesta, were going to go work for a still theoretical Clinton campaign. So did Missouri senator Claire McCaskill's decision to endorse Clinton for president so soon after she left the State Department, since McCaskill had been an Obama diehard in 2008's primary and everyone knew her backing would be read as a stamp of approval for Clinton from ObamaWorld. And didn't it also seem suspicious that Jim Messina, who was now running the super PAC that backed Obama in 2012, was already directing it to support Clinton?

Biden knew he was far from alone in his mounting frustration with the solidifying narrative that Clinton's candidacy, nomination, and presidency were now just a formality—Deval Patrick, the Massachusetts governor and a friend of Obama's, warned on *Meet the Press* in November that "people read inevitability as entitlement." But Biden was still finding it hard not to be personally stung by Obama's apparent hand in it all, never more than when Clinton officially announced her candidacy in April 2015 and he heard the president praise her as "an outstanding secretary of state. She is my friend. I think she would be an excellent president." Biden interpreted it as effectively an endorsement, and he could hardly be blamed for briefly wondering: Did he and Obama just—somehow—have fundamentally different views of the last seven years, or what was needed now?

In Wilmington and at the Naval Observatory, he started muttering about the discouraging dynamic to his most trusted aides, and when he began searching for a new communications director early that spring, he lectured applicants to let them know he was still considering running, sometimes even diving into punditry—*I would have a better shot at winning working-class white men, she has too much baggage*—before pulling back and griping more broadly about the perception that Clinton was a runaway front-runner before he'd even seriously considered his own campaign. No one around him knew if he really wanted to run, but they also knew he wanted nothing less than to be counted out. Not like this, anyway.

Mike Donilon told friends who asked for updates that "the one way to get Joe Biden into this race is for a bunch of people to tell him he can't do it."

Biden still wasn't saying any of this directly to Obama. As Biden later recalled in a book about that year, the president had approached the subject gingerly at one of their lunches in the fall of 2013, wondering if Biden had started considering all the things he could do after leaving the vice presidency—running a foundation or foreign policy organization, say, or making some money. The VP demurred and Obama tried point-blank: Had Biden decided whether to run? Not yet. Obama tried again in February, urging Biden to be careful about a burgeoning draft movement that had started trying to pull him into the race prematurely: "I'm very protective of your legacy, I really mean it," Obama told Biden, who replied that the chatter wasn't coming from his people. Biden revealed that he'd asked his advisors, led by Donilon and Ricchetti, to lay out what he'd need to do to run, just in case he decided to. Obama offered to put Biden in touch with his own advisors, led by Plouffe, and to take a look at the memo Donilon would write.

The tone of their conversations was still, mostly, affectionate, but that was as far as Biden would go with Obama for the time being, and Clinton remained a sensitive topic. When Bill Richardson, who'd been out of politics for a few years, cornered Biden after a reception, he demanded an answer: "Are you going to run?" Biden replied that he was still deciding. "Hillary's telling everybody you're not going to run," Richardson said, promising Biden his support. "I don't care what she does," Biden steamed, saying that actually, he probably would run. Richardson pushed slightly further: What about the reports that Obama was on Team Hillary? "No," Biden shot back. "That's bullshit." What Biden barely told anyone was that he had a good reason for his delay.

* * *

Beau Biden always knew his dad would be president. He was in favor of Joe running every time he considered it, and as a freshman at the University of Pennsylvania back in 1987 he'd been the most reluctant one in the family to let his dad drop out, arguing to his siblings and parents that they couldn't concede the argument that Joe had plagiarized Kinnock and Kennedy. This was still true after Obama and Biden were reelected, when Beau had more influence with the VP than ever. He'd been hanging around the

West Wing plenty and had gotten to know Obama—only eight years his senior—ever since he returned from Iraq in late 2009. Now he was often staying in the room with Joe until the final seconds before important appearances or tough deadlines, even though he had his own duties to attend to as Delaware's attorney general and presumed next governor.

He'd passed on the chance to take his dad's old Senate seat in 2009, preferring to carve his own path, but the family was on board with the loose plan for Beau to spend some time as Delaware's governor before he ran for president himself. At least that was the idea before he fell ill. These days, Beau liked to turn casual conversations with the family and advisors not into chats about his own political future but into Joe 2016 planning sessions by asking leading questions to get the room thinking about a possible campaign. He was central to the inner circle's discussions as they hired a new top political organizing aide and full-time fundraiser.

By the late fall of 2014, though, he was also aware that while some of his father's advisors wanted Joe to announce his presidential campaign at the beginning of 2015, the VP hadn't yet thought it through because Beau's health was still in question and his future uncertain. Beau was struggling with aphasia on top of his chemotherapy, but he insisted that his family have a normal Thanksgiving on Nantucket, where the plan was to spend more time mulling the race. Days away from his seventy-second birthday, Joe was pessimistic when he sat down with his sons, expecting them to advise against it. Clinton didn't just look like a formidable opponent, there was already talk about who'd be in her cabinet two and a half years later. Instead, the Biden sons were both all-in, Hunter ticking through Clinton's political vulnerabilities and Beau arguing that Joe had a duty to run.

This didn't entirely convince Biden, but it shifted his calculus. The truth was that 2016 had always been somewhere in the back of his mind and that he'd been dropping hints about it for years without the supposed experts really paying any attention. This was, in part, because of his age—he'd become the oldest president ever if he was inaugurated at seventy-four—and also because it was widely believed that he'd promised Obama he wouldn't be interested in 2016 way back when he first interviewed for the job in Minneapolis. As the *New York Times* reported when Obama picked him, "At his age, it appears unlikely that Mr. Biden would be in a position to run for president should Mr. Obama win and serve two terms. Shorn of any remaining ambition to run for president on his own, he could find himself in a less complex political relationship with Mr. Obama than most vice presidents have with their presidents."

It was true that he hadn't really let personal politics get in the way of their personal relationship until now, but not that this was inevitable. Just two months into their administration, Biden's spokesman Jay Carney told the *Times* that Biden wasn't "ruling anything in or out" with respect to 2016, a comment that raised plenty of eyebrows in the West Wing but few outside, since it was buried thirty-four paragraphs into the story about his role in the White House. Still, even Obama's inner circle was none the wiser when Biden started holding occasional political strategy sessions at the Naval Observatory in 2011 to discuss his future, and few people in Obama's Chicago HQ even noticed on the morning of election day 2012 when Biden, asked after casting his ballot if it was his last time voting for himself, replied, "No, I don't think so." The Kevin Sheekey and donor sagas felt like ancient history in the heat of campaign season, and still no one cared when Biden then invited Dick Harpootlian, the Democratic Party chairman in South Carolina—an influential early-voting state in the presidential primary process—to his ceremonial swearing-in for the second term in January.

Beau's diagnosis that August had paused Biden's political thinking. For one thing, it was impossible to plan ahead with such a sobering prognosis. For another, as much as Biden had tinkered with the idea of running again, it was really Beau who at that point was supposed to be the future president in the family. If he might not be able to do it, well, *should* Joe think about 2016 more seriously than before?

The reality that he was approaching a possible campaign either consciously or in a kind of sleepwalk became undeniable in the second half of 2013 when he showed up at Senator Tom Harkin's Steak Fry, a traditional stop for presidential hopefuls in Iowa. There, Biden presented himself as a champion of the Obama years, which he insisted had been dedicated to uplifting the middle class, and he nodded to his supposed gaffe from the previous year: "I know a lot of people criticized me for speaking out not long ago about gay marriage," he said. "I could not remain silent anymore. It's the civil rights of our day." Two months later, Biden hired Greg Schultz, Obama's 2012 Ohio state director, as his in-house political fixer. The VP had gotten to know Schultz during a series of trips to far-flung corners of that vital battleground state, where Biden was tasked with keeping the

Democrats' margin of loss as low as possible by appealing to blue-collar voters.

As 2013 wound to a close, Biden started bringing more people into the loose conversation about his future. On an Air Force Two flight to Iowa, Biden abruptly asked Agriculture secretary Tom Vilsack, the state's former governor, why he thought Biden hadn't done better in the state in his previous campaigns. During the holidays, he cautioned advisors that he was still far from making a decision—he knew that some of his closest friends thought he had to think seriously about his age, and his emotional availability with Beau sick. But, he asked them anyway, what could his next two years look like if Clinton didn't end up running? And how long could he wait before he started raising money or campaigning for himself? One easy thing he could do, Greg Schultz, Steve Ricchetti, and co figured, was to find excuses to pop into important states over the next year to get the voters and influencers there thinking about him. This was rarely subtle, but it worked. Three days after Clinton's high-profile return to Iowa the next September, he grabbed headlines by touching down in Des Moines himself to support a group of activist nuns.

And yet, no one in the White House or the top tier of the party quite believed that Biden would actually run. When the DNC needed a new press secretary it hired a former Biden 2008 staffer in what it assumed would be a sign of neutrality in the primary. Meanwhile the crossover from Obama's orbits to Clinton's sped up. Biden was in the Oval Office in early 2015 when Vilsack—who'd backed him in 1987 and then served two full terms alongside him in Obama's cabinet—told the president that his longtime political aide would manage Iowa for Clinton, and that Vilsack would be endorsing her. Biden was crestfallen but didn't say a word. There was no more even pretending that this could all be a coincidence. No one was surprised when Podesta had departed the White House to chair Clinton's campaign, but he was soon joined by a cast of senior ObamaWorld advisors, including White House communications director Jennifer Palmieri, strategist Joel Benenson, ad maker Jim Margolis, organizing guru Marlon Marshall, and pollster John Anzalone. And those were just the senior-most examples—Obama's name dotted résumés up and down her hundreds-strong staff.

But these were all details, and Biden still questioned why Obama was so worried that his—*their*—legacy was so fragile that Clinton needed to protect it. When he had time to himself at home, Biden mused about how his ongoing work in the White House could all feed naturally into the kind of campaign the country really needed. He was, finally, reading the country's political mood more precisely, even if Obama couldn't quite see it. Wasn't there an opening for Biden, as Obama's *actual* natural heir, to make the kind of populist point he'd resisted making nearly three decades earlier? Back then his strategist Pat Caddell had urged him to breathe economic fire and Biden had preferred moderation. Now he could talk about Obama's unfinished business with the middle class.

If a populist turn might look unlikely to casual observers, Biden thought it might bring him back to his roots and highlight his strongest moments as Obama's partner. At one point in 2014 he stood up during an interview with *New Yorker* writer Evan Osnos and read aloud portions of his 2008 convention speech to argue, "we're not talking enough about income inequality." Biden had long fancied himself the White House's in-house champion of regular people, a perception his staff bolstered with occasional leaks about his positioning in some internal debates, like when word trickled out during financial regulation discussions in 2010 that he'd worked with Goolsbee and former Fed chairman Paul Volcker against Larry Summers to push Obama to support the "Volcker Rule," which would stop banks from making certain kinds of risky investments.

He now brought on Don Graves, who'd been the White House's point person on Detroit's recovery and ran Obama's jobs council, and then economist Ben Harris to ramp up his economic policy shop. Their special focus would be on businesses' struggles to plan and support workers for the long term and on their reliance on stock buybacks, as well as to consider the government's tools for combating monopsonies and monopolies. A big part of their jobs was to set up meetings between Biden and experts to get him up to speed on these matters, which he was convinced were important for protecting middle-class Americans, and to consider how to get the federal government thinking about them.

At one session, they gathered a group of economists that included Goolsbee, Council of Economic Advisers chair Jason Furman, and his predecessor, Alan Krueger, to talk about why middle-class wages were stagnating. Krueger stood up and told Biden that Obama had just asked him the same question, and that he'd written him a memo, which he now held aloft for Biden. Wage collusion is rampant both explicitly and tacitly, he told the vice president, who was listening closely, and the administration should go after the practice, which was hurting workers by suppressing their pay. Another time, Biden gathered a group of business leaders including Richard Branson, BlackRock exec Larry Fink, Container Store chairman Kip Tindell, and Business Roundtable leader John Engler (a former Republican governor of Michigan) at the Naval Observatory. Biden began the discussion by asking how business leaders could take a broader stake in communities and society at large, and how they could reconsider their responsibilities with a long-term perspective. For four hours, the group went around the table and told him that he was onto something, and that they were thinking through these questions themselves.

Around Biden it was only obvious that these conversations had a 2016 angle when he spoke about them in public—he chose venues in Iowa and New Hampshire and a DC think tank to do so. But when he got there the actual addresses were rambling and dry, more about economic policy than political red meat. Still, when Donilon handed Biden a long memo about the race in early February 2015, his message was encouraging: with the economy continuing to improve and the public having little question that he'd been a good partner for Obama, the broadest dynamics would favor Biden if he ran. He was increasingly seen as an authentic guy, too, and it might even help that he'd been a miserable fundraiser throughout his career, since voters were getting more disgusted than ever about the role of money in politics.

A few days later, Biden welcomed Clinton to the Naval Observatory for a long overdue tête-à-tête about the race. The conversation was warm but weighted down by their history. Clinton used to say Biden reminded her of her husband, but she had stopped once they actually started working together as VP and secretary of state. For a while, Biden served as a go-between for Obama and Clinton, back when the president and secretary of state were wary of the other's political motives. At the time, Biden was still somewhat skeptical of Clinton's foreign policy chops compared to his own, and though they occasionally strongly disagreed about the use of American military force, the weekly breakfasts they'd held quietly but consistently in the first term eventually drew them close. They'd become allies in most administration debates by the end of Obama's first term, so much so that Clinton had hung up a photo of the pair laughing together in her office. Now, though, she told him he'd been a good vice president but asked directly if he would run against her.

He replied carefully: he hadn't made a decision, he said, but if he did run, it would be *for* the nomination and not actively *against* her. Clinton walked away without much clarity. Biden didn't feel like he could tell her about the real reason he hadn't decided yet: Beau.

Biden summoned Donilon, Ricchetti, and his sons to talk it all through the next Thursday night. Was it realistic to think he could start giving more pointed speeches, then hiring staffers, and maybe announce a campaign in April?

It was, substantively, an encouraging conversation. But as it dragged on, Biden noticed that Beau was uncharacteristically quiet and clearly tired. He wasn't doing well. The meeting ended with no resolution.

* * *

By early 2015, White House newcomers were often taken aback by the place Obama appeared to have in his deputy's heart, and the space Biden took up in Obama's mind. It would've been understandable to assume—as many did—that their familiarity was at least partially an act performed for political purposes, especially considering the way 2016's campaign was clearly unfolding to Clinton's benefit and the way Obama appeared to be behind her, even when you looked at it with no inside knowledge. But with two years left in their administration, Biden felt secure in his role in Obama's regular decision-making process. They were still holding fast to their weekly lunch regimen, which had long since turned into a cornerstone of their schedules, a chance to strategize and bounce ideas off each other, and to make sure neither would ever surprise the other in public. This access had made Biden a uniquely influential vice president in historical terms, but it was the personal warmth between them—built from a fundamental trust they'd been developing for six years—that turned their relationship into an exceptional one in American history. Over lunch, they shared family updates, vented about unhelpful allies and stubborn opponents, and mused about the future. They still started their days together with the President's Daily Brief, and by that point Biden had calculated that they were spending up to seven hours a day with each other. This had been true for most weekdays since January 2009—a particularly grueling half decade, if you asked them, which they believed gave them a mutual understanding no one else could possibly fathom. Biden had recently started telling (and retelling) a version of a story in public that his aides had heard on a loop behind the scenes for years: During one early lunch, Obama looked at Biden and said, "You and I are becoming good friends! I find that very surprising!" Biden replied, "*You're* fucking surprised!"

Internally, Biden was now playing the role of Obama defender and enforcer, like when he took to appearing in meetings about the botched rollout of healthcare.gov to insist on Obama's behalf that the staff hurry up and fix the debacle, which Obama regarded as not just a mess for people who needed coverage but also a huge distraction from the substantive work he was trying to do.

Still, as Obama had grown more comfortable in some aspects of the job, some of Biden's early roles diminished. There were fewer deals left to cut with an uncooperative GOP-driven House and Senate, and though the vice president was still in on high-priority foreign policy meetings and spearheaded a wide range of international projects for the president, from Latin America to Ukraine, Obama no longer relied on his advice as closely as he once had while the administration tried to move on from engagements in Syria and Libya and considered how to confront ISIS. Biden was briefly embarrassed in 2014 when Robert Gates published a memoir and wrote, "Joe is a man of integrity, incapable of hiding what he really thinks, and one of those rare people you know you could turn to for help in a personal crisis. Still, I think he has been wrong on nearly every major foreign policy and national security issue over the past four decades." A few months later, he was caught by surprise when Obama pushed Chuck Hagel, Biden's old friend and colleague, out of the Pentagon, where he'd been serving as defense secretary.

Biden had a mostly serious policy of not complaining about Obama personally, even to friends, even when he disagreed with him on policy or felt out of the loop. The pair was still meeting every week, after all, and they were still sharing personal reflections with each other with the understanding that their lunches would remain fully confidential. Often now, they were talking in more detail about their families—what it was like for their kids and grandkids to go through middle and high school under such a spotlight, for example, and how lucky they were that the younger generations of Bidens and Obamas got along, as did Michelle and Hunter's wife, Kathleen, with whom she was occasionally spotted at SoulCycle and liked to share cocktails at the White House. Once, after the Obama daughters and some of the Biden grandkids were whisked away from Sidwell Friends School and brought to the nearby Naval Observatory because of a security threat that turned out to be nothing, Michelle Obama called Biden to check on her daughters. The VP replied that he had them all under his supervision and that it was too late for her to get them back, or back in school after the threat cleared, since he'd already ordered pizza and they were all hanging out.

And increasingly, they were talking about Beau. Biden's reputation for gregarious extraversion obscured a deep wish for privacy on truly personal matters, forty-two years after his wife and daughter were killed and twenty-six years after his aneurysms—the aftermath of which all played out in the public eye. So Obama understood the weight of the situation, and felt immense responsibility to protect Biden and respect his wish for privacy, when he was one of the first people told about Beau's glioblastoma diagnosis in 2013, and when he and Michelle remained two of the few people outside the Biden family to know about it for most of the next year. Obama knew that Biden's mind was often in Houston, where Beau was receiving care, as his condition grew more serious, and the president felt a new pain of his own as his friend across the table opened up as he described trying to save his son.

The notion that their relationship was primarily a static political partnership of convenience became even more of a relic. At one lunch in 2014, while Beau was finding it especially difficult to communicate proper nouns, Biden confided to Obama that he thought his son might have to resign as state attorney general, and that Joe and Jill would have to take out a second mortgage on their Wilmington home to provide for Beau's family, since he would no longer have his salary. Obama, understanding that Beau was his father's anchor, and that he had been since the 1972 accident, implored Biden not to do that, saying that he would give him the money.

Nonetheless, the world was still turning and Clinton was still approaching her campaign launch, and Obama's concern grew. Not only did he not want to see Biden destroyed by Clinton in a primary, which would be a devastating way to end his career and cast a shadow on their joint project of eight years, but he also thought Biden was far from emotionally prepared for a campaign, which would be draining and brutal in the best of circumstances. A messy primary between his two allies would also be a nightmare for Obama, not least because of the uncomfortable questions it would raise about his legacy and place in the party moving forward. At their first lunch of 2015 in January, Obama tried to get Biden on the record. "If I could appoint anyone to be president for the next eight years, it would be you, Joe," he said according to Biden's published recollection. "We have the same values. Same vision. Same goals. You've earned the right to make a decision based on how you feel about the race." So, he asked, what was Biden thinking? The VP replied, carefully, that it wasn't like he was desperate for the presidency, but he still needed time to make a decision. What he didn't say out loud was that his considerations were still inextricably tied to Beau, who was invested in seeing his father run, and who was doing worse than even Obama knew. As Biden later wrote, "Giving up on the presidential race would be like saying we were giving up on Beau."

With no answer on the presidential race, Obama mused about his own future and asked Biden if he'd at least considered how he wanted to spend the rest of his life. The seventy-two-year-old was taken aback, and again answered cautiously. He said that as he saw the road ahead, he could spend a decade with his family and make real money for the first time in his life, or he could spend ten years trying to change the country for the better. If that option was in reach, he said, he knew he shouldn't give it up. Neither of them pointed out that this timeline ended in 2025, when Biden would be eighty-three; the 2016 race was surely Biden's last chance to be president.

Biden didn't reveal to Obama just how bad Beau's condition had gotten until early that year, and after he did, Obama increasingly played an emotional support role while Biden talked and talked about his son and his doctors, always staying far from the topic of 2016. The outside world still knew essentially nothing of Beau's disease or Biden's pain. For weeks, Biden tried not to cry at the White House, still feeling exposed after doing so when Beau had his first scare half a decade earlier. Obama's worry for Biden grew as he saw his partner struggling to make sense of news from Beau's doctors while he went through surgery and new rounds of treatment. Backstage at one joint event, Obama cornered Donilon, looked at him closely, and asked, "How is he? Take care of him, OK?" He also asked some of Biden's aides to make sure he stayed busy, which Biden himself had also been suggesting to his top advisors.

When he could, Biden threw himself into small tasks, eager for a daily purpose and distracting himself by becoming absorbed in speech prep. Once, when he spent more than two hours preparing for the Yale commencement address, his scheduler tried reminding him of his busy schedule. Kaufman interrupted her and encouraged Biden to keep going with the speech—the process had been more relaxing and engaging than anything Biden had done in months.

Still, it was hard to watch. When, in April, Biden told Obama about an upcoming procedure Beau was having, Obama broke down, too, and told Biden to go to Houston to be with his son, since nothing they were doing in Washington could be more important.

Beau Biden died at the end of May 2015, tended to by two dozen family members who'd come to Walter Reed.

Quietly, in the White House, Obama asked his speechwriter for help writing a eulogy. "Let's make it about what it means to be a good man," he said. "The qualities that go into being a good man." When he got the draft he sat with it for a while, marking it up by pen, as he did for all the speeches he cared about most. He did the same with the second draft, sitting, thinking, and writing.

At the microphone in Delaware at the service on the first Saturday of June, Obama struggled to keep his composure as he described the family. Beau, he said, "learned early the Biden family rule: If you have to ask for help, it's too late. It meant you were never alone, you don't even have to ask, because someone is always there for you when you need them." He revealed that Joe Biden had once told him that he went home to Wilmington every night when his kids were young not because they "needed him. He did it because he needed those kids." And he was clearly talking as much about Beau as Joe when he went on:

> You know, anyone can make a name for themselves in this reality TV age, especially in today's politics. If you're loud enough or controversial enough, you can get some attention. But to make that name mean something, to have it associated with dignity and integrity, that is rare. There's no shortcut to get it. It's not something you can buy. But if you do right by your children, maybe you can pass it on. And what greater inheritance is there? What greater inheritance than to be part of a family that passes

on the values of what it means to be a great parent, that passes on the values of what it means to be a true citizen, that passes on the values of what it means to give back, fully and freely, without expecting anything in return?

As he wound down, he turned to Beau's two children and told them, fighting off tears, that he, Michelle, and their daughters were "honorary members" of their family, and that "we're always here for you, we always will be—my word as a Biden." And then he turned to Joe and Jill. "Michelle and I thank God you are in our lives. Taking this ride with you is one of the great pleasures of our lives. Joe, you are my brother." He paused, and looked him in the eyes.

CHAPTER 13

2015

It was already obvious in June that the summer of 2015 would play an outsize role in the modern American story. Less than three weeks after Beau Biden's funeral, Obama again solemnly addressed a service in front of a nation in need of consoling, this time tearfully singing "Amazing Grace" after a white supremacist killed nine Black South Carolinians at the Mother Emanuel AME church in Charleston. Shortly after the massacre, the Supreme Court upheld the legality of Obama's signature health-care law, only to one-up itself the next day by ruling that same-sex couples had a right to marry across the country. It was all almost enough to distract from reality TV bloviator Donald Trump's xenophobic campaign launch, which itself largely obscured Clinton's sprouting difficulties within her own party as a long-shot challenge from left-wing Vermont senator Bernie Sanders gained unexpected traction.

Inside the White House, Clinton's early struggles to connect with voters were far from a pressing concern, since no one thought there was any real chance she'd lose the primary. (Trump's antics were regarded as even more of a sideshow, so got even less space in the collective West Wing mindshare.) Around Obama, the bigger worry was about how Clinton was approaching his proposed Trans-Pacific Partnership (TPP) trade agreement. She had praised the Asia-focused pact for years before hitting the campaign trail, where she found that voters—especially white working-class men in the Midwest—were skeptical of, or downright hostile to, such international trade arrangements, which they regarded as harmful for American jobs. Obama wanted to make ratification of the deal one of his final top priority pushes, but Clinton was clearly building up to oppose it—which she did in October—without looking too much like a cynical flip-flopper. Paired with her monthslong insistence that she couldn't weigh in on the pending construction of the Keystone XL pipeline because she was a former administration official, only to oppose the Obama-favored project in September when neutrality became politically untenable, it was clear the front-runner was struggling more than expected with how to talk about the administration.

This wouldn't have been such a mounting annoyance if the Obamans didn't think they'd put this all past them the previous summer. That August, Obama had been surprised to read an interview Clinton did with *The Atlantic*'s Jeffrey Goldberg in which she criticized Obama's choice not to get more involved earlier in Syria's civil war, suggesting "the failure to do that left a big vacuum, which the jihadists have now filled." As to Obama's famous formulation that abroad he mostly wanted to avoid doing "stupid shit," she said, "Great nations need organizing principles, and 'Don't do stupid stuff' is not an organizing principle." Obama immediately dispatched a trio of senior aides to tell Clinton's inner circle that this was not helpful, and when Clinton soon called to apologize, he doubled down on the message: "I have enough problems, I don't need this," he said. When they next encountered each other at a party on Martha's Vineyard, in-the-know Democrats watched nervously as Clinton approached Obama, apologized again, and hugged him.

Obama clarified that he wasn't personally affronted, simply that he expected Clinton not to make his life more difficult. By 2015, he was hoping not to have to think so much about the race to succeed him. He was still following it, and when he did talk to Clinton on the phone, he harkened back to their contest in 2008 and invariably urged her, "You've got to pace yourself this time. Work smart, not just hard," repeating the message to Podesta and Abedin to make sure she understood. Their chats seldom got openly political—when she complained about Sanders's persistent campaign, he simply encouraged her to deal with it and to refrain from elevating his profile even further by responding to him. Sanders was her big concern, but Obama still saw him as a fleeting one.

The other looming protocandidate was even less of a worry. When Clinton first mapped out her possible run in 2014, Biden topped a short list of people her top advisors wanted to keep a close eye on, ahead of Elizabeth Warren and Deval Patrick. But by the summer of 2015, he was so nonthreatening that some of them joked about trying to convince him to run for a Senate seat in Pennsylvania instead of the presidency.

* * *

The intuitive idea that the vice president is a natural successor to the president is a neater supposition than a practical reality. No one in Biden's orbit talked much about the inconvenient and underappreciated historical record, but the fact is that throughout American history only four sitting vice presidents—John Adams, Thomas Jefferson, Martin Van Buren, and George H. W. Bush—have been elected directly to the presidency. Biden was still considering attempting something far rarer than it seemed. He was also in a singular position in recent history because of the ambiguity of his political standing: during Reagan's presidency few people had ever doubted that Bush would run for president after their second term, and the same went for Gore; there was never any illusion that Cheney would campaign for the top job. Biden was in a new kind of will-he-or-won't-he limbo, and no one knew how to deal with it.

The uncertainty didn't weigh on him. Instead, he clung to the hope that came with it, the purpose of a possible campaign tethering him to the memory of Beau and giving the family something to rally around amid their grief. When, about a week after the funeral, Obama again raised the matter of 2016 at lunch, he assumed Biden would have now decided against running. Instead, Biden lashed back. He later wrote about the exchange: "Look, Mr. President," he said, plainly in pain. "I understand if you've made an explicit commitment to Hillary and to Bill Clinton," but he said he not only hadn't decided, but also that it might still be a while, since he was grieving. A few weeks earlier, one of Obama's numbers guys had sat Biden down to outline how Clinton's organization was too much of a juggernaut to take on in this environment, and shortly thereafter Plouffe weighed in, too, warning that Biden now stood little chance, and that it could get ugly against Clinton. Now, Biden offered Obama the familiar promise that if he did challenge Clinton their contest would be about policy, not personal matters. He then made clear that they should move on.

Obama would soon see what was inescapable to Biden's closest aides: the VP was in no place to talk about a campaign, let alone much else.

He was finding it hard to get through a meeting or conversation without becoming flooded with emotion over the loss of his son. When Biden flew to Colorado in July to promote Obama's free community college push after a few weeks away from the public eye, he broke down at an Air Force base after hearing one military member call out that he'd served with Beau and the base commander called his son a great American. The family's other struggles were even further from public view but no more distant to Biden's daily worries. They were getting anxious about Hunter, who had a history of addiction problems and was taking his brother's death especially hard.

If it seemed uncontroversial to Biden that he should still be considering running, it was far from the consensus around him. Few aides actively left his fold between 2014 and 2015, but those who did left a mark. Some operatives within the White House took it as a sign he wasn't serious about 2016 when his director of scheduling left to run Clinton's scheduling and advance operation in 2015. No crossover was more meaningful than Ron Klain's. Even Clinton read it as portentous when Klain, a Biden insider for decades, joined her side to help with messaging and debate prep. The move was polemical in Wilmington; some Biden diehards regarded it as a betrayal, and Klain himself fretted that he would become a pariah among his old colleagues.

Biden's innermost circle of real trust was shrinking to be as small as ever, and halfway through the summer he called on two of the few people who could ever honestly say they were truly close to both Biden and Obama. When strategist Anita Dunn and lawyer Bob Bauer arrived at the Naval Observatory in July, the vice president surprised them by insisting he was still serious about his future but simultaneously revealing that he could not run if he had to make the decision that day—he wasn't emotionally ready. Still, he wanted their help in thinking about the political landscape just in case he felt better by the fall. When word leaked that Dunn and Bauer (who are married) had sat with Biden, they were met with incredulity in most corners of ObamaWorld, considering how unseriously many were taking the prospect of a Biden campaign. Not only were Obama's political director David Simas and Plouffe being actively helpful to Clinton, her staff—which itself was even more stacked with former Obama

White House aides these days—was also in regular contact with senior Obama advisor Dan Pfeiffer, his former Iowa state director Paul Tewes, and his former deputy campaign manager Jen O'Malley Dillon.

Yet Dunn and Bauer represented a small, quiet faction that insisted Obama and his hangers-on owed Biden the space and time to work it out. They were joined in this contention by former White House counsel Kathy Ruemmler and Pete Rouse, and Mastromonaco—a onetime Bernie Sanders intern who'd sat in on one of the Vermonter's first planning sessions the previous year—agreed, too. Jon Carson, one of Obama's top organizing aides, connected some Biden staffers to potential hires in strategically important states. Obama himself was still trying to gauge Biden's intent during their lunches, and gathering what he could from his own confidants, who themselves occasionally heard from Biden. In July, the vice president pulled aside Jarrett after a meeting in the Roosevelt Room and confided that he would certainly be running if not for Beau. Beau wanted me to run, he said, but I just don't think I can do it.

And yet it was hard for Biden to watch as Sanders started to gain steam, his working-class-focused message landing with surprising power, considering how far he was from the Democratic mainstream as a democratic socialist. It was almost impossible for Biden not to think that a less raucous version of the message, maybe with some more Catholic-tinged arguments about fairness and some warnings about the danger of reflexive partisanship, would be doing even better from a more famous, more widely acceptable candidate like himself. Clinton would make a great president, Biden kept saying to aides in private, but she was having enough trouble on the trail to give him pause.

So he kept going. It was with all this in mind that he invited Elizabeth Warren to the Naval Observatory in August for a sit-down that he knew would make his 2016 considerations more public when it inevitably leaked. The first-term Massachusetts senator and progressive hero had considered a campaign of her own earlier in the year, but then opened the door for Sanders to run by opting against it. She was now shaping the conversation from the sidelines, eager to push the party toward a more economically populist posture after she believed Democrats had failed to hold Wall Street to real account under Obama. In December, she'd met privately with Clinton and explained her belief that "personnel is policy," then tried to get the presumed front-runner on the record about who she'd surround herself with as a candidate and president, on the lookout for finance industry–adjacent names.

She had a more complicated relationship still with Obama. She'd gotten to know him briefly when she was a Harvard Law professor and later as she pitched the idea of a Consumer Financial Protection Bureau. Harry Reid brought her to Washington to help oversee the government's financial industry rescue work, and Obama soon tried to convince her to join the Treasury Department to advise him and to help set up the Consumer Financial Protection Bureau in 2010. She was skeptical, though, and told him she wasn't going to take a fake job without real responsibilities. She asked to be brought in on his daily economic meeting, an idea that struck Larry Summers as a bad one. "You're jamming me, Elizabeth," Obama once said to close an Oval office meeting that August, before she agreed to join him. On her last day in the role before she launched a Senate campaign, though, she again met with Obama in person. There, she said his economic team had been a disaster—they had no ambition or aggression, and he needed to revamp it. Obama, not totally surprised, asked to keep in touch on housing issues, and told her to ask his secretary for his personal email address once she left the room. It wasn't shocking, but perfectly apropos, when she was then handed his secretary's email, not his.

Obama still liked plenty of what he saw from Warren and appreciated at least the broad strokes of her message, enough to award her the keynote address at the 2012 convention and to speak of her admiringly with advisors. After she became a senator, though, she hadn't let up on him, writing a widely circulated *Politico* Op-Ed in 2013 urging the administration to be wary of hiring too many Wall Street alums, and then blocking his nomination of a banker to be the undersecretary of domestic finance at Treasury. He'd been unamused to hear she was considering running to succeed him as president and was relieved when she passed on the race.

Warren and Biden had their own history of run-ins—in 2005 they'd clashed during a Hill hearing about bankruptcy law, and he'd called her argument "very compelling and mildly demagogic"—but he'd been in the wings for most of her wrangling with Obama, and now she said to Biden basically what she'd told Clinton about personnel. He promised "no one gets in on economics who doesn't get past Ted Kaufman," alluding to Kaufman's reputation as an unbending liberal after he succeeded Warren on the TARP oversight panel, and then as a senator. But mostly, she listened quietly as Biden showed her around the VP's traditional house, pointing out furniture as he spoke about a possible campaign. His message wasn't very tough to decode, but before long he clarified anyway: If I run, I would want you as my running mate.

Donilon sat Biden down around that time and laid out his findings from a sheaf of polling. If Biden wanted to run, said his longtime advisor, he was in a better political position than ever. This was partly because of his own improving reputation as an honest figure, but also largely because Clinton had a huge and worsening trust problem in the public eye. To make matters worse, the party—and especially Obama's administration—was increasingly viewed as elitist, and if anyone could counteract that perception it might be Scranton Joe, whose numbers were best in important states where Clinton (and Obama) were clearly struggling, like Pennsylvania and Ohio. Paradoxically, Obama himself was still popular, and everyone knew they were close, which also helped.

This was enough to nudge Biden toward more active consideration. On one West Coast trip, Biden sat down with a top Obama 2008 campaign fundraiser who asked about his plan and urged him to consider that he'd already go down as the greatest vice president in history, to which Biden replied, "What if I want more?" The donor said he thought Biden had, at best, a 25 percent chance of beating Clinton, and that if he was serious the VP had to enter the race before the end of September—before the quarterly fundraising deadline, and before both the first primary debate and Clinton's scheduled House testimony over the 2012 attack in Benghazi. Biden agreed, and in New York in September he made the time for another only-semisecret meeting with a top Obama moneyman-slash-advisor, investor Robert Wolf. There, though, his indecision took center stage. Now he said he wouldn't decide until after Clinton reported her fundraising numbers—an important gauge of her campaign's strength—testified, and stood on the first debate stage with Sanders. Biden thought he could win if the timing worked, he told Wolf, but he also still wasn't sure he could run because of his grief. He then said something similar in a teary interview with Stephen Colbert, which endeared him to viewers but threw further doubt on his ability to run, even as the host—a fellow Catholic with his own history of family tragedy—seemed to urge him on.

"Nobody has a right, in my view, to seek that office unless they are willing to give it 110 percent of who they are," Biden said.

Nonetheless, when he gathered the usual crowd of advisors, plus Dunn, Bauer, and his new communications chief Kate Bedingfield, by his pool a few days later, they talked logistics. Biden, sitting with his hands on his knees, listened as Dunn talked about a messaging plan and explained that he should be on the first debate stage in October. Fundraiser Michael Schrum discussed the work they needed to do to get big donors on board, especially since they'd already decided to publicly reject super PAC help, and Schultz spoke about how they would build up the staff to compete in Nevada—where they hoped to rely on labor allies—and South Carolina—where they hoped to use Biden's long-standing connections and the benefit of his association with Obama to win over Black voters. They'd effectively skip Iowa and New Hampshire, where it was probably too late to seriously take on Clinton or Sanders, who'd been campaigning there for months. Ricchetti then talked timeline: they'd almost certainly need to announce by the end of September, early October at the latest. Jill Biden, surprised, grabbed her husband's hand and said, "We can't be ready by then." He agreed but wouldn't say that meant he wasn't running.

Over the ensuing days he thought and waited, and let important political invitations—like to the New Hampshire Democratic Party's big fundraising dinner—go unanswered. In conversations with allies, he was keeping the dream alive. Twice when he, Donilon, and Ricchetti met with Chris Coons, who sat in his old Senate seat, they confidently outlined the polling and political path ahead. Then, both times, Biden said, "I'm so glad you're here to bounce some of this off of," before looking away, then looking down, and, quietly and tearfully, adding: "I wish Beau were here."

Obama understood that Biden was in pain, each week's lunch now turning into more of a raw grief-sharing session than a strategy meeting. But by the late summer, this political foot-dragging was a problem. At the DNC's meeting in Minnesota in August, a group trying to draft Biden into the race had shown up and earned headlines for its presence—it passed out chocolate bars and paid for some cheap digital ads—and whispers in high-flying Democratic circles intensified with news that a former Obama political aide from Florida, Steve Schale, was helping the group, and so was Beau Biden's old friend and fundraiser Josh Alcorn.

It put Obama's uncomfortable position into the spotlight, which he couldn't stand, and the drumbeat of speculation distracted from Clinton's campaign and made it seem like her party needed saving. Early that fall, Obama got more forward with Biden about his main concern—he wouldn't stand in Biden's way anymore, but he didn't want to see a hurting Biden get even more emotionally destroyed, or to see his legacy tarnished by a brutal loss. He unreservedly thought that both would happen if Biden tried to run a campaign now. He wasn't breaking through to Biden, though, so asked both Plouffe and Axelrod to separately spell it out for the vice president: at this point, it wasn't just that he was far behind Clinton. He'd probably get wiped out by Sanders, too, and there was no way to spin that result. And that would embarrass Obama, too.

Clinton, meanwhile, was sifting through tea leaves. She grew outright concerned that Biden would get in and make fundraising difficult for her over the summer, when Sanders started beating her in some New Hampshire polls, and she tried flexing her political muscle after another poll had Biden theoretically doing better than she did against some Republican primary candidates. Around the time of the DNC meeting, she had Jake Sullivan, a former Biden national security advisor now on her team, reassure donors, and she touted her support from Vilsack, Biden's cabinet companion and longtime buddy. The main concern wasn't that Biden would necessarily win. Instead, Clinton's internal polling in early-voting states like Iowa showed that he might split the mainstream Democratic vote and widen Sanders's path to the nomination. This was the majority view in Clinton's campaign brain trust, but not the only one. Some advisors who'd worked with Biden reminded her that he'd been incapable of running a disciplined campaign organization in 1987 or 2007, so thought there was no reason to think 2015 would be any different. When the super PAC that Clinton inherited from Obama surveyed Americans about Democratic leaders to gauge their political standing, they asked about both Clintons, Sanders, and Obama. Biden wasn't even on the list.

Biden didn't so much reject the Obama analysis that had been filtered through Plouffe and Axelrod, or Clinton's inconsistent hand-wringing, as let it bounce off him. He was inching forward, but what kept dragging him back was his emotional disintegration, not the threat of political demolition. He was aghast in early October when *Politico* reported that he himself was the source for an August *New York Times* column by Maureen Dowd—ironically the writer who effectively ended his 1987 campaign by exposing the first plagiarism case—revealing that Beau had urged Biden to run, "arguing that the White House should not revert to the Clintons and that the country would be better off with Biden values." Biden couldn't abide what he believed to be the implication that he was using his son's death to set off this latest and most intense round of interest in his potential campaign. So when the pro-Biden group encouraging him to run independently announced plans the next day to place a new ad nationwide invoking the 1972 car accident that killed his wife and daughter, it was a bridge too far for him, and he called for its removal from the air.

Some of Biden's former colleagues found him shaken when he rang to take their temperature. Chuck Hagel had visited Biden at the Naval Observatory while Beau was still sick, and he told the VP that it didn't seem like he was up to it. Now they spoke again, and while Hagel's message hadn't changed, Biden still said he thought he'd be letting Beau down if he didn't run. But he acknowledged the significant challenges that would come with running against Clinton and, when he spoke with Leon Panetta, said he didn't want to stand in the way of the first woman president. Others tried bucking him up. He was buoyed when Harold Schaitberger's International Association of Fire Fighters abandoned its planned Clinton endorsement until Biden made a decision, and Bob Kerrey, a former Senate colleague and ex-candidate himself, urged him to run on competency grounds. Bill Bradley bugged him every few days to convince him, and Chris Dodd, Tom Daschle, and Max Baucus all weighed in positively, too. New York governor Andrew Cuomo—who Biden said reminded him of Beau—told him he should consider running, no matter that Cuomo was publicly endorsing Clinton, and after his Colbert appearance even George Clooney got in touch with Ricchetti to offer his help.

But history was repeating itself as October stretched. As Richard Ben Cramer wrote of the senator's agonizing in 1987, "Joe still couldn't say if he was running. That's all anyone would ask him, for *months*." Yet again, potential campaign hires took other jobs, no longer willing to wait. Still, résumés piled up in Schultz's and Bedingfield's inboxes as the possibility lingered. Biden himself vacillated, sometimes by the day, sometimes wildly enough to scare off natural allies. After talking about the campaign with strategist Larry Grisolano, a longtime Biden fan who'd often told the Obama brain trust they needed to be more middle-class-focused during his tenure on the top rungs of the messaging team in 2008 and 2012, Biden got so excited that he started telling friends in Iowa that Grisolano—whose name he sometimes butchered—would run his campaign. This was news to Grisolano. He'd already talked about Biden with his old business partner Axelrod, and decided he wouldn't join up.

Internal deadlines set by Ricchetti, Schultz, and Dunn slipped, and Biden's fretting grew more profound. In mid-October, with the external speculation and internal questions threatening to overwhelm Biden even more, Kaufman sent an email to a loose network of Biden office and campaign alums. "A lot of you are being asked, and have asked me, about the direction and timing of the Vice President's thinking about a run for President. On the second question—timing—I can't add much, except I am confident that the Vice President is aware of the practical demands of making a final decision soon," he wrote, trying to calm everyone down. But, he added, "I think it's fair to say, knowing him as we all do, that it won't be a scripted affair—after all, it's Joe."

Clinton ran circles around her opponents on the Las Vegas debate stage on October 13. Biden watched closely, just eight days after he'd brought his usual crowd together for what was supposed to be the final judgment call meeting. It wasn't, but it had reinforced to him that he wasn't just running out of time politically, but practically, too. If he wanted to be on the ballot in some states, he needed to declare his candidacy in a matter of days. The debate calmed nerves at Clinton's Brooklyn HQ and among the sizable group of ex–Obama donors who'd pledged their checkbooks to her but still felt bad about ditching Biden.

Now Biden relented and finally agreed to ring potential fundraisers and staffers—Donilon, Ricchetti, Schultz, and Schrum having convinced him that it was now or never. His weekday evenings filled up with the calls, most of which were discouraging, with just three months until voting started. He called the West Coast Obama donor he'd seen a few weeks earlier, told him he would decide in the next few days, and asked: "What do you think now?" The fundraiser replied that he still loved Biden but that he'd said he had only a 25 percent chance when they'd met two months earlier, and the VP had missed the deadline they'd discussed. He had 10 percent odds now, at best, and only if he could answer basic questions like: Who's the team? What's the fundraising plan? The external signs weren't much better. Biden took it hard when Jim Clyburn, the powerful South Carolina congressman with huge influence among Black voters there, said in an interview on Monday, October 19, that he shouldn't run.

By Tuesday morning, Biden was reading drafts of the announcement speech Donilon had scripted for him, finally acknowledging that it was decision time—for real now—and fretting about how he'd let this go on for so long. Either way, he decided, he'd make an announcement on Wednesday, October 21. The moment had him thinking expansively, reflecting on his tenure alongside Obama, and he let it show when he appeared alongside Mondale that afternoon across town. He spoke glowingly of his boss, reminding the crowd just how much time they spent together. Praising Mondale's guidance and example, he said he and Obama never differed ideologically, and were "simpatico" on every major issue. "A vice president is totally a reflection of the president," he said. "There is no inherent power—none, zero—and it completely, totally depends on your relationship with the president."

Biden wasn't just being romantic for the crowd, which included Jimmy Carter and a range of powerful liberals. Obama was still popular among Democrats, and the race was clearly at the top of his mind. Clinton had recently raised eyebrows by lumping "the Republicans" in with the National Rifle Association, health insurance companies, drug corporations, and the Iranian government when asked about her enemies, and now Biden appeared to disagree, though he didn't mention her by name. "It is possible, it is necessary, to end this notion that the enemy is the other party," he said. "End this notion that it is naive to think we can speak well of the other party and cooperation. What is naive is to think it is remotely possible to govern this country unless we can—*that* is what is naive." He also offered an alternate history of the well-known deliberations over the bin Laden raid four years earlier, in which he'd famously been skeptical while Clinton had urged action. "We walked out of the room and walked upstairs," Biden now said of Obama. "I told him my opinion: I thought he should go, but to follow his own instincts."

These pointed statements were confusing—or galling—enough to cause a stir online, but when Biden got back to the Naval Observatory after the event, his tears returned as he gathered his closest confidants for one last conversation about his choice. They went back and forth, agonizing over the timeline and the same old concerns over whether it made any sense. They only adjourned when Donilon, for the first time, looked at Biden and said it wasn't right for him now. Biden retreated to his study to look over the speech with a pen and to, somehow, weigh his final considerations.

Alone with his thoughts, facing either one last excruciating campaign or the effective end of his five-decade political career, he did what he always did when the pressure was on. He called friends. He called family. He waited for the answer to hit him. He made a call to Tony Blinken, his longtime foreign policy aide who was now the deputy secretary of state, and another to Ben Harris, his economic advisor, to fact-check parts of the announcement speech he was still thinking about giving. One person he couldn't call was the one whose political advice he would have wanted most for the majority of their decade-long relationship to that point. Obama was maybe the last person he could talk to now.

Around 11:30 p.m. he called James Smith, a Columbia, South Carolina, lawmaker and veteran in his late forties who reminded him of Beau. He tried out his pitch on Smith, who'd always been a big supporter. He thought the nation was unsettled, he said, and that he'd have to focus on appealing to Rust Belt voters, especially since Clinton seemed too cocky about winning them. Smith was encouraging, and Biden decided to read out the latest draft of the speech. He went populist, describing inequality in Scranton and other places like it, and he bragged that he was known as "Middle Class Joe." He praised Obama's leadership in a time of crisis and touted "the Obama legacy," then riffed about unifying a nation torn apart by partisanship during those same years, about the importance of devotion to country, and about being an American president—not a Democratic one or a Republican one, an apparent allusion to Obama's 2004 convention speech about red and blue states. And, in a nod to Beau, he talked about funding cancer research. Smith was in tears and told him: "Dammit, Joe, you have to run." When Biden didn't immediately reply, Smith briefly panicked. (*Oh no, I just said 'dammit' to the vice president!*) Biden then spoke up, softly, as midnight neared. "Well, James, I'm going to sleep on it."

Biden brought Ricchetti, Donilon, and Bedingfield to the Naval Observatory early the next morning to tell them he wasn't running. He called Obama, who offered to stand with him at the announcement if he wanted, and agreed to let Biden use the White House Rose Garden, as long as his staff OK'd the use of the official space for a political event.

When Biden then got to the White House, Obama helped wrestle the launch speech into another kind of announcement. He then walked out one step behind Joe and Jill, who approached the lectern hand in hand. At the microphones Biden first thanked Obama for letting him use the Rose Garden, then immediately turned to what had taken so long. "As my family and I have worked through the grieving process, I said all along what I've said time and again to others: that it may very well be that that process, by the time we get through it, closes the window on mounting a realistic campaign for president. That it might close. I've concluded it has closed." Obama closed his eyes, which had been glued to Biden.

It was, with only a few tweaks, the speech Biden would've given if he were running.

CHAPTER 14

2016

Obama seldom enjoyed his interactions with the Beltway press corps, whom he by and large regarded as shallow, irresponsible, and easily distracted compared to their investigative and policy-minded counterparts. He did at least sometimes see the upside of the annual black-tie White House Correspondents' Association dinner. Held every spring, it was a celebration of a lot of what was wrong with the decadent DC culture but also a lighthearted chance to be blunt about messages he was trying to get across tactfully the rest of the year. His speeches were always biting, and usually a pretty good reflection of how he actually felt.

In 2015, he had devoted a chunk of his address to the contenders for the Republican presidential nomination. He rolled his eyes at Bush family scion Jeb, mocked right-winger Ted Cruz, and scoffed at hardline social conservative Rick Santorum. He then said, "And Donald Trump is here. Still," to waves of knowing laughter across the Washington Hilton ballroom. That wasn't his first time needling Trump at one of these dinners. Some believed Obama's 2011 ridicule amid Trump's birtherism crusade inspired the reality TV personality to seriously consider presidential politics in the first place. By the end of April 2016, though, Trump was on the verge of becoming the GOP's nominee, and Obama could no longer get away with essentially ignoring him, which he'd been doing for a year and had previously thought was the best way to handle a candidate he considered little more than a laughable carnival barker and an unqualified, corrupt idiot.

Now, Obama displayed his impatience with a press he saw as complicit in Trump's rise, but mostly his contempt for Trump and his feckless party.

Most importantly, he made sure everyone understood that he refused to take Trump or his threat seriously.

"The Republican establishment is incredulous that he is their most likely nominee—*incredulous, shocking*. They say Donald lacks the foreign policy experience to be president. But, in fairness, he has spent years meeting with leaders from around the world: Miss Sweden, Miss Argentina, Miss Azerbaijan," Obama said. He continued with a joke about Trump's business chops, then said to the gathered journalists in his most floridly sarcastic voice, "Alright, that's probably enough. I mean, I've got more material—no, no, I don't want to spend too much time on The Donald. Following your lead, I want to show some restraint. Because I think we can all agree that from the start, he's gotten the appropriate amount of coverage, befitting the seriousness of his candidacy. I hope you all are proud of yourselves—the guy wanted to give his hotel business a boost, and now we're praying that Cleveland makes it through July."

This was basically how Obama talked privately about Trump, too, though his incredulity that Republicans would actually vote for him shifted that spring to confident dismissal of the notion that Americans writ large would seriously consider him in November. Biden was never quite so glib, but among aides and with his boss, he gave no indication of taking Trump terribly seriously either in 2015 or early 2016. When he did talk about Trump, it was to shake his head at his racist provocations, or to shrug that at least now Americans had no choice but to confront uglier parts of their past.

As far as the pair saw it at that point, there wasn't much reason to think harder about the topic. Biden talked a lot about economic dislocation, but surely *that* couldn't explain *this*. Obama, meanwhile, viewed it as an outlier that the Republican standard-bearer, Sanders, and now Clinton were all opposing his trade regime. If Trump's ascension was about anything, it was about a new strain of right-wing lunacy engulfing the GOP. He would clearly be remembered as an even more outrageous Barry Goldwater when this was all said and done, a blip on the way to President Hillary Clinton's inauguration in 2017.

* * *

The Bidens skipped their usual Nantucket Thanksgiving in 2015, opting instead for Rome to distance themselves from memories of the previous year's final trip with Beau. Joe took the occasion for reflection unusually seriously. In Italy and then back in Washington he began mapping out what he hoped would still be an influential role for himself in his last year in office with Obama. He had plenty of goodwill to work with, not just because of his generally positive image and sympathy after the last six months but also because of the implicit comparison with Obama—who was beloved by Democrats but widely regarded by the political class as overly polarizing, even though his approval rating was in the low- to mid-forties, as it often was—and Clinton, who was increasingly seen through a hyperpartisan lens.

Biden identified two openings for himself. First, if the battle for the future of his party wouldn't include him as it grew increasingly ferocious, maybe he could help find a common, hopeful thread to bring the warring liberals, centrists, and progressives together in pursuit of more economic opportunity. He thought they needed a grave reminder that they couldn't take for granted their appeal to people of color and that they were dooming themselves if they gave up on working-class white men. He also wanted to make sure they knew this was no time to swing hard to the socialist left. Second, after hosting Chinese president Xi Jinping in September, he was thinking plenty about China's global influence and—combined with rejuvenated right-wing populism and isolationism in Europe and Trump's stubbornness at the top of the GOP field—the importance of straight-forwardly defending democratic principles that suddenly seemed up for reconsideration. If anyone could credibly tell Western economic leaders they needed to understand the disconnect between their rhetoric and their constituents, he figured, it might be him.

Depending on whom in his office you asked, it was either pitch-perfect or world-historically blinkered when he singled out the upcoming World Economic Forum in Davos, the ultimate gathering of the private-jet-and-ski-jacket elites, as his first chance to do both. He told advisors he wanted to "shake" the plutocrats "to the core," because "they had to wake up, or else folks would storm the gates." (As the *Wall Street Journal* reported that January, at the Swiss conference "a cheeseburger sells for $68 and a Tesla serves as an Uber.") There was no recognition that it was hardly a stretch to interpret this as a slight on Obama's record and engagement style, coming as it did seven years into his term as the leader of the Democratic Party and the Western world.

The vice president spent much of the first days of 2016 in his office with the economist Ben Harris, his national security advisor Colin Kahl, and speechwriter Vinay Reddy, occasionally pausing to reflect, "This is the speech I've put the most work into of any in my entire career." Onstage in the Alps, he tried jarring the executives and presidents in the auditorium, insisting that they "embrace the obligation to your workers as well as your shareholders" and to be wary of the threats of short-term, profit-motivated thinking in a world increasingly upended by automation and what he called "the digital revolution [that] has the potential to exacerbate" the deterioration of public trust in governments and rising extremism. He specifically criticized stock buybacks, an investor-enriching tactic he'd been decrying since 2009, and called for "a more progressive tax code. Not confiscatory policy—not socialism—a tax code" around the world, singling out increasing inequality and the scourge of corporate tax avoidance as long-term risks with immediate consequences, too.

The warning, which lasted nearly an hour, summed up what might be called Late Bidenism, and to the people who'd known him longest his satisfaction with being able to share it with this particular elite audience—the Swiss president and the International Monetary Fund managing director were in the front row—was obvious in the way he grinned and surveyed the crowd. He scarcely noticed that the trickle out of the room started accelerating about twenty minutes in, or that the Americans in the audience were far more concerned with what was happening a world away in Iowa, where a spate of recent polling showed Sanders overtaking Clinton and Trump edging Cruz.

Biden was paying attention to the race, too, but trying to stop himself from obsessing by keeping his mind on his legacy. Early in 2016, he started sitting down a rotating cast of aides for long, introspective conversations about how he wanted to be remembered, both as VP and overall. One conclusion was that he hoped his foreign policy work would define his tenure, so he asked Ricchetti and Kahl to lean in on scheduling a final round of trips abroad—especially to areas of special focus like Latin America and the Middle East, but also sentimental spots like Ireland—before he left office. Unknown to him, Graves had been discussing a cancer research investment project with Obama's advisors since the previous year, and Biden embraced the mission when Obama assigned it to him at his final State of the Union address. Yet with Sanders continuing to gain surprising traction in the primary in the first part of the year, Biden thought there was still no denying that the country's political mood had shifted toward a more blue-collar sensibility, and he told aides outright that he wanted to ensure that the world knew he'd advocated internally for working people, especially union members. As such, he said, they should circle back on some of his early economic initiatives around the recovery and wages to highlight those pushes.

Nowhere did this emphasis come out more explicitly in the final two years of the Obama administration than in its internal negotiations over a new Labor Department rule about overtime pay eligibility. From the start, Biden and Ricchetti sided with Labor secretary Tom Perez against a set of officials on the Council of Economic Advisers whom Biden and Perez referred to as, alternately, Obama's "Ivory Tower" or "Ivy Tower" economists. (In private, it was still common to hear Biden drawing a contrast between his University of Delaware and Syracuse degrees and his boss's Columbia and Harvard credentials.) The central point of tension was the salary level below which businesses would have to pay hourly employees time-and-a-half wages once they'd worked beyond forty hours per week. Obama's economists sought to build a sound economic argument for a reasonable and business-friendly increase on the status quo—an upper bound of $455 per week, or about $23,500 per year—and initially floated a new number under $40,000, which still represented a significant increase.

Perez and Ricchetti, and, increasingly as the debates continued, Biden, advocated for a figure in the high $40,000-to-$50,000 range, arguing that this was a more realistic window to actually cover middle-class workers. When one administration economist at one point pushed back that such a change would be too much for employers to bear and that they would suffer, National Economic Council director Jeff Zients—who was backed by Biden and Perez and who was the only person with an extensive business record in the room—replied that his own experience led him to believe companies could absorb the change far more easily than the economists thought. Biden, who feared that Obama was more susceptible to his economists' modeling than empirical arguments about workers' daily practicalities, kept trying to steer the conversation toward the end goal: they were all trying to help ensure better workplace protections, and ultimately more overtime pay, for middle-class workers, so they should push for as much as they realistically could. They landed at a threshold of $50,000, to which Obama agreed before dropping it to roughly $47,500 to account for lower pay rates in the South. This was still about double the previous limit, making roughly four million workers newly eligible for OT.

Little of this back-and-forth bled into public view at the time. But after Biden decided not to run for president he invited Sanders over for a meeting at the Naval Observatory whose takeaway would undoubtedly become more widely known. They met in January, at which point Biden was wistful enough about the race that on multiple occasions aides asked his family friends in Wilmington to remind him he couldn't keep fantasizing about a long-shot path to the nomination.

Though Sanders and Biden hadn't known each other well on the Hill, the Vermonter appreciated that Biden had at least taken him seriously and never dismissed him as a wing nut, as had plenty of his colleagues. Still, while Sanders also believed Biden understood the point he was trying to make about class on the campaign trail, he thought the VP to be more conservative than Obama on plenty of other matters, and so was surprised when Biden seemed downright sympathetic to a lot of his arguments in person. At the mansion in northwest DC, Biden urged Sanders to bolster his foreign policy chops and told him that he had planned to make a point of not taking super PAC money in his own campaign. Biden suggested that Sanders lean into the campaign finance angle as a point of contrast with Clinton's big-money enterprise, and when the VP sat for a CNN interview two and a half weeks before the Iowa caucuses, his praise for Sanders came across a lot like a series of implicit elbows at Clinton.

"Bernie is speaking to a yearning that is deep and real, and he has credibility on" the topic of income inequality, Biden said, adding that while Clinton had "come forward with some really thoughtful approaches to deal with the issue," nonetheless "it's relatively new for Hillary to talk about that" since "Hillary's focus has been other things up to now, and that's been Bernie's—no one questions Bernie's authenticity on those issues."

What really galled Clinton and some of Obama's political advisors, though, was Biden's defense of Sanders on gun control. It was a central issue on which the favorite had been grilling the upstart for weeks—an offensive that Obama himself had recently joined by promising not to campaign for candidates who wouldn't support "common-sense gun reform." This had been an obvious message for Sanders, who'd previously voted to permit manufacturers immunity when their guns were used in shooting deaths. But "what Bernie Sanders has to do is say that the Second Amendment says—which he has, of late—the Second Amendment says you can limit who can own a gun, that people who are criminals shouldn't have guns," Biden told Gloria Borger. "People who are schizophrenic and have mental illnesses shouldn't own guns. And he has said that." It wasn't a direct defense, but it was close enough to set off heartburn at the White House.

Biden thought Sanders was too far left to be considered a serious contender, and that he had doomed himself electorally by self-identifying as a democratic socialist. He had little doubt that Sanders would be rejected by Black voters in the primary and more conservative white voters in the industrial Midwest, too. Biden would, of course, eventually back Clinton whenever it made most sense politically. But, the vice president muttered to Greg Schultz soon after his meeting with Sanders, "At least he *gets it.*"

* * *

Obama could understand why Clinton stood fast in her politically necessary opposition to his increasingly unpopular TPP trade deal as Sanders effectively tied her in Iowa, demolished her in New Hampshire, and came too close for comfort in Nevada. Her position was even coherent as Sanders started his agonizingly slow and uneven fade once more Black voters began weighing in for Clinton. But throughout the spring and into the early summer, Obama made sure Ben Rhodes and David Simas kept in regular touch with Clinton's lieutenants like campaign manager Robby Mook and policy advisor Jake Sullivan to underscore his insistence on pushing the proposal through, and on Clinton not becoming too forceful in her condemnation even as her opponent and labor leaders pressured her to lean into it.

TPP was a final legacy item for Obama, an international pact he thought would cement the modernization of American relations with Asian-Pacific nations while China—which was not included—flexed its economic power. Obama believed Clinton was in a difficult position. As far as he could tell, she clearly supported the principles behind the deal, which she had promoted as a cabinet member, but she couldn't afford to back it now, given the populist domestic drumbeat about its insufficient worker protections. Still, Obama was fairly sure she would reverse course again when she was elected, recognizing the realities of the globalized economy if not the program's importance to him personally.

There was no obvious reason for Obama to be worried—or even to know—that his own deputy was growing uncomfortable with it, too. That summer, Biden confided to Tim Kaine, now a senator and Clinton's running mate, that some pieces of his Minneapolis agreement with Obama had remained especially important: that they would be candid with each other—brutally, if necessary; that Biden would never surprise Obama on major issues; that Obama would keep Biden in the room as an active participant while decisions were made; and—crucially—that while they would inevitably disagree on some things, Biden would never let Obama read about his private qualms in the press, so long as he never made Biden sell an initiative or position he didn't agree with.

For years, Biden had relished defending Obama to lawmakers, activists, and donors whose criticisms he thought were bullshit. But as their time together wound down, if Biden agreed with allies' complaints, he sometimes looked back and said quietly, "I have four letters in front of my title: V-I-C-E," as if to say the matter was out of his hands. As far as the trade arrangement went, he at first agreed to pitch it to fellow Democrats on the Hill, even though he knew plenty of progressives and labor allies had issues with it. As he heard from more of them over time, though, he kept at his public advocacy but was occasionally less polite in private. With the deal's details becoming political fodder for Clinton, Sanders, and Trump, Biden sometimes grew furious when Obama's staff tried scheduling him to promote provisions that he increasingly regarded as bad for unions and therefore worthy of some of his most piquant profanities.

"Don't ever have me go in on this unless I need to," he instructed his aides that summer, putting them on guard for ObamaWorld requests for help on the topic. He still supported the general principle of countering China's economic influence and improving the American position in the region, and he wanted to help Obama. He just couldn't abide being seen as too eager a salesman for an arrangement that unions were organizing against. In July, on Air Force Two en route to San Diego, he threatened to not deliver a speech about Chinese trade at all. A team of staffers had to remind him that he'd be talking about the World Trade Organization, not the TPP. He kept fuming even after he relented. "Stop pitting me against labor," he said before deplaning.

If none of this felt dramatic in the moment, it was because there was a more immediate problem: Sanders was proving a far more difficult opponent for Clinton to dispatch than anyone had anticipated, just as Trump was running away with the GOP nomination. Simas had been assuring Obama that Clinton would ultimately prevail over Sanders ever since she'd beaten him in South Carolina in March and then largely swept the large southern states. But the president refused to publicly endorse Clinton, which would probably stop the ongoing Sanders challenge in its tracks, until she officially claimed the nomination on her own. And Sanders was promising to contest it until that summer's convention.

Obama's theory was that he, as president, was still the center of political gravity, and that if he stayed publicly neutral then he could maintain his influence with Sanders's backers and help bring the party together after the fractious primary. He had always shied away from intraparty disputes as president, often to his allies' immeasurable frustration. (Reid tried replacing the unpopular DNC chairwoman Debbie Wasserman Schultz with Dick Durbin earlier in the year, for example, but Obama simply couldn't be bothered to approve the maneuver, despite the clear political benefit.) Yet as the Democrats' race approached the late spring—at which point Trump had already won the Republican nomination—and Clinton's popularity kept dipping among Sanders's young, progressive supporters, Obama started getting antsy. Clinton would need those millennial skeptics in the general election.

The president had never really understood Sanders's appeal, and said so regularly to aides when he was off camera. It was clear even to outsiders, though. Obama essentially accidentally endorsed Clinton in a *Politico* podcast interview ahead of Iowa, which came a few months after the site uncovered an old radio interview in which Sanders had mused about running a primary challenge against Obama in 2012. That was shortly before the publication of a book about how Obama had let progressives down that featured a glowing blurb from Sanders on the cover. Among friends, Obama described Sanders as tiresome and disruptive, though once he started winning primaries and kept drawing crowds in the tens of thousands, Obama allowed a grudging appreciation for his ability to build a movement—especially among young people—like he himself had done in 2008.

Still, Mook periodically assured Simas, and Simas assured Obama, that Sanders was simply attracting a younger, smaller faction of the party that was always open to outsider appeals, and that it didn't represent a real threat. Obama adopted and clung to this view even after his older daughter, Malia, started promoting Sanders to him, and he only slightly adjusted it after Clinton failed to win the primary outright in March. But in Obama's eyes, Sanders's surprise wins in states like Michigan, where he campaigned against trade deals, were more about Clinton's struggles to connect with voters than anything else.

It wasn't until June, after Sanders was mathematically eliminated with his loss in California, that Obama summoned him to the White House to usher him out of the race. Obama's annoyance with Sanders wasn't helped by the senator's slightly late arrival. But only when the president and his close advisors noticed that the steps of the Eisenhower Executive Office Building across the street were lined with young government aides stretching to get a glimpse of Sanders did they begin to realize that they had failed to appreciate the true extent of his popularity and resonance. Inside the Oval Office, Obama was relieved that Sanders was polite when the president urged him to drop out and said he should be proud of the good race he'd run.

The conversation between the two was also surprisingly positive a few weeks later when Obama called with an ask that he knew would torment the Vermonter. Criticism of TPP was a central plank of Sanders's campaign, and he was still promising to fight Clinton tooth and nail over the party's platform document, which would be approved at the July convention in Philadelphia. Now, Obama had one nonnegotiable request. When they got to Pennsylvania, he told Sanders, *you can't have your supporters bring up TPP for an up-or-down vote on the convention floor.* Obama wasn't about to let his party oppose his signature deal in writing, even if neither its nominee or its runner-up would back it and had instead spent months making it the target of their public opprobrium—just like their Republican opponent.

* * *

A few times over the course of 2016, Obama decided that he would be wise to try to better understand Trump's motivations, and he called Al Sharpton. The reverend had been squaring off against Trump in New York for decades, and though Obama was still convinced the real estate executive had no real shot at the presidency, he was starting to have more frequent flashes of concern that so much of the country thought otherwise. By the summer, he wasn't the only one reevaluating Trump and the threat he represented, but he still resisted outright fear. Clinton had spent over a year trying to give Trump extra attention as part of a "pied piper" strategy to force Republicans to nominate their most obviously unacceptable candidate and scare off voters, but in May Trump briefly overtook her in public polling and his supporters began showing up for progressively larger and angrier demonstrations outside her events.

The first time Obama called Sharpton on the topic, he asked about the 1989 saga of the Central Park Five, in which five Black and Latino teenagers were falsely convicted of an assault on a white jogger. While Sharpton defended them, Trump had helped drum up intense public anger at the group with a full-page ad in the New York Daily News calling for the use of the death penalty. "Do you think this is an act, or do you think he's really racist?" Obama asked Sharpton. The pair knew each other well and talked often, and Sharpton was blunt: "Mr. President, whether it's an act or not, if you're comfortable with a racist act, you're a racist." Obama acknowledged the point, but otherwise stayed silent.

As puzzled as he was about Trump, Obama was still convinced he couldn't win. The polls occasionally narrowed, but Clinton usually led by a healthy margin, and Obama started campaigning for her in July, immediately becoming her biggest and most reliable draw. As far as he could see, she wasn't a great candidate and had trouble empathizing with regular people—he often talked about the time they were campaigning together in North Carolina and she left a barbecue restaurant early while he was still greeting patrons—but she wasn't *that* bad. She was the most qualified candidate in years, and it wasn't her fault she had the distinct disadvantage of being naturally compared to two of the most overwhelmingly gifted politicians in modern American history, her husband and Obama, while two more generational phenomena—Sanders and Trump—ran against her. Anyway, after his own campaigns Obama was pretty sure any competent Democrat had sufficient demographic momentum working in his or her favor, especially among minorities, young people, and women, that a functioning turnout operation should carry them across the line. Plus, while he knew plenty of people didn't like Clinton and he was well aware of the sexism she faced, he still didn't really get why the negative sentiment about her ran so deep, even if he was annoyed by the scandal over her use of a personal email server, too. (His first rally with her was, coincidentally, just hours after FBI director James Comey ripped into Clinton's security practices but recommended against charges.)

Nonetheless, Obama wasn't too sympathetic when he saw her struggling over how to talk about him and his record. Ever since she had campaigned for down-ballot Democratic candidates in 2014's midterms, Clinton had been worrying out loud to advisors, saying that Democrats had to sharpen their message about the condition of the country, to talk about stagnating wages and the slow recovery without criticizing Obama and his administration. The challenge was that Obama's polling remained through the roof within the party, but perceptions of the economy were far more mixed and Clinton's internal polls showed that even voters who liked Obama were in favor of "a new direction." Clinton was just as sensitive to the idea that she was criticizing Obama as to the notion that she wouldn't be her own, independent president.

In April, she met with pollster Stanley Greenberg, Bill Clinton's old numbers guy, who'd been encouraging Podesta and Mook not to hide from voters' displeasure with the economy, and to ditch her talk about "building on the progress" of the Obama years, her lengthy Obama praise at the top of every speech, and her regular line about how "America is already great," a counter to Trump's "Make America Great Again" slogan. Greenberg said she didn't need to criticize Obama, but to share more about what she was hearing from struggling Americans on the trail, since her party was shedding working-class white voters at an alarming rate and even its base of minority voters was not entirely thrilled with the incumbent administration's economic record. In focus groups, they still talked with scorn about the bank bailouts and tied them to Obama, not Bush.

Still, Clinton vacillated between the more economically populist message that people like Greenberg were pushing—she studied his line of argument in her debate prep, leaning into Trump's plan to enrich himself with tax cuts—and a focus on how she offered continuity while her opponent would make life miserable for different demographic groups. The inconsistency was understandable. Even Obama's own research team held secret focus groups to explore precisely how she should balance assuring his fans that she'd carry on his priorities without letting other voters think she'd simply represent a third term. The pollsters found no simple answer.

Obama understood, but remained unconvinced that this was quite so complicated. He had little doubt that he'd win a third term if he could, happily running on his own record.

* * *

Biden and Obama didn't usually talk about the race over lunch. Biden was still unhappy with how his own considerations had ended the previous year and discouraged with the way Obama had handled it, and Obama sensed correctly that the topic was still raw for him. Plus, Biden was more preoccupied with his grief than with politics, and they both had real work to discuss while they tried cementing as much of their respective and joint legacies as possible.

Biden did, however, still like to bring it up with his other friends. He'd never fully tuned out after his Rose Garden speech, and while he wasn't a *Politico* or political Twitter obsessive, he watched *Morning Joe* and read the *Times* and therefore had plenty of thoughts about why Clinton wasn't running away with the election. The problem was evident, he believed: no one trusted her, and each wave of public polling he saw and each rope line he marinated in simply reinforced this concern. Clinton was turning into a toxic candidate, he griped to allies, sometimes dominating private discussions by rattling off the latest figures on her image and unwinding on her inexcusable email arrangement. Simas insisted to Biden that while her trustworthiness levels were bad, so were Trump's, so the VP shouldn't be so concerned solely on that score. There were plenty of other factors to consider, Simas told him. Biden remained fixated on Clinton's missed opportunities.

Still, he and Obama both stood fast in seeing no reason to step back and consider whether they'd entered a new era of American politics—whether Trump really represented a substantially different phenomenon from the Republicans they dealt with each week and was therefore easy to dismiss, as they believed, or if he was actually the terrifying natural product of the GOP's devolution, and therefore worthy of more serious contemplation. In May, Biden shared an intimate stage with John Boehner at Notre Dame's commencement and decried that politics "has recently become a blood sport full of invective." He only mentioned Trump by implication, but said that he and Boehner "aren't old school, we're the American school." Even now, he insisted, "Progress only comes when you deal with your opponent with respect—listening as well as talking."

Biden began campaigning for Clinton over the summer, usually appearing in Rust Belt cities where she was bleeding support and where he thought he could help persuade workers not to abandon their ancestral Democratic Party. He seldom offered Clinton advice directly but let loose among associates on his flights to and from the campaign stops. After Clinton's first debate with Trump in September, he questioned the immediate consensus that she'd wiped the floor with him, fuming to advisors that she should've simply made a show of turning her back on Trump and directly addressing the cameras to say, "Everyone knows who Donald Trump is. Here's who I am and what I'm going to do for your family." He'd opened private lines of communication with former aides and elected allies in states like Florida and Pennsylvania over the summer, and while they mostly still had good news for him, he took their every qualm as evidence that Clinton needed his help.

Clinton's aides agreed, but only in small, carefully targeted doses. In August, Biden told the Clinton camp that it needed to let him do an event at the United Auto Workers' hall in industrial Warren, Ohio. He went ahead with it even when they warned that no one would show up because of the area's trend toward Trump. As the Clinton team predicted, the attendance was sparse. Biden took it as further evidence of her weakness—the famous enthusiasm gap between her and the Republican—even though Biden himself was the main draw. He grew more alarmed after an event in Cleveland the next month, when volunteers asked him for advice on how to respond to misinformation when they were knocking on doors, since the campaign hadn't given them enough guidance.

By that point, Biden's back-channeling with Clinton's top advisors was growing slightly more fraught. Through Ricchetti, he told them that he respected and liked her, and largely agreed with the common view that Trump was sufficiently repulsive to stop voters from choosing him. But he still felt that they were missing how warily real people viewed her, and he wanted to be convinced they were deploying him the right way. Twice, Mook and Podesta visited Biden at the Naval Observatory to brief him on

Pennsylvania, where his numbers were stratospheric among the white non-college-educated voters and union families among whom Clinton needed to minimize her margins of loss. Biden lit up: "That's right! We're losing those people! It's because none of you know what it's like" in their neighborhoods, he said, hardly giving them any opportunity to object, then agreeing to a series of trips for the ticket. Sometimes, though, when he thought they were on the wrong track, he went dark. In the election's final weeks, Mook asked Ricchetti if Biden would appear for Clinton in Iowa. Biden considered it, but declined. He'd never done well in Iowa, and Trump looked likely to win there anyway.

Almost no one knew that earlier that fall, when Clinton collapsed amid a bout of pneumonia at the September 11 memorial in Manhattan, interim DNC chair Donna Brazile had thought about how to replace Clinton on the ticket if she had to. Biden was her obvious solution, and the day after Clinton fell, Ricchetti called Brazile to see if she had time to talk to the VP. She ultimately decided not to seriously consider removing Clinton. She didn't call Ricchetti back.

As the fall of 2016 lengthened, Obama developed a practice of catching up with some of his former aides who were now working for Clinton and asking what worried them most. When the conversations then turned to his own concerns, he often brought up fake news—disinformation campaigns flying under the radar and poisoning the public's perspective on the race.

Obama's inkling of fear had been growing since the summer, though he hadn't let Clinton know, wary of keeping a strict boundary between his official and political duties. He and aides around him had watched in silence as leaked Democratic Party emails started circulating online, and when Trump interrupted the Democrats' Philadelphia convention with a call for Russia to secure more of Clinton's emails. In August, national security advisor Susan Rice and CIA director John Brennan told Obama about evidence that Vladimir Putin was trying to interfere with the election, and Obama asked the intelligence community for a full assessment of what the Russians were up to.

He briefed the bipartisan group of congressional leaders, but McConnell refused to get on board for a public letter about the findings for weeks, leaving Obama at what he thought was an unsolvable loss. He'd confronted Putin in Hangzhou in September, but even as Democrats demanded to hear from him on the matter he didn't want to say much out loud without GOP support, for fear that he would play into Trump's conspiracy-laden arguments about a "rigged" election fixed by the "deep state." Only in early October did the federal government release a public report led by Jeh Johnson, the secretary of Homeland Security, and James Clapper, the director of national intelligence, revealing that the email leaks had been the result of an effort from the highest-ranking Russian officials. The bulk of the federal government's response, as a result, was on hacking and preparing voting systems, not the disinformation that worried Obama most. Still, even that momentous news was buried within hours by the release of Trump's vulgar *Access Hollywood* tape, which was earthshaking enough to persuade Obama, Biden, and almost everyone around them that Trump's minimal chances were essentially squashed—never mind that WikiLeaks began publishing sensitive emails stolen from Podesta almost immediately after the recording was published that afternoon.

Obama's confidence sprouted cracks about two weeks later, as the leaks kept coming and Comey once again popped up and reminded voters of Clinton's email scandal. Clinton and Mook tried projecting confidence by insisting that they were looking to expand the electoral map into GOP territory—in the fall she visited Arizona, which had gone to the Republican in fifteen of the previous sixteen elections—rather than playing defense. This baffled the president and his advisors. When Clinton's team asked Michelle Obama—the biggest star in the party because of her sky-high favorability ratings and the rarity of her political involvement—to visit Arizona, too, the White House's political staff agreed but asked what Clinton had planned for Michigan, Pennsylvania, and Wisconsin, where she still looked strong, yet which would alone probably be enough to guarantee her the presidency. Obama shrugged, and said it wasn't his campaign, and that they should agree to Clinton's requests. All the punditry and many polls pointed to a blowout. But when he asked his former aides now working for Clinton about the scene in other important states like Florida, Obama was clearly nervous. One advisor said, "I'm cautiously optimistic," to which Obama replied, "I'm probably more cautious than optimistic."

The Obamans were still confident enough to nix what they saw as weird or bad decisions emerging from the Clinton camp in the closing days. At her penultimate rally, a massive outdoor affair featuring both Obamas and both Clintons in Philadelphia, Obama's team stopped Clinton's from playing "Don't Stop"—Bill Clinton's old theme song—considering it to be an out-of-touch throwback. As for Trump, Obama told friends as the election wound down, "He's a fucking idiot." But, he'd say, as miserable as the last year had been, they just had to get through a few more days.

* * *

Election nights are always awkward for people who work in politics, stuck as they are with little to do but wait for news. This is triply true for outgoing presidents who are pretty sure the nation is about to approve of their eight years in power by electing their chosen successor, so Obama opted to distract himself with a movie night at the White House residence with Michelle and Valerie Jarrett. He resisted looking at his phone throughout *Doctor Strange* but picked it up as the movie ended to check the messages pinging in from Simas. The news was less positive than Obama was expecting, and Michelle went to bed while Jarrett walked downstairs to see the political director in person. The president stayed upstairs, staring at his phone and then at his iPad.

Two and a half miles northwest, Biden was wired, surrounded by a busy group of aides who were monitoring results from around the country and handing the VP a rotation of iPhones with elected officials on the other line promising updates on their own races—his primary focus—and sometimes Clinton's—which he'd expected to more or less ignore, given its foregone positive conclusion. As always on nights like this, Biden liked to talk to people he'd campaigned with or known for years, even if they were Republicans. He connected with Rob Portman, a long-serving GOP senator from Ohio, and congratulated him on his easier-than-expected reelection, before turning back to Schultz, Ricchetti, Donilon, and fundraiser Michael Schrum for updates and explanations about why the TV's maps were still looking so red. When ominous results from Florida started flooding in, Schultz texted Steve Schale, Obama's former guru in the state and a Draft Biden alum, to make sense of it. "I don't think it's there" for Clinton, Schale replied, grimly, which Schultz relayed, only to be cut off by Donilon, who insisted there was still time and Clinton still had a path. Schultz texted Clinton's campaign chief in Ohio and got a similarly glum response. Biden, watching the back-and-forth closely, shut off his stream of planned calls after 11:00 and asked for more intel from the ground. He rang Mike Duggan, Detroit's mayor, when he saw Michigan, a state he'd been assured would go blue, wavering. Duggan sounded resigned to a loss and told Biden he should get ready to run in 2020. Biden hung up, suddenly unsure what to believe.

Simas had called Schale a few hours earlier when Volusia County, a mostly Democratic county north of Orlando, started tilting toward Trump. Schale hadn't sounded positive. Obama was surprised but said little, waiting for more news. Simas and Schale kept texting, the White House aide growing more and more resigned to the writing on the wall as midnight approached. Simas now predicted to Schale that Clinton would lose, and Schale relayed the analysis to Schultz, who was with Biden. Schultz then called the Floridian back: the VP and Donilon were still confident that Clinton would pull it out, Schultz said, no matter what Obama's data guys were saying. There was no way they'd all read everything so wrong for so long.

Midnight had come and gone by the time Obama made the call to Clinton. There was no more question that Trump would win, and he told her she couldn't fight it, that dragging out her concession would be bad for the country. He called Podesta to make sure the message was unambiguous.

Biden, who'd been wearing out his living room TV remote flipping between NBC and CNN, rang the White House switchboard at 1:30 a.m. and asked for Obama. "Hey, boss," he said, prompting his aides' ears to perk up, since many of them had never heard him call Obama anything but "Mr. President." They spoke for about two minutes, and Biden barely said a word as Obama said all he could: It was really over, and he'd soon congratulate Trump. The Naval Observatory fell silent around 2:00.

Obama, sitting disbelievingly upstairs at the White House, called Trump, then Rhodes, and then his speechwriter Cody Keenan, who'd been watching the returns with his wife and a few colleagues. "So, that happened," Obama said, speaking slowly as reality crashed in on him. "We're going to have to rework tomorrow's remarks a little bit." Obama hadn't begun processing, but he started dictating anyway.

CHAPTER 15

2016–2017

No one could remember a quieter reception at the White House. Eight years' worth of Obama-era cabinet members and senior staffers had RSVP'd enthusiastically for what they expected to be a November 10 celebration of their old colleague Clinton's victory. Instead, two days after their world imploded they filed into the grand East Room looking for reassurance and a drink or three. Everyone appreciated the hugs, but no one really wanted to be there, Biden included. They were grateful when Obama walked in looking like he had no interest in lingering, either. Mingling only briefly, he told some ex-officials who approached him that he was still thinking about his unsettlingly smiley meeting with Trump earlier in the day, in the Oval Office. The president-elect is a bullshitter, he said, as if anyone could be surprised by that. Obama thought Trump was clueless, too, and he was working through what it would all mean for the country.

At the microphone that Thursday evening, Obama took a more considered tone, distilling his political ethos for a crowd that had heard it before. *The arc of the moral universe is long, but it bends toward justice*, he repeated, as he so often had, citing Martin Luther King Jr. He conceded that history doesn't always proceed in a straight line, and that Trump's win was unexpected. But, he said, trying to spark some enthusiasm for his final two months in office, they'd accomplished a lot—the unemployment rate was down, wars were winding down, health care was more accessible than ever—and they still had some tasks to finish. *Progress moves forward*, he said.

Some of the Democrats in the room sought and found comfort in

Obama's words. The rest could have been forgiven for assuming he was on autopilot, since it all sounded a lot like what he usually said, even before a racist sexual harasser with demagogic tendencies was elected to lead the free world. In truth, Obama was already nearly forty-eight hours into consolation mode. He'd taken it upon himself to buck up his shell-shocked staff with a similar message in a series of meetings starting on the Wednesday morning after election day.

Biden, meanwhile, had started Wednesday in the Naval Observatory and then his West Wing office by questioning everything, beginning with the polls. *How the hell did this happen?* he kept asking his aides before shaking it off with obvious effort and, with Ricchetti at his side, insisting, *This is a democracy. We're going to do our jobs.* They told their own staff, plenty of whom had spent the previous few weeks lining up roles in the Clinton administration, to focus on their day-to-day tasks as much as possible. Biden soon joined Obama in the Oval to confer just as Clinton was giving her concession speech in Manhattan. They didn't watch, and when they emerged the VP joined Obama in reassuring the staff some more. At least, they did as much as they could, considering that they, themselves, could use reassurance, too. No one could give it to them.

Obama's primary concern was his meeting with Trump on Thursday. He spent Wednesday night and part of that morning considering the man as he never had before. He mused that surely Trump was a chameleon who did whatever was in his best interest at any given time. Trump couldn't possibly be as crazy as his campaign persona, and had to be susceptible to some friendly banter, which might at least open him up to Obama's suggestions. *Right?*

In person, Obama first focused on immediate dangers, hoping to scare Trump into responsibility by warning him about the North Korean threat and against hiring Michael Flynn, Trump's preferred national security advisor candidate, a former Defense Intelligence Agency director whom Obama regarded as possibly compromised and certainly a loose cannon. He also tried reasoning with Trump about his own legacy, though he didn't put it that way. Instead, he appealed to Trump's sense of political expediency. The Republican had campaigned on tearing up Obamacare, but the outgoing president suggested he should keep in place its most popular pieces, like protections for preexisting conditions. He tried advocating for programs for people who'd been brought into the country as undocumented minors, too, and for his nuclear deal with Iran. Obama left the meeting unsure if he'd gotten through to Trump, who kept talking about his crowd sizes. But he was hopeful that the new president was as open to guidance as he professed to be. Either way, Obama was convinced it was worth continuing to try to save some of his vulnerable policy wins.

He was mobbed by fellow world leaders two weeks later, at a conference in Lima, Peru. Most were desperate for advice on how to deal with Trump, but Obama still didn't have good answers. Instead, he urged some trusted allies to just keep their joint liberal project going. At one quiet meeting with Australian prime minister Malcolm Turnbull, Obama acknowledged that Trump's ascension would mean the end of the TPP as he'd fought for it. When Turnbull raised the idea of countries like Australia forging ahead with the deal without the United States, Obama replied that he liked the concept but suggested Turnbull refrain from putting his approval in writing. "You never know who is listening," Obama said. He didn't want it to look like he was coordinating with foreign leaders to influence his successor less than a month after the election. Trump probably wouldn't change his mind on much if he saw other countries coming together without him, Obama told his counterparts, but maybe he'd reconsider if he felt real competitive pressure from outside America.

Publicly, Obama insisted that Trump might still be different from what the crowd in Lima feared, and that he could be persuadable. This became a refrain among the gathered leaders, and some of them took to hopefully paraphrasing former New York governor Mario Cuomo: maybe Trump campaigned in poetry; he might govern in prose. Chilean president Michelle Bachelet shut that talk down in a small session away from the microphones. "I didn't notice a lot of poetry in that election," she told her colleagues.

By the time he'd landed in Lima, Obama was deep into an outwardly philosophical but inwardly scattered search for an explanation. In the earliest days after Trump won, he asked some trusted advisors what they thought the election had meant. His own view seemed to waver as he weighed the possibilities. Sometimes he posited that it was just a freak accident, the product of political circumstances no one could have predicted. Other times, it was because people were bored with all the successes of his own administration and Clinton hadn't done a good enough job convincing them. He never let himself take the natural next step and wonder what would have happened had he encouraged Biden, not Clinton, earlier. But maybe, he occasionally mused in angry moments, it was nothing less than a rejection of his own vision of America.

In Peru, he was in one of his dark places. Seeing other leaders' fear juxtaposed with the masses still lining the streets to see him, he considered the possibility that he'd had too optimistic a view of a globalized world and culture, and that he, Clinton, and their followers had underestimated tribal anger, no matter how much they had accomplished for Trump's voters. "Sometimes I wonder whether I was ten or twenty years too early," he admitted to Ben Rhodes, who later recalled the reflection in his memoir.

Back in Washington, Obama's political aides told him about the sheer number of voters who'd backed Trump after supporting him twice, purely because they wanted "change," whatever it meant. He understood this impulse, he said, and started talking about these voters as one key to the surprise.

But even this, a month after the election, wasn't entirely consistent. Obama was still sure that if he could have run for a third term, he would have won.

There weren't many days in the fall of 2016 when Biden wasn't thinking, or gabbing, about what came next for him. Ricchetti had taken Biden's broad-strokes instructions—he wanted not only to stay engaged with international affairs and domestic policy so as not to become suddenly irrelevant after half a century in office but also to make some real money for the first time in his life—and whittled them into arrangements with the University of Delaware and the University of Pennsylvania, a cancer research–funding initiative, plus plans for a speaking tour and a book deal. (He also considered a podcast and a political nonprofit, but decided against both.) Biden was getting excited about this final stage of his life. He would spend more time by the beach in Rehoboth and occasionally pop by DC to visit friends and stay at the house he and Jill were planning to rent in McLean, Virginia, so she could keep teaching at Northern Virginia Community College. So when, about a week and a half before election day, *Politico* reported that Clinton was considering asking Biden to be her secretary of state, he quickly told his aides this was just a float meant to flatter him, and that he wouldn't even consider it.

There wasn't much reconsideration of his retirement the week Trump won, either. What did change was his sanguinity about the plan. Biden was plainly shaken for days after the election, though he wasn't as obvious in his existential searching as Obama. Instead, he appeared to harden in the convictions that had been bubbling inside him for the last year. When former South Carolina Democratic Party chairman Dick Harpootlian visited Biden at the White House a few days after the election, Biden told him he didn't regret not running, since he wouldn't have been able to withstand the emotional rigors of a campaign—especially not one as brutal as 2016's had been. Harpootlian replied that the VP would have to think about running in 2020, to which Biden said his main immediate personal concern was making money, primarily to ensure a comfortable future for Beau's children. But within days, he also started whispering to some senior Democrats he considered allies that Clinton had been the wrong candidate for the moment, and that he would have won if he could have run. When he saw Simas, he thought back to the Obama aide's insistence that Clinton's lack of trustworthiness wouldn't be important, since no one trusted Trump, either. Biden asked him, "Oh, trust doesn't matter, huh?" and kept walking.

Between Biden and Obama themselves, though, waves of intense nostalgia flooded every interaction. Both carefully tried to put the 2015 experience aside and instead reminisced about their near-decade's worth of partnership and personal connection. Biden was moved when, in early January, Obama took time out of his farewell address in Chicago to acknowledge him: "To Joe Biden, the scrappy kid from Scranton who became Delaware's favorite son, you were the first decision I made as a nominee, and it was the best," he said. "Not just because you have been a great vice president, but because in the bargain I gained a brother. And we love you and Jill like family, and your friendship has been one of the great joys of our lives."

Only Ricchetti and Jill knew a greater tribute was coming two days later, when Obama would ambush Biden with a tear-soaked awarding of the Medal of Freedom, at which he recited their joint accomplishments and called Biden, "I believe, the finest vice president we have ever seen. And I also think he has been a lion of American history." Obama went on, expanding on his emotions as he rarely had in public: "To know Joe Biden is to know love without pretense, service without self-regard, and to live life fully."

The surprise ceremony was broadcast live on cable, and Biden—

overwhelmed by the distinction, the abrupt appearance of his family and friends in the White House's State Dining Room, and the presence of a hastily outlined acceptance speech prepared in the last forty-five minutes by the vaguely-clued-in Bedingfield and speechwriter Vinay Reddy—cried more openly than he was used to doing, too, in full view of the world. He understood that the hypersentimental moment would be seen as the cap-stone of their relationship, and also, therefore, of his career. He thanked his family first, at length, before turning to Obama.

Biden had already been thinking about how to thank him, and it all spilled out. "Mr. President, you have more than kept your commitment to me by saying that you wanted me to help govern," he said. "Every single thing you've asked me to do, Mr. President, you have trusted me to do. And that is, that's a remarkable thing," he continued, rambling and overwhelmed. "I don't think, according to the presidential, vice presidential scholars, that kind of relationship has existed. I mean, for real. It's all you, Mr. President, it's all you." He couldn't stop escalating, insisting that the reason he'd been able to be an effective global messenger for Obama was "because we not only have the same political philosophy and ideology, I tell everybody, and I've told them from the beginning—and I'm not saying this to reciprocate—I've never known a president, and few people I've ever met [in] my whole life—I can count [them] on less than one hand—who have had the integrity and the decency and the sense of other people's needs like you do."

In retrospect, the lovefest might have felt incongruous with the pitch-black political environment. The day before, Trump had used his first press conference as president-elect to sharply attack the press corps. But nothing felt off about it inside the White House, where the tears never stopped flowing, or on TV, where the ceremony was mostly treated like the profoundly emotional gathering it obviously was to everyone involved. Obama left the room beaming at having been able to do that for Biden, his uncharacteristic giddiness obvious even to aides who didn't know him well. Biden showed up at a reception hours later back at the Naval Obser-vatory still clutching the medal.

* * *

Bill Clinton didn't want to go to Trump's inauguration, concerned for his safety and uninterested in dignifying the new president. Hillary convinced him to go so they could send a message of continuity for the good of the country—they would just get it over with and get out of there. George W. Bush thought it was "some weird shit." Obama and Biden each felt similarly. They approached the event like a funeral and departed the second they could.

Obama wanted to get far away, and directed his plane to Palm Springs in Southern California, where he intended to unplug and become essentially unreachable for a while. He was ready to get past the ceremony of his departure, and only brought a few people beyond the family—confidants like Jarrett and Rhodes—along for the ride.

Biden, smiling broadly, got on an Amtrak Acela train bound for Joseph R. Biden Jr. Railroad Station in Wilmington, surrounded by a cabin full of cameras, family members, aides, and a retinue of elected officials. It was "full circle," he told the CNN reporter who followed him onboard that afternoon, almost like he was trying to force the final emotional scene of his own biography. "I'm going home to Delaware, the people I owe."

Obama never did a very good job of hiding his romantic notions of New York. He hadn't lived there since graduating from Columbia, but whenever an aide moved there, he grilled them about the neighborhood where they were planning to live and the things they were planning to do, openly fantasizing about walking the city streets anonymously. As president, he liked to linger at restaurants and donors' penthouses when he got to visit, and he often wondered aloud if it would be possible to move to the Upper East Side with Michelle once their post–White House Secret Service detail shrank a bit. The consensus was that it wouldn't be very feasible at all because of their security requirements, though, and the Obamas decided they would stay in Washington at least until Sasha graduated from high school. This dampened the chatter about their next steps for a while, but in the final months of the Obama administration they couldn't help but think about it again, even once they had a home lined up for themselves in northwest DC's Kalorama neighborhood. No one ever thought they would return to Chicago, but maybe they would at least buy a pied-à-terre in New York, the rumors went, or a house in Palm Springs, or even in the mountains of Asheville, North Carolina?

The gossip continued into the early weeks of their post–White House era, the Obamas only effectively putting it to rest by installing a pool at their new home in the capital. The now-former president and first lady rented work space, too, from the World Wildlife Fund in Washington's West End, near Georgetown. They placed nearly two dozen staffers in the suite, which they decorated with dark wood and memorabilia from Obama's time in office, including a photograph of an Obama ancestor that had been presented to him by the Irish government, Norman Rockwell's painting of Ruby Bridges signed by the subject herself, and a framed American flag given to him by the Navy SEALs who killed bin Laden. The Obamas were planning to stay in town for the foreseeable future, never mind that they'd never liked Washington much or that Trump's daughter and son-in-law, Ivanka Trump and Jared Kushner, moved in around the corner.

This wasn't much of a concern because, at least at first, they wouldn't actually be spending much time in the district. Their newfound freedom meant space to vacation with other supercelebrities—Oprah Winfrey, Bruce Springsteen, and Tom Hanks on David Geffen's yacht in French Polynesia on one trip, kitesurfing off Richard Branson's private Caribbean island on another—and also to try to unwind. Obama had bristled at the common impression of him as obsessive and uptight that was burnished by a mid-2016 *Times* profile of his habits. That piece had reported his preferred late-night snack as "seven lightly salted almonds." Among friends, he'd shake his head and say it was usually (but not always) more than seven. Now, he was still seldom without his iPad, but he was just as often playing a Scrabble-like game as reading the *Times* or Vox News, and planning his next round of golf. He took to undoing one extra button on his dress shirts and usually stopped himself from talking about the aspects of the presidency he missed by pointing out that now he was sleeping much more. Sometimes he compared the new, slower pace of his life to the scenes from the *Matrix* movies where Keanu Reeves's Neo character dodges gunfire by perceiving time at a snail's pace.

Back home, he quickly receded from the public eye, eager for privacy but also so wary of hangers-on that he more or less cut off personal contact with anyone who wasn't a genuine friend, a move that had the effect of tightening his inner circle even further than before, since so many of his close advisors and allies left town for New York, San Francisco, or Los Angeles when Trump took over. He hated the belief that he was antisocial even more than the almonds report—"I'm not fucking aloof," he'd say whenever that common description made it into an article he read about himself—but before long, he was having semiregular meals and hangouts at home with Jarrett and Eric Holder and Ron Kirk, his former trade representative, and vanishingly few others.

This was in part a tactical retreat because of his impatience with day-to-day politics and the business of Washington—an exhaustion carried over from his time as president that was now amplified since he believed he no longer had any real power to actually do anything about it all. Plus, he'd conceived of his new, relaxing life as existing in the new economy and international environment he'd helped build and President Hillary Clinton would steward. The previous year he'd thought out loud in an interview about becoming a Silicon Valley venture capitalist and he had planned to take the hands-off approach to politics and his successor that George W. Bush had taken with him. Insofar as he wanted to maintain influence, it was within the culture to encourage the perpetuation of shared liberal values, so he started considering a deal with Netflix—where his friends and donors Reed Hastings and Ted Sarandos were in charge and his former assistant Ferial Govashiri had gone to work—to produce content, while posting "cool dad"–style book, music, and movie recommendations on his Twitter and Facebook pages. This kind of thing was an efficient way for him to make a wide-reaching impact now, he figured, convinced politics could still mostly be behind him, despite all the evidence to the contrary.

He knew that Trump's victory meant this kind of detachment was at least partially a pipe dream—"I feel like Michael Corleone, I almost got out," Rhodes recalled him saying late in his tenure, exasperated that he'd never be able to live an apolitical life with Trump now defining the end of his presidency. But he held fast in refusing even the most innocuous politics-adjacent asks. When the Iowa Democratic Party invited him to speak at the 2017 edition of its big fundraising dinner to mark the ten-year anniversary of his landmark speech that many still thought won him the 2008 caucuses, he turned it down.

Instead, he was determined to stick to the two projects he'd laid out for himself before leaving office, each conceptually similar to ex-presidents' standard post–White House endeavors but both designed to be extraconscious of his theoretical ongoing ambitions. He was leaving office at fifty-five so had decades' worth of endeavors still to come. Obama wanted to get his presidential foundation and library off the ground, and he set off raising money for it almost immediately, aiming to bring in between $500 million and $1 billion with asks of up to $20 million when he met with the country's moguls. (Disney's Bob Iger, filmmaker J.J. Abrams, and Salesforce's Marc Benioff were among the first donors of at least $1 million.)

The idea was to build less of a straightforward nostalgia center than a place for new generations of global leaders to come together and learn, in pursuit of his overall post-presidential goal of empowering young people to step up. The foundation would provide funding for training and grant programs around the world on top of the physical space. Slated for Chicago's Jackson Park, the building itself was designed to function little like a traditional presidential library. Instead of being built around Obama's archives, it would be filled with interactive displays and experiences geared toward encouraging civic engagement.

And, any day now, he'd get to work on his presidential memoir. Penguin Random House hadn't reportedly paid him and Michelle a record $65 million for nothing.

Obama's commitment to closing off interlopers and political intrusions was matched only by Biden's enthusiasm for the real world, which he demonstrated upon his return to Wilmington by catching up with what felt like everyone in his iPhone's contacts list, reading frivolous human interest stories out loud off the Apple News app, beginning a cathartic draft of a book about the year Beau died, and slowly getting started on a much more private book of poems he would write for Jill for Christmas, including some about their relationship. And still, he was restless enough that the half-joke du jour among the informal advisors tasked with determining his next projects was that he should run for a seat on the New Castle County Commission, which he'd left forty-five years earlier. What only his closest friends could see, though, was that his personal preoccupation was more urgent than he let on. He was concerned about providing not only for Beau's family but now also for Hunter's. His younger son had divorced Kathleen, returned to using hard drugs and alcohol, and was disappearing for weeks at a time.

Biden nonetheless balked when he was approached early in 2017 by an agency proposing a four-year, $38 million contract to give a series of speeches. It was far more money than he'd ever even considered, but he'd already agreed with his advisors to operate with an untouchable rule when mapping out his postadministration life: don't sign him up for anything they wouldn't want to see on the front page of a major newspaper. He wasn't explicitly thinking about his political future, but Clinton's struggles to defend her own secretive paid speeches to banks—and the resulting accusations of corruption, which were usually unfair but undoubtedly lacerating—had stuck with him. Nine years after joining Obama's ticket, he was still worried about his brand. The perception of buckraking spooked him, and he laid out even more rules for the appearances he would agree to make, ensuring that he dealt with no controversial hosts and specifying even how the tickets were sold to preclude suspicions that he was peddling access to himself. He turned down the offer.

Obama was less engaged with the politics of the moment, and both he and Michelle were stunned and offended when Elizabeth Warren said in April that she was "troubled" by reports that the former president was due to earn $400,000 from a health-care conference hosted by investment firm Cantor Fitzgerald. (His schedule also had stops at other financial institutions, like Carlyle and Northern Trust.) Warren decried "the influence of money. I describe it as a snake that slithers through Washington and that it shows up in so many different ways here in Washington," and Bernie Sanders chimed in the next day, calling Obama's choice to deliver the speech "distasteful."

Obama had always been hyperaware that others looked to him for behavioral cues, even when he wasn't trying to act as a role model. But instead of using the criticism to reflect on his place in the new, Trump-led political order in which Democrats were still trying to find their footing, he grew defensive and protective of his status as a private citizen, which he thought should now indemnify him from this kind of criticism. When Warren asked to come by his office to talk after hearing that he was upset, he dug in for nearly two hours, almost brooding as he told her he was incredulous that liberals were really still going after each other even with 2016 in the rearview mirror. At the same time, though, he had a bigger concern: he also couldn't believe that Warren and Sanders were demagoguing the private sector, especially after—in his eyes—Sanders's extended challenge had damaged Clinton for her general election against Trump, which he thought raised huge questions about the entire approach.

* * *

A few weeks after his meeting with Warren, Obama landed in Milan. After waving to crowds of onlookers, he ducked into the Park Hyatt for a sit-down with Matteo Renzi, the young and similarly minded former Italian prime minister who was trying to plot a comeback after a few months in political exile. For more than an hour, they caught up about the populist Five Star Movement surging in the country, and about the threat of Russian election meddling, pausing at one point to call new French president Emmanuel Macron to congratulate him on fending off an extremist competitor. The meeting was private, but there wasn't much secretive about it. Most of the details found their way to the pages of the *Times* a few hours later. Obama tried to be careful not to look like a shadow president as Trump's provocations escalated back home, but it was hard not to read the Milanese chat and the call to Paris as the actions of an only barely implicit advocate for a pluralistic liberal world order in the face of rising authoritarianism and extremism.

This impression only stiffened as Obama kept the meetings going—he sat with German chancellor Angela Merkel in Berlin at a forum where he outright said, "We can't hide behind a wall," and when he met with Canadian prime minister Justin Trudeau in Montreal, the photographs of them eating halibut and drinking wine at a trendy restaurant looked almost as if they were staged for a magazine feature about young center-left world leaders. At each stop, Obama made a practice of reassuring his host about the state of the modern order—his very presence often helped prove the point that no apocalypse had yet befallen the Western world—but also privately warning that the American system was resilient enough to survive one Trump term, though perhaps not his reelection. He suspected this was true of some other countries with new right-wing governments, too.

Biden was starting to travel again, as well, but with a lot less fanfare, and with fewer reassurances on offer when foreign leaders would ask him how the world could cope with Trump. Like Obama, his mind went first to the institutions holding up the global system and American democracy. But his concern about their solidity was much more acute than his former boss's, especially on the frequent days that he'd start by watching doom-saying *Morning Joe* broadcasts on MSNBC or reading downcast David Brooks columns in the *Times*. Like any good Democrat, he got worked up daily when he heard of the latest developments in Trump's King Kong act back in DC, but he only called Ricchetti, Donilon, or Bedingfield to consider a public response when he perceived an assault on the country's institutions, like when Trump fired FBI director James Comey for refusing to end the investigation into his Russian ties, making a mockery of the Justice Department's independence. The group would discuss how to react, but they usually passed on making a statement, figuring that Trump would drag Biden into the political gutter, which wouldn't help anyone.

But still, Biden would talk in nearly apocalyptic terms with friends and advisors, warning of a deep shift in the culture. "We've never seen anything like this," he would intone darkly and dramatically. "He's grabbed ahold of this country, and emboldening the strain of the country that is really problematic." When Biden got really grim, he'd admit that Trump made him realize he'd been naive about the country's progress. He'd often recounted the story of telling his children, "Don't tell me things can't change," the morning of Obama's inauguration. Now, he said, that seemed ridiculous: hate and evil only receded, they never disappeared.

It was Obama, though, whose relative silence was most glaring to a country in which his administration was remembered increasingly fondly and almost mournful pleas for his return to the public arena were becoming an accepted feature of #Resistance-era culture. The world felt like it was deteriorating by the minute as horrifying updates dripped out of Trump's Washington, the government suddenly run by a gang of right-wing ideologues and amateurs with a penchant for targeting immigrants, liberals, and commonly held truths. Obama had approached the presidency like a self-conscious preacher of shared morality who understood his own power for summoning communal emotion—with his tears after the Sandy Hook shooting, say, or his rendition of "Amazing Grace" in Charleston—but also the importance of maintaining pride in America's remaining unified principles. Now, though, he had deliberately stepped away. Though this was traditional, there was little that felt standard about the moment, making his absence hard to understand for masses of scared Americans. This was occasionally expressed with humor. One November *Saturday Night Live* sketch had Chance the Rapper singing, "Every night, I turn the TV on and cry / I say why, I feel like we're all gonna die / So come back, Barack / Even though it's not allowed, we want you back somehow." More often, it was plaintive. "We all miss him," said Kobe Bryant of his fellow athletes.

Obama himself was amused by this kind of thing at first but insistent that he had to step back to make space for new Democratic leaders to take charge. And as the pleas got more specific—Why couldn't he do what he did best and give a soaring speech to remind the country of its moral center, or at least lobby against Trump's immigration crackdowns or issue more statements about his nuclear threats?—this insistence turned into outright frustration that well-meaning liberals didn't appreciate what he was trying to do, or didn't respect his wish for some version of personal normalcy after eight years in office, no matter how abnormal things were getting.

It was an ongoing and bigger-picture version of his impatience with the contention sometimes shared by former colleagues like Clinton and Rice that he could have done more to combat Russian interference in 2016. He didn't acknowledge that he was making a bet that the country would survive Trump's sustained attack on its principles. He was, though, wagering that Americans would come to appreciate his careful approach in the long run. He was assuming they could soon meet the new leaders that his distance was enabling to rise up. And he held out faith that in four years Trump would leave office and they would also again witness, and then appreciate, the democracy-strengthening traditions of leadership hand-offs that he had tried perpetuating.

But Obama was also angry, and not nearly as convinced that he knew how to handle this new era as it seemed from the outside. He was still on vacation in Palm Springs when the first crisis hit his post-presidency: Trump had banned immigrants from a handful of Muslim-majority countries, Democrats around the country were speeding to airports to protest the move, and there was no good way for Obama to respond, as he saw it. The small group of aides who had stayed in his employ quickly convened after a day of getting used to their new office, debating the wisdom of putting out a statement from Obama. Saying something so soon would destroy his plan to respect precedent by staying mum about his successor, he worried, but shouldn't he do *something* in the face of such an egregious step? They agreed to release a statement from his press secretary that didn't mention Trump by name, and which praised the protests, but in so doing they established an internal precedent of agonizing over their responses to Trump's provocations. The pattern recurred in the ensuing months, Obama agreeing to put his name to some more statements as time went on but insisting on not mentioning Trump in those written communications, which, for example, defended both the Affordable Care Act Trump wanted to gut and the Paris climate change agreement he was threatening to exit.

The idea was, basically, to keep out of it in public unless something so outrageous happened that Obama had no choice but to speak up. He had more pressing things to do, anyway: he was making only slow progress on his memoir, which he was writing with input from speechwriter Cody Keenan by hand on yellow legal pads during stretches of the day that his aides carved out to encourage him to focus. Meanwhile, he was reading the news coverage of his successor voraciously, searching for signs of eroding democratic norms and shifts in the international order, as well as for more specific indications that Trump would strip immigrants of their rights and citizens of their health-care coverage. He was particularly appalled by reports that the Trump administration was separating undocumented families at the border, and also mortified by Trump's rollback of environmental regulations, since that represented at least four lost years in the fight to mitigate climate change's effects. Yet Obama was convinced that when he weighed in on anything it would spark an immediate explosion of backlash among Trump's followers and instantly render any discussion a partisan wasteland.

That Trump needed a foil to survive politically was obvious to Obama, but even some of Obama's remaining friends in Washington questioned the ex-president's policy of hanging back to deprive the new one of an easy enemy. They wondered how he felt about the possible destruction of his legacy—he always cut off such conversations by saying "Michelle and I are fine" and changing the topic—and whether he truly still believed that the Trump era would be a blip on the long arc of progress. For the most part, he hated this conversation and usually avoided even mentioning Trump by name when old friends and former aides stopped by his office, even though he made clear how little he thought of the president and had no problem expounding at length on the world's ills more broadly. It didn't take long for him to abandon his previous, naive hope that Trump would change and to conclude that he was clearly both a racist and out of his mind, which only fed into his conviction—usually expressed in private with an eye roll or a shake of the head—that Trump was, in fact, an aberration.

It all added up to the most radical handoff of the presidency since Dwight Eisenhower took over from Harry Truman, and it became by far the most hostile in March 2017 when Trump abandoned any pretense of wanting guidance from Obama and accused him on Twitter—with less than no evidence—of wiretapping him. Obama determined that his office needed to reply to this lunacy with cold facts only, hoping to avoid a back-and-forth. The men hadn't spoken since the inauguration—Trump had tried calling Obama when he was flying to Palm Springs, but missed him—and now they certainly wouldn't talk again anytime soon, as Trump turned his wild accusation into an obsession with Obama and undoing his legacy.

Even the bright spots Obama identified in the early Trump days were born out of deep darkness. He was visibly buoyed upon seeing high school students' nationwide activism inspired by the survivors of the February 2018 school shooting in Parkland, Florida. Yet that same interest in upcoming generations also bore a special kind of fury that Obama reserved for Trump's interactions with children. He feared that the new president might infect an impressionable cohort with a kind of amoral coarseness and openness to sexism and racism from which the country would struggle to recover. For months Obama stewed in frustration after reading about Trump's address to the Boy Scout Jamboree in July 2017 in West Virginia, where the new president had—in front of horrified adults—entertained the scouts by mocking Clinton and Obama and telling tales of embarrassing pundits on election night and going to parties with the "hottest people in New York" and promising to "say Merry Christmas again." At the scouts' age, Obama fumed, they were liable to absorb every word of this divisive message. Again, though, he said nothing in public, unsure how he could help fix Trump's damage without starting an unproductive war of words.

Only once did Obama step further back into the fray. Every once in a while, in the earliest Trump days, both Pelosi and Schumer, the Democratic leaders on Capitol Hill, checked in with Obama to get his gut reactions to their strategy, and he occasionally caught up with his remaining senator friends, too. That often meant pinging Tim Kaine for updates on Trump's efforts to dismantle the ACA and on Senate Republicans' initially tortured relationship with the new president.

Within a few months, the reports from Pelosi, Schumer, Kaine, and others were getting alarming. Obama still didn't see how his public involvement could help, so he stayed quiet while Bernie Sanders, an ACA skeptic but nonetheless Democrats' most effective active messenger, took the public lead on rallying support for the law while Republicans put forth a threadbare alternative that was essentially just a repeal. But Obama quietly started advising ex-aides and lawmakers trying to build a public defense, and, when he finally felt that it would help in May, he amplified the pressure campaign by saying during a speech in Boston, "I hope that current members of Congress recall that it actually doesn't take a lot of courage to aid those who are already powerful, already comfortable, already influential." He then added a statement ripping the proposed GOP replacement plan the next month and, watching closely but still treading lightly for fear of galvanizing Republicans, made a few private phone calls, including to Alaska's governor, since the state's Republican senator Lisa Murkowski was a swing vote and he thought he could influence her. When John McCain dramatically doomed his own party's vote to kill Obama's most important accomplishment, Obama called his old opponent to thank him.

* * *

If you asked some of the people who stuck with Biden, he was starting to act a little like he was still in office. A few weeks into what could have been a quiet retirement, the ex-VP started getting restless, feeling disconnected from the day-to-day action and dissatisfied by the news updates he was reading and watching every day. The solution, he determined between speeches, was a series of regular briefings from current and former aides and external policy experts. First, these were weekly updates on legislation on Capitol Hill, but before long they were economic policy sessions, too, and then he started thinking about ways to rally sufficient Senate support for significant infrastructure investments, even though there was no such bill up for debate and he was only in sporadic touch with a small handful of current senators. Soon he was bouncing specific infrastructure program ideas off friends, and then insisting on finding a way to offer Americans two free years of community college, since he and Obama hadn't gotten that push fully over the line before leaving office but he still loved the idea.

This all scratched one itch, but not the one he cared about most. He soon asked a group led by Blinken to start giving him a series of foreign policy updates that at times effectively simulated the President's Daily Brief, just without any classified intel. He asked for news on China, Russia, and the Middle East, but also for updates on international policy debates that were playing out under the radar in DC.

He'd never fully disconnected and was in fact still steaming about 2016, though he tried not to talk about it in public as much as he did in private. Still, his frustration popped out a few times. Speaking at the University of Pennsylvania in March, he griped, "This was the first campaign that I can recall where my party did not talk about what it always stood for, and that was how to maintain a burgeoning middle class." He didn't mention Clinton by name, but continued: "You didn't hear a single, solitary sentence in the last campaign about that guy working on the assembly line making sixty thousand bucks a year and a wife making thirty-two thousand as a hostess in a restaurant." It was vintage Bidenism, focused especially on the working-class guys—like the ones he grew up with, he always said—who'd left his party. The next month, he told a crowd in New Hampshire that Democrats simply hadn't convinced anyone they understood their plight. "Trump was pretty smart, he made it all personal," he said, and enough Democrats had stayed home. "I'm absolutely positive they wanted to be with us, but we have to prove again we understand that hopelessness." At a hedge fund conference in Las Vegas in May, he went a bit further still: Clinton "would have been a really good president," he said, but "I never thought she was a great candidate. I thought I was a great candidate."

Trump had already been president for four months. But how could Biden move on?

The subtext was never particularly subtle with Biden. A few weeks after leaving the vice presidency, Biden gathered a group of advisors at the rented home in Virginia to talk about what came next. Topic number one was how he could stay involved in politics—what donors should he keep in touch with, and should he officially launch a PAC? He let that idea fizzle for now but successfully planted the seed in everyone's mind: Should he be preparing to run for president in 2020? He hadn't really thought about it deeply but knew he had to consider it and that some people in the room would be into the idea. (His brother Frank, who wasn't there, was even publicly tweeting encouraging him to run before reporters found his account.) This was all wildly premature, and Biden was clear that he had a lot of resting and healing still to do before he thought about it seriously. But he wanted the possibility to stay alive.

He had to do something to stay in the conversation, anyway, especially given the way his former boss was talking about what came next. In one interview before leaving office Obama had considered who might become future representatives of the party and mentioned Kamala Harris, who'd just been elected a senator from California; the thirty-something mayor of South Bend, Indiana, Pete Buttigieg; Kaine; and Colorado senator Michael Bennet. A few weeks later, in another interview, he again pointed to Harris and added former Missouri secretary of state Jason Kander, Los Angeles mayor Eric Garcetti, New Orleans mayor Mitch Landrieu, and Atlanta mayor Kasim Reed. It didn't take much decoding to figure out that every person on this list was at least fifteen years younger than the seventy-four-year-old Biden. But then no one, not even him, would call himself the party's "future," exactly.

Still, Biden figured it wouldn't hurt to get a PAC started once he saw coverage of Sanders traveling the country with the new DNC chairman Tom Perez, Obama's former labor secretary, in a springtime "unity tour" that got awful coverage for its attempts to insist all was well within the obviously riven party. Even then, though, the Bidens were finally starting to live a new kind of lifestyle. In their first two years out of office, they made upward of $15 million on their book deals, academic appointments, and speaking gigs. So there was no hurry to dip back into the political pool.

At least not until August.

CHAPTER 16

2017–2018

Biden was at the family's new beach house on the second Saturday in August watching updates pour in from Charlottesville, Virginia, where an unthinkable white supremacist rally was turning violent. The picture darkened as reports circulated that a crowd of counterprotesters had been run over by a terrorist's car, and then that one person had been killed. Biden called Kate Bedingfield. He knew he wanted to put out a statement of some sort condemning it all, and she typed as he dictated the outlines of a draft, then emailed it around to Steve Ricchetti, Mike Donilon, Ted Kaufman, and Greg Schultz. They traded edits and ideas for three days, before Biden, still planted in front of his TV, watched Trump lay blame for the horrors "on both sides." He called Donilon, and together they shaped the loose draft into an essay they published two weeks later in *The Atlantic*. "If it wasn't clear before, it's clear now," Biden wrote. "We are living through a battle for the soul of this nation."

Biden had been using this kind of language for years—especially dedicated students of the man might remember his easily forgotten insistence that "it is time to reclaim America's soul" at the 2004 convention—but it was immediately obvious to the people who spoke with him that week that something different was happening now. Biden suddenly sounded much graver and more purposeful than before, and he latched on to a comparison made by Gitenstein, his longtime friend and a native Alabaman, of Trump to George Wallace, the racist governor and presidential candidate who campaigned on a platform of segregation starting in the 1960s. At once, Biden's generalized dismay about Trump turned specific: he was a poison for the country, which needed an antidote.

To his longest-serving advisors there was something reminiscent here of the internally famous clarifying conversation he'd had with his mother a decade earlier, a neat illustration of his tendency to let his feelings marinate just a tad too long, considering that in his heart he knew what he wanted to do. That talk with Jean had snapped him out of the delusion that he might not want to be Obama's vice president. There wasn't much ambiguity now, either, even if he still wouldn't say it out loud. He was the antidote.

* * *

Biden never doubted that Trump was an aberration; ousting him would be a win for normalcy. Obama, however, had come to see it differently as the Trump era rolled on. The pair agreed that Trump's voters shouldn't shoulder all the blame for the president's outrages—his middle-class supporters "aren't prejudiced, they're realistic," Biden said in Chicago that fall, whereas Obama conceded that "sometimes the backlash comes from people who are genuinely, if wrongly, fearful of change."

Yet "more often it's manufactured by the powerful and the privileged who want to keep us divided and keep us angry and keep us cynical because that helps them maintain the status quo and keep their power and keep their privilege," Obama had continued in his first domestic political speech since leaving office. "It did not start with Donald Trump. He is a symptom, not the cause." This was a far cry from his old insistence that the Republican "fever" would soon break, the product of a reconsideration Obama had been undertaking ever since he started writing his book— which would recall many of his early fights with an increasingly radical right wing—just as Trump was getting used to the White House.

The former partners, however, never discussed this fundamental disagreement about the harrowing Trump-centric moment and, implicitly, what had happened to conservatives—and therefore all of politics—over the last decade. In fact, they hardly talked about current affairs at all these days. Biden spoke to the Chicago Council on Global Affairs just as Obama was hosting his foundation's first summit in town, but neither visited the other's programming. When they did mention each other in public, it was like they were still a pair with a working relationship. But Biden's more personal take—he usually described them essentially as brothers—was more apt when they occasionally caught up in private, usually over the phone, to chat about their families and life out of office. They appeared together only a handful of times, and never to make a point about Trump. Once, Obama made a surprise cameo at a fundraising event for the Beau Biden Foundation, where he spoke briefly about Beau and about dropping Malia off at college. The next year, they popped up at a veteran-focused DC bakery together. It was all warm, and it was also powerful grist for the bromance content mill just when liberals were desperate for some nostalgic comfort.

Obama discussed none of it with Biden, but he was all the while trying harder than ever to understand the origins of the fractures through which Trump had burst. When friends visited him in the West End office and brought up the latest Trumpian outrage they'd seen on cable, he would first make sure they knew he never watched—he was still a *SportsCenter*-first guy as far as TV went—before pointing to a RAND Corporation study about facts' slipping prominence in American life and worrying at length about the widening gulf between Fox News and MSNBC or NPR. He started studying the work of a few popular nonliberals, like libertarian Conor Friedersdorf of *The Atlantic* and conservative Patrick Deneen, author of *Why Liberalism Failed*, and scouring *Times* stories about the latest tactics and demands of his own party's seemingly ascendant left wing, which looked like it had been gaining momentum ever since Sanders fans insisted "Bernie would've won" the day after Clinton lost. As Obama saw it, progressive activists were onto something—stretching the bounds of public debate for the good guys by agitating for a $15 federal minimum wage, say—but their elected politicians were missing the important last step. They had to actually get this stuff into law, and that required political pragmatism and realism about what everyday Americans would tolerate, not reflexive acceptance of activist demands.

This was one piece of a sprawling and quickly intensifying debate about which Obama felt strongly but wanted no active part in. Ever since November 2016, Democrats had been in an existential tailspin. One disagreement was over the degree to which they should resist Trump or try to find room for compromise when good policy was possible—at a closed-door session for terrified liberal donors gathered in south Florida over Trump's inauguration weekend Ron Klain had argued for all-out war while Rahm Emanuel had advocated for picking their spots. Another was about how hard left to tack, and yet another—the one being mindlessly debated on cable each night—was about who, exactly, was leading the party, and who should.

Obama had briefly waded into that fight as he was leaving office, privately convincing outgoing labor secretary Tom Perez to forgo a run for Maryland governor and to run for chairman of the DNC instead. The committee needed a dramatic rehabilitation after being sapped of money and public confidence in recent years, and the only other serious candidate was a Sanders-wing congressman, Keith Ellison, with whom Obama had clashed. The outgoing president figured installing a close ally would keep the party on what he saw as his responsible path. Obama then stepped back, though, only making calls on Perez's behalf to the voting DNC members in the final two days of the race, letting Jarrett, Simas, and a group of staffers including his former deputy campaign manager Jen O'Malley Dillon and longtime aide Yohannes Abraham do much of the work of sending the signal that Obama approved of Perez's candidacy. Biden's endorsement helped, too, but it was the Clintons who stepped up more, first campaigning for Perez and then sitting with him at their home in Chappaqua, New York, for a broader strategy session once he won the close race.

Obama's disengagement during the vote-gathering process was just as well, since his broad popularity among the party's everyday supporters didn't extend to the activists and officials at the committee who actually got a vote in determining the next chair. They blamed him for effectively ignoring the DNC during his presidency, and for at first putting his campaign's resources into his own political group rather than the central office after he ran up against the party's establishment during the 2008 primary. Then there was the fact that he presided over the party's assumption of a technocratic and distant reputation while Republicans—the party of the rich—somehow succeeded in branding themselves the truly sympathetic ones on middle-class economics. But it was his lack of interest in the DNC and in down-ballot work that was most impossible to ignore when you considered how aggressively the party had been hollowed out. Democrats now had nearly a thousand fewer seats in state legislatures than they did when Obama took over.

Obama had acknowledged he deserved some of the blame. "I take some responsibility on that," he told George Stephanopoulos shortly before leaving office. "I couldn't be both chief organizer of the Democratic Party and function as commander in chief and president of the United States. We did not begin what I think needs to happen over the long haul, and that is rebuild the Democratic Party at the ground level." His answer was to help raise cash and occasionally consult on strategy for a group Holder was launching at his advice to combat Republicans' partisan redistricting. Obama spoke little with Perez for the first few months of his tenure at the DNC, and he stepped back even further when the party launched a "unity reform commission" intended to regain trust and fix the DNC's procedures to make sure the presidential nominating process was as fair as possible. O'Malley Dillon was partially in charge of the effort. Still Obama saw no reason to get involved or even follow it very closely.

His bigger concern was the party's possible leftward swing on policy and posture on the Hill, where in September Sanders got sixteen colleagues to go along with his proposal for a "Medicare for All" system. It stood little chance of passing but it did put those Democrats on record arguing they could do better than Obamacare. Obama followed the debate closely because of his pride in the ACA, but when former colleagues asked for his take he was always careful to point out that this was the logical next policy step after his law. He just didn't think that it would work, or that Sanders should try turning it into some kind of litmus test for the left. Obama had told his team eight years earlier that if they were starting from scratch he might want a universal single-payer system like what Sanders was proposing, but that they weren't. They were working with the private insurance market, and Republicans had still accused him of a communistic government takeover. Imagine, Obama sometimes mused, what they'd say if Medicare for All got close to passing, and what a disaster that would be for Democrats as far as regular voters were concerned.

Biden was concerned about Sanders and his acolytes, too, but he had no patience for the argument that the party was in crisis, in no small part because he had no trouble identifying its possible next leader whenever he looked in a mirror. He also thought it was obvious that there was a more immediate threat to deal with. And, he believed, that very threat—of Trump and Trumpism—should make it clear that the party's relative moderates would carry the day with real voters. Biden watched two special elections in particular to test this proposition. Both were personal to him. One, in early 2018, pitted Conor Lamb, a young former marine, against a guy calling himself "Trump before Trump." Donilon was helping Lamb, who reminded Biden of Beau, in the race outside Pittsburgh, a region Biden thought and talked about a lot, especially after his beloved Pennsylvania went for Trump. First, though, there was the 2017 Senate race in Alabama, where his old friend Doug Jones, a US Attorney who'd successfully prosecuted Ku Klux Klan members for the 1963 church bombing in Birmingham, was running an uphill race against a reactionary, hyperconservative judge named Roy Moore who was found to have preyed on underage girls.

Biden kept in regular touch with Jones as his race unfolded, telling him he thought the state—which hadn't elected a Democratic senator in decades—had a chance to redeem its soul and asking about how influential Trump was on the ground against Jones's offer of hope and his promise to avoid the national political back-and-forth. To Biden, the race was a simulacrum of the overall national picture, even though Alabama was far more conservative than the country at large. When Jones narrowly won, Biden told the new senator and his friends that his moderation and promise of steady leadership had fine-tuned a formula for victory. Lamb soon used it, too.

Biden always denied that his interest had anything to do with 2020, but as the Jones race unfolded he also stepped up his casual check-ins with allies in battleground states like Florida, asking increasingly pointed questions about local dynamics in the ensuing months. By the time Lamb won, heralding a possibly big year for Democrats in November's midterms, Biden was reconnecting with a handful of the party's leading donors through his new PAC, including Jeffrey Katzenberg, Steven Spielberg, hedge fund manager James Simons, and Meg Whitman, the former Hewlett-Packard executive and Republican gubernatorial candidate in California. He also started handing out one of a trio of books to people, including possible future supporters, who he thought might be interested. One, *White Working Class* by Joan C. Williams, was about finding empathy for, or at least understanding of, that group of people so often dismissed by liberals in the days after Trump's win. Another, *How Democracies Die*, by Steven Levitsky and Daniel Ziblatt, spoke for itself. So did the third, which came with a title that would seem familiar if you'd been listening at all to Biden in recent months: Jon Meacham's *The Soul of America*, a history of American challenges and how hope won out each time.

* * *

Much of the liberal angst over Obama's relative silence—*he wasn't fund-raising enough! Why wouldn't he say more about Trump?!*—faded as the midterms approached and the party's best campaigner first endorsed vast swaths of candidates up and down the ballot and then returned to the trail to boost Democrats and expose his successor's failings. He was surprised by the appetite for his help.

Biden, meanwhile, never doubted that his endorsement would be in high demand, even though in reality this was because he was viewed by many middle-of-the-road Democratic candidates as an undoubtedly popular but mostly harmless elder statesman, not a dynamo or a particularly influential name to put in their ads. Still, he saw in the promising midterms an obvious opportunity to highlight the political versatility he still felt—his team searched for a diverse group of endorsees all around the country—and to make a point about the moderates' role as the heart of the party, even with progressive energy surging.

Sometimes Biden's decisions about who to back were emotional and intense. When he met with James Smith, the South Carolina legislator who'd been trying to convince him to run for president for years, Biden insisted Smith had to run for governor in 2018. Biden told him he and Jill believed in Smith, and the state senator thanked him for taking the time, as if to end the meeting for Biden's benefit. (*Surely he had other places to be?*) The ex-VP grew agitated. "Come on, man!" he said. "Wait a minute! I'm your friend! That's ridiculous! We're going to do this together!" They talked the race through for another half hour. Other decisions were more strategically careful, especially after Biden sat down with John Anzalone, Obama and Hillary Clinton's old pollster, in the fall of 2018 to talk through what he was seeing. Anzalone focused especially on three of his gubernatorial clients—Gretchen Whitmer in Michigan, Steve Sisolak in Nevada, and Fred Hubbell in Iowa—and told Biden each of those pragma-tist Democrats had a chance to prove there was a moderate path to victory in important states after beating lefty primary opponents. They also high-lighted the gap between real voters' preferences and insiders' and activists' beliefs about what voters needed.

Meanwhile, Biden was using the tour for his new book about 2015,

Promise Me, Dad, to test if he could still handle the travel and constant attention he'd need to endure if he was going to seriously approach another campaign. He quickly grew exhausted but was buoyed at each stop by the diversity—of age, sex, and ethnicity—in his crowds, and he invariably walked off the stage after his emotionally draining appearances and nodded smilingly to his aides, as if to say, "You see that? I've still got it." He extended the book tour, and then did it again, keeping the swing going on and off for over a year.

But it was on this tour that he was also bluntly reminded that 2020's race was already starting to unfold, and that he better hurry up and make some plans if he was serious about it. Before one stop at the University of Montana in Missoula, he sat for thirty minutes with Steve Bullock, the governor who was thinking of running for president as a Bill Clinton–like consensus-maker from a red state. Bullock had been friendly with Beau, thanks to their shared time as attorneys general, and now Biden listened as he said he figured he had something to offer in the race, even though Biden was leading in the way-too-early polling of the theoretical field. Biden was encouraging and told Bullock to make sure his family was ready for the grind of the campaign, but he ended the meeting with a friendly warning: he was still expecting to run if he didn't think anyone else could win. Bullock wasn't the only one to hear this message. As he traveled the country Biden had the same conversation with Ohio congressman Tim Ryan and Los Angeles mayor Eric Garcetti.

Still, Biden didn't appreciate the wall of skepticism he was about to hit. As sure as he was that he was going to run and should be considered the front-runner, most of his party's leading lights were equally convinced he wouldn't go through with it. For one thing, there was the inescapable matter of his age. Sure, Sanders was a year older, but Biden had physically slowed visibly since leaving office, speaking more slowly and less precisely, even though he was still mentally as sharp as ever. He would be seventy-eight when inaugurated, which would make him the oldest president ever to assume the office, and the topic of age and lucidity was a live one with someone as erratic as Trump in power. (One bizarre quirk of presidential history: Trump, Bill Clinton, and George W. Bush were all born in summer 1946. Biden was four years older.) Even if he could surpass that concern, there were immediate practical ones to consider. For one, he hadn't run a presidential campaign of his own since 2008, and that one had been a disaster. Campaign technology had transformed completely even since then, and he hardly had a state-of-the-art digital or data team surrounding him, though he was slowly trying to change that. One of his leading moneymen marveled in 2018 that his children had shown him that campaigns could raise serious money online now. This would've been news to a properly plugged-in Democrat a decade and a half earlier.

This was all before you even considered the state of the party itself—and whether Biden was in step with its modern incarnation at all. When he'd appeared for Jones in Birmingham in 2017, Biden had grown nostalgic for his early days in the Senate. Back then, he said, "the Democratic Party still had seven or eight old-fashioned Democratic segregationists. You'd get up and you'd argue like the devil with them. Then you'd go down and have lunch or dinner together. The political system worked. We were divided on issues, but the political system worked." Speaking for plenty of baffled liberals, longtime blogger and *Daily Kos* founder Markos Moulitsas responded in the *New Republic*, "If Biden's solution to eight years of Republican obstruction and conservative slash-and-burn tactics against him and Barack Obama is to talk about 'bipartisanship' and 'consensus,' then he might as well pack up and go home. Because if he's that stupid to believe that shit, then he's no longer got any business being in the public face." The awkward thing for Biden was that it wasn't just progressives who were eager for new blood. Third Way, the centrist Democratic think tank, didn't even think to invite him to their big 2018 conference aiming to chart a path to 2020 and find an acceptable candidate; a number of Biden's allies were there but the group's leaders instead invited younger pols like Tim Ryan and spent their time trying to woo former New Orleans mayor Mitch Landrieu.

Biden started to grasp the depth of doubt that fall and resolved to use the final stretch before midterm election day to dispel some concerns and to solidify his role as the party's top public counterweight to Trump. In the final weeks, he scheduled far more events for Democratic candidates than any other potential 2020 contender, making an extra point of visiting House districts in out-of-the-way suburbs to prove his value in areas that had been swinging in recent presidential elections. This was on top of the expected visits to traditional battlegrounds like Florida, Iowa, Michigan, Nevada, Ohio, Virginia, Wisconsin, and, of course, Pennsylvania. And he made sure to spend extra time and energy on behalf of candidates in

Missouri and North Dakota—two red states—to clear up any doubt that he was the Democratic surrogate who could go where no other could due to his popularity and crossover appeal. The effort outstripped that of his closest theoretical competitors. Sanders traveled plenty, too, for example, but seldom to the most competitive areas, where many competitive swing-district candidates were spooked by his uncompromising leftism.

Biden spent election night glued to his phone, as usual. Monitoring the results from the rented home in McLean, he talked to most of the candidates he'd campaigned for, and plenty he didn't, either to congratulate or console them, or just to catch up. This time felt better than 2016 had in part because Democrats were winning big, at least in local races and in the House.

But it was also because of a refrain he kept hearing, and not always from the most expected sources. At one point he connected with Mitt Romney, who'd been easily elected to the Senate that night as a rare Trump-opposing Republican. They were warm as Biden cheered Romney's win. Then Obama's old rival got to the point: *You have to run*, Romney said.

CHAPTER 17

2018—2019

Doug Jones visited Biden at the ex-VP's rented office in DC a few months after he became a senator. Biden had been hosting a stream of visitors throughout 2018, showing off his view of the Capitol and musing about his next moves. He caught Jones up on his latest thinking, and asked how he was experiencing the party's leftward sprint, which, aside from Trump, was the talk of the town. Twice, Biden threw off the pace of the conversation by insisting "I'm pretty liberal on this" about policy decisions Jones was working through. The third time, Jones interrupted him. "You need to get out a little more," the Alabaman said with a grin. "Because in this world, you're not a liberal anymore."

Biden thought it was funny, but by that point his confidence about his place in the political landscape was at an all-time high, even amid the unrelenting commentary about a progressive takeover. For months, Biden made a practice of waving around a printed-out report that John Anzalone had put together for him making the case that he was the most popular Democrat still on the scene among a wide group of Americans ("I'm more popular with women than Hillary was!") and that with Trump bulldozing his way around the world, voters were putting a premium on experience. A few months later, in the wake of the successful midterm elections, the pollster wrote another presentation for Biden. This one, which was also designed to allay Jill's latest fears that maybe another run wasn't a good idea, laid out the beginnings of an argument about how Biden might win a crowded presidential primary. It focused on how different 2020 was looking from 2016, particularly because even Sanders's voters thought favorably of Biden, unlike their feelings about Clinton. He followed up with one more deck aimed at dousing BidenWorld's fears that the party really was undergoing a lefty-led revolution that would leave Biden behind, especially after a charismatic and media-savvy twenty-nine-year-old ex-Sanders volunteer named Alexandria Ocasio-Cortez instantly became one of the most recognizable Democrats by upsetting leading House member Joe Crowley in a Bronx-and-Queens-area primary. Anzalone's upshot: real voters in politically important parts of the country weren't as interested in this story line of progressive ascension as the DC media was.

The view from Biden's Constitution Avenue office, however, was only drifting further from the elite consensus that was felt by many professional Democrats and expressed spikily in the press. In December Frank Bruni wrote in the *Times* that Biden's boosters were "of unsound mind" because they believed in "a man who failed miserably at two previous campaigns for the nomination, the first one all the way back in 1988, a year before Alexandria Ocasio-Cortez was born," and who "spent nearly forty-five years in Washington, a proper noun that's a dirty word in presidential politics." (He softened the blow by titling the column, "I Like Joe Biden. I Urge Him Not to Run.") This wasn't long after *Politico Magazine* had called Biden "a deeply flawed candidate who's out of step with the mood of his party" (Headline: "Joe Biden Is the Front-runner. Uh-oh.") and soon before Mehdi Hasan argued in *The Intercept* that Biden would be "an utter disaster both as the Democratic nominee and as president" because of his "shocking inability (refusal?) to see that Trump is a symptom of long-standing Republican nihilism and derangement—not the cause of it."

Unprinted opinions were harsher. Though Biden's possible rivals could also see that he was leading the early polls before anyone had even announced his or her candidacy, they were convinced this was simply a product of nostalgia and Biden's name recognition, and that his standing would slip dramatically as soon as others started introducing themselves, let alone attacking him. Versions of "the first day of his candidacy would be his best" became a common refrain in Democratic circles, as did reminders that no modern Democrat had won the presidency if they'd run before, and that one obvious and related takeaway from the midterms was the party's appetite for new faces.

In response, Biden got both atypically philosophical and predictably defensive. He still believed his go-to aphorism that "in politics you're either on your way up or on your way down," and he had no interest in losing a messy primary only to feel sidelined again in the general election before being forced into retirement. But he had experienced enough real, personal grief for multiple lifetimes; he was, by the end of 2018, a seventy-six-year-old with the weight of not just two failed presidential campaigns but four agonizing near-campaigns under his belt already. It wasn't political loss that worried him. He knew the territory. He disagreed with the prevailing analysis, anyway—he believed Trump, his own profile, and the emerging shape of the primary combined to render comparisons to 1988 or 2008 fatuous.

He kept hearing from people who agreed, and some of them might be legitimately useful allies to have. Biden and Ricchetti both kept in touch regularly with Harry Reid, who was retired in Las Vegas but still in control of his state party's political machinery and holding some power over their influential caucuses. Soon after the midterms Biden also caught up for forty minutes over the phone with Harold Schaitberger, whose firefighters' union had boosted Biden in 2015 by effectively unendorsing Clinton. Schaitberger told him he couldn't promise an endorsement this time before his group went through its formal process, but that he had no doubt his members would be with the ex-VP from Day One. When Brendan Boyle, a young Philadelphia-area congressman, soon visited Biden in DC for what was supposed to be a thirty-minute drop-in, he pointed out that history since the 1970s showed that Democratic primaries tend to be won by the candidate who best appeals to working-class voters, both Black and white. The only time progressive intellectuals got their pick was in 2008, he continued, but that was because African American voters had also backed Obama. Biden, Boyle said, fit the winning mold and could win back Pennsylvania, while all his likely opponents were too much like failed candidates Gary Hart, Paul Tsongas, or Howard Dean.

Biden nodded along as the meeting galloped toward an hour and perked up when Boyle took a step back and warned that a second Trump term would transform the country into something different from the one their Irish ancestors had come to. These bigger-picture appeals were what really stuck with Biden, even when they came from old friends who were themselves no longer relevant politically. He was especially heartened by encouragement from Bill Nelson, who'd lost his Florida Senate seat in

November after a campaign rife with veiled accusations about his own advanced age and fitness for office. (Nelson was only two months older than Biden.)

And yet Biden wasn't really moving forward. He told Boyle in December that he was 60 percent of the way to running, then proceeded to blow through multiple self-imposed deadlines by which to make a final decision as 2019 neared. First it was "by the end of the year," then "around January first," then "after the holidays," before, in December, he said he'd decide "in six weeks to two months," and people close to him started wondering if he wouldn't be wise to wait until after the first quarter of 2019 to avoid fundraising comparisons to other candidates who might launch then with more online fanfare and better preparation. It quickly became exhausting both to members of his inner circle who were readying a campaign and to potential hires, plenty of whom backed out of assumed jobs with a campaign that showed no signs of launching, leaving Biden without staffers lined up in strategically necessary states. On days when Biden sounded like he was 75 percent of the way there, he would talk to advisors and potential donors about how ready he was to squash Trump's ideology; on days when it was more like 25 percent he still sounded worried about whether he was making the right decision, since he risked sacrificing his role as beloved elder statesman and making his final career chapter a depressing failure rather than the triumph of the Obama years. He knew a primary would be bruising even if he won it, and that he'd almost certainly have to answer for his former bank-friendly position on bankruptcy policy and his role in the Anita Hill hearings. He also clearly couldn't avoid a public reevaluation of his 1994 crime bill, widely regarded as the source of disproportionate incarceration rates of Black Americans and one of Sanders's favorite punching bags. Biden had no doubt he was ready to meet the moment. But had the moment already left him behind?

In Wilmington and Virginia, he was still acting like a candidate-to-be, discussing donor outreach and possible endorsers, and also spending far more time than was rational making policy plans—on taxes, health care, and Russia, among other topics—for a campaign that clearly wouldn't be fought along wonky lines. In private he talked so much like he thought he was already president that aides had to specifically make sure he knew he couldn't slip and accidentally mention a campaign in public, since that would ruin their rollout plans and trigger the legal process formally declaring his candidacy. But at the end of some hours-long policy-focused sessions in McLean, Schultz and Bedingfield would still stand in the driveway and wonder aloud: What did that meeting mean? Had he fully decided to run yet?

* * *

From the perspective of an innocent liberal bystander, it might have been reasonable to assume at this point that a restoration was on deck—that the theoretically thriving political partnership that had been in power for eight years would return and fulfill its natural conclusion to save the country from Trump. Now, perhaps, was the moment where Obama could step in and take Biden arm in arm back to the White House, the retired inspirer emerging to vouch for the old romantic promising to calm the waters and heal the nation's wounds. The reality, however, wasn't just less fantastic but almost surgical in its choreographed distance, all thanks to Obama.

Biden, of course, wasn't alone. By late 2018 the list of Democrats who were thinking about running for president at least somewhat seriously— either out of a real conviction that they could win or a more casual "If Trump can do it, so can I" attitude—stretched beyond four dozen, by far the largest field of potential candidates in modern American history. Considering Obama's pledge to empower a new generation of leaders post–White House, he couldn't exactly regard this as a bad thing, even if the primary looked like it might devolve into chaos if the roster of contenders—which ranged from governors to mayors to TV lawyers to bored billionaires—didn't edit itself down a bit. Still, with little interest in playing a determinative role at this stage in the prerace but also feeling a lingering urge not to exit the game entirely, Obama offered himself up as a consultant to the Democrats considering a run. He made it known via whispered word of mouth that he'd be willing to meet and offer some advice on running a campaign in his West End office for a session that some started calling "the pilgrimage" and a younger cohort compared to "office hours" with a professor.

Neither Obama nor his remaining staff, spearheaded by political and comms advisor Eric Schultz, ever reached out to any of the candidates directly, figuring that if they were serious they would know how to find him. They recognized the precarity of these meetings—Obama knew his every utterance was being dissected and that any leaks or misconstrued comments could dramatically change the primary's direction—so before the visitors arrived, Schultz or one of his deputies would warn their staff that they were not to say a word about the sessions. When the Democrats would then get to the building, they'd usually sit on the sofa in Obama's inner office for around an hour, more if it was going well, and pick his brain from across the coffee table. He usually started with the same shtick, whether he knew his visitor or not. He'd caution them not to run unless they thought they could win, urge them to consider what a campaign could do to their family, and counsel them solemnly that they refrain from going any further if they didn't think they were the best person to be president in the first place. Thus came and went a steady stream of senators—Kamala Harris, Michael Bennet, Elizabeth Warren, Bernie Sanders, Cory Booker, Kirsten Gillibrand, Jeff Merkley, Amy Klobuchar, to name a few—governors—Jay Inslee, John Hickenlooper, Steve Bullock—mayors—Eric Garcetti, Mitch Landrieu, Pete Buttigieg—members of Congress, and others.

Obama had been thinking about 2020 ever since Trump had won, of course, but he'd always kept his cards close to the vest and rarely said anything about specific potential candidates to anyone, especially leery of having his private handicapping become public knowledge. In person in the office, he rarely strayed from the script unless he already knew his visitor, or if someone caught him on an oddly introspective day or asked especially good questions.

In those cases, he liked to talk about his own experience—it took him about a year before he hit his campaign stride in 2007, he said to some, but added that he didn't fully appreciate how hard the experience would be for himself or for Michelle or their daughters. If the candidates appeared to be onto something, or asked for logistical advice, Obama directed them to Plouffe, but he insisted that if they were really going to do this they'd better be fully convinced of their plan, since there was no such thing as a half-assed campaign.

The thickest-skinned and naivest of the bunch asked Obama to evaluate their strengths and weaknesses. Obama rarely held back, and sometimes this tough talk gave the visitors pause. He was discouraging with Garcetti, for one, figuring the LA mayor wasn't well known enough and didn't have a clear enough vision. Garcetti opted against running. More often, they insisted they had what it took no matter what Obama said. After meeting with a procession of wannabes, Obama was unconvinced that many were anywhere close to as prepared for a campaign as he'd been as a novice senator, which was saying something. Some, he thought, had promise but needed to figure out how exactly they would make their appeal. This described Harris. Others still had impressive records but essentially no recognition beyond their jurisdiction, so were bordering on delusional. To Bullock, Obama warned, "The problem is nobody knows you. They know you as much as this guy named Pete."

This wasn't a total insult—Obama had actually been impressed by the brains, charisma, and chutzpah of the thirty-something mayor of a small midwestern city. When they'd met, Buttigieg, who is gay, had asked Obama about the nuances of talking about identity on the campaign trail, and spoke confidently about how the party could reach overlooked voters. Obama just doubted it would all add up to viability in a presidential campaign where image and fame mattered immensely—he thought Buttigieg was too short and, as a former volunteer for Obama in 2008, seemed too young—and where such a large field would make breaking through that much harder.

Still, with long-shot candidates he previously knew he was slightly less biting, if still honest. He told Julián Castro, his former housing secretary, that when he had launched his own campaign he figured he had a 30 percent chance of winning. So, he suggested to the candidate with far slimmer odds than that, you never knew what could happen. When he met with Bennet, a quiet but serious senator who wasn't particularly well known but whom Obama had once considered for secretary of education, the ex-president was encouraging when it came to the actual substance of the presidency. Bennet could be good at it, he said. But, he warned, the Coloradoan had no obvious role to play in a rollicking campaign. How exactly did he propose to stand out? This was going to be a three-ring circus.

Biden didn't pay it much mind when he heard Obama was taking these meetings. So were both Clintons and so, for that matter, was he. Obama, however, read 2018's positive midterm results as vindication of his strategy of stepping back from the daily fray for the party's benefit, and he started telling visitors more openly that he had no intention of getting actively involved in the presidential primary at all once it started in earnest—especially not to endorse. Biden had always been realistic about this. No one expected him to get his old boss's formal endorsement from the start, given Obama's distance from politics these days. But there was also no way around the fact that Obama's posture was at least a bit of a slight—however implicit—since supporting anyone else would mean rejecting his longtime partner, and he was at least theoretically staying open to it as long as he didn't explicitly back Biden. It meant he was making the active and ongoing decision not to support Biden. Obama denied this whenever anyone surfaced the notion, of course, invariably insisting that his own tough primary against Clinton had only improved his candidacy, so why shouldn't he encourage a lively one?

But even beyond the matter of Biden, neutrality was complicated territory for Obama, who had two other close friends considering campaigns, as well. Eric Holder, for one, was talking about 2020, though only preliminarily. The other was former Massachusetts governor Deval Patrick, a close Obama ally who was also friends with Jarrett. Axelrod and Plouffe had worked for him and used his 2006 campaign to test digital organizing methods ahead of Obama's presidential run. He was Simas's old boss, too. Obama, though, had a good reason for staying quiet even beyond the awkwardness of his personal relationships. He didn't want to be seen as putting his thumb on the scale after Sanders's fans believed the party's institutions had unfairly handed Clinton the nomination in 2016 and plenty then soured on the Democrats. The party couldn't afford to see this dynamic repeated.

What Obama did want, however, was to make sure his party picked a winner, and in some of his longer conversations with potential candidates from his technocratic liberal side of the party he mused about how to reckon with the newly empowered left. Even relatively moderate candidates would have to be willing to stretch their usual policy boundaries now, he said, and even if they weren't comfortable getting all the way to supporting something like Medicare for All, they had to be careful not to diminish the goal of such a proposal. "We're now in a world where you can't rule out policies because they're expensive," he would point out, a fact he found to be theoretically encouraging but mostly frustrating, considering his insistence on practicality and the political limitations he had faced in 2009 and 2010. Still, Obama was coming around to some new ways of thinking, albeit gingerly. In his first political speech out of office, in September 2018, he'd praised Medicare for All and a handful of Warren's priorities, like putting workers on corporate boards, as "good new ideas." Off mic, he was wary about being left behind politically just as his legacy was starting to be debated in the party—he wanted to make clear that he knew he'd been elected a political lifetime ago. The ACA, he would say, was intended to be like a starter home, not a final policy, and the presidency was like a relay race. Progress was the whole point. Still, he'd always end those chats in his office by insisting that a race to the left wasn't the way to win over real primary voters with real everyday concerns beyond MSNBC's horse race coverage. He said as much to the victorious House Democrats after the midterms, and tried reminding them that they would, eventually, need to worry about the price tags of their proposals—which at the time included a hotly debated Green New Deal framework proposing historic climate-focused investments—now that they were in power.

His meeting with Sanders was cordial, though their stylistic and ideological differences had only grown since 2016, with Sanders in the Hill trenches and Obama detached from the fray. The senator wanted to make sure Obama wouldn't weigh in against him, and Obama reassured him and pivoted to his central question: How was the Vermonter planning on persuading people who didn't already agree with his call for a political revolution? Sanders disagreed with the skepticism embedded in Obama's question—he thought he would win if he could get as much turnout as possible from usually marginalized groups and disaffected voters—but said he appreciated that it was a rational concern. Obama's two-hour sit-down with Warren was warmer, which was surely helped by the ex-president's daughters becoming big fans of the senator and letting him know it. It was a welcome turnaround from his uncomfortable 2017 encounter with Warren. He walked away from the session believing she obviously had more talent than anyone else who might run, and probably more intelligence. He just couldn't figure out how she was going to win over working-class voters.

As Obama saw it, the challenge for all these candidates was going to be replicating his coalition—blowing out turnout by appealing enough to young voters and minorities without losing too many older whites—which he considered Democrats' obvious avenue to victory, not a path unique to his talents, profile, and moment. He still hadn't decided which candidate he thought could get this done by late 2018, and he answered most attempts to figure out the one he favored by insisting he simply wanted to lift up the party's future leaders, like forty-five-year-old Stacey Abrams in Georgia and thirty-nine-year-old Floridian Andrew Gillum, who'd both narrowly lost midterm gubernatorial races, but neither of whom was running for president. Still, some of his old political staffers were starting to place their bets. Anzalone and Anita Dunn were with Biden, but ad maker Jim Margolis and pollster David Binder signed up with Harris, digital strategist Joe Rospars with Warren, and organizing chief Mitch Stewart, who'd kept close with Obama after he left office, was advising Michael Bloomberg, who was still thinking about running.

In Obama's innermost circle, however, attention was mostly elsewhere. Obama had watched with interest in the midterms as lanky forty-six-year-old Texas congressman Beto O'Rourke had come shockingly close to winning a Senate seat, raising unheard-of sums of cash and livestreaming his skateboard-and-rock-music-heavy campaign to the masses while building a national following in the process. He was now considering whether to spin that near-success into a presidential run, and some Obama White House alums made no secret that they saw in O'Rourke some traces of Obama's capacity to inspire, so started emailing around a bumper sticker mockup mashing his "BETO" campaign logo up with the famous O design from Obama's 2008 bid. Obama dispatched Plouffe to meet with O'Rourke, and the two started talking often, roping in Obama's former Iowa guru Paul Tewes for sessions in El Paso. Some of Obama's top donors bought in, too: private-equity exec Mark Gallogly flew to Texas to meet with him and ex-ambassador to the UK Louis Susman started building a network of Obama fundraisers for him on Wall Street. Dan Pfeiffer, the former senior Obama White House advisor, wrote an article making "The Case for Beto O'Rourke," and as O'Rourke got closer to announcing a campaign he also called Robert Wolf, the former bank exec and Obama economic advisor turned golf buddy.

Some of this was happening in public, or close to it, and was being widely read as implied support from Obama himself. He wouldn't go that far, but in private he did tell friends that O'Rourke's Senate campaign had impressed him and he talked to Jen O'Malley Dillon, who was considering taking a job running the campaign, about the importance of stepping up to defeat Trump. She started in El Paso soon after.

Obama's closest allies weren't just lining up behind O'Rourke, though. Buttigieg was cultivating a healthy contingent of his own Obamans, largely thanks to his growing relationship with Axelrod, who was talking him up to anyone who would listen. Axelrod saw him as a plausible answer to the question he always asked when evaluating candidates: Who is the remedy to the incumbent? It didn't take long for Larry Grisolano and Joel Benenson to sign on with Buttigieg, too, or for Obama's former fundraising chief Rufus Gifford to argue that "Obama was the Pete or Beto candidate in 2007: He was new, he was talking about the future, he was very nontraditional."

It was Patrick, though—an Obama Foundation board member who kept in regular touch with Obama, Jarrett, and Simas—who got perhaps the most meaningful nod despite being frequently ignored by pundits because he'd been out of office for a while. A few months into Trump's presidency, Wolf hosted a panel at a hedge fund conference in Las Vegas and gave his two participants, Jarrett and Jeb Bush, a heads-up before they began: he would ask them whom Democrats would nominate next. Bush named Biden, who was also at the conference. Jarrett also knew that Biden was there. She still predicted Patrick.

Her answer raised eyebrows, including Biden's. He'd started making a show of reading articles about ObamaWorld's interest in O'Rourke, Buttigieg, and Patrick in particular. "You believe this shit?" he'd ask whoever was around.

* * *

He believed it. Obama and Biden had, for about a year, been trying to make a point of talking every few weeks. The chats were still mostly casual and usually over the phone—they laughed about the publication of a murder mystery novel starring the two of them, which Biden proudly displayed at home—but just as Obama had spent much of 2014 and 2015 trying to divine Biden's intentions about 2016, he was now trying to work out just how definite his plans were for 2020. Biden sure sounded like he was running, but when their calls turned to politics he used Obama more as a therapist or sounding board than as a political advisor or equal partner. As 2019 approached, Obama could tell Biden was probably going to run, and he told his aides that the ex-VP deserved a serious hearing.

But he had plenty of questions, and even more concerns that couldn't be easily answered. Obama had whispered to friends that he strongly doubted Biden could create the kind of inspiring connection with the first-to-vote Iowans and New Hampshirites that Obama once had, and which he would need to seriously compete. Obama struggled with what to do with that belief, in part since he hated getting too involved with campaigns that he didn't think would win—*especially* in Democratic primaries—and his worry only increased when he asked Biden about who he'd hired for his prospective campaign and heard about only the old, predictable names. It was not, he griped privately, "an A-team" like the one Biden would probably need to get back in touch with the modern party and discourage his worst habits—like his loquaciousness and lack of interest in fundraising—which had helped doom his last campaigns.

Obama was particularly certain that Biden and his advisors simply didn't understand internet-era campaigning, and he and his own aides remained especially unimpressed by a series of self-consciously corny tweets Biden's staff had been sending every once in a while from his official account depicting a pair of children's friendship bracelets reading JOE and BARACK. There were obvious political dynamics to consider, too: Obama knew well, and often repeated, that no Democrat older than fifty-five had been elected to the presidency in six decades. And though Obama remained skeptical of Sanders's wing of the party, he had no doubt about it being where the energy was. So wouldn't Biden quickly be exposed as out of touch? When Obama bounced these notions off his advisors, no one disagreed.

What occupied him more, though, was Joe himself. Obama had thought his old VP seemed tired ever since they'd first caught up after leaving office, and the prospect of him going through a draining campaign seemed unthinkably painful. His concern was reputational, too. Obama figured that if Biden's campaign failed, which seemed likely, the former VP's legacy and ultimately his memory would be painted by that embarrassment—as would Obama's. Wouldn't he want to go out on top, with the public's final memory of him more "Medal of Freedom" than "1 percent in Iowa"? The problem, as Obama saw it, was that he couldn't say anything like this to Biden himself, not after the way 2016 had ended. Biden hadn't forgotten their searing White House chat about how Biden wanted to spend the rest of his life, even though Obama didn't resurface it. Surely Obama couldn't bring the topic back up, he felt. He could tell Biden was still sure that he could have saved the country from Trump had his personal circumstances been different in 2015—and had Obama, and especially his political advisors, just gotten out of his way.

As a result, Obama felt his hands were tied. He was left sitting in his office quietly, wondering if maybe some other candidate would catch enough fire before Biden even launched to dissuade him from trying.

So when they finally started talking about it outright, Obama's message was crafted to be caring, not calculating, even if his hope to convince Biden was obvious to the ex-VP. Obama asked Biden if he thought he really wanted to go through with a campaign, since he *really* didn't have to. *You don't have anything left to prove,* he insisted, trying not to make it seem like he was strong-arming Biden out of running so much as hoping to provide him with breathing room to make the correct decision away from the heat of the political moment. Obama outlined his worries about Biden's legacy and emotions—he just didn't want to see him get hurt, he said—but Biden had no trouble decoding Obama, and stood fast. He wasn't going to go through this again. He had a chance to remove Trump from office, he said, and simply couldn't abide passing that up.

Late in January 2019, Biden pulled Obama's old friend and advisor Al Sharpton aside for a gut-check. He was in New York City for the reverend's annual Martin Luther King Jr. Day breakfast event, and, standing in the green room before his speech with Sharpton and Martin Luther King III, he started talking solemnly about Charlottesville, then said he was thinking about running. Sharpton replied by posing Obama's question more directly than the president had. "You have to make up your mind: Do you really want it?" he asked Biden. "Because right now you'll go down in history as the vice president at an epochal moment. Do you want to risk that if you lose?" Biden seemed unfazed. Sharpton was right, he said, "But we've got to do something about the direction of the country." He'd started repeating this point whenever anyone asked him about 2020, and soon added an addendum: he would happily step aside if he was given reason to believe any of his prospective competitors could actually beat Trump.

To Biden, Trump was a monster with one special political power: defining people, especially enemies, in the public eye. That meant it would take someone with a precemented reputation to take Trump on, he figured, and his advisors were starting to believe the primary itself would be shaped by the question of who seemed best positioned to win the general election. So sure, Biden was as impressed as anyone by Buttigieg, but he also thought everyone was kidding themselves. The guy had gotten destroyed in the piddling race for DNC chair in 2017, so how was he going to be the party's presidential nominee? And Beto? He was good, but he lost his Senate race to Ted Cruz, the most hated senator around. Plus, Biden suspected O'Rourke had thrown the race away by refusing to hire a pollster. What was the realistic case for Booker? Warren? Harris? During the midterms Biden had pitched himself as the guy best positioned to excite Obama-missing liberals while winning back former Democrats who'd gone for Trump, and he proposed to do the same now for a national audience by focusing on the fight for the soul of the nation while his opponents waged a different, smaller battle for their party's heart.

He no longer thought he had good arguments not to do it, and he started telling confidants that he felt called to run as he finally began building out a full-size team under Greg Schultz. He just had to make a few fundamental decisions, like whether he should heed the unsolicited and mostly unwelcome advice he'd been getting from some quarters and announce preemptively that he'd only serve for one term, promising to retire at eighty-two. It was worth discussing, he supposed, but he mostly hated the notion. Or maybe he should announce a running mate from Day One to get buzz and distract from his age, an updated version of his briefly considered 2007 ploy for attention. Without even telling him, some of his allies zeroed in on Stacey Abrams, the dynamic speaker and voting rights crusader who'd nearly become the country's first Black woman governor in November 2018. But Biden hadn't changed, so of course he just kept the idea vaguely alive, but unaddressed, long enough for it to fizzle.

* * *

And then Obama did something uncharacteristic. He ever so briefly got excited. As spring 2019 approached and dozens of candidates kept piling into the race, he finally conceded that there were no two ways around it: Biden really was going to run, and if that was going to happen, Obama at least wanted to know what his friend, the man who had some claim to his record, was up to. The problem was that Biden's launch looked like it was happening in slow motion, so Obama summoned Anita Dunn to the West End and asked her to bring the people in charge of Biden's comms and digital operations.

When Dunn and Bedingfield arrived with a pair of midlevel aides it quickly became apparent that their job was to reassure the ex-president.

Obama opened the meeting by laying out his worries: the political environment was brutal these days, so he wanted to make sure Biden's image would be protected aggressively in what was likely to be his final act as a public servant. Obama had an hour marked off on his calendar for the session, and he launched into a back-and-forth with Dunn and Bedingfield. He asked for details: What would the kickoff look like, and how were they planning to make the case for Biden? They explained that the idea was to argue that Biden was the "antidote" to Trump, to which Obama replied that they might still run into problems with the party's progressives on big issues like immigration, where activists had sometimes clashed with their administration. Dunn and Bedingfield agreed, and admitted that their challenge would be to present Biden as a change agent after his long, well-documented career. After two hours Obama was more satisfied but he made sure his visitors understood that if this all unraveled they wouldn't be disappointing just Biden, they'd be letting Obama down, too.

A less diplomatic staff-to-staff conversation followed. Obama had already explained to Biden his reasoning for staying away from an endorsement, and Eric Schultz had been keeping in touch with Bedingfield and others as a general quality-control check on Obama's behalf and to coordinate their message as journalists wrote about the Obama-Biden relationship ahead of the campaign launch. Now they just had to work out the nuts and bolts of how Biden could talk about Obama in public, a politically fraught proposition for the pair that was outwardly insisting there was no substantive distance between them, even as Obama withheld his endorsement, and even as Biden's verbal discipline showed no signs of improving. They settled on a plan to hand the 2012 campaign's email list over to Biden and to have Obama's spokeswoman Katie Hill issue a rare statement praising Biden once he launched his campaign—something no other candidate got. Biden, in turn, would be free to invoke Obama as he made nostalgic appeals and discussed their record, but he had to be vigilant about not implying that he had his ex-boss's support. He could use video and images of them, too—everyone knew he would obviously deploy the emotional Medal of Freedom speech prominently, considering how he still talked about what "we" had accomplished and even used Obama's signature walk-up music at his appearances during the midterms—but only if the clips and pictures were already publicly available and unaltered.

Both Obama and Biden signed off on the plan, and Biden started talking differently about Obama in private, clearly chuffed to be back in more frequent contact and thrilled to be working on something like a joint project with him again—so much so that a few times during planning sessions in Delaware he ostentatiously started to describe conversations he'd had with "Barack—I mean President Obama" only to cut himself off and say, "actually, I'll keep that between us."

But the flurry of activity had the opposite impact on Obama, who felt himself getting dangerously close to straying from his long-held insistence on not weighing in on intraparty fights. He was also running up against his revulsion at becoming a political football if the extent of this coordination leaked. He and his team pulled back a bit to maintain neutrality, and the calls slowed back to a trickle. When asked, they offered an explanation that could easily have been read as a rationalization: Obama wouldn't be doing Biden any favors by putting his finger on the scale for him. Biden would emerge stronger if he did it alone.

Biden's slowly growing political team figured this wasn't much of a problem, at least to start, since while his ties to Obama were an important part of his support levels among Black voters especially, research undertaken separately by Anzalone and fellow pollster Celinda Lake showed most Americans had little grasp of what, exactly, he'd done as VP. Anyway, the shape of his appeal was fundamentally different from what Obama's had been. He struggled with younger voters but did better with old ones, especially white ones, and was more convincing when he leaned on his empathy rather than messaging about making change. He could talk about Obama plenty, but he couldn't run as an Obama retread even if he wanted to.

Instead, he set out in the early spring to gather an arsenal of endorsers for a show of force to present himself as the party's juggernaut. He tried recruiting Terry McAuliffe, the ex–Virginia governor and DNC chair who was considering a run of his own, to lead his fundraising efforts. He asked Reid for his support, as he also wooed House Majority Whip Jim Clyburn, the most influential Democrat in South Carolina, and labor leaders like AFL-CIO president Richard Trumka. That this approach smacked of old-school, antiquated campaigning ("That's so Hillary," said one Obama friend, sighing) wasn't as troubling to Biden's supporters as the fact that almost none of his top targets signed on, with the exception of Schaitberger's firefighters.

And, as always, Biden's family loomed larger than his underwhelming political maneuvering. He'd been trying to keep the latest painful developments extraquiet, even as far as Obama was concerned. Kathleen and Hunter had split in 2016 as his drug use and infidelity spiraled following Beau's death, and for a while he and Hallie, Beau's widow, then became a couple. Joe Biden only found out when the *New York Post*'s *Page Six* started sniffing around, and he and Jill issued a quick statement professing to be happy for them without mentioning Kathleen—an omission that offended her friends, a group that still included Michelle Obama. The intervening years hadn't been much better for Hunter, whom Biden had trouble contacting for days at a time until he checked into rehab in February 2019. That didn't take, though, and Hunter grew furious and bolted from Wilmington when Joe and Jill then tried holding an intervention for him a few weeks later.

It was within these unsettled waters that Biden approached his campaign launch in fits and starts, first considering kicking off with a rally in either Scranton, Pittsburgh, Gettysburg (Donilon's favored option), or Charlottesville, which seemed like a natural fit. Quickly, though, the inner circle second-guessed itself: Could they be certain neo-Nazi protesters wouldn't show up if he appeared there? He couldn't pop up in town and film an announcement video unnoticed, could he? (No.) They finally settled on a video *about* Charlottesville, in which Biden insisted, "I believe history will look back on four years of this president and all that he embraces as an aberrant moment in time," before an informal kickoff at a union hall in Pittsburgh and then a bigger rally in Philadelphia meant to hammer home his message of unity and his intention to vanquish Trump's ideology. Biden was rusty overlooking the crowd of about six thousand, which was significant in size but still noticeably smaller than the opening audiences drawn by some of his competitors. A chair that had been reserved for Hunter remained empty. But Biden hit his stride when he brought up Obama as a contrast to Trump. "Barack Obama is an extraordinary man, I watched up close, his character, his courage, his vision. He was a president our children could, and did, look up to," he said while pitching himself as the natural next step, earning his biggest applause of the afternoon whenever Obama's name was mentioned.

It didn't take long before Biden's team rolled out a video featuring the Medal of Freedom ceremony, after briefly considering using it as the launch clip. By then Biden's campaign Instagram accounts featured the pair laughing together, and Obama's face peppered his Facebook ads, too. This was just days after Biden had laughed off a reporter's question about his ideology by replying, "I'm an Obama-Biden Democrat, man."

Obama, all the while, stayed silent, even when Biden insisted to his press pack at Wilmington's Amtrak station, "I asked President Obama not to endorse," before slipping over his own words. "He doesn't want to—this—we should—whoever wins this nomination should win it on their own merits." Watching from Washington, Obama couldn't help but laugh.

CHAPTER 18

2019

Obama told anyone who asked that he wasn't following the primary that closely: He'd tune in fully when the general election came around, but he had better things to do than dedicate himself to the daily back-and-forth until then, and he wasn't about to start watching cable news again after avoiding it for years. This was true in spirit, and the explanation usually worked. Friends tended to change the subject after they invariably shared their own punditry and realized it was futile to try to get his take. It was also true that the ex-president wasn't exactly setting his schedule around the never-ending parade of debates. But it might have been hard to find anyone who was reading the *Times*' coverage more closely on their iPad every day, or who was quicker with an eye roll and an exhaled "this is a shitshow" whenever he did walk by a TV that an aide had tuned to CNN in the office.

Part of the problem was that the candidates weren't letting him ignore them. At one early debate both Julián Castro and New York City mayor Bill de Blasio laid into his administration's record of deporting undocumented immigrants, and Hawaii congresswoman Tulsi Gabbard argued that his signature health-care law had been written by "big insurance companies and big pharmaceutical companies who've been profiting off the backs of sick people"—an especially inflammatory version of an argument that others were implicitly making: Obama's approach to health care had been too conservative, and perhaps this was true for plenty of other matters, too. Obama's allies were outraged. DNC chief Tom Perez told some of the candidates they were being idiots and, considering how popular Obama still was, alienating the party's most important voters. At home in Kalorama, Obama didn't let Castro, de Blasio, or Gabbard offend him personally. They didn't matter; they clearly had no shot at winning.

What bothered him more was the direction of the overall conversation, especially as Sanders's Medicare for All proposal became a focal point of debate, and the ACA came in for hours of sidelong but nonetheless nationally broadcast pokes. Obama was encouraged by the energy coursing through the contest but couldn't see how any of this talk was particularly productive toward the end goal of beating Trump. He started conceding to confidants that he was still unimpressed with the field, unconvinced that any of the Democrats were proving they could win. And though some of them—Harris, Buttigieg, O'Rourke, and Minnesota senator Amy Klobuchar included—called him every once in a while for general advice, they almost never had specific questions that might actually help them, and he couldn't figure out why. It also didn't help that his thoughts on the primary were proceeding on two separate tracks. The first was broad: *Is anything happening that will hurt the eventual nominee, no matter who it ends up being?* The second was more directed: *What's going on with Joe?*

The answer to the latter question was even less encouraging by summertime 2019, when the debates began. Due to the sheer size of the field, the candidates split into two separate nights for the first showdown in Miami, and Biden was randomly put on the second stage. He was still the national polling leader by a wide margin, but few of his opponents or analysts in the press—or Obama—had seen any reason to revise their dim view of his prospects in the campaign's opening months. So when the first ten candidates squared off, not one even mentioned the theoretical front-runner's name. As far as they were concerned, it wasn't worth it—Biden was still a popular enough guy that attacking him might backfire among rank-and-file voters. But that's all he was; no one saw him as their biggest real long-term threat. It seemed so likely that he would soon fade from relevance that they could simply wait for his supporters to drift away from him without going to the trouble of even alluding to him.

He was, they were pretty sure, hopelessly retrograde and out of touch with an electorate he hadn't faced without Obama in over a decade. Earlier in June he'd told a glitzy fundraiser crowd at the Upper East Side Carlyle Hotel that, when he would set out to combat income inequality as president, "No one's standard of living will change, nothing would fundamentally change." His horrified opponents and critics read the comment as a promise not to dramatically reshuffle the American economy and society, which they considered necessary. It was of a piece with his oft-repeated pledge to return the country to a pre-Trump "normal," which also put him at odds with most of his opponents and, they assumed, their voters. They wanted progress, not restoration.

It wasn't just the politics that made him look like he'd beamed in from another era. Even before launching his campaign he'd had to defend his heavily tactile style after a handful of women said they felt he'd touched them inappropriately through the years. He said that while he had always been affectionate, he understood standards of personal space had changed, and promised to adapt. Only in June did he reverse his long-held position on the Hyde Amendment, now opposing the measure that prohibits federal funding for most abortions—a stance many Democrats and most progressives had held for years. That wasn't long after he'd called Anita Hill to apologize for her treatment in front of his committee nearly three decades earlier, though she hadn't accepted it. And he'd also just recently apologized after once again reminiscing at the Carlyle fundraiser about his decades-old work with segregationist senators while trying to make a point about bipartisanship. "I was in a caucus with James O. Eastland. He never called me 'boy,' he always called me 'son,'" Biden had said of the former Mississippi senator, also bringing up former Georgia senator Herman Talmadge. "At least there was some civility," he said. "We got things done. We didn't agree on much of anything. We got things done, we got it finished. But today, you look at the other side and you're the enemy." Cory Booker of New Jersey, a rival candidate and one of just three Black senators, led the criticism of Biden this time, arguing that he was clearly missing the gravity of what he was saying about cooperating with racists.

Biden thus walked into his final days of debate prep as if on eggshells, internalizing specific warnings from aides to be careful about how he addressed women and minority candidates in Miami to avoid more accusations of insensitivity. Four times in his last practice sessions he walked through ways to discuss his complicated record on school busing, figuring that it might arise in the context of the segregationists. But he was still caught off guard when it did come up, surfaced as it was by a candidate he considered an ally. He'd gotten to know Kamala Harris, after all, through Beau—they'd worked closely together as state attorneys general—and he couldn't believe she was the one to essentially accuse him of being on the wrong side of civil rights history, a wound that felt even deeper when he learned after the debate that it was all planned out: her campaign had T-shirts designed around the exchange ready to post online for sale.

This was standard modern politics, but nonetheless a jarring wake-up call for Biden, who took the opportunity to step back and survey a scene that, he could no longer deny, was far more bitter and emotional than he'd anticipated or previously experienced. None of it stopped him from trying to remain jovial and chummy, like a friendly uncle, backstage at the debates. He greeted some other candidates like old friends, always chatted with the support staff, and even once ribbed Booker about dragging his feet on proposing to his then-girlfriend, actress Rosario Dawson. But in prep he was warier, more careful about recognizing the unforgiving landscape. It became clear that not even the rhetorical device he'd been using to stop himself from rambling would cut it anymore. Onstage in Miami he'd tried to forestall questions about his age and tendency to talk and talk and talk by repeating a line whenever he sensed himself going on too long. Now, though, it scanned as a bit too on-the-nose. He had to stop saying "Anyway, my time is up, I'm sorry."

The perception that Biden was plummeting didn't come just from the debate stage. His political troops had begun the campaign by openly laying out his path to the nomination: no matter what happened in Iowa and New Hampshire, he'd do well enough in Nevada, and then especially South Carolina, to sweep to victory. The idea was to narrow the field to him and just one other candidate, presumably Sanders, after South Carolina, at which point Black voters would be able to flex their political might within the Democratic Party and crown Biden following "Super Tuesday," when a huge proportion of delegates toward the nomination would be awarded from states with more diverse populations. So the inner circle was shaken after Harris's attack—she could, presumably, dislodge his support among his key voters—but then heartened when their first postdebate focus group with Black South Carolinians revealed the opposite. Everyone at that table told the moderator a story about their family's interactions with the state's longtime segregationist senator Strom Thurmond and some said that they agreed with Biden: his ability to work with those old racists was evidence that he could bring people together, and no one thought he himself was a racist after his time with Obama. Greg Schultz started calling the campaign's South Carolina state director after each debate for a gut-check of the older Black women she'd watch it with. They stuck with Biden. Still, the ex-VP had to get as far as South Carolina in the first place for this to matter electorally. And his central case to the pundit class—and eventually to voters—that he could be uniting and reassuring enough to beat Trump in the general election became harder to make as his numbers dropped in New Hampshire, and then Iowa.

If no one was surprised that progressive New Hampshire was inter-ested in its lefty neighbors, Sanders and Warren, Biden's Iowa problem was more severe. He'd lost out on several top hires by dragging his feet on announcing his campaign, and the team he did end up with was largely out of practice in the state. The guy running the operation wasn't even a full-time resident anymore, leading to a creaky infrastructure—no one told Biden he was sitting next to the state party's influential chairman at one event until Tom Vilsack did it for them—and instead of camping out in the disproportionately Catholic industrial hot spots in the eastern part of the state, as Iowa pols expected, Biden's travel seemed scattershot. He was proving a lackluster campaigner, too, both talking way longer than he should at town halls and getting agitated when progressive activists inter-rupted his events to insist on more urgency on climate change or immi-gration. His crowds thinned, and local headlines darkened enough that by the fall old Biden friends who'd gone out to campaign for him were calling his aides back east furiously demanding a reset. Even after a top deputy was then dispatched to Iowa, the scene remained grim. How could Biden become the nominee if he had a freshman congresswoman, Abby Finkenauer, charged with cutting him off when he rambled for too long, or when Vilsack—who hadn't been governor in twelve years—was closing his events for him?

This was no fun to watch from afar, but at least Obama's committed neutrality was working for him, leaving him free to candidate-surf and devour different campaigns' proprietary polling when they shared it. He was convinced that he needed to fully understand the field, since he still figured he'd be called upon to unite the fractious party around the nominee—whoever it was—after the primary.

So while Obama wasn't surprised to see Biden struggle—*Hadn't twenty-six other candidates predicted this, too, and therefore decided to run against him?*—he figured he had good reasons not to say anything about it out loud, even when some of his old friends wished he would. ("I think the turnout tonight demonstrates the high regard in which the vice president is held in the extended Obama family, and I think that message is not out as far as it should be," Pete Rouse told a crowd of about four dozen administration alums at a fundraiser he helped organize for Biden late in 2019.)

This posture also gave Obama an excuse not to engage too much with any single campaign, though his interest in others did fluctuate. He'd been mildly disappointed to see O'Rourke flame out, unable to translate his Texas energy into national momentum. Yet Obama watched with particular interest as Buttigieg gained unexpected support by leveraging an Obama-style speaking cadence and argument about outsidery but pragmatic inspiration. The thirty-something candidate had become a strong contender out of relative obscurity and openly looked up to Obama—who had always been happy to take his calls ever since naming the mayor one of the party's up-and-comers three years earlier. Obama thought Buttigieg was clearly tapping into some hope-adjacent vein, which was what the party needed to do in his mind. But he stopped short of active encouragement, turned off by Buttigieg's apparent inability to win over nonwhite voters. For a while Obama then grew especially interested in Harris, the candidate who outwardly appeared to have the best shot at mirroring his rise and voter coalition. However, her campaign operation itself was a shambles, rife with competing power silos, and she never seemed to find the right register to connect with Iowans, so she lost Obama's attention by late summer.

This was just as well, since Obama was careful never to assess, let alone praise, any of the candidates around anyone who might ever repeat it. Not only did he not want to lose his political capital with a big chunk of the party, but he also didn't want to give Trump the opening to further divide Democrats. "I'm not going to hand Trump an excuse," he told one friend who wanted him to speak up as the primary threatened to drag on with no end in sight. "I'm his favorite bogeyman."

Biden sat with a small group of aides the day after the debate-night disaster in Miami. He had something on his mind, and it wasn't Harris's surprise attack—his aides back in Philadelphia campaign HQ were dealing with that, insisting to reporters that her point on busing was inconsistent and ahistorical. Instead, he asked Donilon, Ricchetti, Dunn, Schultz, and Bedingfield if they could believe how his opponents were going after Obama out there. This group had heard the shtick hundreds of times by now, but Biden unspooled it once more: *Barack Obama was one of the greatest presidents in the history of the country. He walked into one of the greatest crises in history, we inherited everything except the locusts, and the locusts were coming.* What America were his rivals living in? This was Twitter's fault, wasn't it? To some of the people in the conversation, this attitude was reflective of a broader problem with the activist left, too. They remembered how progressive bloggers had insisted Obamacare would be a massive failure if it didn't include a public option, no matter how many millions more people were covered because of it.

It was all unfair, Biden continued, and he wanted to do something about it. Donilon chimed in supportively, and suggested that Biden cling even closer to his old boss in public to blunt the suggestion that he was out of step with the modern center-left and progressives. Obama was the most popular Democrat by far, and this would be a good way to keep Biden's core voters, especially older Black ones who didn't like seeing Obama criticized. It would feed into an argument undergirding his whole appeal: it was Biden's opponents who were misreading today's party, not him.

They resolved to amp up the Obama factor as they prepared for the next debate, in Detroit, and Biden was ready this time when the shots came—even on matters that had nothing to do with the ex-president, like his own criminal justice record in the Senate. "I find it fascinating, everybody is talking about how terrible I am on these issues. Barack Obama knew exactly who I was, he had ten lawyers do a background check and everything about me on civil rights, and he chose me and said it was the best decision he ever made," Biden said. This only annoyed most of his opponents. (Booker: "You invoke President Obama more than anybody in this campaign. You can't do it when it's convenient and dodge when it's not.") But Biden dug in when they pressed him again on the administration's record of deportations. "I think the president of the United States, Barack Obama, went out of his way to try to change the system and he got pushed back significantly," Biden replied. He kept going with his unflinching defense and blame-dodging the next morning. He'd expected the criticism, he told reporters, but "I was a little surprised how much of the incoming was about Barack." He figured he was onto something. "I hope the next debate we can talk about our answers to fix things Trump has broken, not how Barack Obama made all these mistakes. He didn't."

Biden then hugged Obama even tighter in Houston, countering War-ren's embrace of Sanders's Medicare for All plan ("I'm with Bernie") with an obvious retort: "Well, I'm for Barack," which led a frustrated Warren to insist she was only trying to build on Obama's work and legacy. She, like everyone else onstage, could see what Biden was doing and understood Obama's popularity, even if she didn't agree with plenty of his individual decisions.

When the conversation returned to immigration and Biden shrugged off his own role in the administration's policy by insisting he wasn't the one to make the decisions, his former colleague Castro used Booker's line of argument. "Every time something good about Barack Obama comes up, he says, 'Oh, I was there, I was there, I was there, that's me, too!'" Biden couldn't "take credit for Obama's work but not have to answer to any questions," Castro said. Biden had long before decided there was a simple answer to this: "I stand with Barack Obama all eight years, good, bad, and indifferent." When Castro then said, "I'm fulfilling the legacy of Barack Obama and you're not," Biden was unamused. "That would be a surprise to him," the ex-VP replied.

If invoking Obama felt like a cure-all for Biden on the debate stage, the same was true for his political team back east. They took to deploying the Medal of Freedom video online anytime the candidate hit a rough patch, even though Biden confided to friends that he hated the part of the clip that showed him crying, figuring it looked weak, so demanded his cam-paign use as little of that bit as possible. At times, the embrace was over-whelming enough that Eric Schultz, Obama's advisor, would call or email Biden's campaign manager Greg Schultz (no relation) and ask him to have Biden back off a bit, wary of allowing the impression that Obama was in on it. Even some of the people around Biden rolled their eyes at his one-note appeal sometimes. When he would talk about "Barack, I mean Pres-ident Obama" at events, they suspected he hadn't really slipped and was rather just trying to remind voters of the friendship, since he was loath to actually call Obama by his first name, even in person. They also knew he was, at times, claiming more agency in the administration than he'd actu-ally had, like when Warren talked about dreaming up and passing the law creating the Consumer Financial Protection Bureau and Biden cut in to insist: "I got you votes! I got votes for that bill! I convinced people to vote for it!" In reality he was far from central to that push. But Biden's numbers were still sinking in the first two states, and polling and focus groups conducted by Anzalone and Lake over the summer showed that while mentioning Obama wasn't sufficient to keep Biden afloat, it at least reminded people that they liked Biden. So he wasn't about to let up.

The thing is, there was nothing subtle about this. The upside of invoking Obama was clear, even if Biden wasn't a skilled enough campaigner to ride it to victory. One person who'd also been thinking about it plenty was Deval Patrick, the Obama Foundation board member and ex-governor who'd passed on a run earlier in 2019 because his wife was sick, but who'd spent the ensuing months unimpressed with the field, just like the ex-president. So Obama wasn't outright encouraging, but also wasn't at all surprised, when Patrick decided to try jumping into the race after all in November, making no secret of their friendship. Obama was surprised, though, when Bloomberg, who'd also decided against running earlier in the year, then announced his own late candidacy, promising to spend untold hundreds of millions, even billions, on it, because he thought Biden was doomed.

This was frustrating not just to Biden—who'd become close allies with Bloomberg in the latter years of the Obama administration—but also to Obama, since Bloomberg began saturating airwaves around the country with ads that made it seem like the tycoon and the ex-president were extremely close. Biden griped at a Central Park South fundraiser that with "the advertising I've seen, you'd think Mike was Barack's vice president." Some voters did, in fact, get the mistaken impression that Obama was now backing Bloomberg thanks to all the ads. A handful approached Axelrod to ask why the ex-president had thrown in his lot with the ex-mayor of all people, and Plouffe tweeted that it wasn't just political types: "Someone at my gym in California asked me why Obama chose Bloomberg over the rest of the field." It was all especially galling to the Obama confidants who remembered that Bloomberg had appeared with both Obama and John McCain back in 2008 and had cast doubt on Obama's preparedness for the presidency, then criticized Obamacare and dragged his feet on endorsing him for reelection four years later, only to turn around and blame him for racial divisions in 2016.

But by late 2019, Obama-bashing was out, the field having recognized that they weren't getting anywhere with most real people by criticizing the man so many—especially Black voters—still thought of with intense nostalgia. Obama-hugging was in. His image started popping up not just in Biden's and Bloomberg's ads, but also in the ones paid for by billionaire environmentalist Tom Steyer, and then Warren's, too, and before long even in Tulsi Gabbard's. Obama thought this was all a bit funny and slightly embarrassing for some of them, considering the tone of the debates just a few months earlier. But he also took to noting, archly, that none of these campaigns were asking for his team's permission or approval when they rolled out new clips featuring his face or his voice. This was fine, they didn't need permission. It was just, well, funny that none of them, or their staffs, had asked.

Well, none of them except for Biden's. Joe always asked permission.

* * *

There was still one more candidate who kept catching Obama's attention late into the year. Warren had become a fixture near the top of early-state polls after rebounding from a slow start to her campaign, and with an emphasis on publishing ambitious and aggressive policy proposals based around her plan to tax the richest Americans, she was clearly still gaining momentum among highly educated liberals. Obama had put most of their disagreements behind him by September 2019 and, when asked about Warren, he often responded with some variation of "Liz Warren is smart as shit." He read with interest the stories about her powerhouse organization of young staffers and suburban volunteers in Iowa and New Hampshire, and—still spooked by Castro's plan to decriminalize illegal border crossing and O'Rourke's proposal for a mandatory buyback program for assault weapons—he appreciated that her crusading progressivism tended to appear more realistic than Sanders's, for example. Still, he couldn't shake the worry that her wing of the party was tugging the rest of the Democrats away from the median voter—Warren ended up siding with Castro on border policy and with Sanders on the need for a single-payer health-care plan. And, much like his concern about Buttigieg, he was still waiting for evidence that Warren could appeal to Black and Latino voters.

The imperative to find that evidence grew more urgent as Biden slipped further from the race's focus—by November he appeared to be in a dog-fight with Buttigieg, Warren, and Sanders, who was recovering from a heart attack, in the first two states, and the momentum was decidedly not on the ex-VP's side. For one thing, he hadn't been able to shake the criticism that he was just too damn old for the job. At one point during the debate in September Castro accused him of "forgetting what you said two minutes ago." The audience was loud enough that Biden actually missed what Castro said, and he had to subtly ask Sanders, who was standing next to him, to repeat it for him. Biden thought it was ridiculous, and commentators broadly wondered aloud if Castro had gone too far. (In fact, Biden hadn't reversed himself as Castro implied, though it was true that he hadn't been clear.) Yet Biden didn't help matters by, that same night, encouraging parents to "make sure you have the record player on at night," an embarrassing anachronism that had the effect of reminding some viewers of thirty-eight-year-old California congressman Eric Swalwell's insistence at an earlier debate that Biden "pass the torch" to a new generation.

Biden knew he'd get plenty of questions about his fitness for the job, but he also took heed when his advisors reminded him that, despite his interest in winning young voters as Obama had, his strength was actually with older voters, and that they would be offended by these kinds of attacks. Still, his annoyance with them only grew over time—Sanders and Bloomberg (both seventy-seven) and Warren (seventy) weren't getting the same criticism. After getting another round of it at another debate, one of his rivals heard him muttering in frustration that the press, activists, and long shots were just looking for faults in the candidates at this point, and were exaggerating them. Stomping offstage, he listed two examples of what was apparently the matter with some of his rivals before blurting, "And everybody thinks I have Alzheimer's!" When Swalwell dropped out over the summer, Biden called him and said, "You're right I want to pass the torch to you, but if Trump's president there's no torch to pass."

Still, his campaign team knew he had a problem, and Biden's eventual concession that he would be a transitional figure—empowering the new generation to serve under and alongside him as president—wasn't enough to fix it. In focus groups with Iowans, his aides tried out a new tack. When the caucus-goers suggested Biden had lost a step because of his halting speaking style, the moderators would ask whether they knew he had overcome a debilitating stutter and taught himself to talk without one. That information tended to completely reverse the Iowans' opinions of Biden's mental acuity. The problem was that Biden had always been extremely sensitive about the subject, refusing to talk about it much even seven decades after he'd gotten over the stutter and left behind the schoolyard taunts that he wasn't smart. Even when *The Atlantic* published a long, touching article about Biden's stutter and the writer's own to widespread acclaim, Biden was upset. He told Bedingfield and Schultz that he didn't like the piece because it implied that he still stuttered. Only reluctantly did he consent to letting his team boost the message to voters.

This still didn't solve his bigger problem, which was that for all his team's insistences that "Twitter isn't real life" and that he was campaigning for real voters, not progressive activists, he was still at least slightly out of line with the party's zeitgeist as it negotiated how far left to veer ahead of the caucuses in Iowa. That was an ideologically confused state where one 2016 poll had shown that nearly half of Democrats considered themselves "socialists" before a 2019 survey said over half wanted a moderate Democrat to win—and where thirty-one counties voted for Trump after supporting Obama. Biden, with his history of political contortion to find the center of the party, might have been well prepared for such an electorate, but he instead focused on disproving the growing public perception that he was an outright conservative within the party. He was indignant when Warren suggested that perhaps he was "running in the wrong presidential primary" after he criticized her support for a Medicare for All policy. It shouldn't have been so hard to understand that he was just where average Democrats were ideologically, he thought. And here's the issue, Biden took to griping in private: the reporters covering him were just too young! How could they understand the party's evolution, let alone the context around his bankruptcy positions, or the practically ancient busing fight? (Only his longest-serving confidants remembered that he'd had the same complaint when he was running twelve years earlier.)

But far more recent history was also causing him trouble. At one debate he touted his deal with Mitch McConnell to avoid the 2012 fiscal cliff, only for Michael Bennet, who'd been one of just two Democratic senators to vote against that agreement, to step in. It had been a "complete victory for the Tea Party," Bennet said. "We had been running against this for ten years. We lost that economic argument because the deal extended almost all those Bush tax cuts permanently and put in place the mindless cuts we still are dealing with today." It wasn't a blockbuster moment, but Biden was stung by the implication that his dealmaking at Obama's request was counterproductive—he didn't even engage with the idea that he had unwittingly helped reset the broader debate over the parties' economic sympathies. "Man," he sighed to Bennet privately afterward, "we agree on almost everything."

Still, this was all more annoying to Biden than it was a sign of the walls closing in, and he sent the message even to his midlevel staffers that they should stop with their obvious gloom even as his polling kept slipping within the states. At times his sister, Val, showed him some of the sky-is-falling-style fundraising emails his campaign was sending out and he'd make a call: "What the fuck is this?" he would demand, unamused to be told that this kind of appeal was standard in modern politics. "Why are you sending emails saying *I'm* worried I'm going to lose?"

He had a point. For all the dire signs in the first two states, his national lead had barely budged—on December 19, the RealClearPolitics average of national polls had him at 27.8 percent to Sanders's 19.3 percent. Exactly one year earlier, it was 27.5 to 19.0. There was no national primary, of course, but it wasn't like voters around the country were turning against him en masse, even if things were looking dispiriting on the ground in early states. The depressing atmosphere around him was beginning to get annoying, and he started trotting out a new line whenever someone near him seemed too pessimistic, or when he saw especially dark coverage on TV. He finally said it in public when he met with the *Times*' editorial board and detected unrelenting negativity from the journalists. "I'm not saying that it's guaranteed I win, but name me a nominee who's taken as many hits from the beginning of them announcing—even [though] I announced late—who has taken the hits," he said. He leaned back, an unbelieving look crossing his face as his eyes widened and he spread his arms. "You all declare me—not *you*, [but] editorially, in a broad sense—declare me dead. And guess what? I ain't dead. And I'm not gonna die!"

This still wasn't particularly convincing to anyone paying close attention who was outside Biden's closest orbit. The *Times* essentially treated it as a punch line, joining the chorus in calling on Biden to "pass the torch to a new generation of political leaders" as it endorsed Warren and Klobuchar. (Biden thought it proved his whole point that the *Times*' editorial board had rejected him while the elevator attendant in its building had gushed over him.) His staff got the message that even Obama was particularly worried when a series of ex-aides known to be close to him began popping up in meetings. Jeff Zients, the businessman who'd run both the Office of Management and Budget and the National Economic Council in his White House, appeared in budget sessions to help the campaign organize and plan its finances, and to assist in getting its dwindling cash flow situation sorted, but occasionally also to bring up the reality that Biden's campaign—which was starting to seriously hurt for funds—needed to set aside half a million dollars if it wanted to shut down properly. At this point, back in Washington, Obama wasn't concerned just with Biden's feelings. He was starting to actively fret about Sanders.

Obama had been more or less sanguine about the senator from Vermont for most of 2019, reminding freaked-out donors and moderates that even Sanders's brand of democratic socialism would be a huge improvement on Trumpism, and that while he rarely saw eye to eye with Sanders about party priorities, the importance of foregrounding pragmatism, or the best ways to make change, he would campaign for him in the general election if Sanders won the nomination. At least he respected the rule of law, wasn't a raging sexist or racist, and had an unquestioned ability to get young people engaged. He said a more positive version of this to Sanders directly, too, and made sure that Schultz stayed in regular contact with Faiz Shakir, Sanders's campaign manager, so no one could think Obama was actively opposing them. That wasn't Obama's style, Obama and Schultz both pointed out whenever the progressives called them for reassurance that Obama wasn't going to bigfoot them before Iowa.

But by late 2019, Obama was finding this posture to be much easier described than kept. His assurances for the last year had largely come alongside the assumption that Sanders couldn't actually win the nomination—he'd mostly wanted to make sure no one could accuse him of favoritism and split the party. Yet with Sanders remaining at or near the top of polling in Iowa, New Hampshire, and also Nevada, thanks to his underrated strength with Latino voters, and with so many other candidates refusing to drop out and therefore dividing the more moderate vote, his path to victory was no longer unthinkable. Obama had genuinely come to respect Sanders's movement and found him to be reasonable in private conversation, but he thought it was obvious that a socialist who hated compromising on his priorities or offering serious olive branches to voters who wouldn't agree with him stood little chance in a general election, even against Trump.

As Obama saw it, he had always preserved the option of stepping in if things got especially dangerous. First, though, he owed it to the party to try nudging the candidates back in a productive direction before he went nuclear. He tried at an Obama Foundation summit in Chicago in October. "The idea of 'purity,' and you're never compromised, and you're always politically woke, and all that stuff, you should get over that quickly," he said. "The world is messy, there are ambiguities. People who do really good stuff have flaws." When this was greeted by a wave of commentary about Obama's sometimes surprising cultural conservatism instead of a broader reckoning in the primary, he tried again, scheduling a sit-down conversation with friendly voting rights activist Stacey Abrams at a conference for liberal donors in Washington two weeks later, where he would be clearer.

There was no mistaking Sanders, and also Warren, as his targets now that he finally, clearly spoke up about the party at the Mandarin Oriental. He got expansive, feeling free to riff as long as he didn't mention anyone by name. "Voters, including Democrats, are not driven by the same views that are reflected on certain left-leaning Twitter feeds, or the activist wing of our party," he said. "And that's not a criticism to the activist wing—their job is to poke and prod and text and inspire and motivate. But the candidate's job, whoever that ends up being, is to get elected."

To be a successful candidate, he continued, the contenders had "to pay some attention to where voters actually are, and how they think about their lives. And I don't think we should be deluded into thinking that the resistance to certain approaches to things is simply because voters haven't heard a bold-enough proposal, and as soon as they hear a bold-enough proposal that's going to activate them. Because you know what? It turns out people are cautious, because they don't have a margin for error."

Truth be told, Obama couldn't believe he had to say all this stuff, it was so central to his understanding of national politics and the lessons of his administration. But he spelled it out unmistakably anyway. "The average American doesn't think we have to completely tear down the system and remake it," he said. The country "is less revolutionary than it is interested in improvement."

His words hit like an earthquake, and he got a call from Sanders the next day, demanding to know if Obama was now standing against him. Obama said the coverage had overplayed it a bit—he wasn't railing against Sanders or Warren specifically, just trying to urge realism and aiming to calm the party down a bit amid its latest freak-out about the large field. This mollified the senator.

But Obama hadn't been entirely misinterpreted. For good measure, he tried making the point one more time at a Northern California fundraiser a few days later. This time, he might as well have said Sanders's name, he was so clearly referring to him. "We will not win just by increasing the turnout of the people who already agree with us completely on everything," he said. "Which is why I am always suspicious of purity tests during elections. Because, you know what? The country is complicated."

CHAPTER 19

2020

These were the depths to which the former vice president had fallen as 2019 gave way to 2020: the impeachment of the current president was a sordid saga built around Trump's attempt to strong-arm the president of Ukraine into supporting his false and reckless accusations that Hunter had undertaken corrupt work there and Biden had covered it up. And it really seemed to help. Sure, Biden's name was being dragged through the rancid partisan mud and his troubled son was thrown into the blinding international spotlight. But wasn't Trump revealing his desperation to derail Biden? Wasn't this proof that even Republicans thought he stood the best chance at taking back the White House? It sure seemed like it to Biden's staff, judging by the uptick in donations and media attention, and in the internal poll numbers, just weeks before Iowa's caucuses.

Biden himself, though, was unconvinced. He'd spent a few years now worrying about Hunter, often unsure of his whereabouts or the state of his drug use, though things at least seemed to be getting a bit better, now that he was recently remarried. (Not that Biden had ever met Hunter's new wife before the wedding—six days after the couple met—or that he even knew about it before it happened.) Trump's circus couldn't be good for Hunter. It also couldn't be good for his campaign, Biden figured, since even though all the metrics were finally pointing in the right direction, his own message was getting drowned out. He was convinced the country yearned for his promise of cooperative post-Trump healing, they just couldn't hear it over the din. Meanwhile he couldn't help but wonder why no one was defending him from the president's ludicrous accusations, the ones Trump had abused his power to pursue. Why wouldn't Obama even put out a statement rubbishing the allegations, since the supposed misdeeds theoretically happened on his watch?

Biden would still never let himself get fully mad with Obama. He turned his ire on the DNC and had aides make the point in a whisper campaign: Why wouldn't Tom Perez, the party chairman, get on TV to defend him? How could the party's leaders just claim to be pursuing neutrality? Wasn't it obvious that they should run record-correcting ads to counter the flood of bile coming from the White House? This was a matter of defending the last Democratic administration!

You could read the situation—and all the pursuant questions—as a bit of a debacle. You could also read it as just another inconvenience, yet another exasperating obstacle thrown up by doubters who just didn't see that Biden was still going to win. On his better days that's how he saw it, anyway, and he didn't much want to hear from anyone who disagreed. Shortly before caucus day, in frozen Des Moines, his brain trust walked his top donors through the latest thinking. A few things were true at the same time, they said: Iowa and New Hampshire were heavily white states, not the kinds of places where Biden would eventually do best. This was the standard line for anyone looking to lower expectations, as was their insistence that Biden was the only candidate who didn't *have* to win Iowa since he'd do well in Nevada and South Carolina, especially. But Team Biden reassured the financiers who'd dropped in to knock on Iowans' doors for the campaign that the race there was still virtually tied, and that even New Hampshire wasn't *actually* looking so bad for him, especially if he did well in Iowa first.

Biden believed it, so he never budged from his demand to always be talking about presidential policy, no matter how far he seemed from the Oval to commentators and rivals, and no matter what else was going on in the political world. He just didn't see the point of chatting about attack ads or impeachment votes, and definitely not precinct strategy, at this point. He'd listened as his advisors debated—then ditched—the idea of skipping Iowa altogether when it looked especially forbidding, and he'd chosen to ignore the mixed messaging they were sending out about the state's importance to him, buying into Ricchetti's belief in the final weeks that he really could win it. He'd even brushed it off when he learned that John Kerry had been overheard the day before the early February caucuses musing about jumping into the race himself to stop Sanders. (The former secretary of state insisted he'd been misheard, and that he still fully believed in the ex-VP.) Why would Biden want to get caught up in it all? If things really were going so poorly around him—poorly enough to unravel his final bout of presidential ambition—well, they'd see about that when the voting started. That would be a conversation for after Iowa. Even on the eve of the caucuses, his final opportunity to sprint around the state lining up potential voters after a year of mad campaigning, he watched the Super Bowl with about a dozen friends from the Senate and his many campaigns, only wanting to discuss the importance of passing infrastructure legislation, branding it well, and selling it around the country.

It wasn't until late on caucus night that it was no longer possible to deny that something was clearly going wrong. Reality flooded in: Biden was completely unprepared for this precise political moment. He sat at the hotel, surrounded by Ricchetti, Schultz, Bedingfield, and a rotating cast of family members, as the numbers sputtered in slowly, too slowly, and rumors started flying that the software used for reporting the results wasn't working, so no one could trust what they were seeing on TV or Twitter.

And *surely* it wasn't working, because Biden's numbers looked terrible. He wasn't just not winning, he was well behind Sanders. And also well behind Buttigieg. And he was trailing Warren. Impossibly, he was in a close race for fourth—*fourth!*—with Amy Klobuchar. (*Amy Klobuchar?!*) He sat there as the campaign team dialed into conference calls about how to make a legal challenge to the results because of the vote-counting disaster, and then, slowly, he agreed that he'd have to say something that night to reassure his voters, even though he still didn't know what the hell was happening. But his family was running all over the place, and he wouldn't leave the suite without all the grandkids, and he couldn't find one of them, and before he knew it there was Klobuchar on TV effectively acting like she was declaring victory. (*What?!*) Only then did he get in front of a mic. He promised, unconvincingly, "Folks! Well, it looks like it's going to be a long night, but I'm feeling good."

He couldn't know it then, and he couldn't know it when his general counsel that night sent the party a stern letter demanding "full explanations and relevant information regarding the methods of quality control you are employing, and an opportunity to respond, before any official results are released." But the caucus-tallying software's implosion saved him. It had stolen the spotlight.

The numbers, after all, were right, even though they took forever to add up. If the system hadn't fallen apart that night, it sure seemed like all anyone would have been talking about was how Biden, the national front-runner and elder statesman—the beloved nostalgic hawking a return to the calm, comforting Obama years—had somehow limped into fourth place, destroyed by a socialist and a mayor half his age and beaten even by the person he'd once wanted as his Number Two.

There was no good way to spin it when Biden and his campaign team met in New Hampshire the next morning: they were almost out of money and this iced-over state looked even worse for him than the last one. If he was still the front-runner, he was the weakest one anyone could remember, his pitch of steady leadership now looking as outmoded as it was naive, with Sanders in pole position. This was unacceptable, Biden decided, but rather than taking time to feel personally chastened or at fault, he demanded action. He charged Anita Dunn with taking the campaign's reins from Greg Schultz and considered the team's debate over how to handle New Hampshire, which voted in a week, and where the national press was now on Biden death watch. Ricchetti wanted to go all-in and try to do well there, and Biden agreed to at least give it a shot, since it would be hard to explain abandoning the state altogether. Biden and allies leaned hard on Maggie Hassan, one of the state's senators and its former governor, to promise him an endorsement, and they believed they would get it.

But his crowds were thinner than ever, his polling got worse, and Hassan, reading the writing on the wall, decided against backing Biden publicly. A week wasn't enough to right the ship, and two days before the primary the brain trust gathered once again. It was clear Biden was going to lose New Hampshire in embarrassing fashion, and that he needed at least a respectable showing in Nevada, which voted ten days later, in order to survive until South Carolina, a week after that. That's where the comeback would start if there was one, but even that now seemed like a desperate stretch. How could he justify staying in the race if he kept losing brutally, draining his campaign funds as he spiraled? New Hampshire's public polls were fluctuating between putting Biden in fourth and—unthinkably—fifth place, and the campaign was in dire enough financial shape that it had almost entirely stopped paying for daily polling of its own.

There were no good options left, but Biden, still struggling to believe that this shit was really happening yet unsure who to blame, agreed that they might as well try avoiding another mortifying night in front of a listless crowd in Manchester, and just go straight to South Carolina. That would mean acknowledging what everyone already knew: he'd lose badly in New Hampshire and a big win in the South was his only hope at this point—and maybe moderates' last chance to halt Sanders. Biden called John Lynch, a former governor of New Hampshire, to make sure he wouldn't be offending anyone by skipping town, and then departed. Enough of Iowa and New Hampshire. He never wanted to run in either of these states's primaries again.

Biden was hardly in a better mood in Columbia, but at least the crowds there were diverse, and they seemed to appreciate him. Recognizing that it was now or never for the campaign's survival, Dunn redirected all the money it was spending on states that would vote in March. Those resources would now go to Nevada, where, after a quick spurt of issue polling paid for by leftover cash, Team Biden decided to lean on a message of taking gun control seriously in a final bid to leap past Buttigieg, Warren, and Klobuchar—all of whom did beat Biden in New Hampshire—and at least make things competitive with Sanders, who'd crushed him with more than three times as many votes in the Granite State.

It was a lot to take in, even for the people zoomed all the way in on the campaign minutiae for a year now. Obama, getting antsy back home in Washington, was as surprised as anyone when it actually worked. He knew some of his advisors were in touch with a pro-Biden super PAC, urging it to pump as many resources into ads in Nevada as possible, and he understood Dunn's contention that a second-place finish out west would be good enough to at least keep Biden in the game for South Carolina.

But Biden's runner-up finish in Nevada was also reason enough for Obama to reconsider some bigger-picture things. Maybe the modern party wasn't as hopelessly captive to its young lefty energy as Obama was starting to suspect. Then again, he'd remained in irregular contact with Biden, seldom offering real advice but agreeing to stay on the line as the candidate ranted about the new political environment and fretted about what would happen if Sanders won. So Obama at least understood Biden's old-school view of the political landscape. He'd never quite pulled for him but never entirely abandoned him either. Obama had never *fully* bought into the idea that Biden was a total relic.

Still, Obama remained unwilling to do anything overt to trip up Sanders, who won Nevada and still seemed close to being unstoppable. If he was going to win, Obama wanted to maintain a productive relationship with him. And that still felt like it might be in the cards, though Biden's small, initial step toward a comeback—he beat Buttigieg and Warren and Klobuchar in Nevada! *That was something!*—was reason enough to keep some hope alive for his old friend.

Biden's phone rang one morning four days before the South Carolina primary, as he and his fellow candidates made last-minute preparations for February's final Democratic debate that night. He'd been awful in the last few debates, and he knew it—he was tired, fed up, and struggling to land an effective punch on Sanders. But now Obama was unexpectedly on the line on a debate day for the first time since 2012.

The ex-president shared no secret tips, unveiled no hidden strategy. He figured he might simply buck his old partner up. Listen to your team, Obama said: stay tight, and keep yourself above the fray. Biden just had to stay alive and remain a plausible savior for regular, exhausted people who weren't on board for Sanders's brand of change but sure as hell weren't down with Trump.

For years Biden's friends believed he carried himself differently after good conversations with Obama, and this was no exception. His old partner's words of encouragement rang in his ears as he approached the stage that night. *Go out there*, Obama had said, and *be president.*

Biden wouldn't put it this way, since he insisted that he deserved some more credit, but the next seven days' procession of unlikely events was as compelling a testament to the power of luck—and the importance of forcing luck to go as far as it can—as he'd experienced in his already winding career in politics.

First, there was the vote in South Carolina, where he was feeling good after a solid debate. A stream of reports still suggested that Sanders could actually compete with Biden in South Carolina, and everyone knew that if Sanders got too close there, it would be near-impossible to dislodge him from the nomination. Biden was always going to win South Carolina, but he needed it to be by a serious margin to make a convincing case that he could still consolidate the party's Sanders skeptics around him. In later months he would attribute the last-minute public endorsement by James

Clyburn, the beloved civil rights activist and congressman, as the catalyst for the state's heavy swing toward him. But behind the scenes, too, Clyburn helped pause some of Sanders's momentum.

The morning after the debate, Sharpton had been preparing to make huge political waves by throwing his support behind Sanders, who would welcome the backing of an unquestionably influential Black leader with a huge audience that had historically been unsure about the Vermonter. Clyburn, however, approached Sharpton at a breakfast the Rev was hosting to reveal that he'd soon be endorsing Biden, who was also standing there. Sharpton—who'd discussed the race with Obama earlier in the primary and took his own role as endorser seriously—understood the encounter to be a signal that the tides were turning. "Oh?" he replied, taken aback by Clyburn's faith in the ex-VP so many were leaving for dead. "Well, you just froze me. I can't go against you." Biden thanked him, also recognizing the weight of the dramatic about-face. Still unconvinced by Biden but willing to hope for a miraculous comeback and to trust Clyburn, Sharpton replied, "I'm doing this for Jim and Jim's late wife. They paid too many dues."

When Biden then won nearly half the state's vote even though six other candidates remained in the race—some of them paying for a near-constant loop of Obama-hugging campaign ads on South Carolina TV—he took a moment to revel. "To all those of you who've been knocked down, counted out, left behind, this is your campaign. Just days ago, the press and the pundits had declared this candidacy dead," he told a rollicking room in Columbia, standing between Jill and Clyburn. It was the first presidential primary he had ever won, over four decades after he first started really thinking about it. Suddenly the idea of his return to the White House no longer seemed so ridiculous. Just like he told the *Times*, he wasn't going to die.

He knew he still had to defeat Sanders, and then oust Trump, to get there, but this was a moment for reflection. He'd done this alone, and no one could pretend the doubters hadn't been out in force, he thought and later told friends. No one could say this was because of Obama's political magic—his old boss had thought he was out of touch, and hadn't been convinced of Biden's "battle for the soul of the nation" pitch or his emphasis on compromise. But Obama had been wrong, no matter how often he'd played pseudotherapist on their occasional calls. And these voters had chosen Biden because he'd spent years cultivating them, he was sure, not because of loyalty to anyone else. "Now, thanks to all of you, the heart of the Democratic Party, we just won, and we've won big because of you," Biden said to cheers.

It was, however, one of the last times he'd hear such cheers for months, thanks to yet another unanticipated dynamic crashing in to his surprise benefit. Biden had been monitoring reports of a virus spreading in China and Europe for weeks and felt lucky to have Ron Klain back at his side as an advisor after their 2015-era political estrangement. Klain had run the Obama administration's response to a 2014 Ebola outbreak in West Africa and could now whisper in his ear about how seriously to take this thing. It was the kind of issue Biden liked to talk about—not necessarily sexy, but understandable to real people and, he thought, all about basic competence in government. He'd written a *USA Today* Op-Ed to that effect back in January. (Opening line: "The possibility of a pandemic is a challenge Donald Trump is unqualified to handle as president.")

Now it was starting to become *the* issue, and people were scared—not just to show up to events with thousands of others, but also about how this would hit their workplaces and homes. Suddenly the issue that had always animated many Democratic primary voters—*Who could beat Trump?*—became the only subtext to the campaign, the president's mismanagement of the pandemic's early days understood as a given by this crowd. The prospect of a long, drawn-out primary that might not end until that summer's convention now looked even less acceptable to voters than it had a few days earlier.

Watching from Washington as the campaign trail suddenly started shuttering—the candidates unsure of what to do with themselves after South Carolina amid worries that they might infect one another or their voters when they brought them together—Obama couldn't help but conclude that the primary had to end. He couldn't say so out loud with Sanders still going strong, but voters were in need of reassurance, and he identified only one plausible candidate who could offer it at that point.

The calculus from here was simple, as he saw it. March 3, Super Tuesday, when a huge chunk of delegates would be awarded, was four days after South Carolina, and too many candidates were still in the race. This threatened to split the delegates up and keep the nomination technically undecided but likelier to go to Sanders for weeks longer, if not months. Obama's role, now, was to step in and ensure the kind of smooth end to the primary he'd been promising to facilitate. He was deft enough to know he couldn't demand that anyone drop out, but he could argue to some of the remaining candidates that they had to seriously consider what their path forward looked like, and how—realistically—they wanted the primary to end. By this point Biden knew more or less what Obama was thinking but didn't quite know what he was going to do.

Nor did Biden know that his old boss had been keeping up an occasional dialogue with Buttigieg in recent weeks, which made Obama's call to the Hoosier that much easier after South Carolina. Buttigieg was on his way back to South Bend after a stop to see Jimmy Carter in Georgia and a swing through Selma, Alabama, when he got the call. Obama's message was careful. He didn't need to spell out to Buttigieg that he had essentially no remaining path to victory, and that his supporters would presumably back Biden instead of Sanders—and possibly propel the ex-VP to the nomination—if he left the race. Instead, the former president said the young ex-mayor now had a chance to shine, to make clear he knew that the party and future were bigger than his political aspirations, to build his capital with the next president, and to leverage his new following to the greatest possible effect. Obama called Klobuchar next, with much the same message.

By that Monday night, the former rivals were at Biden's side in Dallas, joined by Beto O'Rourke. Neither ever credited Obama with pushing them across the line to drop out or endorse the ex-VP—they'd both already been considering it. No matter: by the night after that, Biden was nearly sweeping Super Tuesday, even winning states like Klobuchar's Minnesota, where he hadn't spent a dime. Voters were suddenly rallying to his side, with no better options and a pandemic bearing down, after a year of dismissing him. Before Sanders even arrived at his Tuesday night rally in Vermont, Biden looked to nearly have the nomination in hand.

No one on TV or on any stage that night thought to say anything about Obama. No one knew how closely he was watching or what he'd done behind the scenes. This was finally Joe's moment.

* * *

This final major act of the partnership was as unlikely as it was unusual: it would be the one time in their decades orbiting each other that Obama and Biden effectively switched roles, the generationally gifted speaker who'd once seemed like a herald of a new era now necessarily playing the part of behind-the-scenes fixer and expert while the onetime sidekick eager for assignments assumed the mantle of national mass-reassurer and moral leader—the part of the presidency and its pursuit he'd always known was important but that he had always been content to leave to the more politically rousing Obama.

Their first task was sticking the party back together by making nice with the skeptical and shell-shocked left that had just days earlier appeared ascendant. Sanders was still in the race and Warren only dropped out after Super Tuesday. Both Sanders and Biden called to congratulate her on her campaign and to angle for an endorsement, but it was Obama who kept her on the phone for an hour complimenting her, asking for ideas about how to keep her younger voters engaged, and—subtly, he hoped—making sure she didn't have any notion of backing Sanders at that late point. The Vermonter was the harder problem to solve, insistent as he was on sticking to the race even as the pandemic deepened and the remaining states almost uniformly fell to Biden, who figured he had to tread lightly on pushing Sanders aside, lest he infuriate Sanders's voters and doom himself for November. Obama, however, was getting impatient, especially after Sanders answered a journalist's question about his timeline by insisting he was focused on combating the spread of the virus, not the wind-down of his campaign. Obama and Sanders had started talking every few days, and Eric Schultz and Sanders's campaign manager Faiz Shakir were now in constant contact, too. Obama understood that Sanders felt the COVID-19 situation vindicated his politics—who could now deny that the country needed a truly universal health-care system? But Obama also wanted to avoid a redux of 2016, when Sanders didn't exit the race until he was mathematically eliminated, long after it was obvious Clinton would win. The ex-president still blamed that decision for poisoning Clinton's image and therefore her chances. And he knew that when he spoke, Sanders listened, even if he didn't always like what he heard.

On the phone, Sanders agonized not just about COVID-19 but also about the next steps for the movement of millions that he'd built in the last half-decade. How could he just disappear on them? Obama replied that he sympathized, having struggled to keep his own movement intact once he became president, and that he understood Sanders wanted to see a concrete way to keep the fight going before he formally left this campaign. Off the line, Obama spitballed ideas with his aides and friends until he came up with one that Sanders might like. Sanders clearly wanted the promise of policy concessions out of Biden before he quit, Obama thought, so what if he and Biden both assigned some allies to work cooperatively on task forces on a set of issues? They could come up with proposals for Biden and the party at large. Biden's team got just a quick heads-up from Obama's office that he'd signed them up for such an endeavor before Sanders agreed to the plan.

Biden was willing to make it work. He had in fact already been intentionally loud about a few initial policy shifts to his left—on bankruptcy policy, student loan debt relief, and health-care funding—as he sought to send the message to Sanders's and Warren's backers that he was modernizing and trying to understand where they were coming from. This was also to maintain good relations with Sanders himself. The pair had never exactly been friends in Washington, but they'd always liked each other and Sanders had appreciated that Biden never condescended to him like other senators had. Now top Biden advisors like Dunn were in frequent touch with Sanders's political and policy teams to coordinate the primary's denouement, and, in the final days before Sanders finally agreed to concede, Obama reconnected with him, reminding him how much he respected his movement and insisting that he should have a big role in campaigning against Trump. Biden and Obama had already agreed on this, and when Sanders dropped out in April, Biden reiterated it to him repeatedly.

The Obama-Biden coordination was far more extensive than publicly appreciated at the time, and even most political pros only started to get a taste of the way Obama was reengaging when, in early May, a group of Obamans led by Jarrett and Plouffe held a virtual fundraiser for the campaign that brought in ten times its initial goal of $150,000. Once again, though, the truth was even more intense backstage. Obama had been speaking occasionally with O'Malley Dillon, one of his old political aides, ever since encouraging her to take the job running the ill-fated O'Rourke campaign the previous year, and their talks had been more regular since Dunn had asked O'Malley Dillon to run Biden's Nevada effort in February. Now she was considering taking over the entire campaign, and Obama pushed her toward the job, promising to be a resource not just in helping her define the ideal relationship between campaign manager and candidate but also by sharing his analysis and advice about the race and his former VP whenever it was needed.

Over the ensuing weeks, then months, Obama commenced a series of calls with O'Malley Dillon and Dunn, both separately and together, to review the campaign's strategies and metrics, and occasionally to discuss ways to best deploy Biden as a campaigner. Obama hadn't wanted to get too involved for months, but now he was all the way in. Almost no one outside this trio, including Biden, knew about the depth of the calls. Occasionally Obama used the sessions to step back and get a measure of the candidate—sometimes to ask if it would be useful for him to call Biden to relay a message, and sometimes to make sure Biden was following their advice. To the people who were closest to the former president and to the nominee, the sudden frequency of their own one-on-one calls was near-on farcical, considering the careful distance they'd maintained for the previous year-plus.

Then again, it was an unsettling time for everybody.

Biden, for one, suddenly found himself the nominee of his party for the first time while cooped up inside the Wilmington home overlooking a lake that could hardly have felt farther away from the factory floors of Detroit, the cafés of Miami, or the union halls of Las Vegas—the places he'd been expecting to ply his emotional style of face-to-face campaigning, and where, he often liked to say, he was "always the last one off the rope-line." He didn't let himself wallow, insisting on exercising every morning before he dressed in a suit despite never leaving home and instead spending all day on calls with advisors. But he missed the road, especially after his first few virtual events were marred by technical problems that threw into serious question his ability to communicate with the outside world. He did, however, finally get to relax after a year of draining campaigning, which not only helped give him some perspective but also gave him a chance to recharge and shrug off the increasingly explicit allegations coming from Trump's backers that, at seventy-seven, he was growing senile or at least not up to the job. Biden had in fact been struggling at times to keep his speech crisp by the end of long campaign days, but this was a matter of exhaustion more than anything else, and the time at home with his family and German shepherds helped.

Obama, meanwhile, left DC for Martha's Vineyard, hunkered down, and counseled Biden to do the same, occasionally joking (until his staff got him to stop) that he'd basically been living in lockdown for a decade, but mostly arguing that keeping Biden healthy was the most important thing. This was not an obvious point. Worries immediately arose that Trump was doing a much better job of being omnipresent, even if his daily COVID briefings were chaotic, than Biden, who was swiftly accused by Republicans and fearful liberals of "hiding in his basement." But a quick round of focus groups and message testing aligned with Obama's presumption—that putting up a responsible, stable face and modeling good pandemic behavior would be more effective than trying to outdraw Trump. One TV clip of Biden insisting the best way to get the shocked economy back on track was to get control of the pandemic tested especially well. The campaign doubled down on the message, aiming to emphasize the contrast between Trump's daily yellathons and Biden's occasional interviews and scripted speeches—a contrast in styles that the campaign found resonated in particular with women voters.

It came as a shock to Biden, O'Malley Dillon, Dunn, and the rest of the senior team when in early May the *New York Times* published an Op-Ed written by Axelrod and Plouffe insisting that he change course. Biden's "most memorable moments on the campaign trail have come through spontaneous, intensely moving encounters with people who, like Mr. Biden, have endured searing struggle and loss. His authentic sense of empathy is a quality uniquely suited to this agonizing moment," they wrote. Now, they continued, "Mr. Biden finds himself on the outside looking in. Governors and mayors have taken center stage in the only story that matters." They argued that he needed to be more creative and increase the tempo of his campaign, to be more experimental with his use of the internet and to rely more on surrogates. "While television remains a potent force, YouTube, Facebook, Twitter, Instagram, Snapchat and TikTok are all essential in a COVID-19 world in which candidate travel and voter contact will be severely limited. In many respects, they *are* the campaign, not an important part of it."

Confusion, and then downright annoyance, reigned in Biden's inner orbit. For one thing, Plouffe had just appeared at an online fundraiser for Biden alongside O'Malley Dillon, and had established himself as a useful validator for Biden when he needed it—that fundraiser was just a few hours after the candidate had appeared on *Morning Joe* to defend himself against an accusation of sexual assault leveled by a staffer who'd worked for him in the early 1990s. (Valerie Jarrett had opened the fundraising event by pointing out that Biden had passed Obama's vetting process in 2008.) Plouffe hadn't said a thing about this Op-Ed then. For another, it seemed clear that this could be read as an urgent message from Obama himself. O'Malley Dillon was personally offended: Axelrod and Plouffe had her number and knew how to reach her if they really wanted to share advice. So did Obama.

Obama, however, hadn't gotten a heads-up about the piece, and was mortified by the assumption that he was sending messages to Biden in the *Times*. He was, in fact, worried about some of the things Axelrod and Plouffe warned about, and had even shared those concerns with Sanders, who'd called Obama to insist that Biden force himself back into the national conversation. But Obama's preferred method of sending messages was still his direct private calls, and Biden's capacity to claim attention online had been one of their main topics from the start. Obama had, for example, sought to craft his own official endorsement of Biden to maximum effect on the internet. Eric Schultz coordinated closely not only with Dunn but Shakir, too, to make sure they used and distributed Obama's tidily filmed monologue to bring in voters who weren't sure about Biden but remembered the former president fondly. Later in the summer, they followed it up with a sixteen-minute video of a conversation between Obama and Biden—who both carefully emerged from isolation to film in Washington—which the Obama side insisted should be more cinematically interesting than your average campaign clip, for maximum attention. The *Washington Post*'s film critic reviewed "its sleek production values and swift, assured editing" glowingly: "As a portrait of one of American politics' most beautiful friendships, the video works as an appealing, wonkily satisfying bromance reboot. As a fond look back at presidential comportment, intelligence and well-regulated emotions, it's a welcome whiff of nostalgia."

That was just the public stuff. Obama had been thinking critically about the dangers of disinformation campaigns and social media companies' inability to regulate them ever since 2016, and even back then he'd confronted Facebook's Mark Zuckerberg after Trump won and insisted the CEO start taking it seriously. Now Obama told O'Malley Dillon and Dunn that they needed to be thinking carefully about how Trump would take advantage of the internet's power to divide people, and that their digital team must prepare to fight back. The campaign nearly quintupled its digital investments after Obama's initial assessment, and he sent in his own team to help, too: suddenly Jason Goldman, a former digital advisor in Obama's White House and a longtime tech industry figure, started discussing digital strategy with Biden aides at the ex-president's behest. Before long Obama had Goldman, along with ex–Google chairman Eric Schmidt and LinkedIn cofounder Reid Hoffman, create a secret council of high-powered tech executives to offer their advice, like embracing influencer marketing campaigns. Obama also knew he could help even more directly by using the improved team's digital event platform, once they got the kinks out. His first online fundraiser for Biden in June brought in $11 million, by far the biggest haul of the campaign. The band sure looked back together.

* * *

The backdrop for the most dramatic ideological expansion of Biden's long life was incongruously peaceful. He sat in his well-appointed study and sometimes on his deck overlooking the lake sprouting from Little Mill Creek as he took hours of conference calls with economic and public health advisors in the early months of the pandemic and reconsidered what it meant to remain a heat-seeking missile for the center of the party just as that center was moving as fast as it ever had. This was a response to the state of the country: the economy appeared on the verge of collapse just as thousands upon thousands were dying and, before long, a racial reckoning was nigh.

For one thing, it meant a readjustment of how he thought about 2009. Biden had spoken of his work shepherding Obama's stimulus as reason to trust his recovery chops. He'd done it before. But with no end in sight to the lockdowns or misery as the spring of 2020 stretched on, he started pushing his economic advisors not to let the political concerns of that era color their prescribed response. First, he began saying, this looked like it could be a depression worse than the Great Recession. That changed one spring morning when he said 2009's level of federal spending might fall far short, and that they should be thinking on the scale of World War Two and the Great Depression. Biden toyed with sharing this message out loud—"I think it's probably the biggest challenge in modern history, quite frankly. I think it may not dwarf but eclipse what FDR faced," he said on

CNN in April. In practice, it meant abandoning mainstream Democratic orthodoxy of the last few decades, especially the early Obama years, when deficit spending was a massive concern, and not just because Republicans demanded it. This wasn't a quick or easy shift—in August Ted Kaufman publicly warned that deficits would make it difficult to spend too much in 2021—but in his economic meetings Biden took to blowing past such worries because of what he perceived to be the need to spend massive amounts on relief programs as quickly as possible to get people back on their feet. This wasn't just a rejection of early Obama-era thinking but a crisis-born break even from Obama's warning about fiscal responsibility to House Democrats as recently as 2019.

The circumstances, of course, had changed dramatically, and Biden let himself dream big about using the opportunity to make some serious changes to the American economy with the recovery effort. He started talking about huge health-care, education, and climate programs, figuring that the appetite for such change would never be higher. "The blinders have been taken off because of this COVID crisis," he told a small virtual donor gathering. "I think people are realizing 'My Lord, look at what is possible,' looking at the institutional changes we can make, without us becoming a 'socialist country' or any of that malarkey." It was a far cry not only from when Obama sought to downplay the transformative nature of the 2009 stimulus spending in the face of GOP opposition but also from Biden's own 2019 contention to donors that "nothing would fundamentally change." Biden hadn't suddenly forgotten how Capitol Hill worked, of course, and he knew that even in the best of times modern presidents only likely got one or two big legislative pushes through before their party was wiped out in their first midterm season. But the crisis looked like it was politically punishing not just Trump but also all Republicans and Biden seemed likely to become president with healthy Democratic margins in the House and Senate, which would presumably help him push through big-ticket items packed with liberal priorities. He'd also started talking quietly every other week or so with Warren, who'd become an unlikely advisor after they'd reconnected following the death of her eldest brother from COVID, about the need for broad populist economic shifts and aggressive recovery spending.

And Obama was never far, either. If he'd been down on Biden's ability to adapt to modern politics earlier in the campaign, he was gratified now as his old partner ditched the mantle of sober restoration in favor of something a bit more inspiring. Still, Obama was cautious about the degree of change Biden was now publicly discussing, as if moderation were no longer electorally relevant in the face of a deadly pandemic, economic suffering, and an incumbent president apparently gone mad, if Trump's unhinged daily briefings were any indication. Biden's conception of what was needed from a modern president appeared to be changing, going beyond even what they had done together twelve years earlier to now responding to what he saw as much bigger schisms in the country.

Nonetheless, when the schisms became so much more agonizingly clear with the late-May murder of George Floyd in Minneapolis, and the ensuing demonstrations about racial justice, Biden again called Obama for advice on how to respond. He was recognizing Obama's unique position as the first Black president but also remembering how he wrestled with what to say after the 2014 protests of Michael Brown's killing by a police officer in Ferguson, Missouri, in particular. Obama sided with the Biden advisors—most prominently Symone Sanders and Louisiana congressman Cedric Richmond, the two highest-ranking Black strategists on his team—who counseled him on a passionate but measured response, and argued that he should make his first pandemic-era trip a visit with the Floyd family in Houston ahead of Floyd's funeral. In Texas Biden spoke quietly with the family, including Floyd's six-year-old daughter, and confided that he saw the moment as another sign that America was at an inflection point. To Obama, this was the right approach. Biden didn't need to break new political ground or make the story about himself, but to be empathetic and demonstrate that he understood the pain and inequality on display. He should promise change to comprehensively face up to systemic racism, a promise that would in fact go further than any nominee ever had. Obama thought Biden's refusal to embrace lefty activists' calls to reduce police funding was appropriate, too—both saw "defund the police" as a politically toxic message to add to the precarious moment, and Biden in fact believed in increasing funding for training.

The experience also hardened Biden's views of Trump on race, and the backlash to Black Lives Matter protests gave him reason to second-guess his 2017-era insistence that the president's voters weren't racially motivated. "They have real fears. It's not based on race, they voted for a Black man two times," he'd said then. Now, though, there was little point in arguing that there wasn't a hefty element of racism involved for some of them. Obama agreed, and both fretted later in the summer that, after unrest in Kenosha, Wisconsin, following yet another police shooting of a Black man, Jacob Blake, Trump would succeed in turning the campaign into a racist, 1960s-style referendum on "law and order." Biden had little choice but to argue that voters knew better than to think of him as a violence-supporting and cop-threatening radical, but Obama still worried that the entire project of American cohesion was in the balance. He'd started talking more openly about protecting the rule of law itself after Trump had ordered Lafayette Square, in front of the White House, forcibly cleared of protesters as he marched to a church across the way with the chairman of the Joint Chiefs of Staff, in uniform, at his side.

This was all on Obama's mind as he prepared his eulogy for civil rights hero and congressman John Lewis at the end of July. Obama had been trying to think critically about his own record for years as he wrote the first volume of his memoir, and he kept running into the notion that Republican refusal to cooperate had gotten in his way at every turn, and that he could have seen this more clearly. Yet it was the experience of the last few months, especially, that had started to push him even further, toward the conclusion that structural changes were needed to ensure a fair political system—an argument he had long resisted. He thus decided that the funeral was the right time to argue that honoring Lewis meant passing new voting rights legislation, "and if all this takes eliminating the filibuster—another Jim Crow relic—in order to secure the God-given rights of every American, then that's what we should do."

Biden's advisors had known that Obama would endorse the end of the filibuster while promoting his book, but it wasn't due to come out until after the election, and they were uneasy when told the former president would call that summer for the effective elimination of the sixty-vote threshold in the Senate to pass major legislation. Biden wasn't ready to go that far and turn his beloved chamber into a simple-majority-rule body, so this felt like Obama was putting him in the uncomfortable situation of looking like a hidebound traditionalist unwilling to consider change. This wasn't precisely Obama's intention, but he succeeded in forcing a debate in broader terms about GOP obstruction, and in at least persuading Biden to think about it.

They were both evolving, but at different speeds, and on different matters—Obama faster on tactics and dealing with the opposition after reviewing his own eight years in power, Biden more swiftly on how to appeal to voters amid the crisis, thanks to his time on the campaign trail. As Democrats appeared to be on track for big enough majorities that he'd have plenty of leverage over Republicans, the candidate was spared a real interrogation of his continued insistence that he, with his decades of Senate experience, could get some of them to go along with him. To many in his party, it was unthinkable that after his time as vice president, and after the searing Trump years, he might still have hope in the modern GOP's willingness to compromise.

CHAPTER 20

2020–2021

It was inevitable. Obama knew that there was no way Biden *wouldn't* be hearing from everyone who'd ever had his phone number. He needed to find a running mate, and everyone who's anyone had an opinion to share—that's just how this works every four years. What Obama didn't anticipate was that they would be calling him, too, which wound up involving the ex-president in the process far more than he'd expected as it inched along for months, deep into the summer of 2020. Really, it was fair enough, and not just because everyone around Biden thought he'd done a pretty good job of picking a running mate himself. By that point Obama was increasingly likely to be found on the line with the nominee himself on any given day. Biden was eager to talk it all through, and he could finally pick Obama's brain again, mostly unencumbered by awkward politics for the first time in five years. The distance between them—their half-calculated and fully stressful semiestrangement—had been impossible to ignore just a year prior. Now it could hardly have felt more like ancient history, although the power in the relationship had unmistakably shifted, and a distinct wariness lingered on both sides of the calls.

Biden set out straightforward instructions for his vice presidential search committee, which was led by Eric Garcetti, Chris Dodd—who'd spent most of his post-Senate years as the movie industry's top lobbyist—Delaware congresswoman Lisa Blunt Rochester, and Biden's former aide Cynthia Hogan, Apple's chief lobbyist. Part one was simple: they should look for a woman, since Biden had pledged to pick one in his final primary season debate. They should take seriously Biden's role as leader of a diverse and shifting party, and talk to elected officials, labor groups, constituency organizations, and anyone else who might have thoughts on whom he should consider. The eventual finalists would have to pass a vet and would have to perform well in the secret polling Celinda Lake would be undertaking to gauge their images. They'd also have to meet his most important personal criteria: that they be prepared to do the job if something happened to the seventy-seven-year-old—who would be the oldest president ever inaugurated but who was promising to be a "bridge" to a new generation of leaders—and that they be "ideologically simpatico" with the nominee, even if they disagreed on some details or methods of making change.

The advice started trickling in, some welcome and much unbidden, almost as soon as Super Tuesday. It opened into a flood after Sanders dropped out. Dunn first asked for the senator's input, but he demurred and said that while he'd prefer a progressive, they really just needed to pick someone who would help Biden beat Trump. This was a common refrain, but with Biden's lead appearing to build by the day, less of a daily concern to his team than it usually is for nominees, who tend to need more political help. Sharpton offered his take repeatedly. In March in Selma, he made a point of acknowledging "our vice president" in the congregation at a church gathering, publicly clarifying to Biden, who was there, that he was referring to Abrams, who was also in the audience. By the summer he was on the record encouraging Biden to choose a Black woman, and he wasn't alone—Klobuchar removed herself from the running in June and urged him to pick a woman of color. When Biden and Sharpton spoke at a soul food restaurant in Houston for half an hour before the nominee's meeting with George Floyd's family, they talked about Abrams, Orlando area congresswoman Val Demings, and Kamala Harris. Any one of them would be the first Black VP as well as the first woman in the job.

Biden was slow to narrow down his long list, which started at over a dozen names and stayed uncommonly long for weeks. This sometimes led to uncomfortable conversations with allies offering their views. Once a politically influential friend suggested Biden look closely at Michelle Lujan Grisham, the governor of New Mexico and a former congresswoman, and Biden replied, blankly, "Who?" before he remembered she was on the list. A similarly unfamiliar dynamic surrounded mentions of Rhode Island governor Gina Raimondo early in the process, and Biden occasionally brought up others to gauge associates' temperature on them, too. Before she removed her name from contention, that included Nevada senator Catherine Cortez

Masto (Harry Reid's suggestion and the favorite of some Latino groups, as well as an old ally of Beau's), Illinois senator Tammy Duckworth—who had the backing of veterans' groups—and, later in the process, Congressional Black Caucus chair Karen Bass of California, whom many progressives liked.

This was all secret. But his private conversations mirrored the public ones in one important way: they always came back to one name, not unlike how Obama kept gravitating back to Biden twelve summers earlier. This situation was more fraught, however, because of how the campaign had played out. Biden had trained himself over many years in the Senate not to hold grudges whenever he could avoid it, so Jill took it upon herself to be the family grievance-keeper when she felt it was necessary. And while the ex-VP saw the makings of a loyal partner in Kamala Harris, with whom he always caught up chummily when they saw each other backstage and at private airport terminals on the campaign trail, his wife was far slower to come around to the idea. She still felt betrayed by what she saw as Harris's debate ambush the previous June. The issue was that Harris had genuinely been close to Beau thanks to their collaboration on mortgage settlements as attorneys general, and that the Bidens had thought of her as a friend. Candidate Biden had moved on, understanding that Harris didn't feel that she could apologize and reverse her position on busing, but believing that she was eager to put the topic behind her entirely, given how little traction it had ultimately gotten her and how unable she'd been to follow up her initial attack.

Yet it took his wife longer to come around to the idea, and some Harris allies even met with Biden aides late in the process after hearing that Dodd, too, wasn't over it. (Biden, for his part, acknowledged privately that this was a problem and sought to calm the waters by convincing others of his equanimity on the matter; he was photographed holding a talking-points note card with the reminder "DO NOT Hold Grudges.")

Harris was clearly a top-tier choice no matter how you sliced it: she and Biden had similar political viewpoints as consensus-first liberals, though she was more sensitive to the influence of lefty activists. She would be a historic and exciting pick, too, not just the first female vice president but also the first Black VP and the first Asian American one. And her campaign launch, at least, showed that she could create buzz like few others—she'd drawn over twenty thousand in Oakland in January 2019. Schumer counseled Biden to seriously consider her, as did Kaine. Biden never downplayed the chatter around her, and his allies could be forgiven for reading into it when, in April, he thanked her for her support in front of a star-studded group of about fifty donors: "The idea, Kamala, that you ran a hell of a race and endorsed me—it means a lot. It's not an easy thing to do, but, you know, thanks for making the time and for being so loyal," he said. "And I'm so lucky to have you as part of this, this partnership going forward, because I think we're going together we can make a—we can make a great deal of difference, and the biggest thing we can do is make Donald Trump a one-term president. So I'm coming for you, kid."

She made sense, too, to Obama, who by the summer was happily watching from afar in the Martha's Vineyard home that he and Michelle bought in late 2019. He hadn't been impressed by Harris's campaign in the end, but he'd admired her from afar for years, even offering her a chance to be considered for attorney general in 2014 (she declined). He told Biden as much, but Obama still didn't see his job as recommender-in-chief.

Instead, he wanted to guide Biden along as much as would be useful, but only when Biden asked. So he was happy to lay out his own advised criteria for the job. As had been the case for them, Biden's pick should have complementary strengths to his, but Obama didn't think Biden needed to worry as much as he had about finding a political match to fill his electoral holes, since he figured the life-or-death stakes of the race guaranteed maximum turnout and intense partisanship anyway. He was happy, too, to offer advice as Biden considered names to sit on his selection committee and later as he wanted a sounding board to talk through some candidates' pros and cons. Obama was even fine with answering the phone when some of the contenders themselves came calling, though he didn't have much advice for them and he came away thinking they were just trying to get him to recommend them to Biden. He grew most interested and involved when Biden started saying he was looking for "his own Biden"—that he was trying to replicate their relationship as much as possible, believing it to be the gold standard. On repeated calls, Obama agreed with Biden's general wish but cautioned him to remember that it took time for them to grow close, and to feel like they had a connection of both head and heart, to put it in Bidenese. This relationship, he kept saying, will feel different no matter what.

Still, Obama was on Biden's mind often as he assessed the people who had a real shot at the position. The shape of their bond and their general ideological agreement were front and center as he thought about Warren, who openly wanted the job and had been advising Biden regularly for months, but who was still further left than Biden was comfortable with, even though she said she was willing to go along with his policy prescriptions since he'd won. And Obama was surprised when Susan Rice, his friend and old national security advisor with no history in electoral politics, became a finalist. Biden came to see her as a serious option because of her experience in Obama's White House, and Obama was intrigued but thought her lack of political reps made her too risky a pick. Biden also took Michigan governor Gretchen Whitmer far more seriously than was publicly appreciated, especially once Anzalone and Emanuel told him they were fans. But he was shaken out of the Whitmer reverie by the reminder that she was too politically similar to him—a fellow unflashy white moderate with a Rust Belt focus—and wouldn't necessarily be a complementary pick, like Obama had advised.

When the time finally came for Biden and Harris to have a formal interview over video chat, Biden was delighted that she quickly made clear she wanted a relationship like his and Obama's, too. This was an obvious thing to say to Biden, but he indulged her and laid out the reality that this would be his expectation for their entire term. Unlike when Biden met with Obama in Minneapolis in 2008, Harris brought no conditions for how to structure their interactions, instead just a general pitch for herself as a partner. It wasn't a hard case to make, since Biden was already looking for parallels to Obama's search for him, and there were plenty here. Even if it didn't feel urgent, she could help with voters who might still need convincing, like Biden had done for Obama—this time, well-educated white suburban women who needed a push, and some Black voters who remained on the fence about voting. She didn't know it, but she'd also aced Lake's poll test by being seen as the most qualified of the contenders to take over on Day One if needed—a metric Biden cared a lot about, and which was perhaps the most important reason Obama had picked him. Biden didn't even mind that Harris's campaign had ended in embarrassment. So had his in 2008, and Harris had at least had the wisdom to drop out before Iowans rendered their verdict. (It had taken a while for the extent of Biden's good fortune to sink in back in 2008—he was the first VP candidate ever to run in the primaries and get picked for the ticket after finishing lower than the runner-up. Harris would be the second.)

Yet as Biden grew more comfortable with the idea of Harris, he also saw a chance to correct a wrong that still lingered from 2008 to 2016 to now. There would be no room for ambiguity this time, if he had his way: Harris would almost certainly run for president again, and he absolutely thought she represented the future of the party. She seemed to recognize the significance of Biden implying this when they first appeared together as a ticket in Wilmington in August, and he underscored the point that he saw obvious parallels here to his own arrangement by saying, "I asked Kamala to be the last voice in the room." He also bestowed on her an honor he'd previously given to Obama: he said she'd been "an honorary Biden for quite some time."

* * *

If Obama's political origin story centers on his star turn at a convention and the story of Biden's political career could plausibly be mapped through his eleven convention experiences—from beside-the-point hotshot on the sidelines to also-ran to prime-time speaker who still couldn't get top billing—perhaps it was fitting that Biden's twelfth one and his crowning event looked so different from the rest. There was little realistic talk of holding the ceremony in person in Milwaukee as scheduled thanks to the virus. Biden had barely ventured out of his house, and Trump's first big in-person rally in June after the initial lockdowns was a cautionary tale—a fiasco that appeared to cause a huge spike in COVID infections in Tulsa and perhaps the death of 2012 Republican candidate Herman Cain, who was there and died of the virus about a month later. But no one knew what a fully virtual convention should look like, and the prospect rattled Obama, in particular, who kept repeating throughout the summer that Biden needed to keep in mind that politics were visceral—voters needed to feel the Democratic passion and not think they were being too cautious or too precious by playing it overly safe pandemic-wise.

Obama was sure Biden had better things to worry about than programming—like planning his fall campaign—and that it might play better to his strengths than Biden's anyway. He also knew he could get anyone to pick up his calls and he was getting slightly bored on the Vineyard. So he rang Steven Spielberg, who agreed to help consult with the team as they tried to make the show as engaging as possible. The director and the ex-president gathered a Hollywood advisory panel, envisioning rotating hosts, coast-to-coast speeches, and a quick pace that would make Trump's drawn-out super-spreader event on the muddy White House lawn look like a gothic relic. Getting excited by the project and the mandate to make Biden look as presidential as possible so voters could remember what it was like to have a seminormal and responsible commander in chief, Obama even got involved with setting the speaking schedule in conjunction with his old aide Stephanie Cutter, who was running the convention planning. He agreed with Biden's team that Michelle should be the first night's main speaker, and he liked the idea of Jill taking the next night. But when presented with the plan to have him close the third night, Obama and his staff thought it would instead be wise to instead lift Harris's voice and have her finish the evening, after he spoke. That way he could draw as many viewers as possible for her time in the spotlight.

Obama's speech was still the big story, though, landing not just as a touching endorsement of the man he described as his "brother," but as by far his most powerful takedown yet of Trump as he prepared to campaign for Biden through the fall after years of holding back about the forty-fifth president. "I never expected that my successor would embrace my vision or continue my policies. I did hope, for the sake of the country, that Donald Trump might show some interest in taking the job seriously, that he might come to feel the weight of the office and discover some reverence for the democracy that had been placed in his care," Obama said, beaming onto TV screens from Philadelphia, hoping to defend the nation's core principles at the place of its founding. "But he never did. For close to four years now, he's shown no interest in putting in the work, no interest in finding common ground, no interest in using the awesome power of his office to help anyone but himself and his friends, no interest in treating the presidency as anything but one more reality show that he can use to get the attention he craves. Donald Trump hasn't grown into the job because he can't."

For most voters the headline of the week was the Obamas' full reengagement with national electoral politics, and how Democrats tore into Trump's handling of the pandemic. This was to be expected with the threat of a second Trump term so present and with no end in sight to the virus's rampage. Yet the intentionally broad programming meant to unify voters behind Biden also inadvertently highlighted just how far Biden had traveled so quickly as a politician to claim the nomination—and, as was evident to those around him, how he was still coming to terms with this distance.

For one thing, as eager as he'd been to embrace policy positions pushed by Warren and Sanders, who both spoke at the convention, he was equally excited by the chance to include former Republican officeholders who opposed Trump, too, like former Ohio governor John Kasich and former secretary of state Colin Powell. As a matter of pure politics, there was nothing surprising about this attempt to prove Biden was serious about establishing "unity" against Trump, their common antidemocratic threat. But behind the scenes his aides also pushed back against Sanders's when they insisted Alexandria Ocasio-Cortez get a chance to speak. The Biden side considered the progressive star too polarizing and critical of him, and then only granted her one minute on-screen when Sanders doubled down. To some on Sanders's side, this was a bad sign, even though Biden was being accommodating on so much else.

The worry wasn't that Biden was simply renting the left for the election—he had clearly bought into many of its priorities—but that he was still unrealistic about how much GOP buy-in he'd get for his agenda, and that he might be willing to give up too much to appease them. Some of his friends had heard him muse about building a bipartisan cabinet, perhaps an even more ideologically mixed one than Obama's—a few worried he'd even take seriously some of the suggestions put forward by *Times* columnist Thomas Friedman, whom he read closely and who in April proposed an administration that included Ocasio-Cortez and Warren, but also Romney, Ohio's Republican governor Mike DeWine, and the CEO of Walmart. Biden scoffed at the spirit of the inquiry whenever anyone asked about his faith in Republicans—he wasn't naive, he always said, but he would then insist that he still talked to more Republican officials than people assumed. He'd been saying it out loud less recently—he was now more likely to rhetorically elbow McConnell—but early in his campaign he'd predicted that "the thing that will fundamentally change things is with Donald Trump out of the White House. Not a joke." He'd gone further: "You will see an epiphany occur among many of my Republican friends."

The obvious follow-up question was what had changed for the better since the Obama years, back when his boss had predicted repeatedly that the "fever" would break, only to give up on that hope after the death of 2013's gun reform push. That hope was truly buried by 2016, when McConnell refused for nine months to hold a vote on Obama's Supreme Court nominee Merrick Garland to replace the deceased Antonin

Scalia, keeping the court at eight justices until Trump won. The hope was a distant memory for most by now as the overwhelming majority of that party lined up behind Trump and did his bidding with nary a question for four years, from local nobodies to senior senators like Biden's old friend Lindsey Graham, who'd cried on camera about what a good guy Biden was in 2015 and who was now out there attacking Hunter to appeal to Trump and his voters.

Even Obama told the *New Yorker* that summer, "If you asked Joe and I what regrets we might have, or what lessons we learned from my administration, it's not that we were insufficiently bold in what we proposed. It's that we continued to believe in the capacity of Republicans in Congress to play by the rules, and to be willing to negotiate and compromise." He continued: "Through its actions, the Republican Party has discredited the old-style negotiations and compromises that existed in Congress when Joe first came in. And it's probably taken him a little time to let go of that, because I think he has experience of being able to get stuff done."

Biden's answer to this point rarely changed. *Just trust me*, he'd say. *I know what I'm doing.* Anyway, that was a long-term concern. He had an election to win first. None of this would matter if he lost.

When Ron Klain started drawing up Biden's game plan for the fall debates against Trump, he had Ronald Reagan in mind. Reagan's first debate against Carter in 1980 was the ideal example for ousting an incumbent, and Biden could reasonably replicate the approach against an increasingly unhinged Trump: the ex-VP would defend himself when necessary, but for the most part he would focus on staying above the bickering and not engaging with the president's louder provocations. But that was June, and as the summer progressed Trump detached further from any simulacrum of normal presidential behavior (June: clearing Lafayette Park by force; July: considering the possibility of adding himself to Mount Rushmore; August: turning the White House lawn into a tool of the Republican National Committee). As Biden, Klain, and Dunn pored over presentations from debate coach Michael Sheehan about Reagan's performance and Trump's debate patterns in 2016, another comparison became more apt. Perhaps Biden should approach this as his old friend John Kerry had in 2004 and embrace the fighting spirit. A scrap was clearly coming whether he liked it or not, and Biden started ravenously consuming tapes of that year's show-downs. Then, in the final mock debate session before the first debate in late September, Klain asked attorney Bob Bauer, who was playing the role of Trump, to go totally crazy so Biden could practice interrupting and derailing even the most unhinged version of the president, and so he could go over a few prepared lines insisting Trump couldn't push him around.

Bauer's clown act was still no match for the real thing. Trump's real-life rage onstage in Cleveland was shockingly incoherent and a great adver-tisement for Biden's promise of a return to normal, especially as fears rose that Trump might not accept the results of the election were he to lose. But while Biden's team was happy to display Trump's erratic behavior com-pared to Biden's relative calm (they hadn't practiced the ex-VP's interjec-tion of "Will you shut up, man?" but they had no issue with it) and to highlight the incumbent's unwillingness to disavow the white supremacist Proud Boys, there was still the concern that Trump's posse largely refused to wear face masks in the theater. Few, thus, were all that surprised when the president revealed he tested positive for COVID soon thereafter, was hospitalized, and pulled out of the next debate.

* * *

Shortly after Biden won the Democratic nomination the previous spring, a small group of his confidants gathered to complete an exercise they thought might be useful as they considered how to set up his presidency. Clearly the political, economic, environmental, and social landscapes that Biden was now facing were as unforgiving as any of them could remem-ber. But how many realistic unconventional challenges could they plan for, whether that meant an out-of-control pandemic that hamstrung their ability to coordinate a transition or an outgoing president who stonewalled their efforts and encouraged violence after he lost? The group kept build-ing the list, but stopped counting when it hit seventy possible roadblocks. The veteran Democratic pros didn't want to discourage themselves.

Still, for months the central campaign team had quietly been talking about the possibility of a democratic emergency far more serious than the recount in Florida at the end of the 2000 election, which plenty of them, led by Klain, had worked on themselves. As the fall progressed and Trump delighted in refusing to rule out the possibility of rejecting the election results, Biden's advisors gathered a team of the party's top lawyers to prepare for the worst, though it was hard to imagine what that could look like. They figured that the results would take a while to come in, so the legal war room in Washington was unsurprised to be stuck on standby, on the lookout for chicanery and intimidation, through the Saturday after election day. No one, however, was prepared for Trump's claims to be taken quite so seriously by such a wide swath of Republicans, and no one predicted full-on violence.

Heading into it, the easiest way to look at the transition was as a redux of Obama's in 2008 and 2009 amid an economic collapse and an untrustworthy and untrusting world, and with an ideologically opposed president leaving office. That spring Biden tapped a group of advisors to run his operation with the expectation that the lessons of that experience would be baked into their approach. He first asked his old friend and advisor Ted Kaufman to take charge, considering he literally wrote the law governing transitions, and in concert with Mark Gitenstein they aligned on bringing in Zients—a trusted Obama hand who'd become integrated into BidenWorld during the campaign—and Yohannes Abraham—a longtime Obama loyalist who'd risen steadily in the White House, helped lead the Obama Foundation, and taught about transitions at Harvard's Kennedy School—to run the day-to-day.

But almost immediately they agreed that their task would be far more complicated than 2008's had been in part because they had so little control of their circumstances. For one thing, they were still stuck to conducting business from afar, with Klain—Biden's pick to be his White House chief of staff, twelve years after he became his top vice presidential aide—the only advisor regularly in Wilmington throughout the transition. More importantly, even if Biden was able to immediately pass economic relief, there would still be an international pandemic with no magic bullet available to stop it and also plenty more to consider, for example, a huge threat of climate change after four years of environmental recklessness. They organized their work into four streams—COVID, economic recovery, climate, and racial equality—and set out to hire 1,100 people ready to take over on Day One (conducting eight thousand interviews in the process), in case they needed to seize control of the government from uncooperative Trumpists as the outgoing president's increasingly unhinged claims to have won the election escalated and became gospel to many of his supporters.

Obama had come to realize that the presidency was isolating and crisis-focused by design as the weight of the Great Recession bore down on him in the 2008 campaign's final days. Biden had been taking controlled trips to see small tested and masked crowds for months, but he was now starting to make the same discovery much more literally, nine months into his effective isolation at home. He did, however, have the benefit of an advisor who'd been through it himself. Obama not only found Biden calling regularly in the days and weeks after he won while he considered whom to name to what cabinet and White House job, but Obama also checked in with Zients and Abraham to ask for updates and offer guidance.

Obama also sought to insert some realism into the political conversation, especially after the publication of the first volume of his memoir two weeks after election day. As he saw it, one central theme of *A Promised Land* was how he ran into structural roadblocks time and again as president and had to find ways around them and make progress anyway. Now, he hoped to use his press tour to argue that Biden could make change with many of the same, and some new, obstacles in place—a case he expected to land well because of the predictable foot-dragging Trump's team was doing in relinquishing control of the government. Biden's transition team had prepared for Trump to refuse to allow "ascertainment," the technical maneuver that starts the handover of power between administrations by allowing the incoming teams access to federal resources. They had even talked scores of exhausted government bureaucrats out of retiring in the final months of Trump's term to help facilitate the transfer of power. (They got past the ascertainment delay but considered themselves lucky that there was no serious threat to Biden's safety that required the cooperation of Trump officials, unsure if it would have ever come.)

Obama was surprised, though, that his warning also resonated because of the unexpectedly close nature of the election results, not just in Biden's race but down-ballot, too. Democrats had expected to enter the Biden administration with majorities not just in the House but also the Senate. Yet Pelosi's majority had shrunk and Schumer's was now contingent on Democrats winning both overtime elections in traditionally conservative Georgia in January, which would still get them to only fifty seats, meaning

Harris would have to break ties in the Senate. Even if that happened, which felt unlikely, Biden was entering office with a significantly slimmer path to passing major legislation than Obama had, and less of a clear mandate for the rest of his party.

Still, Biden didn't want to signal any peeling back of ambition and his charges happily took and consulted Sanders's list of recommended personnel, and embraced Warren's, too, even tapping one of her close allies, congresswoman Deb Haaland, to be the first Native American cabinet secretary by nominating her to run the Interior Department. When progressives had major objections to floated picks, Biden tended to listen—opting against Emanuel, whose term as Chicago mayor had been marred by a police shooting cover-up scandal, for transportation secretary, and against Gina Raimondo, who was seen as insufficiently progressive, for Health and Human Services, for example. (He wasn't entirely convinced to stay away from lefties' targets: Emanuel later became his ambassador to Japan and Raimondo his Commerce secretary.) It was, in many ways, the most typically Biden approach imaginable: he hadn't reinvented himself so much as located the center of the increasingly motivated, but still somewhat cautious, Democratic Party now that it was approaching power again. For a few weeks, Biden seemed content to send the message that the world wouldn't return to the Obama-era status quo overnight, but that at least America could sleep again.

Biden's allies could be excused for their confusion over the president-elect's inconsistent feelings about whether he wanted an effective Obama redux. In truth, as much as he was insistent on running his own show and didn't like the implication that he couldn't do it on his own, he also thought swaths of the Obama record and style were close to unimpeachable, so worth replicating and building on. He'd said as much repeatedly on the campaign trail, especially in the primary. Nowhere was this clearer—and nowhere did this hit closer to home—than with his expectations for and treatment of Harris.

For one thing, he had assigned Harris a new team entirely during the campaign, recognizing—as Obama had for him—that her inner orbit wasn't cutting it. She was annoyed, like he had been. But he was intentional about trying to build a personal relationship with her from the start, and he was thrilled when Harris's extended family sat for an early Zoom with his grandkids, and then when she and her husband, Doug Emhoff, started coming through Delaware for occasional dinners with the Bidens even before election day. (Face time was one benefit of not needing to be on the campaign trail 24/7; the pair ended up speaking almost daily, far more than Biden and Obama had in 2008.) The political benefit of picking her had been clear from the start—the campaign and DNC reported raising almost $365 million the month she joined the ticket, which broke all sorts of records—but she was eager to prove her substantive worth, too, and many of her incoming staffers read parts of Walter Mondale's memoir as well as a book on the modern vice presidency by scholar Joel K. Goldstein. This was happening just as Biden's team, which included three former vice presidential chiefs of staff in Klain, Ricchetti, and Bruce Reed, also considered how to optimize her role, and Biden asked her to sit in on his early meetings and pressure-test his staff's recommendations, especially on racial equity in COVID-19 vaccine distribution, voting rights, and the contours of the first economic recovery package.

Conscious that their dynamic would be different from Biden's with Obama when it came to dealing with the globe and the legislature—he still had more experience on those fronts, but now he was the one in charge—the incoming president sought to use Harris's prosecutorial (and limited senatorial) experience by giving her massive briefing books and asking her to help lead interviews as he built his administration in nonstop meetings at The Queen, an event space in Wilmington. Like Biden had twelve years earlier, though, she held back on most specific personnel recommendations, only noting that she hadn't always had a great relationship with Xavier Becerra, her successor as California attorney general who nonetheless became Biden's health secretary, arguing for the elevation of Michael Regan, who took over the Environmental Protection Agency, and pushing for Ohio congresswoman Marcia Fudge to be Agriculture secretary. (She ended up with the Housing and Urban Development job.)

What got far less attention than Harris's role on the team was an important way Biden had chosen to differ from Obama, apparently having learned his lesson. There were, in the end, no Republicans in this cabinet. This was also a crisis presidency, but it was time to push in the opposite direction—to be as aggressively Democratic as possible. Privately Biden had even been talking to Sanders about making him Labor secretary, suggesting through Klain that he would back him to be a nontraditional official empowered to walk picket lines, speak out about his own opinions, and establish a center of influence of his own in the administration for his career's final act. From the start, however, Biden warned Sanders that the job would be contingent on the results of the Senate races in Georgia. Sanders was the only senator he was seriously considering for a job at all because of the precarious balance of the chamber, Biden told him, but he was willing to choose him because he wanted to be ambitious. Yet on the off chance the Democrats somehow won the seats in Georgia, Biden couldn't afford to imperil his tiny Senate majority by removing Sanders from it. The Vermonter understood and agreed.

Neither had any reason to think that this would be the least of their concerns as the Georgia runoffs approached on January 5.

Obama was in Hawaii on January 6, unsure what to make of the news alerts pinging in, since he wasn't watching TV. He'd been surprised but happy that the Georgia races had gone well the previous day, but he hadn't anticipated paying any more attention to DC, where the only important thing expected to happen that Wednesday was the formalizing of Biden's win, one last procedural stamp.

Ever since September his plan had always been to hang back and offer himself as a resource if things got hairy due to Trump's lies about the legitimacy of the election and to let Biden, the president-elect, take the lead in responding. He hadn't fathomed the kind of violent insurrection—an attempted overthrow of the democracy—that his aides were now describing in a rolling set of email updates, and as the situation escalated it became obvious that he would have to say something. All the living presidents would, for the sake of continuity. They checked, using the loose lines of communications that ex-presidents had long maintained: George W. Bush would release a statement, too, and so would Bill Clinton, plus even ninety-six-year-old Jimmy Carter.

For once, finally, Obama let his anger show after four years of building fury and impatience with his successor, who not only hadn't let him live a normal, detached postpresidency but who had recklessly imperiled the world order and now threatened to finish the job. Still, the main response had to be Biden's, so Obama—still getting used to deferring to his old deputy—stuck to releasing a statement laying the blame for the deadly riot at the feet of "a sitting president who has continued to baselessly lie about the outcome of a lawful election." It was "a moment of great dishonor and shame for our nation," he continued, yet "we'd be kidding ourselves if we treated it as a total surprise," since Republicans and right-wing media had been complicit in Trump's lie, he wrote. "Their fantasy narrative has spiraled further and further from reality, and it builds upon years of sown resentments. Now we're seeing the consequences, whipped up into a violent crescendo." He put the challenge to GOP leaders: "They can continue down this road and keep stoking the raging fires. Or they can choose reality and take the first steps toward extinguishing the flames."

Biden, meanwhile, had been watching it all unfold from Delaware, where he'd started the day expecting to give a talk about his plans for the economy. When he connected with his brain trust, he told the aides he absolutely had to speak out on the theme he'd been considering daily since 2017's white supremacist rally in Charlottesville, Virginia: Trump's assault on American institutions. On camera, he called on Trump to call off the rioters and insisted this was not "true America," but rather the work of "extremists dedicated to lawlessness." But, he conceded, "our democracy's under unprecedented assault, unlike anything we've seen in modern times. An assault on the citadel of liberty, the Capitol itself." The storming of the Capitol, he said, "borders on sedition." For the first time in over a decade, it no longer made sense for him to call Barack for guidance or a gut-check or a heads-up midcrisis. He didn't need to call Honolulu.

Nor did he peel back on his transition work over the next two weeks. Yet in private, when he could steal a second away, he was quieter than ever, not quite seething but clearly restless. Eventually, he conceded to friends that he was now conscious that every time he opened his mouth he would be speaking for history, not just the next day's *Washington Post*. This was his new reality not just as the incoming president but also as the nation's leader at one of its perilous junctures. He was thinking of Obama's example still, but now also Lincoln's and Washington's.

The once-ubiquitous comparisons to the calamitous circumstances Obama had faced in January 2009 no longer felt so apt. Not only did Biden think he needed to speak for an ailing country—the night before he was inaugurated, he and Harris visited the Lincoln Memorial to honor the victims of the pandemic, now up to 400,000 in the United States alone—but now also for democracy itself.

He was, at this point, comfortable thinking of the moment in these historical terms, and therefore with the idea that his inaugural address, composed with Donilon and historian Jon Meacham, would be remembered as a defense of basic democratic values against an unprecedented assault and a promise of healing, both medical and social. He wouldn't say a word about Trump's second impeachment, determined to move on and not to get dragged back into the muck even while his colleagues on Capitol Hill investigated.

The imperative to send this message only strengthened when, a week before the inauguration, security concerns forced Biden to scrap plans to take an Amtrak train to Washington for the ceremony, just like he'd done for much of his career. He was facing a new challenge. Yet few people but he and Obama remembered that they had also taken a train into Washington for their own inauguration a dozen Januarys earlier.

AFTERWORD

Biden had always been big on symbolism, especially when it came to his work spaces. As a senator he'd treasured the table that was handed down to him from the Philippine government via Harry Truman and then a pair of anti–civil rights movement senators because he thought it represented progress, diplomacy, and bipartisanship. He displayed it prominently. As VP, he'd preferred his room in the West Wing to his larger office across the street in the Eisenhower Executive Office Building and his ceremonial one in the Capitol. He enjoyed pointing out that it was just down the hall from Obama's, and he often noted its portraits of Thomas Jefferson and John Adams, the men who first defined the vice presidency and then took the top job. When it was finally his turn to decorate the Oval Office, he saw little reason for subtlety.

Excising the cold air of Trump and replacing it with homages to liberal-minded advancement was the obvious part. With help from his brother Jimmy and Meacham, he substituted out a portrait of Andrew Jackson for one of Benjamin Franklin and arranged busts of Cesar Chavez, Bobby Kennedy, Martin Luther King Jr., Abraham Lincoln, Rosa Parks, Eleanor Roosevelt, Truman, and Daniel Webster around the room, which he also dotted with his own family photos. The more politically pointed choice was to replace the art above the fireplace, directly across from the president's desk. Each of his predecessors dating back to Richard Nixon had looked up at portraits of George Washington. Lyndon Johnson, however, had Franklin Roosevelt on that wall half a century earlier, and Biden decided he liked the way Johnson, the architect of the "Great Society" program, had thought. Biden had been considering LBJ and FDR a lot since the previous spring, for months progressively making his stated vision for the country's pandemic recovery sound more and more like a comprehensive New Deal–style plan composed not only of trillions of dollars in spending on economic stimulus but also infrastructure financing and climate investments. He returned Roosevelt to the mantel and moved Washington a few feet away.

He was even using Bill Clinton's carpet, but there was no explicit nod to Obama in the decorations. That probably would have been superfluous. No one who came across Biden in those days could possibly doubt that his old boss took up significant real estate in his head as he conceived of his task, in both purposeful and unconscious ways. Biden sat in the exact same spot Obama had for eight years when he gathered aides for meetings at the couches in the Oval, and for a while Biden referred to his predecessor's accomplishments, or White House procedures he remembered, as "the way we did it" in "our administration."

For the first six months of his presidency, too, he and his aides—many of them holdovers from the Obama years—openly spoke of learning the hard lessons of that administration and leveraging them to far greater effect this time. This seemed like an obvious approach to everyone, and the upsides to acknowledging it seemed clear to loyalists of both presidents, as well. "For them to go back four years later, with the benefit of eight years of White House–based political experience—it's an advantage I don't think any administration has ever had," Pfeiffer told the *Washington Post* that spring. The mission appeared to be not just on track but also ahead of schedule when Biden signed a nearly $2 trillion COVID-targeted relief bill in March full of easy-to-understand and popular provisions. It was regularly compared to Obama's 2009-era stimulus of roughly $800 billion, which, in its day, was considered unfathomably enormous and therefore politically dubious.

As Biden then set out to add another roughly $3 trillion in spending on social programs and infrastructure, however, he ran into some of the same kinds of limitations that had bedeviled Obama, starting with a Republican Party categorically opposed to collaborating on his programs. He was also hamstrung by his tiny margins in both the House and Senate, which limited his capacity for progress, no matter how much time he spent trying to play his old-school Capitol Hill schmoozing card. Public sympathy, however, was in short supply as he repeatedly thudded up against the unmoving limits of the presidency to effect change unilaterally. He was both a victim of his own floridly set expectations about a new FDR-inspired era—which came from a time just months earlier when he'd expected to be working with a more heavily Democratic Senate, but which he didn't temper as he took office—and a man unable to reinvent himself politically yet again so late in his career. After the last decade it simply didn't seem realistic to those around him to think he could now approach the office in some entirely different way to adapt to this latest unforgiving moment. He couldn't easily bring himself to choose more attainable priorities that fell far short of his campaign pledges, just as he couldn't now reconsider either the public conception of his refusal to compromise on Afghanistan or the ramifications of his stubbornness. Similarly, it was an inexcusably big ask to reset benchmarks for how the exhausted country could begin to move on from an emergency footing even as the pandemic persisted, he thought. Any such concession seemed unthinkable to him for his first year in office, an admission of disappointment he wouldn't countenance.

It was possible to read Biden's first twelve months, thus, as either something of a microcosm of the Obama years or as their frustrating natural next step in the face of unrelenting right-wing attacks not just on his government but also on the legitimacy of the democratic system itself. Biden's overpromises were hardly a mortal political sin, but his inability to convince an aggressively riven populace that it was still on a positive post-Trump track felt painfully similar to the lead-up to the 2010 midterms and Obama's famous "shellacking," never mind how much historic legislation both presidents signed in Year One. This was largely thanks to protracted negotiations within the Democratic Party itself as it searched first for its post-Bush, and now, much more urgently, post-Trump identities.

Still, though Biden hated when people put it like this, there was always an argument to be made that no matter what he accomplished in office, his legacy would first and foremost be Trump's defeat. That would, in fact, be enough for so many to consider Biden a success, both in the immediate sense of day-to-day threat elimination and for years to come in terms of the world's stability. Yet the defining question of his first year was how to convince Americans and a few recalcitrant counterparts-cum-roadblocks in DC that there was still so much more on offer—so much more *needed*—after he swept into office promising not just to eradicate Trumpism in the

White House but also to heal the nation more broadly. For evidence that this wasn't just a theoretical concern, he had to look no further than the many states where GOP legislators, still in Trump's thrall, were working on bills to make voting harder, and possibly to lay the groundwork for overthrowing elections altogether.

Obama saw the problem as structural, as he had for so many of the presidency's ills for a few years now. In his view that structure—modern DC and its Republican-driven political culture—needed exposing, then renovating. He wouldn't blame Biden for trying to make compromises in office, he told one of his favorite columnists, *New York* magazine's Jonathan Chait, in December 2020, but "there comes a point where you have to clearly communicate over and over again for the American people what the cause is for gridlock. Why something is not happening. That I think is a good lesson for them to learn." Biden, eventually, professed to embrace the lesson, and promised to implement it, at a White House press conference marking his first year in office. His approval rating was only slightly above where Trump's had been at a comparable moment, a far cry from the previous summer, when over half of Americans were happy with his performance. "I'm going to get out of this place more often, I'm going to go out and talk to the public," he said, also promising to listen to more external perspectives and to campaign more for Democrats. He wanted people to know "Mitch [McConnell] has been very clear he's going to do anything to prevent Biden from being a success," and to ask, "What's he for? What's he proposing to make anything better?" Biden continued, asking of Republicans, "What are they for?" It was a good question, but one that even Obama, a far better communicator, had strained to get across during his tenure. It was still hard to make the case after a year of the Biden administration that simply raising the question would be anything more than a first step back toward progress.

* * *

Biden never saw any use in obscuring the ways in which he was drawing inspiration from the Obama years, even when some members of his administration were worried by the prospect of a right-wing conspiracy campaign insisting that Obama was really pulling the strings. (The conservative *New York Post*'s salty April 2021 headline after Jen Psaki showed no interest in talking about how often the presidents were speaking privately:

PSAKI SAYS OBAMA, BIDEN TALK REGULARLY BUT REFUSES TO SAY HOW OFTEN.) It was true that in closed-door meetings Biden often insisted that his team discuss the Obama experience, but Obama wasn't there and Biden usually just wanted to ask what they could do better this time, knowing what they now knew. Biden was still sensitive to the ideas, occasionally shared on cable, that Obama had somehow carried him to the presidency or that he would simply be Obama 2.0. But he was also still equally proud of his predecessor's record and so would occasionally admit to allies that he was constantly chagrined to learn how much of the Obama years' progress had been unwound by Trump. He found himself occupied with the question of how to first restore it, and then how to cement his own accomplishments to ensure they couldn't be rolled back by the next Republican president.

As a result, one of his most frequent contentions was that he had to be far more intentional about selling the stuff he was passing to keep it popular, a point he'd tried making to Obama back in 2009 but had conceded as their political standing sagged and other crises arose. Shortly after his own rescue bill first passed the House in late February, Biden appeared virtually for a gathering of Democratic members of Congress and promised the crowd—whose political fortune was tied to his—that he wouldn't repeat Obama's error. "We didn't adequately explain what we had done. Barack was so modest, he didn't want to take, as he said, a 'victory lap.' I kept saying, 'Tell people what we did.' He said, 'We don't have time. I'm not going to take a victory lap.' And we paid a price for it, ironically, for that humility," Biden recalled, unwilling to even winkingly recognize that he was obviously criticizing his old boss.

Biden's bill's passage had actually been a rapid-fire display of how to learn from one's errors. For one thing, it was hard to find anyone left in Democratic politics who would say Obama had been right to wait so long for Republicans to join him while he was trying to pass Obamacare. Now Biden took one meeting with Senate Republicans and rejected their proposal to cleave the bill into about a third of its $1.9 trillion size. He figured this measure needed to pass as soon as possible and he knew it could become law through a simple-majority vote rather than needing sixty votes because of Senate rules for spending legislation. He thus determined it would have to move ahead quickly with or without Republicans onboard. The image of bipartisanship just wasn't relevant here because of how urgently Americans needed the funds, and neither, really, were deficit concerns or worries about the price tag for purely political reasons. There was no redux of the Emanuel and Summers arguments from 2008 to slim down that bill, because the political moment was so different now. (Biden had agreed then, but now scoffed at such arguments when pundits floated them, though he also dismissed economists' prescient worries that so much spending would contribute to inflation a few months down the road.) Meanwhile, after seeing how fickle public opinion was a decade earlier, Biden this time figured as many programs would have to fit in this one bill as possible. He was now under no illusion that they could return to the drawing board for a second round of funding legislation if they needed to.

He hoped they wouldn't need to in part because he had other priorities to get to, and in part because he expected the bill's components would get enough people back on their feet, designed as they were to jump-start the national recuperation from the pandemic. As such, Biden not only ordered an array of his new cabinet secretaries to start talking up the provisions to make sure people knew about them, but also leaned into the point that it was all intended to be immediately useful—far more so than its 2009 analogue, which was more focused on longer-term investments and which contained smaller one-time payments to residents. "We didn't do enough to explain to the American people what the benefits were of the [2009] rescue plan," Psaki said in March. "We didn't do enough to do it in terms that people would be talking about it at their dinner tables. And that's one of the reasons we—of course—have been trying to break down the impact of the American Rescue Plan into key components that will impact people directly: the direct checks, you know, ensuring funding to help expedite vaccine distribution, and of course reopening of schools."

The results were, indeed, felt quickly, as the $1,400 checks began arriving in many bank accounts and the child tax credit almost immediately slashed child poverty rates around the country. Dunn, who'd spent enough time around Obama to know his regrets well, at the same time encouraged a group of Biden allies outside the White House to launch a political organization that could raise money and pay for ads promoting the president's agenda all over the country, something Obama never had, even after the Supreme Court's *Citizens United* decision made it possible, but could have used.

For a while, it looked like Biden had cracked a code, his half century in DC adding up to unlikely but real political success in a brutally divided nation where his immediate predecessor was still insisting he'd won the last election. Some Democrats allowed themselves to briefly believe that the dream of another FDR was still a stretch but maybe not as far-fetched as they'd once thought. People close to both Biden and Obama had long known that racism was one massive reason for the forty-fourth president's demonization in right-wing circles, but they were nonetheless prepared for Biden to be framed by those same people as senile or a puppet of the left. Instead, Republicans found themselves mostly unable to tar Biden with any negative narratives that stuck. The welcome soporific effect of Biden's brand of unflashy but functional governance sans inspirational speeches or noteworthy partisan battles even had some liberals now improbably thinking of Obama with a more skeptical eye in retrospect.

Obama himself never said a word about it all, and Biden wouldn't let any of his charges bad-mouth his old partner in front of him. But to some of the former president's remaining loyalists outside the new administration, this celebratory posture six months in was a bit premature. They were rooting for Biden, of course, but they didn't think pundits were properly remembering just how inhospitable the political and economic environment had been in 2009. Obama's task hadn't been easy. And, in private conversations, they didn't find Biden's display of learning his lessons particularly revelatory or groundbreaking. *Of course* he'd learned from the Obama years, and *of course* he was making progress, some took to almost-whispering to friends and, occasionally, journalists. Wasn't that the whole point of electing him?

* * *

Obama couldn't find many good reasons to return to DC these days. Sasha was now away at college and both he and Michelle were loving their lives out on Martha's Vineyard, where they had a private chef, memberships at two golf courses, and a solid group of friends, including Eric Holder. He flew back and forth but dropped into his office in the West End less than ever, having reorganized it after Biden won to be less concerned about the day-to-day and more conscious of defining his legacy and how his postpresidency could shape it. Practically that meant leaning further into his role as a cultural—not primarily political—figure, at least until the midterms approached or the presidential library opened. He especially enjoyed recording a personal podcast with Bruce Springsteen about unity, hopes for a new generation, and modern American masculinity. It was all part of his wish to be a popular influence on society and to tamp down the polarization around his every last move. The publication of a coffee table book based on the podcast completed the project. As he saw it, the ideal version of his new role was to pop up on occasion to keep folks hopeful and optimistic, and to advocate for liberal, pluralistic values when needed.

What he was very consciously not doing was golfing with Biden. That had never been their thing, and it would've just felt unnatural for them to start socializing like that now that Joe was president and Barack had nothing but time. This was fine with Obama—content as he was to believe from afar that he'd played a critical role in putting his former partner in the Oval, even if Biden didn't quite see it that way, and to muse about how his tenure had proven to be ahead of its time as far as the political culture was concerned. This was where he'd landed in his reflections about how Trump had succeeded him. In this version of events Biden made perfect sense as the figure to usher society back into the present from the Stone Age before it rediscovered the future. Obama felt no need to start texting Biden a stream of unbidden advice in January—he'd usually hold off until he was asked—and he scaled back the cadence of his calls with Dunn, O'Malley Dillon, and others who were now in the West Wing. They knew how to get in touch when they needed him, and either way they were keeping Obama's remaining aides plenty apprised of what was going on.

It was with considerable exasperation, then, that he found himself dragged back into the DC sludge when, that summer, the party for his six-tieth birthday became an issue. The drama was mostly self-inflicted before it spiraled out of control. Obama had been planning a bash on the island for roughly five hundred celebrities and longtime friends deep enough into the summer and the administration's vaccination drive that the out-door festivities felt uncontroversial over the months of planning. The summertime's rise of the dangerous Delta variant of the virus had other plans, however, and as the spring ended whispers were flying in Wash-ington's Democratic circles about whether Obama would go ahead with the party, considering Biden's insistence on modeling responsible behav-ior throughout the pandemic and his administration's public retreat from its confident claim of near-victory over the virus in July. Meanwhile, if there was any one issue on which Obama was still especially engaged with the White House, it was in helping spread the word about vaccinations, a public endeavor he vigorously embraced for months on end even as he tried retreating from politics. All this surely outweighed one party. When Obama then did cut back the guest list at the last minute but went ahead with a slightly scaled-back affair, the reaction in the conservative press was radioactive. (Fox News: "Mainstream Media Silent While Obama Dances Maskless in a Crowded Tent.")

But it was unsparing even in some corners of the media the two presidents cared more about. In the *Times*, Maureen Dowd was scathing on both aesthetic and political grounds, calling the ex-president "Barack Antoinette" and, comparing him unfavorably to Jay Gatsby, writing, "Obama gave a big, lavish, new-money party at his sprawling mansion on the water because he wanted to seem cool. Being cool is important to him." Worse, she wrote, "As president, he didn't try hard enough on things we needed. He was a diffident debutante with a distaste for politics. Post-presidency, he is trying too hard on things we don't need." This felt unignorable and like an annoyance Obama was sure he didn't need at this stage in his life. It was not, however, a moment for introspection in his eyes.

Biden's White House, for its part, held an official position that looked like mild discomfort bordering on annoyance of its own, but mostly because aides had to answer questions about this in the first place. Biden wasn't ever going to attend—no sitting president could make time for something like that, let alone security arrangements. But Klain and Donilon had been invited, and Kathleen and some Biden grandkids were expected. (The aides skipped the party; the family went.) And Biden had recorded a warm birthday video that played for the guests, in which he revealed that he still thought all the time about Obama and what he would do in certain situations. Biden was, thus, sympathetic but unamused to have this new headache on top of the one he was already dealing with amid the virus's resurgence, just as he had been hoping to put it behind him.

But some people around Obama were frustrated by this, too. It wasn't just that everyone should have more important things to worry about than his party. They knew that everything he did was political by definition and that this didn't look great. Yet maybe this was a sign of what the administration was failing to do, and running up against, nationwide. Some wondered aloud: Couldn't they at least have defended Obama a bit more by saying this is what responsible gatherings could look like? He had a vaccine requirement and it was all outside! Wasn't he an example? The good kind?

Even in the moment, everyone knew the party was a sideshow. Much bigger things were happening in the White House, and this time Obama was watching closely. He had been onto something in June when he argued in a podcast interview that "Joe and the administration are essentially finishing the job." Biden sometimes still bristled at this characterization of his work, but that was in fact how he was approaching the war in Afghanistan, which he'd been promising to finally, really, truly end, and which was at long last winding down when he entered office after the Trump administration struck a deal with the Taliban to withdraw troops.

He started a review of Afghanistan policy almost as soon as he was inaugurated, pretty sure he would actually have the chance to do what he'd basically wanted to do all those years earlier. This war was on the hands of a whole generation of leaders now, he believed, and he wasn't much interested in arguments that he had a duty to extend it as it approached its third decade. Never had this been clearer than the previous February, when CBS News's Margaret Brennan asked if he bore "some responsibility for the outcome if the Taliban ends up back in control and women end up losing the rights." He was clearly exasperated by the question after all these years. "No, I don't!" he'd said, arguing that the country can't keep a military presence everywhere it detects injustice. "Do I bear responsibility? Zero responsibility. The responsibility I have is to protect America's national self-interest and not put our women and men in harm's way to try to solve every single problem in the world by use of force." The American people also appeared to be on his side. Fatigue with the war was widespread, and poll after poll showed nearly two-thirds of citizens approved of the plan to remove the troops.

His order to proceed with a full troop withdrawal was thus not surprising to his foreign policy advisors—especially not to Blinken, his longtime aide who was now his secretary of state a dozen years after having a firsthand view of the 2009 debates with Obama, Hillary Clinton, Robert Gates, and the generals over the war's future. None of Biden's military aides should have then been surprised when, as the drawdown proceeded, Biden remained unmovable in the face of their arguments that he should keep a residual force in Afghanistan or send in more support for Afghans who'd helped the US and now needed help escaping. The intelligence was starting to show that the Taliban could take over much more quickly than they'd expected, imperiling the plan for an orderly exit by September. Yet Biden—still wary of the Pentagon's advice even now that it was run by his own defense secretary, the former Central Command leader and Iraq mission general Lloyd Austin—refused to budge.

The increasing chorus of DC foreign-policy types questioning his strategy only hardened him, convinced as he was that this was the crowd that had been so wrong for so long about the war. The effect was to deafen him to the increasingly desperate pleas for help from within the country. He'd called Obama to tell him he was ending the American presence, and Obama, who still felt some weight on his shoulders over the war's prolonged denouement, was supportive. No one knew better than Obama how deeply Biden felt about it. He determined it was best to tread lightly here, not just because of Biden's conviction and their complex history on the matter but also because he felt strongly that the country should only have one president at a time and he didn't want to overstep his role. (Biden had called George W. Bush, too, as a courtesy.) "There's going to be no circumstance where you see people being lifted off the roof of an embassy of the United States from Afghanistan," the president insisted as worries proliferated that he'd end up with an evacuation similar to the retreat from Vietnam. Yet he did concede briefly and send three thousand troops on a temporary mission to secure the airport in Kabul and make sure embassy staff could evacuate. Images like the ones he said were out of the question started to surface.

Still, though, he refused to change course, sticking with his line that "the likelihood there's going to be the Taliban overrunning everything and owning the whole country is highly unlikely." Even as this was proving to be clearly false, the Afghan army folding across the country, he wouldn't reconsider the withdrawal. Instead, he believed that the Taliban's speed in taking over was a massive indictment of the war effort itself, considering how much time, energy, and resources had been put into training and propping up the local soldiers over many years. He'd been right all along, he thought.

In truth, he also believed he had more time and that his plan to pull out troops would make for an orderly withdrawal. He was surprised when it became clear that the Taliban had a clear path to overtaking Kabul, and that mass confusion was starting to turn Hamid Karzai International Airport into a disaster zone with Afghans straining to get out. Yet two weeks out from the withdrawal deadline, as the situation was turning into an international fiasco and it became clear that Afghanistan would immediately fall back into full Taliban control once the last US soldier left—but before an ISIS suicide bomber killed nearly two hundred people, including thirteen American troops—he sought to try to get his own country to have some perspective.

"We went to Afghanistan almost twenty years ago with clear goals: get those who attacked us on September 11, 2001, and make sure al-Qaeda could not use Afghanistan as a base from which to attack us again. We did that. We severely degraded al-Qaeda in Afghanistan. We never gave up the hunt for Osama bin Laden, and we got him. That was a decade ago. Our mission in Afghanistan was never supposed to have been nation-building," he said. With some tweaks it could have been a monologue from the old debates with the generals. "Our only vital national interest in Afghanistan remains today what it has always been: preventing a terrorist attack on American homeland. I've argued for many years that our mission should be narrowly focused on counterterrorism—not counterinsurgency or nation-building. That's why I opposed the surge when it was proposed in 2009 when I was vice president. And that's why, as president, I am adamant that we focus on the threats we face today in 2021—not yesterday's threats."

What much of Washington—and certainly its press—was reading as stubbornness and an appalling inability to reassess even in the face of calamity, Biden believed was a principled insistence on finishing the job that Americans would appreciate. He could either withdraw the troops or escalate by sending thousands more back into combat, he said. "After twenty years, I've learned the hard way that there was never a good time to withdraw US forces."

He'd been thinking plenty about his extended Situation Room and Oval Office disagreements with Obama's military advisors, and how that saga had shaped his vice presidency, which had led him here. Two days earlier, he shared out loud a thought that he kept having about the war the US had clearly lost, though he wouldn't say it like that. "I was the fourth president to preside over an American troop presence in Afghanistan. Two Republicans, two Democrats," he said. "I would not, and will not, pass this war onto a fifth."

The dam broke.

With even Democrats now openly questioning Biden's handling of the Afghanistan debacle and press coverage of Biden turning brutal for the first extended period in his administration, Republicans began hammering at a message that cut right at Biden's central claim as president. He was incompetent, they began arguing, and as if the botched withdrawal was a flipped switch, his approval rating began sliding.

It wasn't all, or even mostly, about Afghanistan. The country was slipping into a nasty malaise thanks to COVID's persistence, increasing prices, and the rise of conspiracy-driven right-wing antivaccination sentiment, too. Indicators of Americans' sense of optimism slumped throughout the late summer and into the fall.

Biden's problem now was that he didn't have anything flashy and new to show off, and—just like Obama had all those years earlier, but with far less capacity to captivate the country rhetorically and even less room to maneuver on Capitol Hill—he was finding it difficult to argue to voters that despite how they felt, things were actually getting much better. He was having a hard time getting agreement even within his party as its members debated the ambitious spending plans he'd proposed covering both physical infrastructure and investments on things like childcare, fighting climate change, and housing. With most focus on the Senate, where he had no margin for error with just fifty seats on his side, attention was especially trained on Joe Manchin, the conservative West Virginia Democrat, and Kyrsten Sinema, an unpredictable first-term Arizonan. Both expressed some discomfort with the sheer amount of spending Biden still had on the table—over $4 trillion in total—and both shuttled in and out of the White House and administration aides' ears for weeks, and then months, at a time.

This dynamic had been foretold when Manchin held up the COVID relief bill's passage at its final moment back in March with an objection to how many unemployment benefits it would pay out, and when both he and Sinema joined a few others in voting to strip out a provision raising the minimum wage. The parallel to Obama's years of struggle with his era's numerous conservative Democrats was clear to the ex-president, who didn't envy his successor's position but wasn't surprised by it after Biden had first won the presidential primary on a platform of restoration and then the general by promising systemic change. With progressives furious at the pair of senators and some of their centrist counterparts on the House side, and with no room to alienate either side if he wanted to pass any piece of his agenda, Biden was stuck in the middle of the debate over his party's identity, which he'd been avoiding for more than a year.

What unsettled Obama, though, was how unavailable one way out of this—focusing on obstreperous Republicans—appeared to be. It was eye-opening how little anyone seemed to care, now that Republican leaders weren't even pretending to want to compromise on most of what Biden was proposing. This was simply an assumed feature of Washington now. Biden once liked to point out that McConnell had given a tribute to him on the Senate floor about their mutual trust before Biden left the vice presidency, and had even named a cancer research funding provision of a bill after Beau. Four months into Biden's presidency, though, McConnell had said "one hundred percent of our focus is on stopping this new administration," an echo of his 2010 pledge to ensure Obama served only one term, but with almost none of the ensuing uproar. There wasn't much more outrage a few weeks later when John Barrasso, the third-ranking Republican senator, followed up. "McConnell came under a lot of criticism for saying at one point he wanted to make sure that Barack Obama was a one-term president," he said. "I want to make Joe Biden a one-half-term president. And I want to do that by making sure they no longer have the House, Senate, and White House." This was just politics now. You couldn't really blame Biden for focusing so much on his own party, even when he obviously wanted to keep crossing the aisle, just like he had his whole career.

* * *

After all this time, Biden wasn't sure if he'd ever quite get used to the trappings of the White House. He loved being president, of course, but he felt self-conscious being waited on so attentively and confined without the ability to roam freely or to easily sit outside. He immediately decided he'd continue his senatorial and vice presidential practice of going home to Wilmington, or to the beach, or, he supposed, to Camp David, most weekends.

His daily life in the office would look little like Obama's, even if the political patterns were repeating themselves. He took to starting his mornings slightly later, after catching up on the CNN and MSNBC breakfast shows Obama dismissed as insider babble, and to calling aides until later into the night. He preferred a constant stream of advice and debate from an only-slightly-expanded version of his longtime inner circle to the silence Obama often wanted after hours.

Biden relied less obviously on his vice president, too, though internally this was not as dramatic a shock as the dire news coverage that Harris received in her first year made it seem. More conscious than anyone of the VP's positioning, from the first day of their tenure Biden made sure the White House's official communications included Harris's name, and he made a practice of ensuring she got to speak before him at major events. He tried giving her more explicit assignments early on than he'd had, telling her, for example, that when he assigned her the task of tackling the root causes of migration surges from Central American nations that it meant a lot to him, since he'd worked on the matter himself for Obama. And he appreciated that she wasn't just blindly following his example—she'd had her own conversation with Mondale about the job shortly before he died in April, and she was sitting for weekly meetings with Klain, now the White House chief of staff, to try to keep herself integrated in the West Wing's operations. She also approached her weekly lunches with Biden as more of a working meeting than he had with Obama; she used one of them to ask for the administration's voting rights portfolio.

Yet mistrust lingered between some of their aides and they were slower to become genuine friends, in part because it took both longer to adapt to the pressures of their offices and partially because of the even bigger gap in age and experiences. Her assignments were unforgiving, too—progress on voting rights reform was slow, and Central American violence and corruption wasn't going anywhere anytime soon—and she both found it hard to penetrate Biden's brain trust at times and didn't offer him the same immediate experience he'd been able to provide for Obama. As a result, she wasn't as strategically vital to winning votes, which he thought of as a central part of the job after his own tenure. Yet he insisted she remain the final person in the room with him for big decisions—that was real—even when he was convinced he already knew exactly what he was doing.

This was often when it came to negotiating with lawmakers, a task he predictably gravitated to with far more relish than his old boss had, inviting a parade of Democrats by his new digs to talk strategy. When Jon Tester came through in February, the Montana senator grew emotional, never having been in the Oval Office before, which some people around Biden thought revealed plenty about Obama's style, considering how politically important Tester was. This was still little help with Manchin and Sinema, though. The negotiations over Biden's agenda dragged on until he split his proposal into one infrastructure bill that would get wide support and another, bigger plan that would take longer and need whittling down thanks to Manchin's souring relationship with Biden and Klain. They eventually pegged him as unreasonable, and risked tanking the entire social spending agenda by releasing a furious statement about Manchin when the West Virginian kept expressing doubts.

It was a measure of just how high Biden had set the expectations for his presidency that when he did succeed in signing a years-in-the-making $1 trillion infrastructure law in November 2021, even winning Republican votes in the process, his public image barely budged. Many Americans no longer thought they felt the effects of his initial recovery bill and they gave him no bump for the post-lockdown economic rebound. Neither did he get credit for ending the "forever war" in Afghanistan, or, a year on, for ridding them of Trump. Like Obama had, Biden felt too besieged by the world to spend enough time selling his accomplishments, though he knew he should.

Within a few days of moving into the White House, Biden started confiding to friends that he felt a heavy sense of history following him around the building at all times. This only added to the urgency he'd been feeling since winning the Democratic nomination, a tension he insisted had everything to do with the country's dire circumstances and nothing to do—as some of his longtime allies nonetheless suspected—with his age and a tacit acknowledgment that he'd waited long enough to make big decisions. This didn't mean he suddenly learned to make choices quickly, rather that he weighed them that much more carefully and agonizingly, and that he had less patience for the kind of rambling and hobnobbing he once loved. His phone calls with friends were getting shorter and more abrupt, his briefings with policy experts dragging on longer.

Obama started to feel something similar as Biden's first year as president progressed, but the mood expressed itself more soberly around the ex-president. Both were now thinking less of immediate news cycles and more about the meaning of their legacy and their shared political era. Yet as Obama thought more about the long arc of progress that he often mentioned, the weight of evidence sometimes made it look like it was forbiddingly long and far from bending. He resolved to focus only on the most tectonic of threats these days, reconnecting both with tech industry leaders to consider what their field's role could be in combating disinformation—he gathered some of them to discuss this issue in Palo Alto in June 2021—and with climate experts to insist on America's seriousness about the globe's future, no matter how dismissively Trump had treated it. He made a rare appearance at that November's international climate conference in Glasgow to make that case.

Back home, though, Obama's thoughts on the state of the world rarely strayed far from his immediate successor and his antidemocratic threat with Trump remaining in the political picture and keeping the Republican Party wrapped around his finger. Obama calculated, thus, that while he still had no interest in getting involved in daily politics again, lending a loud voice in favor of the voting rights push could only help. He started over the summer, arguing in his first Biden-era appearances for Holder's redistricting-focused group that passing legislation to protect voting rights should be obvious and a matter of basic American values. He found himself saying things that he didn't think would need to be said out loud in 2021, they felt so obvious: "As bad as January 6 was, if we had to repeat in future elections, in which, let's say, the Republican-controlled Pennsylvania legislature decided 'We're not going to certify all those votes coming out of Philadelphia because we think that those urban votes are shady,' imagine what would have happened. We would have had a worse constitutional crisis than we did," he said at a fundraiser with Pelosi for the organization. If they didn't change the laws to protect against such manipulations, he continued, "We are going to see a further delegitimizing of our democracy, and not only are we going to see more unfairness in terms of results and who is represented and who isn't, but we are going to see a breakdown of the basic agreement."

The fight, in other words, was epochal. Slowly it seemed Biden was coming to agree that this was the horrid outgrowth of the battle he'd waged in 2020—when he'd put it in almost Manichean terms—and that he must address the matter of voting access and election protection after months of pressure from civil rights leaders. He had a closing window to make a politically viable push on the matter before midterm season arrived. There was, however, no realistic way to pass as sweeping a law as he wanted with any Republican votes, which meant he'd need to finally call for the abolition of the sixty-vote filibuster rule on voting legislation so Democrats could pass it themselves. To make the case, he finally directly engaged with the threat of Trump, something he'd avoided doing for a year to fulfill his promise of restoring some degree of normalcy.

On the one-year anniversary of the January 6 attack, Biden visited the Capitol to insist Trump and his associates still held "a dagger at the throat of America" with their comportment over the past year. "The former president of the United States of America has created and spread a web of lies about the 2020 election. He's done so because he values power over principle, because he sees his own interest as more important than the country's interest and America's interest, and because his bruised ego matters more to him than our democracy or our Constitution. He can't accept he lost." Less than a week later, he laid out the specifics in Atlanta, arguing for the removal of the filibuster on voting bills before challenging lawmakers: "Do you want to be on the side of Dr. King or George Wallace? Do you want to be on the side of John Lewis or Bull Connor? Do you want to be on the side of Abraham Lincoln or Jefferson Davis?"

But just two days later, as Biden prepared to make his case one more time, Sinema refused to go along with the plan, effectively killing it. He insisted he was undeterred. But it would not have been completely unfair to ask what, at this point, there was left for him to do aside from pivoting to unilateral but perhaps impermanent executive actions, given his political constraints and capabilities.

* * *

The presidency, as a general rule, is not a particularly productive venue for introspection, coming as it does with all the pressures in the world. It does, however, force all of its responsible occupants to reconsider their priorities, theories of effecting change, and conceptions of their role in the country's broadest arc.

One year into his administration, fourteen years into his partnership with Obama, and forty-nine years into his life in Washington, Biden had contemplated all of the above, and appeared to have encountered a series of familiar walls. The fully polarized end of 2021 and beginning of 2022 were testing the outer bounds of the office and his own political abilities, his triumphant rescuing of the republic from Trump and his hyperproductive first sprint meeting a cynical opposition and a skeptical public unwilling to be won over by his brand of persuasion. The 2022 midterms looked like they offered little hope of a Democratic revival to change any of this; the question of whether Biden, at eighty-one, would run for reelection in 2024—possibly against Trump—loomed over his every move, even as he insisted he would.

Discouragement, thus, might seem to be an obvious response from both the commander in chief and his longtime partner. Obama especially seemed prone to moments of gloom. For years, it had seemed that Obama's tenure represented the soul of a new political era, a post-Reagan age inching toward progress, interconnectedness, and liberal-minded mutual understanding around the world. But the Trump experience also made it easier to view the recent years as the dawn and maturation of a darker time typified by greed, mistrust, and fractured information ecosystems.

Yet neither the forty-fourth nor the forty-sixth president ever let himself go all the way down that road, both of their political philosophies still rooted in the necessity of long-term optimism even after all of the forty-fifth's work to destabilize it.

Obama, in the end, had never gone terribly far. He was happy to live in semiretirement, only evaluating the new administration from a distance when he wanted to. But he still sometimes heard from Klain, occasionally as often as every two or three weeks, with asks for advice, White House progress reports, and requests for favors. He was a general advisor, not quite monitoring Biden's government like a big brother but at times offering help and certainly making his presence felt when he felt like it.

And privately, quietly, without almost anyone knowing, Obama and Biden started calling each other again just about as often.

The conversations were as much political therapy as they were about specific counsel. The chats could be anchors for the president, privileged above his phone calls from anyone else, and reflective moments for his old boss, a solemn responsibility and opportunity to hold the ear of the leader of the free world on anything from Afghanistan to Republicans to voting regulations. They were not always happy catch-ups, or especially nostalgic. Biden didn't have time for that, though he could make it if he wanted.

But whenever they hung up, it was clear to everyone around both of them that it wasn't an ordinary call. Each had just spoken with the only other person who could possibly begin to understand.

A NOTE ON SOURCES

This book is primarily the product of hundreds of interviews conducted over the course of 2021 with an array of people who shared with me their firsthand knowledge of, and experience with, the nearly two-decade relationship depicted in these pages. To portray the fullest possible picture, I spoke with colleagues, aides, rivals, confidants, allies, and eyewitnesses from every stage of the presidents' careers since 2003. Contemporary notes, private correspondences, and campaign files provided by these sources were indispensable, as were publicly available (if sometimes byzantine) government records and newspaper archives.

As indicated in the notes, at times I also relied on the memoirs of actors in the narrative, and occasionally on previously published reported accounts—some of which are invaluable resources if you want to comprehensively understand specific sagas that this book only briefly unwinds through the relatively focused lens of the Biden-Obama interactions. The following stand out: Samantha Power's *The Education of an Idealist* (2019), Susan Rice's *Tough Love* (2019), Robert Gates's *Duty* (2014), and Ben Rhodes's *The World as It Is* (2018) for their illumination of important personalities, internal dynamics, and thought processes in the Obama administration, and Mark Gitenstein's *Matters of Principle* (1992) for its detailed reconstruction of Biden's formative 1987 experiences. Richard Ben Cramer's classic *What It Takes* (1992) is also essential for its depiction of Biden at that time. Biden's own book about the year of Beau's death, *Promise Me, Dad* (2017), lays out valuable and underappreciated details of his consideration of the 2016 election. David Mendell's *Obama* (2007) offers a rare view of the man as a Senate candidate, Bob Woodward's

Obama's Wars (2010) painstakingly reconstructs the debates over the war in Afghanistan, Sasha Issenberg's *The Engagement* (2021) is unparalleled in its excavation of the administration's "evolution" on marriage equality (and on the matter more broadly), and Jonathan Cohn's *The Ten Year War* (2021) is exhaustive in its reconstruction of the fight to pass a universal health-care law. Finally, John Dickerson's *The Hardest Job in the World* (2020), Joel K. Goldstein's *The White House Vice Presidency* (2016), and Mark K. Updegrove's *Second Acts* (2001) helped shape my understanding of the jobs Obama and Biden have occupied.

The majority of the interviews for this book were conducted using "background" or "deep background" ground rules, usually meaning I could write about the material shared but not attribute it directly to its source. Of course, memory can be fickle, especially when the topic is ten or more years in the past. And politicians can have strategically convenient memories. Whenever possible I have verified facts, stories, exchanges, and context with multiple people who have personal experience with them, and if I've quoted something directly then it is publicly discoverable or I have unearthed the words from someone with direct knowledge of them. When someone's words are rendered in italics, that indicates an approximation based on the memories of sources who did not recall exact wordings.

Neither President Biden nor President Obama agreed to speak with me for this book, but I have tried to re-create their decisions, motivations, beliefs, hopes, and concerns to the most precise and most intimate degree possible using the extensive recollections of their many associates. These people were tremendously generous with their time and memories for the benefit of the historical record and readers' understanding of the modern presidency.

NOTES

Epigraphs

ix **"A vice president is totally a reflection":** Julyssa Lopez, "Joe Biden and Walter Mondale Discuss 'New Modern Vice Presidency,'" *GW Today*, October 21, 2015, https://gwtoday.gwu.edu/joe-biden-and-walter-mondale-discuss-%E2%80%98new -modern-vice-presidency%E2%80%99.

ix **"I am president. I am not king":** "Transcript of President Barack Obama with Univision," *Los Angeles Times*, October 25, 2010, https://latimesblogs.latimes.com/washington /2010/10/transcript-of-president-barack-obama-with-univision.html.

Preface

xvii **"We won!":** Hunter Biden, *Beautiful Things* (New York: Gallery Books, 2021), 248.

xviii **The younger Bush ended up hiring an array:** Mark K. Updegrove, *The Last Republicans* (New York: Harper, 2017), 295.

xviii **"the ability to pick up where we left off and keep on going":** Jonathan Chait, "In Conversation with Barack Obama," *New York*, December 9, 2020, https://nymag.com /intelligencer/2020/12/in-conversation-with-barack-obama.html.

xviii **focus on government experience:** Gabriel Debenedetti, "A Biden Style of Government Is Emerging: Lowest Drama Possible," *New York*, December 20, 2020, https:// nymag.com/intelligencer/2020/12/joe-biden-cabinet.html.

xviii **The list grew:** Debenedetti, "A Biden Style of Government Is Emerging: Lowest Drama Possible."

xxi **He was in Milwaukee:** "CNN Presidential Town Hall with Joe Biden," CNN, February 16, 2021, https://transcripts.cnn.com/show/se/date/2021-02-16/segment/01.

Chapter 1: 2003–2004

3 **she'd run every one of his races:** Ben Schreckinger, *The Bidens* (New York: Twelve, 2021), 16.

4 **She got up and found a Sharpie:** Jill Biden, *Where the Light Enters* (New York: Flatiron Books, 2019), 149–50.

5 **he tried coming up with a list of Republican senators:** Joe Biden, *Promises to Keep* (New York: Random House, 2007), 354–55.

7 **he'd been profiled in the *New York Times*:** Fox Butterfield, "First Black Elected to Head Harvard's Law Review," *New York Times*, February 6, 1990, https://www

.nytimes.com/1990/02/06/us/first-black-elected-to-head-harvard-s-law-review
.html.

7   **he'd gathered about a dozen close allies:** Michelle Obama, *Becoming* (New York: Crown, 2018), 211–13.

8   **Shomon refused . . . Axelrod, urged him to think:** David Mendell, *Obama* (New York: Amistad, 2007), 182, 157.

8   **who spurned the advances:** Mendell, 168–72.

9   **"I don't oppose all wars":** Barack Obama, "Transcript: Obama's Speech Against the Iraq War," NPR, January 20, 2009, https://www.npr.org/templates/story/story.php?storyId=99591469.

9   **The first one featured a slogan . . . about union jobs:** Mendell, *Obama*, 229–31.

10 **the revelation that Hull was accused:** David Mendell, "Hull's Ex-Wife Called Him Violent Man in Divorce File," *Chicago Tribune*, February 28, 2004, https://www.chicagotribune.com/chi-0402280192feb28-story.html.

10 **wasn't far behind:** "Public Attitudes Toward the War in Iraq: 2003–2008," Pew Research Center, March 19, 2008, https://www.pewresearch.org/2008/03/19/public-attitudes-toward-the-war-in-iraq-20032008/.

12 **Mary Beth Cahill, had been trying to convince:** David J. Garrow, *Rising Star* (New York: William Morrow, 2017), 930.

12 **he told Axelrod he wanted to tell his own story:** David Axelrod, *Believer* (New York: Penguin Books, 2015), 156.

13 **"Tonight, our country stands at the hinge of history":** "Democratic National Convention, Day 4 Evening," C-SPAN, July 29, 2004, https://www.c-span.org/video/?182721-2/democratic-national-convention-day-4-evening.

13 **They caught a bored-looking Hillary Clinton:** "Democratic National Convention, Day 4 Evening."

14 **Here was retired general Wesley Clark:** "Democratic National Convention, Day 4 Evening."

15 **Obama had seen Harold Ford Jr. flop:** Mendell, *Obama*, 269–70.

15 **Gibbs replied by sending Obama copies:** Mendell, 270.

15 **He read the speech as it printed:** Axelrod, *Believer*, 156.

15 **another consultant dove in on the first of more than a dozen rounds:** Garrow, *Rising Star*, 930–31.

16 **Russert caught Obama off guard by asking:** *Meet the Press*, "Transcript for July 25," NBC News, July 25, 2004, https://www.nbcnews.com/id/wbna5488345.

17 **The strategist tried reasoning with the candidate:** Axelrod, *Believer*, 158.

17 **Obama walked into the FleetCenter:** Mendell, *Obama*, 2.

18 **he took Gibbs's tie:** Garrow, *Rising Star*, 936–37.

18 **Axelrod walked him up to the edge of the stage:** Axelrod, *Believer*, 159.

19 **"It is that fundamental belief . . . all of us defending the United States of America":** "Illinois State Senator Barack Obama 2004 Democratic National Convention Keynote Speech," C-SPAN, July 27, 2004, https://www.c-span.org/video/?182718-3/illinois-state-senator-barack-obama-2004-democratic-national-convention-keynote-speech.

20 **As Axelrod later recalled:** Axelrod, *Believer*, 160.

21 **he was more taken by its focus on everyday Americans:** Joe Biden, *Promise Me, Dad* (New York: Flatiron Books, 2017), 57–59.

22 **Ryan, imploded amid news:** John Chase and Liam Ford, "Ryan File a Bombshell," *Chicago Tribune*, June 22, 2004, https://www.chicagotribune.com/news/ct-xpm-2004-06-22-0406220247-story.html.

22 **he only agreed to pay for a campaign SUV:** Mendell, *Obama*, 256.

22 **this kind of attention was probably mostly confined:** Barack Obama, *A Promised Land* (New York: Crown, 2020), 52.
23 **thirty-nine cities in five days:** Mendell, *Obama*, 286–87.
23 **"Must've been a pretty good speech":** Valerie Jarrett, *Finding My Voice* (New York: Viking, 2019), 130.

Chapter 2: 2004–2006
26 **he was already planning:** Joe Biden, *Promises to Keep*, 356.
26 **Biden held off on saying anything:** Jules Witcover, *Joe Biden* (New York: William Morrow, 2019), 363.
28 **A reporter asked him:** Garrow, *Rising Star*, 964.
29 **They could get a simple Italian dinner . . . no dinner scheduled:** Joe Biden, *Promise Me, Dad*, 57–59.
31 **he was at first worried:** David Remnick, *The Bridge* (New York: Alfred A. Knopf, 2010), 427.
31 **finance and agriculture panels:** Garrow, *Rising Star*, 960; Barack Obama, *A Promised Land*, 60.
31 **he had started informally and secretly discussing:** Jarrett, *Finding My Voice*, 131.
32 **reporters overheard his daughter Malia:** Mendell, *Obama*, 303–4.
32 **Teddy had joined him that year:** Schreckinger, *The Bidens*, 25.
32 **Biden ran for president with even more explicit attempts:** Richard Ben Cramer, *What It Takes* (New York: Vintage Books, 1993), 258.
33 **privately loved finding out that the desk he'd been assigned:** Remnick, *The Bridge*, 423.
33 **Obama and Clinton met at her office in Russell:** John Heilemann and Mark Halperin, *Game Change* (New York: Harper, 2010), 24–25.
34 **his advisors assumed he'd be able to grow close:** Mendell, *Obama*, 299–300.
34 **"I am absolutely convinced . . . with the election process":** "Obama First Speech Ohio Electoral," C-SPAN, January 6, 2005, https://www.c-span.org/video/?c4931976/obama-speech-ohio-electoral.
35 **developed a practice of carving out time:** Samantha Power, *The Education of an Idealist* (New York: Dey Street, 2019), 152.
35 **Obama would be on any nominee's short list:** Mendell, *Obama*, 305.
36 **national polling showed that the nation was still roughly split:** "Public Attitudes Toward the War in Iraq: 2003–2008," Pew Research Center.
36 **Schieffer kept at that topic . . . "I'm not sure":** *Face the Nation*, CBS News, June 19, 2005, https://www.cbsnews.com/htdocs/pdf/face_061905.pdf.
37 **"Joe Biden is a decent guy, but man":** Axelrod, *Believer*, 167.
37 **Obama handed a staffer a note:** Remnick, *The Bridge*, 427.
37 **he looked at Samantha Power:** Power, *The Education of an Idealist*, 153.
38 **he griped, it was often on bullshit:** Garrow, *Rising Star*, 969.
39 **His proposal . . . signed off in January:** Garrow, 983.
39 **He wrote in the popular *Daily Kos*:** Barack Obama, "Tone, Truth, and the Democratic Party," *Daily Kos*, September 30, 2005, https://www.dailykos.com/stories/2005/9/30/153069/-.
39 **As Obama saw it:** Matt Bai, *The Argument* (New York: Penguin Books, 2007), 235–38.
39 **Obama framed the modern American economic challenge . . . more funding for research:** "Commencement Address: Barack Obama," Knox College, June 4, 2005, https://www.knox.edu/news/president-obama-to-visit-knox-college-speak-on-economy/2005-commencement-address.
40 **arranged private debates among aides:** Power, *The Education of an Idealist*, 154.
40 **They should wind down the war by splitting Iraq:** Joseph R. Biden Jr. and Leslie H.

Gelb, "Unity Through Autonomy in Iraq," *New York Times*, May 1, 2006, https://www
.nytimes.com/2006/05/01/opinion/01biden.html.

44 **Reid, meanwhile, had been convinced . . . stuck with the Nevadan:** Harry Reid with
Mark Warren, *The Good Fight* (New York: Berkley Books, 2009), 299.

44 **Reid told Obama he should think:** Barack Obama, *A Promised Land*, 67–69.

44 **Obama replied, "I don't know":** Reid with Warren, *The Good Fight*, 300.

44 **He'd assumed Reid would be with Clinton:** Remnick, *The Bridge*, 461; Heilemann
and Halperin, *Game Change*, 36.

44 **Daschle, for one, said something similar:** Brian Abrams, *Obama* (New York: Little A,
2018), 5–6.

45 **Kennedy said Obama didn't have the luxury:** Barack Obama, *A Promised Land*, 67–69.

45 **On the car ride back to Washington:** Axelrod, *Believer*, 185.

45 **Russert played the tape:** *Meet the Press*, "Transcript for October 22," NBC News,
October 22, 2006, https://www.nbcnews.com/id/wbna15304689.

Chapter 3: 2007–2008

47 **When long-serving senators ran for president, he warned:** "Edward E. (Ted)
Kaufman," United States Senate Historical Office, *Oral History Project*, August 17–
September 27, 2012, https://www.senate.gov/artandhistory/history/oral_history
/KaufmanEdwardE.htm.

48 **"the first mainstream African-American who is articulate and bright and clean
and a nice-looking guy":** Adam Nagourney, "Biden Unwraps '08 Bid with an Oops!"
New York Times, February 1, 2007, https://www.nytimes.com/2007/02/01/us/politics
/01biden.html.

48 **Biden tried to clean his message up further:** Nagourney, "Biden Unwraps '08 Bid
with an Oops!"

50 **Axelrod would remind him:** Abrams, *Obama*, 19.

51 **handing out at events copies of the text of his 2002 speech:** David Plouffe, *The
Audacity to Win* (New York: Penguin Books, 2009), 104.

51 **he said that Ronald Reagan had been more transformative:** Nancy Gibbs and
Michael Duffy, *The Presidents Club* (New York: Simon & Schuster, 2012), 507.

52 **"Hello, Chicago!":** Michelle Obama, *Becoming*, 246.

52 **"that on-the-job training for a president can be a dangerous thing":** Joe Biden,
Promises to Keep, 133.

52 **George Stephanopoulos opened:** "TRANSCRIPT: The Democratic Debate," ABC
News, August 23, 2007, https://abcnews.go.com/Politics/Decision2008/story?id
=3498294&page=1.

53 **Biden spent his first restless years in the Senate trying to establish himself:** Kitty
Kelley, "Death and the All-American Boy," *Washingtonian*, June 1, 1974, https://www
.washingtonian.com/1974/06/01/joe-biden-kitty-kelley-1974-profile-death-and-the
-all-american-boy/.

53 **he'd temporarily been given a seat on the Senate floor between colleagues from the
North and the South:** Joe Biden, *Promises to Keep*, 109–10.

53 **he dipped his toe in national waters by backing:** Schreckinger, *The Bidens*, 60.

54 **Biden entertained serious pitches from party operatives:** Joe Biden, *Promises to
Keep*, 135, 139.

54 **Supreme Court Justice Lewis Powell's retirement meant he had to run the hearings:**
Mark Gitenstein, *Matters of Principle* (New York: Simon & Schuster, 1992), 23, 31.

54 **his private polling showed him climbing in Iowa:** Gitenstein, 13.

54 **"I'm angry with myself for having been put in the position—put myself in the position—of having to make this choice":** Jon Margolis and Elaine Povich, "Biden Admits

Errors, Drops Out," *Chicago Tribune*, September 24, 1987, https://www.chicagotribune .com/news/ct-xpm-1987-09-24-8703120482-story.html.

55 **He'd surveyed Delaware voters:** "Edward E. (Ted) Kaufman," United States Senate Historical Office.

55 **Jill walked in on a priest delivering last rites:** Jill Biden, *Where the Light Enters*, 119–20.

55 **"I made a mistake, and it was born out of my arrogance":** Evan Osnos, *Joe Biden* (New York: Scribner, 2020), 47.

55 **Richard Ben Cramer wrote about the "connect," or the "Biden Rush":** Cramer, *What It Takes*, 254.

56 **"Yes.":** "South Carolina Democratic debate transcript," NBC News, April 27, 2007, https://www.nbcnews.com/id/wbna18352397.

57 **"Get the fuck out of the car":** Jeff Connaughton, *The Payoff* (Westport, CT: Prospecta Press, 2012), 192.

57 **Obama was, Biden had said, on "everyone's Number Two list":** Witcover, *Joe Biden*, 374.

57 **"I was the Barack Obama!":** Witcover, 387.

58 **once split the cost of a private jet from Washington to New Hampshire:** Witcover, 383.

60 **He would spend the rest of the year planning his party's new vision for the new era as the committee's chair:** Brian Katulis, "Biden Reboots U.S. Foreign Policy," *Liberal Patriot*, January 21, 2021, https://theliberalpatriot.substack.com/p/biden-reboots-us -foreign-policy.

Chapter 4: 2008

61 **In public, Obama's publicity team dismissed the effort:** Alexander Mooney, "McCain Ad Compares Obama to Britney Spears, Paris Hilton," CNN, July 30, 2008, https:// www.cnn.com/2008/POLITICS/07/30/mccain.ad/index.html.

61 **his research aides quickly found that the clip backfired and offended the women voters they were targeting:** Plouffe, *The Audacity to Win*, 280.

62 **Edwards, whose personal life would soon explode in sordid scandal, had made the same offer to Clinton, who also turned him down:** Plouffe, 158–59.

62 **he mused that the presidency wasn't the best job in the world, but the ex-presidency was:** Plouffe, 294.

63 **I think Joe Biden might be the right guy:** Axelrod, *Believer*, 281–82.

63 **"Did you find our magic bullet candidate yet?"** Plouffe, 285.

64 **an initial list of twenty possibilities:** Plouffe, 285.

64 **Harry Reid floated Bush defense secretary Robert Gates and Ted Kennedy urged Obama to consider Kerry:** Axelrod, *Believer*, 295–96.

64 **removed longtime DC insider James Johnson:** John M. Broder and Leslie Wayne, "Obama Aide Quits Under Fire for His Business Ties," *New York Times*, June 12, 2008, https://www.nytimes.com/2008/06/12/us/politics/12veep.html.

65 **When Biden again refused, Obama asked him to at least talk to his family first:** Joe Biden, *Promise Me, Dad*, 59–65.

66 *Let me get this straight,* **she said:** Joe Biden, *Promise Me, Dad*, 59–65.

66 **They back-channeled on a strategy to convince him:** Jill Biden, *Where the Light Enters*, 154–55.

67 **he told his mother he was going to meet the Queen of England and Jean replied, "Don't you bow down to her":** Joe Biden, *Promises to Keep*, 11.

67 *Does anyone even remember who Lincoln's vice president was?* **Biden liked to ask:** Osnos, *Joe Biden*, 55–56.

67 **"smarter than their secretary of state":** Witcover, *Joe Biden*, 389.

67 **"Absolutely, positively, inequitably, Shermanesquely, no":** Witcover, *Joe Biden*, 389.

68   **At his final meeting with the vetting lawyer in his Senate office, Biden paused:** Joe Biden, *Promise Me, Dad*, 59–65.

68   **Most infamously, Wright had said "God damn America" for "killing innocent people":** Brian Ross and Rehab El-Buri, "Obama's Pastor: God Damn America, U.S. to Blame for 9/11," ABC News, March 13, 2008, https://abcnews.go.com/Blotter /DemocraticDebate/story?id=4443788&page=1.

68   **grappling as it did with the legacy:** "Transcript: Barack Obama's Speech on Race," NPR, March 18, 2008, https://www.npr.org/templates/story/story.php ?storyId=88478467.

71   **the two had actually first discussed the vice presidency in 1976:** "Edward E. (Ted) Kaufman," United States Senate Historical Office.

71   **wondered about Lyndon B. Johnson until he read Robert A. Caro's *The Passage of Power*:** Osnos, *Joe Biden*, 60–61.

71   **Mondale had gotten Carter to understand:** Walter F. Mondale, *The Good Fight* (New York: Scribner, 2010), 171–76.

72   **She gave the three finalists internal code names:** Alyssa Mastromonaco and Dan Pfeiffer, "Obama's Staff Reveals How a Vice President Is Selected," Crooked Media, June 30, 2020, YouTube video, 49:54, https://www.youtube.com/watch?v=IODyGZdTeIU.

72   **kicked off the meeting by counterintuitively explaining:** Barack Obama, *A Promised Land*, 164.

73   **This all sounded good, Obama said, but he wanted to make sure of one more thing:** Jonathan Alter, "Biden's Unified Theory of Biden," *Newsweek*, October 3, 2008, https:// www.newsweek.com/bidens-unified-theory-biden-91693.

73   **he assured Obama: he was sixty-five:** Osnos, *Joe Biden*, 99.

73   **Jill and Beau picked the Davids up at the airport:** Jill Biden, *Where the Light Enters*, 155–56.

73   **he nevertheless amazingly kicked off the meeting:** Plouffe, *The Audacity to Win*, 290–94; Axelrod, *Believer*, 297–98.

73   **Plouffe thought Biden could do well:** Plouffe, *The Audacity to Win*, 289.

74   **To throw the press pack off the scent in the final days, Obama's aides leaked that Chet Edwards, a Texas congressman, had been vetted:** Mastromonaco and Pfeiffer, "Obama's Staff Reveals How a Vice President Is Selected."

74   **Axelrod and Plouffe agreed to reaffirm to Obama that the choice was obviously up to him:** Plouffe, *The Audacity to Win*, 294.

75   **Biden picked up while in a dentist's waiting room as Jill underwent a root canal:** Jill Biden, *Where the Light Enters*, 156–57.

75   **he wouldn't, for example, wear any funny hats:** Heilemann and Halperin, *Game Change*, 411.

75   **Dukakis and a tank:** Josh King, "Dukakis and the Tank," *Politico Magazine*, November 17, 2013, https://www.politico.com/magazine/story/2013/11/dukakis-and-the-tank -099119/.

75   **"Dad, this is hope and history":** Joe Biden, *Promise Me, Dad*, 65–66.

Chapter 5: 2008

77   **Biden's boisterous swarm:** Michelle Obama, *Becoming*, 297.

79   **Obama campaign ad that suggested McCain was old:** Sarah Lai Stirland, "Obama Campaign Mocks McCain's Computer Illiteracy," *Wired*, September 12, 2008, https:// www.wired.com/2008/09/obama-campaign-4/.

79   **Biden's praise of the Republican:** Jimmy Orr, "Biden Praises McCain and Slams Obama? New McCain Ad Released," *Christian Science Monitor*, August 23, 2008, https://www.csmonitor.com/USA/Politics/The-Vote/2008/0823/biden-praises -mccain-and-slams-obama-new-mccain-ad-released.

79 **Obama had joked to his campaign team:** Joe Biden, *Promise Me, Dad*, 72.

81 **Biden had no clue who she was:** Axelrod, *Believer*, 304–5.

82 **"You can put lipstick on a pig":** Kate Snow and Jake Tapper, "Obama Says 'Enough' About 'Lipstick' Smear," ABC News, September 10, 2008, https://abcnews.go.com /Politics/Vote2008/story?id=5769091&page=1.

82 **"Um, all of 'em":** Katie Couric, "CBS Exclusive: Gov. Sarah Palin," CBS News, October 31, 2008, YouTube video, 28:33, https://www.youtube.com/watch?v=-ZVh_u5RyiU.

83 **Biden let loose slightly:** Heilemann and Halperin, *Game Change*, 411–14.

83 **Obama then called Biden himself:** Axelrod, *Believer*, 317.

83 **Obama told Biden he didn't need:** Connaughton, *The Payoff*, 6–7.

83 **McCain's campaign quickly started running an ad:** Alexander Mooney, "McCain Target Biden's Comments in New Ad," CNN, October 24, 2008, https://politicalticker .blogs.cnn.com/2008/10/24/mccain-targets-bidens-comments-in-new-ad/comment -page-22/.

83 **Whenever reporters or pundits surfaced:** "Edward E. (Ted) Kaufman," United States Senate Historical Office.

87 **As the campaign lurched to a close:** Axelrod, *Believer*, 316.

87 **after he and Obama climbed down from the stage:** Mark Halperin and John Heilemann, *Double Down* (New York: Penguin Press, 2013), 70–79.

88 **Joe and Jill held a laptop up to the crowd:** Jill Biden, *Where the Light Enters*, 160–61.

Chapter 6: 2008–2009

89 **"attending state funerals":** Connaughton, *The Payoff*, 6–7.

90 **"manhood is not negotiable":** Connaughton, 6–7.

90 **"I am nothing, but I may be everything":** Joel K. Goldstein, *The White House Vice Presidency* (Lawrence: University Press of Kansas, 2016), 1.

90 **Johnson's deputy, Hubert Humphrey, whom Biden knew from the Senate, had hated it:** Goldstein, 35.

90 **"being naked in the middle of a blizzard with no one to even offer you a match to keep you warm":** Goldstein, 282–83.

90 **he'd only ever been to the Naval Observatory—the vice president's residence— twice:** Greg Jaffe, "The War in Afghanistan Shattered Joe Biden's Faith in American Military Power," *Washington Post*, February 18, 2020, https://www.washingtonpost .com/politics/2020/02/18/biden-afghanistan-military-power/.

91 **he had to stop talking about how much better qualified for the top job he'd been:** Chuck Todd, *The Stranger* (New York: Little, Brown, 2014), 32–33.

93 **he'd been reading about Franklin D. Roosevelt's legendary first hundred days:** Ron Suskind, *Confidence Men* (New York: Harper Luxe, 2011), 296.

93 **two-thirds of Americans approved of him, according to Gallup:** "Presidential Job Approval Center," Gallup, 2021, https://news.gallup.com/interactives/185273 /presidential-job-approval-center.aspx.

94 **"Where the fuck," he took to loudly asking, "is our honeymoon?":** Abrams, *Obama*, 59.

95 **2008 ended as the worst year for job loss since the end of World War Two:** David Goldman, "Worst Year for Jobs Since '45," *CNN Money*, January 9, 2009, https://money .cnn.com/2009/01/09/news/economy/jobs_december/.

95 **"Jesus," Biden replied, not quite under his breath:** Barack Obama, *A Promised Land*, 235–36.

95 **The economists had already been debating the size of the relief package among themselves:** Noam Scheiber, "EXCLUSIVE: The Memo That Larry Summers Didn't Want Obama to See," *New Republic*, February 22, 2012, https://newrepublic.com /article/100961/memo-larry-summers-obama.

96 **Obama turned to Biden to see what he thought:** Obama, *A Promised Land*, 237; Axelrod, *Believer*, 333–34.

96 **When he later recalled the moment:** Barack Obama, *A Promised Land*, 239.

97 **Biden, in particular, started hearing early in the transition from a handful of his former Republican Senate colleagues:** Michael Grunwald, *The New New Deal* (New York: Simon & Schuster, 2012), 207–10.

98 **Gregg—the Republican New Hampshire senator who'd already recused himself from the stimulus vote—decided against taking the commerce secretary gig:** Jeff Zeleny, "Gregg Ends Bid for Commerce Job," *New York Times*, February 12, 2009, https://www.nytimes.com/2009/02/13/us/politics/13gregg.html.

99 **"I do not work for Barack Obama":** Rachel Weiner, "Harry Reid: 'I Don't Work for Obama,'" *Huffington Post*, February 7, 2009, https://www.huffpost.com/entry/harry -reid-i-dont-work-fo_n_155838.

99 **he still used the Senate gym:** James Traub, "After Cheney," *New York Times Magazine*, November 24, 2009, https://www.nytimes.com/2009/11/29/magazine/29Biden-t.html.

99 **Emanuel, meanwhile, saw himself, not necessarily Biden, as the administration's primary go-between:** Grunwald, *The New New Deal*, 192.

103 **it was common to see young Democrats carrying marked-up copies of *Dreams from My Father*:** Ben Rhodes, *The World as It Is* (New York: Random House, 2018), 12.

104 **Biden's son Hunter was especially wary:** Schreckinger, *The Bidens*, 161.

105 **"My memory is not as good as Justice Roberts's":** Chris Good, "Biden Jokes About Roberts' Memory," *The Hill*, January 21, 2009, https://thehill.com/blogs/blog-briefing -room/news/other/39441-biden-jokes-about-robertss-memory.

105 **He said as much at their lunch soon after:** Goldstein, *The White House Vice Presidency*, 167.

106 **Biden often winked to guests that his Senate office had been fancier:** Traub, "After Cheney."

Chapter 7: 2009

107 **back in Washington, he told Obama as much:** Jaffe, "The War in Afghanistan Shattered Joe Biden's Faith in American Military Power."

107 **multiplied the American military presence:** Michael R. Gordon, "Troop 'Surge' Took Place amid Doubt and Debate," *New York Times*, August 30, 2008, https://www .nytimes.com/2008/08/31/washington/31military.html.

107 **deadliest year yet:** "2008 marks deadliest year for U.S. troops in Afghanistan," CNN, September 11, 2008, https://edition.cnn.com/2008/WORLD/asiapcf/09/11/afghan .troop.deaths/.

108 **Biden saw no evidence of a long-term plan:** Bob Woodward, *Obama's Wars* (New York: Simon & Schuster Paperbacks, 2010), 67–69; David E. Sanger, *Confront and Conceal* (New York: Broadway Paperbacks, 2012), 23.

108 **Ask ten different people to describe the US goal in Afghanistan, he said, and you'll get ten different answers:** Fred Kaplan, *The Insurgents* (New York: Simon & Schuster, 2013), 294–96.

111 **Petraeus and Ryan Crocker, the US ambassador to Iraq, spent an hour . . . shouldn't stop them from exiting:** Barack Obama, *A Promised Land*, 157–59.

111 **he recruited Bush's defense secretary Gates to stay on:** Woodward, *Obama's Wars*, 24.

112 **Biden was, in fact, surprised:** Traub, "After Cheney."

112 **the trio had discussed the necessity of assigning Iraq to someone who could cut across agencies:** Goldstein, *The White House Vice Presidency*, 143.

112 **he was straightforward in his regret:** Joe Biden, *Promises to Keep*, 342.

113 **Gates—who'd served under seven, now eight, presidents—had recommended**

replicating George H. W. Bush's model: Robert M. Gates, *Duty* (New York: Alfred A. Knopf, 2014), 282–83.

113 **"He Who Knows All World Leaders":** Traub, "After Cheney."

113 **belief that foreign relations is simply "a logical extension of personal relationships," just with higher stakes:** Gabriel Debenedetti, "Secretary Swell on a Pissed-Off Planet," *New York*, March 30, 2021, https://nymag.com/intelligencer/article/antony-blinken -foreign-policy.html

114 **everyone involved hoped:** Vanda Felbab-Brown, "The 2009 Afghanistan Elections and the Future of Governance," Brookings Institution, August 13, 2009, https:// www.brookings.edu/opinions/the-2009-afghanistan-elections-and-the-future-of -governance/.

114 **The president opened the meeting by reminding the room . . . before they talked in such terms:** Woodward, *Obama's Wars*, 79–81.

115 **On his flight back from Munich a few days later, Biden insisted to a group of reporters:** Gates, *Duty*, 338.

115 **Mondale had a pattern of stepping back to protect Carter from having to side with either him or a cabinet member:** Goldstein, *The White House Vice-Presidency*, 99.

115 **Biden kept thinking back to Hubert Humphrey:** Ryan Lizza, "Biden's Brief," *New Yorker*, October 13, 2008, https://www.newyorker.com/magazine/2008/10/20/bidens -brief.

116 **"Joe, I want you to say exactly what you think. I want every argument on every side to be poked hard":** Jaffe, "The War in Afghanistan Shattered Joe Biden's Faith in American Military Power."

117 **Mullen replied that this approach wouldn't solve the root problems . . . little patience for an extended investment:** Kaplan, *The Insurgents*, 297–98.

117 **"disrupt, dismantle, and defeat":** "FACTBOX: Highlights of Obama's Speech on Afghanistan," Reuters, March 27, 2009, https://www.reuters.com/article/us -afghan-obama-quotes-sb/factbox-highlights-of-obamas-speech-on-afghanistan -idUSTRE52Q44R20090327.

117 **few allies were willing to hear out his pleas to increase their own troop levels:** Rhodes, *The World as It Is*, 41.

117 **fraudulent disaster:** Sabrina Tavernise and Abdul Waheed Wafa, "U.N. Official Acknowledges 'Widespread Fraud' in Afghan Election," *New York Times*, October 11, 2009, https://www.nytimes.com/2009/10/12/world/asia/12afghan.html.

118 **"McChrystal: More Forces or 'Mission Failure'":** Bob Woodward, "McChrystal: More Forces or 'Mission Failure,'" *Washington Post*, September 21, 2009, https://www .washingtonpost.com/wp-dyn/content/article/2009/09/20/AR2009092002920.html ?hpid=topnews.

118 **"What I know concerns me. What I don't know concerns me even more. What people aren't telling me worries me the most'":** Gates, *Duty*, 299–300.

118 **Obama pulled Gates and Mullen aside in the Oval:** Obama, *A Promised Land*, 432– 35.

118 **"The military doesn't fuck around with me":** Bob Woodward and Robert Costa, *Peril* (New York: Simon & Schuster, 2021), 336; John Kerry, *Every Day Is Extra* (New York: Simon & Schuster, 2018), 371.

119 **it was obvious from the way they presented it that the military expected him to choose the middle option:** Hillary Rodham Clinton, *Hard Choices* (New York: Simon & Schuster, 2014), 133.

119 **He still argued that Afghanistan and Iraq were fundamentally different and thus required significantly separate approaches:** Clinton, 138.

120 **the president insisted on distinguishing between the Taliban and al-Qaeda:** Woodward, *Obama's Wars*, 185–87.

120 **Obama told the general to cut out the open disagreements:** Sanger, *Confront and Conceal*, 32.

121 **he sometimes asked presidential historians about LBJ's path:** Sanger, 26–27.

121 **"I am probably the first president who is young enough that the Vietnam War wasn't at the core of my development":** Woodward, *Obama's Wars*, 377.

121 **he'd never been part of the protest movements:** Jaffe, "The War in Afghanistan Shattered Joe Biden's Faith in American Military Power."

121 **he wasn't against it ideologically:** Traub, "After Cheney."

121 **when she was in high school Jill Biden had even known one of the students later shot at Kent State:** Jill Biden, *Where the Light Enters*, 34.

121 **Leaving Afghanistan was a necessity:** George Packer, *Our Man* (New York: Alfred A. Knopf, 2019), 531.

123 **That Wednesday, Obama told his advisors this was the hardest choice he'd yet made:** Woodward, *Obama's Wars*, 301–02.

123 **Biden, however, was in Nantucket:** Hunter Biden, *Beautiful Things*, 90–91.

123 **He returned to the White House ahead of schedule that Sunday:** Woodward, *Obama's Wars*, 324.

123 **Obama said it wasn't necessary:** Jaffe, "The War in Afghanistan Shattered Joe Biden's Faith in American Military Power."

Chapter 8: 2009–2010

126 **his personal approval rating remaining shockingly high:** "Presidential Job Approval Center," Gallup.

129 **CNBC personality Rick Santelli went on a televised rant:** The Heritage Foundation, "CNBC's Rick Santelli's Chicago Tea Party," February 19, 2009, YouTube video, 4:36, https://www.youtube.com/watch?v=zp-Jw-5Kx8k.

129 **his time leading the health-care committee in the Illinois state senate:** Jonathan Cohn, *The Ten Year War* (New York: St. Martin's Press, 2021), 69.

129 **an individual mandate to buy insurance:** Cohn, 79–81.

131 **GOP pollster Frank Luntz circulated a twenty-eight-page memo:** Gabriel Debenedetti, "Democrats Are Moving Fast on the Filibuster. Biden Isn't Yet," *New York*, September 25, 2020, https://nymag.com/intelligencer/2020/09/joe-biden-senate-filibuster.html.

131 **They should avoid mentioning Obama directly:** Randy James, "How Republicans Should Talk About Health Care," *Time*, May 7, 2009, http://content.time.com/time/nation/article/0,8599,1896597,00.html.

132 **Gibbs compared the town hall disruptions:** Ian Urbina, "Beyond Beltway, Health Debate Turns Hostile," *New York Times*, August 7, 2009, https://www.nytimes.com/2009/08/08/us/politics/08townhall.html.

132 **"If we're able to stop Obama on this it will be his Waterloo. It will break him":** Ben Smith, "Health Reform Foes Plan Obama's 'Waterloo,'" *Politico*, July 17, 2009, https://www.politico.com/blogs/ben-smith/2009/07/health-reform-foes-plan-obamas-waterloo-019961.

132 **Sarah Palin started claiming in August that the proposed law would include "death panels":** Andy Barr, "Palin Doubles Down on 'Death Panels,'" *Politico*, August 13, 2009, https://www.politico.com/story/2009/08/palin-doubles-down-on-death-panels-026078.

134 **Biden, on the sidelines of some meetings, marvel at the economic team's detachment:** Dan Balz, *Collision 2012* (New York: Viking, 2013), 28.

134 **self-consciousness he'd felt ever since getting a job at a law firm out of Syracuse Law:** Joe Biden, *Promises to Keep*, 39.

134 **"river of power":** Cramer, *What It Takes*, 501.

134 **"We had about thirty-five jobs to fill—and about 2,500 applicants, most of them**

from Harvard Law or the University of Chicago or Stanford": Joe Biden, *Promises to Keep*, 75.

136 **the *New York Times Magazine* explored in November whether "Joe Biden [could be] the Second-Most Powerful Vice President in History":** Traub, "After Cheney."

136 **Lieberman said on *Face the Nation* that he was against a public option:** David Morgan, "Lieberman: Public Option Is 'Wrong,'" *Face the Nation*, CBS News, November 1, 2009, https://www.cbsnews.com/news/lieberman-public-option-is-wrong/.

137 **Schumer at this point again argued that they should back off the health-care push in favor of a middle-class economics emphasis:** Jeffrey Toobin, "The Senator and the Street," *New Yorker*, July 26, 2010, https://www.newyorker.com/magazine/2010/08/02/the-senator-and-the-street.

137 **the president gathered his VP and a small group of senior aides:** Barack Obama, *A Promised Land*, 424–25.

138 **Dodd resolved to retire:** Abrams, *Obama*, 153–54.

138 **who at one point ran an ad insisting she wasn't a witch:** David Gura, "'I'm Not a Witch,' Republican Candidate Christine O'Donnell Tells Delaware Voters," NPR, October 5, 2010, https://www.npr.org/sections/thetwo-way/2010/10/05/130353168/-i-m-not-a-witch-republican-senate-candidate-christine-o-donnell-says-in-new-ad.

139 **At particularly difficult times, he turned to Emanuel:** Michael D. Shear, "Obama After Dark: The Precious Hours Alone," *New York Times*, July 2, 2016, https://www.nytimes.com/2016/07/03/us/politics/obama-after-dark-the-precious-hours-alone.html.

139 **delightedly high-fiving:** Pete Souza, *President Barack Obama and Vice President Joe Biden High-Five*, February 27, 2010, photograph, The White House, https://obamawhitehouse.archives.gov/photos-and-video/photo/2015/04/president-barack-obama-and-vice-president-joe-biden-high-five.

Chapter 9: 2010–2011

141 **Obama shared the politically acceptable half of his thoughts at a press conference:** Liz Halloran, "Obama Humbled by Election 'Shellacking,'" NPR, November 3, 2010, https://www.npr.org/templates/story/story.php?storyId=131046118.

143 **"There's no goddamned way I'm going to stand here and talk about the president like that!":** Helene Cooper, "As the Ground Shifts, Biden Plays a Bigger Role," *New York Times*, December 11, 2010, https://www.nytimes.com/2010/12/12/us/politics/12biden.html.

144 **"Shirtless Biden Washes Trans Am in White House Driveway":** "Shirtless Biden Washes Trans Am in White House Driveway," *The Onion*, May 5, 2009, https://www.theonion.com/shirtless-biden-washes-trans-am-in-white-house-driveway-1819570732.

144 **"Biden Enjoying Role as Vice President, Close Friendship with Obama":** "Biden Enjoying Role as Vice President, Close Friendship with Obama," *PBS NewsHour*, January 28, 2011, https://www.pbs.org/newshour/politics/the-morning-line-the-obama-biden-relationship.

145 **In mid-April Gates gave him reason for extra concern:** Gates, *Duty*, 540–42.

145 **Leon Panetta, the CIA director, was most in favor of a Navy SEAL–led raid:** Clinton, *Hard Choices*, 192.

145 **Gates now said he actually wanted to consider the drone option:** Gates, *Duty*, 543.

145 **He then doubled down on the argument with Obama one-on-one after the meeting:** Leon Panetta with Jim Newton, *Worthy Fights* (New York: Penguin Books, 2014), 318.

145 **He understood the calls for caution but worried that Biden and Gates were both too scarred:** Barack Obama, *A Promised Land*, 686.

146 **Obama opened the session by lowering expectations . . . Biden's turn:** Garrett M. Graff, "I'd Never Been Involved in Anything as Secret as This," *Politico Magazine*, April 30, 2021, https://www.politico.com/news/magazine/2021/04/30/osama-bin-laden-death-white-house-oral-history-484793.

146 **He was—as always—just trying to stretch Obama's options:** Rhodes, *The World as It Is*, 129.

146 **Both asked first about the SEALs but then thought privately about Carter:** Axelrod, *Believer*, 438.

147 **In one letter bin Laden encouraged al-Qaeda fighters to kill Obama:** Lee Ferran, Rhonda Schwartz, and Mark Schone, "Bin Laden: Kill Obama to Make Biden President," ABC News, May 3, 2012, https://abcnews.go.com/Blotter/osama-bin-laden-letters-al-qaeda-leader-frustrated/story?id=16268578.

147 **After a series of debates not unlike the 2009 ones:** Gates, *Duty*, 555–65.

148 **Biden argued that the "middle class has been screwed":** Corbett Daly, "Biden: The 'Middle Class Has Been Screwed,'" CBS News, October 9, 2011, https://www.cbsnews.com/news/biden-the-middle-class-has-been-screwed/.

148 **"I understand the frustrations being expressed":** Devin Dwyer, "Obama: Occupy Wall Street 'Not That Different' from Tea Party Protests," ABC News, October 18, 2011, https://abcnews.go.com/blogs/politics/2011/10/obama-occupy-wall-street-not-that-different-from-tea-party-protests.

149 **at one point Plouffe called Messina:** Abrams, *Obama*, 235–37.

149 **the *New York Times Magazine* published a cover story:** Nate Silver, "Is Obama Toast? Handicapping the 2012 Election," *New York Times Magazine*, November 3, 2011, https://www.nytimes.com/2011/11/06/magazine/nate-silver-handicaps-2012-election.html.

149 **"This is a make-or-break moment":** "Remarks by the President on the Economy in Osawatomie, Kansas," The White House, December 6, 2011, https://obamawhitehouse.archives.gov/the-press-office/2011/12/06/remarks-president-economy-osawatomie-kansas.

149 **The *New York Times*' editorial board called the speech "a relief ":** "Obama in Osawatomie," editorial, *New York Times*, December 6, 2011, https://www.nytimes.com/2011/12/07/opinion/president-obama-in-osawatomie.html.

150 **Plouffe and Messina noticed that Biden's deputy chief of staff Alan Hoffman had quietly added:** Glenn Thrush, "Joe Biden in Winter," *Politico Magazine*, March/April 2014, https://www.politico.com/magazine/story/2014/02/joe-biden-profile-103667/.

152 **"Hillary Clinton Should Be Obama's Vice President":** Sally Quinn, "Hillary Clinton Should Be Obama's Vice President," *Washington Post*, June 18, 2010, https://www.washingtonpost.com/wp-dyn/content/article/2010/06/17/AR2010061703463.html?nav=rss_opinion/columns.

152 **Bob Woodward said on CNN:** Heather Horn, "Woodward: Clinton-Biden Switch Is 'On the Table,'" *The Atlantic*, October 6, 2010, https://www.theatlantic.com/politics/archive/2010/10/woodward-clinton-biden-switch-is-on-the-table/343915/.

152 **"completely unfounded, completely unfounded, completely unfounded":** Laura Meckler, "Obama: No Biden-Clinton Switch," *Wall Street Journal*, October 19, 2010, https://www.wsj.com/articles/BL-WB-24781.

Chapter 10: 2012

157 **Pelosi, for example, had announced in February:** Chris Geidner, "EXCLUSIVE: Nancy Pelosi Supports 2012 Democratic Platform Including Marriage Equality," *Metro Weekly*, February 15, 2012, https://www.metroweekly.com/2012/02/exclusive-nancy-pelosi-support/.

157 **He warned them that if some reporter asked him:** Axelrod, *Believer*, 447.

157 **he warned that with North Carolina set to vote in May:** Sasha Issenberg, *The Engagement* (New York: Pantheon Books, 2021), 688–95.

158 **He'd campaigned in 2008 in opposition of the Defense of Marriage Act:** Jake Tapper, Sunlen Miller, and Devin Dwyer, "Obama Administration Drops Legal Defense of 'Marriage Act,'" ABC News, February 23, 2011, https://abcnews.go.com/Politics /obama-administration-drops-legal-defense-marriage-act/story?id=12981242.

158 **Privately he said this was all about trying to be practical:** Issenberg, *The Engagement*, 672–77.

159 **David Gregory teed Biden up . . . moved onto other matters:** *Meet the Press*, "May 6: Joe Biden, Kelly Ayotte, Diane Swonk, Tom Brokaw, Chuck Todd," NBC News, May 6, 2012, https://www.nbcnews.com/id/wbna47311900.

162 **"Well, Joe, you told me you weren't going to wear any funny hats or change your brand":** Joe Biden, *Promise Me, Dad*, 67–68.

162 **All that mattered was that their relationship stayed intact:** Halperin and Heilemann, *Double Down*, 299–300.

162 **Biden's initial follow-up statement minimizing the differences:** Issenberg, *The Engagement*, 688–95.

162 **he, too, was for marriage equality:** Sarah Burke, "Education Secy Arne Duncan Endorses Same-Sex Marriage," ABC News, May 7, 2012, https://abcnews.go.com/blogs /politics/2012/05/education-secy-arne-duncan-endorses-same-sex-marriage.

162 **he'd leave it to Obama:** Kathleen Hennessey, "Carney Refuses to Comment on Obama's Gay Marriage Stance," *Los Angeles Times*, May 7, 2012, https://www.latimes .com/politics/la-xpm-2012-may-07-la-pn-carney-refuses-to-comment-on-obamas -personal-gay-marriage-stance-20120507-story.html.

162 **"I had hesitated on gay marriage in part because I thought civil unions would be sufficient":** "Transcript: Robin Roberts ABC News Interview with President Obama," ABC News, May 9, 2012, https://abcnews.go.com/Politics/transcript-robin-roberts -abc-news-interview-president-obama/story?id=16316043.

165 **"Osama bin Laden is dead, and General Motors is alive!":** Rodney Hawkins, "Biden: We Are Better Off, 'Bin Laden Is Dead and General Motors Is Alive,'" CBS News, September 3, 2012, https://www.cbsnews.com/news/biden-we-are-better-off-bin-laden-is -dead-and-general-motors-is-alive/.

165 **"the trees are the right height":** Mark Trumbull, "Another Mitt Romney Clunker? 'Ann Drives a Couple of Cadillacs, Actually. . . . ,'" *Christian Science Monitor*, February 24, 2012, https://www.csmonitor.com/USA/Politics/The-Vote/2012/0224/Another -Mitt-Romney-clunker-Ann-drives-a-couple-of-Cadillacs-actually.

165 **the VP told a largely Black crowd in Danville, Virginia, that Romney's deregulatory agenda:** Rodney Hawkins, "Biden Tells African-American Audience GOP Ticket Would Put Them 'Back in Chains,'" CBS News, August 14, 2012, https://www.cbsnews .com/news/biden-tells-african-american-audience-gop-ticket-would-put-them-back -in-chains/.

166 **an old image of Romney and his colleagues holding wads of cash was a killer:** Balz, *Collision 2012*, 59.

166 **"there are forty-seven percent of the people who will vote for the president no matter what, alright?":** David Corn, "SECRET VIDEO: Romney Tells Millionaire Donors What He REALLY Thinks of Obama Voters," *Mother Jones*, September 17, 2012, https://www.motherjones.com/politics/2012/09/secret-video-romney-private -fundraiser/.

166 **"the middle class," he said, had "been buried the last four years":** Andrew Grossman, "Biden: Middle Class 'Buried' for Past Four Years," *Wall Street Journal*, October 2, 2012, https://www.wsj.com/articles/BL-WB-36270.

167 **Some turned away from their computers within the first ten minutes:** Axelrod, *Believer*, 467.

167 ***BuzzFeed News* declared Romney the winner:** Ben Smith, "How Mitt Romney Won the First Debate," *BuzzFeed News*, October 3, 2012, https://www.buzzfeednews.com /article/bensmith/how-mitt-romney-won-the-first-debate.

168 **"How is Obama's closing statement so fucking sad, confused and lame?":** Andrew Sullivan, "Live-Blogging the First Presidential Debate 2012," *The Dish*, October 3, 2012, http://dish.andrewsullivan.com/2012/10/03/live-blogging-the-first-presidential -debate-2012/.

168 **Obama would have no problem explaining his own record at length but then would get defensive:** Axelrod, *Believer*, 464–65.

169 **he brushed aside Klain's offer to resign from the debate team the next morning:** Balz, *Collision 2012*, 312.

Chapter 11: 2012–2013

177 **Hannity had exited the Romney experience:** Rachel Weiner, "Sean Hannity: I've 'Evolved' on Immigration," *Washington Post*, November 8, 2012, https://www .washingtonpost.com/news/post-politics/wp/2012/11/08/sean-hannity-ive-evolved -on-immigration/.

178 **"if we're successful in this election":** Sam Stein, "Obama: Republican 'Fever' Will Break During My Second Term," *Huffington Post*, June 1, 2012, https://www.huffpost .com/entry/obama-republican-fever_n_1563539.

179 **thinking . . . "not as a president but as anybody else would, as a parent":** Megan Slack, "President Obama Speaks on the Shooting in Connecticut," The White House, December 14, 2012, https://obamawhitehouse.archives.gov/blog/2012/12/14/president-obama -speaks-shooting-connecticut.

179 **It was the only time he ever requested that Michelle join him in the Oval:** Michelle Obama, *Becoming*, 376–77.

179 **Obama briefly addressed the nation:** Slack, "President Obama Speaks on the Shooting in Connecticut."

180 **Obama announced that he would back legislation . . . arms trafficking:** Philip Rucker and Ed O'Keefe, "Obama's Far-Reaching Gun-Proposals Face Uncertain Fate in Divided Congress," *Washington Post*, January 16, 2013, https://www.washingtonpost .com/politics/obama-unveils-gun-control-proposals/2013/01/16/58cd70ce-5fed -11e2-9940-6fc488f3fecd_story.html.

183 **in hopes of forcing an agreement with Obama:** Deirdre Walsh, Dana Bash, and Craig Broffman, "Boehner's Plan B Fiscal Cliff Bill Pulled amid Dissension in GOP Caucus," CNN, December 21, 2012, https://www.cnn.com/2012/12/20/politics/fiscal-cliff /index.html.

185 **"'Why don't you get a drink with Mitch McConnell?'":** Chris Cillizza, "President Obama's Speech at the White House Correspondents Dinner," CNN, April 28, 2013, https://www.washingtonpost.com/news/the-fix/wp/2013/04/28/president-obamas -speech-at-the-white-house-correspondents-dinner/.

186 **He had a story about Biden's nonstop talking:** Mitch McConnell, *The Long Game* (New York: Sentinel, 2016), 209–10.

186 **he liked to show off a huge table:** "Edward E. (Ted) Kaufman," United States Senate Historical Office.

186 **"the single most important thing . . . one-term president":** Glenn Kessler, "When Did Mitch McConnell Say He Wanted to Make Obama a One-Term President?" *Washington Post*, January 11, 2017, https://www.washingtonpost.com/news/fact-checker /wp/2017/01/11/when-did-mitch-mcconnell-say-he-wanted-to-make-obama-a-one -term-president/.

188 **"Joe Biden: The Most Influential Vice President in History?":** Michael Hirsh, "Joe Biden: The Most Influential Vice President in History?" *National Journal*, December 31, 2012, https://www.theatlantic.com/politics/archive/2012/12/joe-biden-the-most -influential-vice-president-in-history/266729/.

188 **Team USA basketball game:** Matt Compton, "Taking In Team USA," The White House, July 17, 2012, https://obamawhitehouse.archives.gov/blog/2012/07/17/taking -team-usa.

188 **Michelle likened Biden to a "big brother":** Tierney McAfee, "The Bromance Is Real: Barack Obama and Joe Biden 'Really Love One Another,' Their Wives Say," *People*, December 9, 2016, https://people.com/politics/president-obama-joe-biden-bromance -real-wives/.

188 **He'd always thought of Beau . . . version of himself:** Hunter Biden, *Beautiful Things*, 38, 47.

189 **Beau was saying he could hear music:** Hunter Biden, 12–13.

189 **"a death sentence":** Hunter Biden, 14–15.

189 **"those two hours would have been more productive had I spent them napping":** McConnell, *The Long Game*, 214–17.

189 **"dance partner":** Leigh Ann Caldwell, "'Fiscal Cliff' Deal Rests with Two Old Negotiating Partners: Biden and McConnell," CBS News, December 31, 2012, https://www .cbsnews.com/news/fiscal-cliff-deal-rests-with-two-old-negotiating-partners-biden -and-mcconnell/.

Chapter 12: 2013–2015

192 **the world's most admired woman for eleven years running:** "Most Admired Man and Woman," Gallup, accessed November 18, 2021, https://news.gallup.com/poll/1678 /most-admired-man-woman.aspx.

192 **Obama and Clinton sat together for a chummy *60 Minutes* interview:** *60 Minutes*, "Obama and Clinton: The 60 Minutes Interview," CBS News, January 28, 2013, https:// www.cbsnews.com/news/obama-and-clinton-the-60-minutes-interview/.

193 **Clinton then visited Obama for jambalaya:** Hillary Rodham Clinton, *What Happened* (New York: Simon & Schuster, 2017), 52–55.

193 **he wouldn't say anything to that effect out loud:** Clinton, 52–55.

194 **A typical CNN poll:** "CNN|ORC POLL," CNN, December 2, 2014, http://i2.cdn .turner.com/cnn/2014/images/12/02/cnnorcpoll12022014.pdf.

194 **Obama, in turn, heaped praise on Biden as a partner, but then pivoted:** CBS *This Morning*, "Obama and Biden Discuss 2016, Political Future," CBS News, April 17, 2014, https://www.cbsnews.com/video/obama-and-biden-discuss-2016-political-future/.

195 **McCaskill's decision to endorse:** Katie Glueck, "McCaskill Endorses Clinton for 2016," *Politico*, June 18, 2013, https://www.politico.com/story/2013/06/hillary-clinton -2016-claire-mccaskill-092959.

195 **directing it to support Clinton:** Nicholas Confessore, "Huge 'Super PAC' Is Moving Early to Back Clinton," *New York Times*, January 23, 2014, https://www.nytimes.com /2014/01/24/us/politics/biggest-liberal-super-pac-to-fund-possible-clinton-bid.html.

195 **Deval Patrick, the Massachusetts governor and a friend of Obama's, warned on *Meet the Press*:** *Meet the Press*, "Meet the Press Transcript-November 30, 2014," November 30, 2014, https://www.nbcnews.com/meet-the-press/meet-press-transcript -november-30-2014-n258491.

195 **Biden interpreted it as effectively an endorsement:** Joe Biden, *Promise Me, Dad*, 163–65.

196 **the president had approached the subject gingerly at one of their lunches in the fall of 2013 . . . Donilon would write:** Joe Biden, 87–90.

196 **he'd been the most reluctant one in the family:** Gitenstein, *Matters of Principle*, 263.

197 **Instead, the Biden sons were both all-in:** Joe Biden, *Promise Me, Dad*, 21–22.

197 **"At his age, it appears unlikely that Mr. Biden would be in a position to run for president should Mr. Obama win":** Adam Nagourney and Jeff Zeleny, "Obama Chooses Biden as Running Mate," *New York Times*, August 23, 2008, https://www.nytimes.com /2008/08/24/us/politics/24biden.html.

198 **Biden's spokesman Jay Carney told the *Times* that Biden wasn't "ruling anything in or out":** Mark Leibovich, "Speaking Freely, Biden Finds Influential Role," *New York Times*, March 28, 2009, https://www.nytimes.com/2009/03/29/us/politics /29biden.html.

198 **"No, I don't think so":** Arlette Saenz, "Let 2016 Begin: Joe Biden Says Not Last Time Voting for Himself," ABC News, November 6, 2012, https://abcnews.go.com/blogs /politics/2012/11/let-2016-begin-joe-biden-says-not-last-time-voting-for-himself.

198 **Biden presented himself as a champion of the Obama years:** Philip Rucker and Dan Balz, "At Iowa Steak Fry, Biden Defends Obama, Stokes Speculation about 2016 Candidacy," *Washington Post*, September 15, 2013, https://www.washingtonpost.com /politics/at-iowa-steak-fry-biden-defends-obama-stokes-speculation-about-2016 -candidacy/2013/09/15/ee56bd48-1ca4-11e3-a628-7e6dde8f889d_story.html.

199 **he grabbed headlines by touching down in Des Moines:** Jennifer Jacobs, "Biden, Nuns in Des Moines for Voter Turnout Tour," *Des Moines Register*, September 16, 2014, https://www.desmoinesregister.com/story/news/politics/2014/09/17/biden-nuns-bus -voter-turnout-tour-des-moines/15758671/.

200 **strategist Pat Caddell had urged:** Gitenstein, *Matters of Principle*, 33.

200 **read aloud portions of his 2008 convention speech:** Osnos, "The Biden Agenda," *New Yorker*, July 20, 2014, https://www.newyorker.com/magazine/2014/07/28/biden -agenda.

202 **Biden noticed that Beau was uncharacteristically quiet and clearly tired:** Joe Biden, *Promise Me, Dad*, 112–18.

202 **Biden had calculated:** Zeke J. Miller, "Biden: Clinton 'Naive' for Calling GOP the Enemy, Hoping to Govern," *Time*, October 20, 2015, https://time.com/4080728/joe -biden-clinton-naive-for-calling-gop-enemy-hoping-to-govern/.

203 **During one early lunch, Obama looked at Biden:** Osnos, "The Biden Agenda."

203 **"Joe is a man of integrity, incapable of hiding what he really thinks":** Gates, *Duty*, 288.

204 **At one lunch in 2014, while Beau was finding it especially difficult to communicate proper nouns:** Joe Biden, *Promise Me, Dad*, 76.

205 **At their first lunch of 2015 in January, Obama tried to get Biden on the record:** Joe Biden, 77.

205 **Obama mused about his own future and asked Biden if he'd at least considered:** Joe Biden, 77–79.

205 **Biden tried not to cry at the White House, still feeling exposed after doing so when Beau had his first scare half a decade earlier:** Joe Biden, 158–59.

206 **Obama broke down, too:** Joe Biden, 158–59.

206 **Beau Biden died at the end of May 2015:** Hunter Biden, *Beautiful Things*, 9.

206 **Obama struggled to keep his composure:** "Remarks by the President in Eulogy in Honor of Beau Biden," The White House, June 6, 2015, https://obamawhitehouse .archives.gov/the-press-office/2015/06/06/remarks-president-eulogy-honor-beau-biden.

Chapter 13: 2015

209 **she did in October:** Jessica Taylor, "Clinton Breaks with Obama to Oppose Asia Trade Deal," NPR, October 7, 2015, https://www.npr.org/sections/itsallpolitics/2015/10/07 /446672839/clinton-breaks-with-obama-to-oppose-trans-pacific-partnership.

209 **only to oppose the Obama-favored project in September:** Monica Alba and Carrie

Dann, "Hillary Clinton: I oppose the Keystone XL Pipeline," NBC News, https://www
.nbcnews.com/politics/2016-election/hillary-clinton-n431781.

209 **she criticized Obama's choice:** Jeffrey Goldberg, "Hillary Clinton: 'Failure' to Help
Syrian Rebels Led to the Rise of ISIS," *The Atlantic*, August 9, 2014, https://www
.theatlantic.com/international/archive/2014/08/hillary-clinton-failure-to-help-syrian
-rebels-led-to-the-rise-of-isis/375832/.

209 **"You've got to pace yourself this time":** Clinton, *What Happened*, 83.

210 **Obama again raised the matter of 2016 at lunch . . . made clear that they should
move on:** Joe Biden, *Promise Me, Dad*, 206–7.

213 *Politico* **Op-Ed in 2013 urging the administration to be wary:** Elizabeth Warren,
"Avoiding Wall St. Shuffle's Perils," *Politico*, January 24, 2013, https://www.warren
.senate.gov/newsroom/op-eds/2013/01/24/avoiding-wall-st-shuffle-and-039s-perils-1.

213 **blocking his nomination:** Ben White, "Warren Wins on Weiss Nomination," *Politico*,
January 12, 2015, https://www.politico.com/story/2015/01/antonio-weiss-pulls-out
-treasury-undersecretary-114191.

213 **"very compelling and mildly demagogic":** Chuck Todd, Mark Murray, and Carrie Dann, "Biden and Warren Had a Long History of Squabbles Before 2020," NBC
News, September 12, 2019, https://www.nbcnews.com/politics/meet-the-press/biden
-warren-had-long-history-squabbles-2020-n1052996.

214 **He then said something similar in a teary interview:** Michael D. Shear, "Joe Biden, in
Colbert Interview, Expresses Doubt About Bid for President," *New York Times*, September 10, 2015, https://www.nytimes.com/2015/09/11/us/politics/joe-biden-in-colbert
-interview-expresses-doubts-about-bid-for-president.html.

215 **like to the New Hampshire Democratic Party's big fundraising dinner:** Gabriel
Debenedetti, "Biden Yet to RSVP for New Hampshire Jefferson-Jackson Dinner,"
Politico, August 24, 2015, https://www.politico.com/story/2015/08/joe-biden-no-rsvp
-jefferson-jackson-dinner-new-hampshire-121666.

217 **He was aghast . . . "better off with Biden values":** Edward-Isaac Dovere, "Exclusive:
Biden Himself Leaked Word of His Son's Dying Wish," *Politico*, October 6, 2015, https://
www.politico.com/story/2015/10/joe-biden-beau-2016–214459; Maureen Dowd, "Joe
Biden in 2016: What Would Beau Do?" *New York Times*, August 1, 2015, https://www
.nytimes.com/2015/08/02/opinion/sunday/maureen-dowd-joe-biden-in-2016-what
-would-beau-do.html.

217 **called for its removal:** Michael A. Memoli, "Source: Biden Hopes New Draft Biden
Ad Won't Air," *Los Angeles Times*, October 8, 2015, https://www.latimes.com/nation
/politics/trailguide/la-na-trailguide-10082015-htmlstory.html.

217 **International Association of Fire Fighters abandoned its planned Clinton endorsement:** Noam Scheiber and Amy Chozick, "Firefighters' Union Backs Away from Endorsement of Hillary Clinton," *New York Times*, October 2, 2015, https://www.nytimes.com
/2015/10/03/us/politics/firefighters-union-backs-away-from-endorsement-of-hillary
-clinton.html.

217 **even George Clooney got in touch:** Joe Biden, *Promise Me, Dad*, 240–41.

217 **"Joe still couldn't say if he was running":** Cramer, *What It Takes*, 312.

219 **Clyburn . . . said in an interview:** Howard Fineman, "Key Democrat's Advice For
Biden: Don't Run," *Huffington Post*, October 19, 2015, https://www.huffpost.com
/entry/james-clyburn-joe-biden_n_562549f5e4b08589ef486907.

219 **"A vice president is totally a reflection":** Lopez, "Joe Biden and Walter Mondale Discuss 'New Modern Vice Presidency.'"

220 **Donilon, for the first time, looked at Biden and said it wasn't right for him now:** Joe
Biden, *Promise Me, Dad*, 234–36.

220 **Around 11:30 p.m. he called James Smith . . . "going to sleep on it":** Gabriel Debenedetti, "How Joe Biden Became President-Elect," *New York*, November 7, 2020, https://

nymag.com/intelligencer/article/2020-election-how-joe-biden-became-president
.html.

221 **turned to what had taken so long:** "Full Text: Biden's Announcement That He Won't
Run for President," *Washington Post*, October 21, 2015, https://www.washingtonpost
.com/news/post-politics/wp/2015/10/21/full-text-bidens-announcement-that-he
-wont-run-for-president/.

Chapter 14: 2016

222 **He rolled his eyes:** "Remarks by the President at White House Correspondents' Association Dinner," The White House, April 25, 2015, https://obamawhitehouse.archives
.gov/the-press-office/2015/04/25/remarks-president-white-house-correspondents
-association-dinner.

222 **Now, Obama displayed his impatience:** "Here's the Full Transcript of President
Obama's Speech at the White House Correspondents' Dinner," *Time*, May 1, 2016,
https://time.com/4313618/white-house-correspondents-dinner-2016-president
-obama-jokes-transcript-full/.

224 **"a cheeseburger sells for $68 and a Tesla serves as an Uber":** Carol E. Lee, "Biden
Plies a Mixed Agenda in Davos," *Wall Street Journal*, January 21, 2016, https://www.wsj
.com/articles/biden-plies-a-mixed-agenda-in-davos-1453408972.

225 **Onstage in the Alps:** "'Middle-Class Joe' Biden tells Davos Bosses to Look After
Workers," Reuters, January 20, 2016, https://www.reuters.com/article/us-davos
-meeting-biden/middle-class-joe-biden-tells-davos-bosses-to-look-after-workers
-idUSKCN0UY2FY.

227 **making roughly four million workers:** Scott Horsley, "Millions to Be Eligible for
Overtime Under New Obama Administration Rule," NPR, May 17, 2016, https://www
.npr.org/2016/05/17/478463549/millions-to-be-eligible-for-overtime-under-new
-rule-obama-administration-rule.

227 **Biden urged Sanders to bolster his foreign policy chops:** Jonathan Allen and Amie
Parnes, *Lucky* (New York: Crown, 2021), xx.

227 **promising not to campaign:** Barack Obama, "Guns Are Our Shared Responsibility," *New York Times*, January 7, 2016, https://www.nytimes.com/2016/01/08/opinion
/president-barack-obama-guns-are-our-shared-responsibility.html.

228 **"what Bernie Sanders has to do is say":** Kevin Liptak, "Biden Praises Sanders on
Income Inequality, Calls Clinton 'Relatively New' to the Fight," CNN, January 12,
2016, https://www.cnn.com/2016/01/11/politics/joe-biden-bernie-sanders-hillary
-clinton-income-inequality/index.html.

230 **Obama essentially accidentally endorsed Clinton:** "Full Transcript: POLITICO's
Glenn Thrush Interviews President Barack Obama on Iowa, 2016, and the Choice
Between Hillary Clinton and Bernie Sanders," *Politico*, January 25, 2016, https://www
.politico.com/story/2016/01/off-message-podcast-transcript-obama-218167.

230 **uncovered an old radio interview in which Sanders had mused:** Gabriel Debenedetti, "Sanders' Challenge: Winning over Obama Supporters," *Politico*, October 10,
2015, https://www.politico.com/story/2015/10/sanders-obama-supporters-214636.

230 **publication of a book about how Obama had let progressives down:** Dan Merica, "Sanders's Campaign Stands by Book Blurb About Progressive Discontent with
Obama," CNN, February 4, 2016, https://www.cnn.com/2016/01/30/politics/bernie
-sanders-democrats-obama-progressives-hillary-clinton/index.html.

231 **lined with young government aides stretching to get a glimpse of Sanders:** Rhodes,
The World as It Is, 387.

232 **Clinton had spent over a year trying to give Trump extra attention:** Gabriel Debenedetti, "They Always Wanted Trump," *Politico Magazine*, November 7, 2016, https://www
.politico.com/magazine/story/2016/11/hillary-clinton-2016-donald-trump-214428/.

233 **who'd been encouraging Podesta and Mook not to hide:** Stanley B. Greenberg, *RIP GOP* (New York: Thomas Dunne Books, 2019), 223.

233 **Greenberg said she didn't need to criticize Obama:** Greenberg, 229.

234 **Biden shared an intimate stage:** Allie Malloy, "Biden, Boehner Lament Negative Politics in Notre Dame Addresses," CNN, May 15, 2016, https://www.cnn.com/2016/05/15/politics/joe-biden-john-boehner-notre-dame/index.html.

236 **Brazile had thought about how to replace Clinton:** Donna Brazile, *Hacks* (New York: Hachette Books, 2017), 114–16.

236 **national security advisor Susan Rice and CIA director John Brennan told Obama:** Susan Rice, *Tough Love* (New York: Simon & Schuster Paperbacks, 2019), 441.

236 **He'd confronted Putin:** Greg Miller, Ellen Nakashima, and Adam Entous, "Obama's Secret Struggle to Punish Russia for Putin's Election Assault," *Washington Post*, January 23, 2017, https://www.washingtonpost.com/graphics/2017/world/national-security/obama-putin-election-hacking/.

237 **Obama's team stopped Clinton's from playing "Don't Stop":** Rice, *Tough Love*, 455.

238 **Michelle went to bed while Jarrett walked downstairs:** Michelle Obama, *Becoming*, 410–11; Jarrett, *Finding My Voice*, 287.

239 **"So, that happened":** Rhodes, *The World as It Is*, 401–2.

239 **"We're going to have to rework tomorrow's remarks a little bit":** Abrams, *Obama*, 386.

Chapter 15: 2016–2017

241 **the outgoing president suggested he should keep in place its most popular pieces:** Cohn, *The Ten Year War*, 211.

242 **At one quiet meeting:** Malcolm Turnbull, *A Bigger Picture* (Richmond, Victoria, Australia: Hardie Grant Books, 2020), 535.

242 **Chilean president Michelle Bachelet shut that talk down:** Turnbull, 535.

243 **In Peru, he was in one of his dark places:** Rhodes, *The World as It Is*, xvi–xvii.

243 **Obama's political aides told him about the sheer number of voters who'd backed Trump after supporting him twice:** Edward-Isaac Dovere, *Battle for the Soul* (New York: Viking, 2021), 8.

243 *Politico* **reported that Clinton was considering asking Biden to be her secretary of state:** Edward-Isaac Dovere, "Clinton Eyes Biden for Secretary of State," *Politico*, October 28, 2016, https://www.politico.com/story/2016/10/clinton-biden-secretary-of-state-230428.

244 **he also started whispering to some senior Democrats:** Gabriel Debenedetti, "How Does Obama Feel About Biden's Candidacy? It's Complicated," *New York*, May 24, 2019, https://nymag.com/intelligencer/2019/05/joe-biden-and-barack-obamas-one-sided-embrace.html.

244 **Obama took time out of his farewell:** "President Obama's Farewell Address," The White House, January 10, 2017, https://obamawhitehouse.archives.gov/farewell.

244 **Obama would ambush Biden:** "Remarks by the President and the Vice President in Presentation of the Medal of Freedom to Vice President Joe Biden," The White House, January 12, 2017, https://obamawhitehouse.archives.gov/the-press-office/2017/01/12/remarks-president-and-vice-president-presentation-medal-freedom-vice.

246 **George W. Bush thought it was "some weird shit":** Yashar Ali, "What George W. Bush Really Thought of Donald Trump's Inauguration," *New York*, March 29, 2017, https://nymag.com/intelligencer/2017/03/what-george-w-bush-really-thought-of-trumps-inauguration.html.

246 **It was "full circle":** Dan Merica and Jeff Simon, "'Full Circle': Joe Biden Reflects on His Life During a Train Ride Back to Delaware," CNN, January 20, 2017, https://www.cnn.com/2017/01/20/politics/biden-amtrak-inauguration-day/index.html.

246 **a house in Palm Springs:** Rosalie Murphy, "The Obamas Are Returning to Palm Springs. Will They Finally Make a Home Here?" *Desert Sun*, January 17, 2017, https://

www.desertsun.com/story/money/real-estate/2017/01/17/obama-rancho-mirage -house/96678406/.

246 **even in the mountains:** Casey Blake, "#AvlNews: Obamas Moving to Asheville?" *Citizen Times,* June 9, 2014, https://www.citizen-times.com/story/news/local/2014/06/09 /avlnews-obamas-moving-asheville/10242673/.

247 **They placed nearly two dozen staffers in the suite:** Gabriel Debenedetti, "Where Is Barack Obama?" *New York,* June 2018, https://nymag.com/intelligencer/2018/06 /where-is-barack-obama.html.

247 **Oprah Winfrey, Bruce Springsteen, and Tom Hanks on David Geffen's yacht:** Debenedetti, "Where Is Barack Obama?"

247 **"seven lightly salted almonds":** Shear, "Obama After Dark: The Precious Hours Alone."

248 **he'd thought out loud in an interview about becoming a Silicon Valley venture capitalist:** John Micklethwait, Megan Murphy, and Ellen Pollock, "The 'Anti-Business' President Who's Been Good for Business," *Bloomberg Businessweek,* June 27, 2016, https://www.bloomberg.com/features/2016-obama-anti-business-president/.

248 **"I feel like Michael Corleone":** Rhodes, *The World as It Is,* xix.

249 **a record $65 million:** Hilary Weaver, "Barack and Michelle Obama Land Reported $65 Million Book Deal," *Vanity Fair,* March 1, 2017, https://www.vanityfair.com/style /2017/03/barack-michelle-obama-land-book-deal.

249 **book of poems he would write for Jill:** Jill Biden, *Where the Light Enters,* 69.

249 **he was approached early in 2017 by an agency proposing a four-year, $38 million contract:** Gabriel Debenedetti, "Why Joe Biden Turned Down $38 Million," *New York,* December 11, 2018, https://nymag.com/intelligencer/2018/12/will-joe-biden-run-for -president-in-2020.html.

250 **Warren said in April that she was "troubled":** Eugene Scott, "Warren 'Troubled' by Obama's Big Wall Street Speech Payday," CNN, April 27, 2017, https://www.cnn .com/2017/04/27/politics/barack-obama-elizabeth-warren-speech/index.html; Debenedetti, "Where Is Barack Obama?"

250 **Sanders chimed in the next day:** Eleanor Mueller, "Sanders: Obama's Paid Wall Street Speech 'Distasteful,'" CNN, April 28, 2017, https://www.cnn.com/2017/04/28/politics /bernie-sanders-obama-wall-street-speech/index.html.

250 **After waving to crowds of onlookers, he ducked into the Park Hyatt:** Jason Horowitz and Stephanie Strom, "Obama Speaks in Milan, with Food as Text and Politics as Subtext," *New York Times,* May 9, 2017, https://www.nytimes.com/2017/05/09/world /europe/obama-food-milan-seeds-chips.html.

251 **the photographs of them eating halibut:** Jonathan Montpetit, "The Liverpool House Summit: What Did Obama and Trudeau Talk About?" CBC News, June 7, 2017, https://www.cbc.ca/news/canada/montreal/obama-trudeau-montreal-restaurant -dinner-1.4149097.

252 **He'd often recounted the story:** Evan Osnos, "Can Biden's Center Hold?" *New Yorker,* August 23, 2020, https://www.newyorker.com/magazine/2020/08/31/can-bidens -center-hold.

252 **One November *Saturday Night Live* sketch had Chance the Rapper singing:** *Saturday Night Live,* "Come Back, Barack - SNL," November 19, 2017, YouTube video, 3:20, https://www.youtube.com/watch?v=ZkPSbp3zTfo.

252 **"We all miss him":** Ben Strauss, "What Kobe Bryant Misses Most About Obama," *Politico Magazine,* June 6, 2017, https://www.politico.com/magazine/story/2017/06 /06/what-kobe-bryant-misses-most-about-obama-215233/.

255 **Trump's address to the Boy Scout Jamboree:** Helen Regan, "Read the Full Transcript of President Trump's 2017 Boy Scout Jamboree Speech," *Time,* July 25, 2017, https:// time.com/4872118/trump-boy-scout-jamboree-speech-transcript/.

256 **But Obama quietly started advising ex-aides and lawmakers:** Debenedetti, "Where Is Barack Obama?"

256 **he amplified the pressure campaign:** Greg Toppo, "Obama: There's No 'Courage' in Aiding the Already Powerful," *USA Today*, May 7, 2017, https://www.usatoday.com /story/news/2017/05/07/speech-obama-takes-aim-trump-republicans/101419626/.

257 **Speaking at the University of Pennsylvania in March, he griped:** Dan Merica, "Joe Biden Indirectly Knocks Clinton's Failed Campaign," CNN, March 31, 2017, https://www .cnn.com/2017/03/30/politics/joe-biden-donald-trump-hillary-clinton/index.html.

257 **The next month, he told a crowd in New Hampshire:** MJ Lee, "Biden Returns to New Hampshire as 2020 Rumors Swirl," CNN, April 30, 2017, https://www.cnn.com/2017 /04/30/politics/joe-biden-new-hampshire-2020/index.html.

257 **At a hedge fund conference in Las Vegas:** Aaron Blake, "Biden Disses Clinton: 'I Never Thought She Was a Great Candidate. I Thought I Was a Great Candidate.'" *Washington Post*, May 19, 2017, https://www.washingtonpost.com/news/the-fix/wp/2017/05/19 /biden-disses-clinton-i-never-thought-she-was-a-great-candidate-i-thought-i-was-a -great-candidate/.

257 **In one interview before leaving office:** David Remnick, "Obama Reckons with a Trump Presidency," *New Yorker*, November 18, 2016, https://www.newyorker.com /magazine/2016/11/28/obama-reckons-with-a-trump-presidency.

258 **A few weeks later, in another interview:** Michelle Ruiz, "Who Is the Future of the Democratic Party?" *Vogue*, January 27, 2017, https://www.vogue.com/article /democratic-party-rising-stars.

258 **In their first two years out of office, they made upward of $15 million on their book deals:** Osnos, *Joe Biden*, 8.

Chapter 16: 2017–2018

259 **"on both sides":** Dan Merica, "Trump Says Both Sides to Blame amid Charlottesville Backlash," CNN, August 16, 2017, https://www.cnn.com/2017/08/15/politics/trump -charlottesville-delay/index.html.

259 **"If it wasn't clear before":** Joe Biden, "'We Are Living Through a Battle for the Soul of This Nation,'" *The Atlantic*, August 27, 2017, https://www.theatlantic.com/politics /archive/2017/08/joe-biden-after-charlottesville/538128/.

260 **his middle-class supporters "aren't prejudiced":** Joe Biden and Ivo H. Daalder, "Joe Biden on Global Engagement in an Age of Uncertainty," Chicago Council on Global Affairs, November 1, 2017, https://www.thechicagocouncil.org/events/joe-biden-global -engagement-age-uncertainty.

260 **Obama conceded that "sometimes the backlash comes . . . fearful of change":** "Full Speech: Obama Brands Trump as 'Symptom Not the Cause of Division,'" NBC News, September 7, 2018, https://www.nbcnews.com/video/full-speech-obama-brands -trump-as-symptom-not-the-cause-of-division-1315294787749.

261 **Obama made a surprise cameo:** Esteban Parra, "Former President Barack Obama Surprises Attendees at a Beau Biden Foundation Fundraiser," *News Journal*, September 25, 2017, https://www.delawareonline.com/story/news/local/2017/09/25/former -president-barack-obama-surprises-attendees-beau-biden-foundation-fundraiser /702496001/.

261 **popped up at a veteran-focused DC bakery:** Dartunorro Clark, "Obama and Biden Reunite at Washington Bakery That Supports Veterans," NBC News, July 30, 2018, https://www.nbcnews.com/politics/politics-news/obama-biden-reunite-washington -bakery-supports-veterans-n895931.

261 **pointing to a RAND Corporation study . . . *Why Liberalism Failed*:** Debenedetti, "Where Is Barack Obama?"

262 **"I take some responsibility":** "*This Week* Transcript: President Barack Obama," ABC

News, January 8, 2017, https://abcnews.go.com/Politics/week-transcript-president
-barack-obama/story?id=44630949.

264 **Biden was reconnecting with a handful of the party's leading donors:** Debenedetti,
"Why Joe Biden Turned Down $38 Million."

267 **When he'd appeared for Jones in Birmingham:** Debenedetti.

267 **Speaking for plenty of baffled liberals:** Graham Vyse, "Biden Wants 'Compromise.' Progressives Don't Want to Hear It," *New Republic*, October 6, 2017, https://
newrepublic.com/article/145199/joe-biden-wants-compromise-progressives-dont
-want-hear-it.

267 **Third Way . . . trying to woo former New Orleans mayor Mitch Landrieu:** Gabriel
Debenedetti, "Undaunted Democratic Centrists Ready to Fight Trump and Bernie
at Same Time," *New York*, July 23, 2018, https://nymag.com/intelligencer/2018/07
/democratic-centrists-ready-to-fight-trump-and-bernie.html.

267 **In the final weeks:** Gabriel Debenedetti, "Decoding the Recent Travel Schedules of
Democrats with Designs on 2020," *New York*, November 6, 2018, https://nymag.com
/intelligencer/2018/11/decoding-the-travel-schedules-of-democratic-2020-hopefuls
.html.

Chapter 17: 2018–2019

270 **In December Frank Bruni wrote:** Frank Bruni, "I Like Joe Biden. I Urge Him Not
to Run," *New York Times*, December 8, 2018, https://www.nytimes.com/2018/12/08
/opinion/sunday/biden-2020-dont-run.html.

270 *Politico Magazine* **had called Biden:** Charlie Mahtesian, "Joe Biden Is the Front-
Runner. Uh-oh," *Politico Magazine*, April 16, 2018, https://www.politico.com/magazine
/story/2018/04/16/joe-biden-2020-front-runner-problem-217995/.

270 **Mehdi Hasan argued in** *The Intercept*: Mehdi Hasan, "Joe Biden Won't Blame the
Republicans for Trump. That Should Disqualify Him," *The Intercept*, May 6, 2019,
https://theintercept.com/2019/05/06/joe-biden-trump-republicans/.

272 **Biden had no doubt he was ready to meet the moment:** Debenedetti, "Why Joe Biden
Turned Down $38 Million."

277 **In his first political speech out of office:** "Read Obama's Full Speech from the University of Illinois," NBC Chicago, September 7, 2018, https://www.nbcchicago.com/news
/local/obama-university-of-illinois-full-speech/173866/.

278 **Some of Obama's top donors bought in:** Gabriel Debenedetti, "Wall Street Democrats
Are Absolutely Freaking Out About Their 2020 Candidates," *New York*, April 28, 2019,
https://nymag.com/intelligencer/2019/04/wall-street-democrats-2020-candidates.html.

278 **Pfeiffer . . . wrote an article making "The Case for Beto O'Rourke":** Dan Pfeiffer,
"The Case for Beto O'Rourke," *Crooked*, November 26, 2018, https://crooked.com
/articles/beto-president-2020/.

279 **Gifford to argue that "Obama was the Pete or Beto":** Debenedetti, "How Does
Obama Feel About Biden's Candidacy? It's Complicated."

280 **self-consciously corny tweets:** Allison Quinn, "Joe Biden Shares Photo of Matching
'Joe-Barack' Friendship Bracelets on Twitter for #BestFriendsDay," *Daily Beast*, June
9, 2019, https://www.thedailybeast.com/joe-biden-shares-photo-of-matching-joe
-barack-friendship-bracelets-on-twitter-for-bestfriendsday.

283 **even used Obama's signature walk-up music:** Dovere, *Battle for the Soul*, 90.

284 **He tried recruiting Terry McAuliffe . . . Trumka:** Gabriel Debenedetti, "How Joe
Biden Plans to Steamroll the 2020 Democratic Field," *New York*, April 24, 2019, https://
nymag.com/intelligencer/2019/04/how-joe-biden-plans-to-steamroll-the-2020
-democratic-field.html.

285 **"That's so Hillary":** Debenedetti, "How Joe Biden Plans to Steamroll the 2020 Democratic Field."

285 **Kathleen and Hunter had split:** Margie Fishman, "Divorce Filing Details Split of Kathleen, Hunter Biden," *News Journal*, March 2, 2017, https://www.delawareonline .com/story/news/2017/03/02/kathleen-biden-files-divorce-hunter/98638454/.

285 **They finally settled on a video *about* Charlottesville:** Alexander Burns, "Joe Biden's Campaign Announcement Video, Annotated," *New York Times*, April 25, 2019, https:// www.nytimes.com/2019/04/25/us/politics/biden-campaign-video-announcement.html.

285 **A chair that had been reserved for Hunter remained empty:** Schreckinger, *The Bidens*, 8.

285 **Biden hit his stride:** Molly Nagle, "Joe Biden Gives Pitch on Uniting the Country in Philadelphia," ABC News, May 18, 2019, https://abcnews.go.com/Politics/joe-biden -heads-philadelphia-give-pitch-uniting-country/story?id=63089272.

286 **"I'm an Obama-Biden Democrat, man":** Marc Caputo and Natasha Korecki, "Joe Biden Is Running as Obama's Heir. The Problem: He's Not Obama.," *Politico*, April 25, 2019, https://www.politico.com/story/2019/04/25/biden-obama-2020-relationship -1287353.

286 **"I asked President Obama not to endorse":** Sean Rossman, "Joe Biden Says He Asked Barack Obama Not to Endorse Him in 2020 Presidential Campaign," *USA Today*, April 25, 2019, https://www.usatoday.com/story/news/politics/elections/2019/04/25/barack -obama-praises-joe-biden-but-doesnt-offer-2020-endorsement/3571729002/.

Chapter 18: 2019

287 **Julián Castro and New York City mayor Bill de Blasio laid into his administration's record:** Jeff Zeleny and Kevin Liptak, "Blistering Criticism of Obama Highlights Dramatic Shift Inside Democratic Party," CNN, August 2, 2019, https://www.cnn.com /2019/08/01/politics/obama-legacy-democratic-primary/index.html.

287 **"big insurance companies and big pharmaceutical companies who've been profiting off the backs of sick people":** Stephen Stromberg, "Do Democrats Think They Can Win by Attacking Barack Obama?" *Washington Post*, July 31, 2019, https:// www.washingtonpost.com/opinions/2019/08/01/do-democrats-think-they-can -win-by-attacking-barack-obama/.

289 **He said that while he had always been affectionate:** Colby Itkowitz, "'I Get It': Joe Biden, Accused of Inappropriate Physical Contact by Multiple Women, Says He Will Change His Behavior," *Washington Post*, April 3, 2019, https://www.washingtonpost .com/politics/joe-biden-accused-of-inappropriate-physical-contact-by-multiple -women-says-he-will-change-his-behavior/2019/04/03/05b5ea58-5643-11e9-814f -e2f46684196e_story.html.

289 **Only in June did he reverse his long-held position on the Hyde Amendment:** Katie Glueck, "Joe Biden Denounces Hyde Amendment, Reversing His Position," *New York Times*, June 6, 2019, https://www.nytimes.com/2019/06/06/us/politics/joe-biden-hyde -amendment.html.

292 **"I think the turnout tonight demonstrates the high regard in which the vice president is held in the extended Obama family":** Alex Thompson, "'The President Was Not Encouraging': What Obama Really Thought About Biden," *Politico Magazine*, August 14, 2020, https://www.politico.com/news/magazine/2020/08/14/obama-biden -relationship-393570.

293 **"I find it fascinating, everybody is talking about how terrible I am on these issues":** Tara Golshan, "Barack Obama Was Joe Biden's Guardian Angel at the Democratic Debate," *Vox*, July 31, 2019, https://www.vox.com/2019/7/31/20749525/barack-obama -joe-biden-democratic-debate-2020.

293 **"I was a little surprised how much of the incoming was about Barack":** Veronica

Stracqualursi and Sarah Mucha, "Biden Surprised by 'Degree of Criticism' Obama Took at Democratic Debate," CNN, August 1, 2019, https://www.cnn.com/2019/08/01/politics/biden-obama-attacks-democratic-debate/index.html.

294 **"I'm with Bernie":** "Full Transcript: Democratic Debate in Houston," NBC News, September 12, 2019, https://www.nbcnews.com/politics/2020-election/full-transcript-democratic-debate-houston-n1053926.

294 **"Every time something good about Barack Obama comes up":** Jonathan Martin and Alexander Burns, "Attacks on Biden in Debate Highlight Divide over the Obama Legacy," *New York Times*, September 12, 2019, https://www.nytimes.com/2019/09/12/us/politics/democratic-presidential-debate-recap.html.

294 **"I got you votes!":** *The Fix* team, "The October Democratic Debate Transcript," *Washington Post*, October 16, 2019, https://www.washingtonpost.com/politics/2019/10/15/october-democratic-debate-transcript/.

295 **"Someone at my gym in California asked me":** David Plouffe (@davidplouffe), "The power of saturation advertising. Someone at my gym in California asked me why Barack Obama chose Bloomberg over the rest of the field," Twitter, February 14, 2020, 11:26 a.m., https://twitter.com/davidplouffe/status/1228354858224431106.

295 **It was all especially galling to the Obama confidants:** Gabriel Debenedetti, "What Obama Is Saying in Private About the Democratic Primary," *New York*, February 17, 2020, https://nymag.com/intelligencer/2020/02/what-obama-is-saying-in-private-about-the-democratic-primary.html.

297 **commentators broadly wondered aloud if Castro had gone too far:** Suzanne Gamboa, "Julián Castro Accused Joe Biden of 'Forgetting.' Did He Go Too Far?" NBC News, September 13, 2019, https://www.nbcnews.com/news/latino/juli-n-castro-accused-joe-biden-forgetting-did-he-go-n1054061.

297 **Swalwell's insistence at an earlier debate that Biden "pass the torch":** Paul LeBlanc, "Swalwell Urges Biden to 'Pass the Torch,' Biden says 'I'm Still Holding onto That Torch,'" CNN, June 28, 2019, https://www.cnn.com/2019/06/27/politics/swalwell-biden-debate-pass-the-torch/index.html.

298 *The Atlantic* **published a long, touching article about Biden's stutter:** John Hendrickson, "What Joe Biden Can't Bring Himself to Say," *The Atlantic*, January/February 2020, https://www.theatlantic.com/magazine/archive/2020/01/joe-biden-stutter-profile/602401/.

298 **That was an ideologically confused state:** Gabriel Debenedetti, "One of These People Could Beat Trump, Right?" *New York*, January 20, 2020, https://nymag.com/intelligencer/2020/01/2020-iowa-caucus.html.

298 **"running in the wrong presidential primary":** Katie Glueck, "Biden Attacks Warren as a 'My Way or the Highway' Elitist," *New York Times*, November 5, 2019, https://www.nytimes.com/2019/11/05/us/politics/joe-biden-elizabeth-warren.html.

298 **At one debate he touted his deal with Mitch McConnell to avoid the 2012 fiscal cliff:** Matthew Yglesias, "A Quiet Joe Biden Debate Moment That Deserved More Attention," *Vox*, June 28, 2019, https://www.vox.com/policy-and-politics/2019/6/28/18955310/democratic-debate-2019-biden-bennet.

299 **For all the dire signs in the first two states, his national lead had barely budged:** Gabriel Debenedetti, "National Democratic Primary Polls: Bernie and Biden Are Back Where They Started," *New York*, December 21, 2019, https://nymag.com/intelligencer/2019/12/primary-polls-bernie-and-biden-are-back-where-they-started.html.

299 **"I'm not saying that it's guaranteed I win . . . I'm not gonna die!":** "Joe Biden," editorial, *New York Times*, January 17, 2020, https://www.nytimes.com/interactive/2020/01/17/opinion/joe-biden-nytimes-interview.html.

299 **The *Times* essentially treated it as a punch line:** "The Democrats' Best Choices for President," editorial, *New York Times*, January 19, 2020, https://www.nytimes.com /interactive/2020/01/19/opinion/amy-klobuchar-elizabeth-warren-nytimes -endorsement.html.

301 **He tried at an Obama Foundation summit:** Juana Summers, "Obama Says Democrats Don't Always Need to Be 'Politically Woke,'" NPR, October 31, 2019, https:// www.npr.org/2019/10/31/774918215/obama-says-democrats-dont-always-need-to -be-politically-woke.

301 **He got expansive:** Gabriel Debenedetti, "Obama Tells His Party's Elites to Relax," *New York*, November 15, 2019, https://nymag.com/intelligencer/2019/11/obama-addresses -democratic-elites-about-the-election.html.

302 **"We will not win just by increasing the turnout of the people":** Brian Slodysko, "Obama Warns Against 'Purity Tests' in the Democratic Primary," Associated Press, November 22, 2019, https://apnews.com/article/5411b7bd9c414b36b4cf35dead3b75be.

Chapter 19: 2020

303 **Not that Biden had ever met:** Nadine Shubailat, "Exclusive: Hunter Biden Talks Getting Married After 6 Days and Why His Life Is in 'The Best Place I've Ever Been,'" ABC News, October 17, 2019, https://abcnews.go.com/Politics/exclusive-hunter-biden -talks-married-days-life-best/story?id=66333924.

304 **Kerry had been overheard:** Jonathan Allen and Allan Smith, "John Kerry Overheard Discussing Possible 2020 Bid amid Concern of 'Sanders Taking Down the Democratic Party,'" NBC News, February 2, 2020, https://www.nbcnews.com/politics/2020-election /john-kerry-overheard-discussing-possible-2020-bid-amid-concern-sanders-n1128476.

305 **He promised, unconvincingly:** Al Weaver, "Biden to Iowa Supporters: 'It's Going to Be a Long Night,'" *The Hill*, February 3, 2020, https://thehill.com/homenews/campaign /481313-biden-to-iowa-supporters-its-going-to-be-a-long-night.

305 **sent the party a stern letter:** Ursula Perano, "Biden Campaign Demands Answers from Iowa Democrats over 'Quality Control,'" Axios, February 4, 2020, https://www .axios.com/biden-iowa-caucuses-campaign-technology-results-e91e3647-bccb-46ac -9c4c-5c93dbd6dc64.html.

309 **took a moment to revel:** Asma Khalid and Deirdre Walsh, "'Very Much Alive': Biden Projected to Win South Carolina," NPR, February 29, 2020, https://www.npr.org/2020 /02/29/810477647/biden-wins-south-carolina-primary-ap-projects.

310 **He'd written a *USA Today* Op-Ed:** Joe Biden, "Trump Is Worst Possible Leader to Deal with Coronavirus Outbreak," *USA Today*, January 27, 2020, https://www.usatoday.com /story/opinion/2020/01/27/coronavirus-donald-trump-made-us-less-prepared-joe -biden-column/4581710002/.

312 **Sanders answered a journalist's question:** Tim O'Donnell, "Bernie Sanders Is Focused on the 'F—ing Global Crisis," *The Week*, March 18, 2020, https://theweek.com /speedreads/903213/bernie-sanders-focused-fing-global-crisis.

313 **Obama reconnected with him:** Gabriel Debenedetti, "How Biden Is Trying to Win Over Bernie's Supporters," *New York*, April 9, 2020, https://nymag.com/intelligencer /2020/04/how-biden-is-trying-to-win-over-bernies-supporters.html.

314 **insisting on exercising every morning:** Gabriel Debenedetti, "Biden Is Planning an FDR-Size Presidency," *New York*, May 11, 2020, https://nymag.com/intelligencer/2020 /05/joe-biden-presidential-plans.html.

315 **in early May the *New York Times* published:** David Axelrod and David Plouffe, "What Joe Biden Needs to Do to Beat Trump," *New York Times*, May 4, 2020, https:// www.nytimes.com/2020/05/04/opinion/axelrod-plouffe-joe-biden.html.

316 **candidate had appeared on *Morning Joe*:** Katie Glueck, Lisa Lerer, and Sydney Ember, "Biden Denies Tara Reade's Assault Allegation: 'It Never Happened,'" *New York Times*,

May 1, 2020, https://www.nytimes.com/2020/05/01/us/politics/joe-biden-tara-reade
-morning-joe.html.

316 **The *Washington Post*'s film critic reviewed:** Ann Hornaday, "Biden and Obama Just
Showed Us the Future of Movies in the Covid-19 Era," *Washington Post*, July 24, 2020,
https://www.washingtonpost.com/lifestyle/style/biden-and-obama-just-showed-us
-the-future-of-movies-in-the-covid-19-era/2020/07/23/87d47aee-ccf4-11ea-b0e3
-d55bda07d66a_story.html.

316 **he'd confronted Facebook's Mark Zuckerberg:** Gabriel Debenedetti, "A 21st Century
Breakup," *New York*, September 18, 2019, https://nymag.com/intelligencer/2019/09
/facebook-silicon-valley-democratic-party.html.

317 **His first online fundraiser for Biden in June brought in $11 million:** Melanie
Mason, "Obama and Biden, Reunited Again, Rake In More Than $11 Million at Virtual
Fundraiser," *Los Angeles Times*, June 23, 2020, https://www.latimes.com/politics/story
/2020-06-23/biden-obama-fundraiser.

317 **That changed . . . in April:** Debenedetti, "Biden Is Planning an FDR-Size Presidency."

318 **Kaufman publicly warned that deficits would make it difficult:** Ken Thomas
and Eliza Collins, "Joe Biden United the Democrats—It's Not Likely to Last," *Wall
Street Journal*, August 19, 2020, https://www.wsj.com/articles/biden-united-the
-democratsits-not-likely-to-last-11597847147.

319 **"They have real fears":** Edward-Isaac Dovere, "Biden Rips Trump as 'Charlatan,'"
Politico, November 1, 2017, https://www.politico.com/story/2017/11/01/biden-rips
-trump-in-chicago-speech-2020-244425.

320 **honoring Lewis meant passing new voting rights legislation:** Clare Foran and Ted
Barrett, "Obama Calls Filibuster 'Jim Crow Relic' That Should Be Eliminated if Necessary to Enact Voting Rights Legislation," CNN, July 30, 2020, https://www.cnn.com
/2020/07/30/politics/obama-filibuster-jim-crow-voting-rights/index.html.

Chapter 20: 2020–2021

323 **he made a point of acknowledging "our vice president":** Dovere, *Battle for the Soul*, 395.

324 **who had the backing of veterans' groups:** Gabriel Debenedetti, "Joe Biden's
VP Search Is Turning into an Open Audition," *New York*, May 21, 2020, https://
nymag.com/intelligencer/2020/05/joe-bidens-vp-search-is-turning-into-an-open
-audition.html.

324 **Jill took it upon herself to be the family grievance-keeper:** Jill Biden, *Where the Light
Enters*, 25.

324 **Harris allies even met:** Christopher Cadelago and Natasha Korecki, "Harris Allies
Granted Call with Biden Campaign After Dodd Blowup," *Politico*, July 31, 2020,
https://www.politico.com/news/2020/07/31/harris-allies-biden-call-dodd-389848.

324 **"DO NOT Hold Grudges.":** Bill Barrow and Andrew Harnik, "Biden's Notes: 'Do Not
Hold Grudges' Against Kamala Harris," Associated Press, July 28, 2020, https://apnews
.com/article/virus-outbreak-election-2020-ap-top-news-ca-state-wire-politics-d3fc8b
88cde56bac9f1e7b5e494fb019.

326 **she'd also aced Lake's poll test:** David Axelrod, "Why Kamala Harris Won the VP Contest," CNN, August 11, 2020, https://www.cnn.com/2020/08/11/opinions/why-kamala
-harris-won-vp-content-axelrod/index.html.

326 **he was the first VP candidate ever to run:** Goldstein, *The White House Vice Presidency*, 220.

327 **when they first appeared together as a ticket:** Gabriel Debenedetti, "Kamala Harris's
Expected Vice-Presidency Keeps Getting Bigger," *New York*, October 6, 2020, https://
nymag.com/intelligencer/2020/10/kamala-harriss-vice-presidency-keeps-getting
-bigger.html.

328 **beaming onto TV screens from Philadelphia:** *Los Angeles Times*, "Read President Obama's Speech at the 2020 Democratic National Convention," August 20, 2020, https://www.latimes.com/politics/story/2020-08-20/president-obama-speech-dnc-2020.

329 **Thomas Friedman . . . who in April proposed an administration:** Thomas L. Friedman, "What America Needs Next: A Biden National Unity Cabinet," *New York Times*, April 7, 2020, https://www.nytimes.com/2020/04/07/opinion/biden-campaign-covid.html.

329 **"the thing that will fundamentally change things is with Donald Trump out of the White House":** Eric Bradner and Gregory Krieg, "Joe Biden Predicts a Post-Trump 'Epiphany' for Republicans," CNN, May 14, 2019, https://www.cnn.com/2019/05/14/politics/joe-biden-republicans-trump-epiphany/index.html.

330 **Lindsey Graham, who'd cried:** Scott Conroy and Jon Strauss, "Watch Lindsey Graham Choke Up Talking About Joe Biden," *Huffington Post*, July 2, 2015, https://www.huffpost.com/entry/lindsey-graham-joe-biden_n_7714708?1435860129=.

330 **"If you asked Joe and I what regrets we might have":** Osnos, "Can Biden's Center Hold?"

330 **clearing Lafayette Park:** Jonathan Allen, Dartunorro Clark, and Rebecca Shabad, "Police, National Guard Clash with Protestors to Clear Streets Before Trump Photo Op," NBC News, June 1, 2020, https://www.nbcnews.com/politics/politics-news/after-night-significant-damage-d-c-mayor-bowser-imposes-earlier-n1221126.

330 **considering the possibility:** Jonathan Martin and Maggie Haberman, "How Kristi Noem, Mt. Rushmore and Trump Fueled Speculation About Pence's Job," *New York Times*, August 8, 2020, https://www.nytimes.com/2020/08/08/us/politics/kristi-noem-pence-trump.html.

330 **turning the White House lawn:** Jordyn Phelps and Ben Gittleson, "Trump Steamrolls Norms with White House Convention Speech, Raising Ethics Concerns," ABC News, August 24, 2020, https://abcnews.go.com/Politics/trump-steamrolls-norms-white-house-convention-speech-raising/story?id=72569119.

336 **laying the blame for the deadly riot:** Laurel Wamsley, "Obama: 'A Moment of Great Dishonor and Shame for Our Nation'—But Not a Surprise," NPR, January 6, 2021, https://www.npr.org/sections/congress-electoral-college-tally-live-updates/2021/01/06/954218662/obama-a-moment-of-great-dishonor-and-shame-for-our-nation-but-not-a-surprise.

337 **he called on Trump:** Kate Sullivan and Eric Bradner, "Biden Says US Democracy Under 'Unprecedented Assault' and Calls on Trump to 'Demand an End to This Siege,'" CNN, January 6, 2021, https://www.cnn.com/2021/01/06/politics/joe-biden-riots-capitol-speech/index.html.

338 **security concerns forced Biden to scrap plans:** Alexandra Jaffe and Zeke Miller, "Biden Forgoing Amtrak Trip to Washington over Security Fears," Associated Press, January 13, 2021, https://apnews.com/article/biden-inauguration-train-security-ba7bcefad3a65bf9432e9178633baadd.

Afterword

339 **he substituted out a portrait of Andrew Jackson for one of Benjamin Franklin:** Larry Buchanan and Matt Stevens, "The Art in the Oval Office Tells a Story. Here's How to See It," *New York Times*, May 5, 2021, https://www.nytimes.com/interactive/2021/05/05/arts/design/oval-office-art.html; Annie Linskey, "A Look Inside Biden's Oval Office," *Washington Post*, January 21, 2021, https://www.washingtonpost.com/politics/2021/01/20/biden-oval-office/.

340 **"For them to go back four years later":** Annie Linskey and Marianna Sotomayor, "The Biden Do-Over: Democrats Get a Chance to Try Again on Obama Defeats,"

Washington Post, March 28, 2021, https://www.washingtonpost.com/politics/biden
-obama-do-over/2021/03/28/4792b04e-8d8e-11eb-a6bd-0eb91c03305a_story.html.

342 **He wouldn't blame Biden:** Chait, "In Conversation with Barack Obama."

342 **His approval rating:** "Presidential Job Approval Center," Gallup.

342 **"What are they for?":** "Remarks by President Biden in Press Conference," The White House, January 19, 2022, https://www.whitehouse.gov/briefing-room/speeches-remarks
/2022/01/19/remarks-by-president-biden-in-press-conference-6/.

343 PSAKI SAYS OBAMA, BIDEN TALK REGULARLY: Steven Nelson, "Psaki Says Obama, Biden Talk Regularly but Refuses to Say How Often," *New York Post*, April 8, 2021, https://nypost.com/2021/04/08/psaki-says-obama-biden-talk-regularly-but-wont-say
-how-often/.

343 **"We didn't adequately explain":** "Remarks by President Biden at the House Democratic Caucus Virtual Issues Conference," The White House, March 3, 2021, https://www
.whitehouse.gov/briefing-room/speeches-remarks/2021/03/03/remarks-by-president
-biden-at-the-house-democratic-caucus-virtual-issues-conference/.

344 **"We didn't do enough":** "Press Briefing by Jen Psaki, March 5, 2021," The White House, March 5, 2021, https://www.whitehouse.gov/briefing-room/press-briefings/2021/03
/05/press-briefing-by-press-secretary-jen-psaki-march-5-2021/.

347 **"Mainstream Media Silent While Obama Dances Maskless in a Crowded Tent":** Lindsay Kornick, "Mainstream Media Silent While Obama Dances Maskless in a Crowded Tent," Fox News, August 8, 2021, https://www.foxnews.com/media/mainstream-media
-silent-obama-dances-maskless-crowded-tent.

347 **Maureen Dowd was scathing:** Maureen Dowd, "Behold Barack Antoinette," *New York Times*, August 14, 2021, https://www.nytimes.com/2021/08/14/opinion/barack
-obama-birthday.html.

348 **"Joe and the administration are essentially finishing the job":** Ezra Klein, "Obama Explains How America Went from 'Yes We Can' to 'MAGA,'" *New York Times*, June 1, 2021, https://www.nytimes.com/2021/06/01/opinion/ezra-klein-podcast-barack-obama
.html.

348 **CBS News's Margaret Brennan had asked:** "Transcript: Joe Biden on *Face the Nation*, February 23, 2020," *Face the Nation*, CBS News, February 23, 2020, https://www
.cbsnews.com/news/transcript-joe-biden-on-face-the-nation-february-23-2020/.

348 **nearly two-thirds of citizens approved:** Ariel Edwards-Levy, "Most Americans Favor Afghanistan Withdrawal but Say It Was Poorly Handled," CNN, August 23, 2021, https://www.cnn.com/2021/08/23/politics/polls-afghanistan-biden/index.html.

349 **"There's going to be no circumstance":** "Remarks by President Biden on the Drawdown of U.S. Forces in Afghanistan," The White House, July 8, 2021, https://www
.whitehouse.gov/briefing-room/speeches-remarks/2021/07/08/remarks-by-president
-biden-on-the-drawdown-of-u-s-forces-in-afghanistan/.

350 **"Our only vital national interest":** "Remarks by President Biden on Afghanistan," The White House, August 16, 2021, https://www.whitehouse.gov/briefing-room/speeches
-remarks/2021/08/16/remarks-by-president-biden-on-afghanistan/.

350 **"I was the fourth president":** "Statement by President Joe Biden on Afghanistan," The White House, August 14, 2021, https://www.whitehouse.gov/briefing-room
/statements-releases/2021/08/14/statement-by-president-joe-biden-on-afghanistan/.

352 **even named a cancer research funding provision:** Daniella Diaz, "Senate Holds Emotional Vote to Rename Cancer Bill After Joe Biden's Late Son, Beau," CNN, December 5, 2016, https://www.cnn.com/2016/12/05/politics/joe-biden-cancer-mitch-mcconnell
-beau-biden/index.html.

352 **"one hundred percent of our focus":** Allan Smith, "McConnell Says He's '100 Percent' Focused on 'Stopping' Biden's Administration," NBC News, May 5, 2021, https://

www.nbcnews.com/politics/joe-biden/mcconnell-says-he-s-100-percent-focused
-stopping-biden-s-n1266443.

352 **"McConnell came under a lot"**: Dartunorro Clark, "No. 3 Senate Republican John Barrasso Vows to Make Biden a 'One-Half-Term President,'" NBC News, June 15, 2021, https://www.nbcnews.com/politics/politics-news/no-3-senate-republican-john -barrasso-vows-make-biden-one-n1270960.

354 **grew emotional:** Maritsa Georgiou, "Tester Discusses Stimulus Proposal Talks, First Visit to Oval Office," NBC Montana, February 3, 2021, https://nbcmontana.com/news /local/tester-discusses-stimulus-proposal-talks-first-visit-to-oval-office.

354 **and risked tanking:** Amber Phillips, "The White House's Extraordinary, Furious Statement About Joe Manchin," *Washington Post*, December 19, 2021, https://www .washingtonpost.com/politics/2021/12/19/white-house-statement-joe-manchin/.

355 **reconnecting both with tech industry leaders:** Theodore Schleifer, "Can Laurene Powell Jobs Save the World?" *Puck*, October 14, 2021, https://puck.news/can-laurene- powell-jobs-save-the-world/.

356 **"The former president"**: Peter Baker, "Biden Condemns Trump as Washington Splits over Legacy of Jan. 6 Attack," *New York Times*, January 6, 2022, https://www.nytimes .com/2022/01/06/us/politics/biden-jan-6-capitol-attack.html.

356 **"Do you want to be on the side"**: Michael D. Shear, "Biden's Longtime Defense of Senate Rules Withers Under Partisan Rancor," *New York Times*, January 11, 2022, https:// www.nytimes.com/2022/01/11/us/politics/biden-filibuster-senate-history.html.

ACKNOWLEDGMENTS

No work of reporting can get anywhere without good sources, and this book would have been impossible without the extraordinary cooperation of the hundreds of people who shared with me their recollections, notes, and records. I can't name them here, but I am indebted to each of them. Special thanks go to the individuals who agreed to speak with me repeatedly over the course of months, taking many hours and reaching deep into their memories and files to make sure I fully understood the whole story. Plenty of them surely had more entertaining things to do with their time.

Hanna Park helped make sure that I always got the story straight with agility and a sensitive eye for detail.

Howard Yoon answered a random email many years and multiple book ideas ago, and his expertise, guidance, calm wisdom, and friendship in the intervening time have been essential. I could hardly ask for more in an agent, or agency—thanks, too, to Gail Ross, Shannon O'Neill, Noah Rosenzweig, and the rest of the talented team at Ross Yoon.

No one really teaches you what to expect from an editor or publisher when you write a book for the first time, so I was delighted and thankful to find that Serena Jones and her team at Holt were unfailingly flexible, curious, and incisive as this project came together. Serena's good humor and finely tuned sense of what's really important helped shape my thinking from the start. Thanks especially to Sarah Crichton and Amy Einhorn for their insights and encouragement, and to Anita Sheih, Molly Bloom, Shelly Perron, Carolyn O'Keefe, Christopher Sergio, and Alex Camlin for all their hard work to make this book a reality. Henry Rosenbloom, Bella Li, and their Melbourne-based team at Scribe were also a pleasure to work with.

I'm lucky to have editors at *New York* who were nothing but supportive as I pursued this project while covering the aftermath of the 2020 election and the first year of the Biden administration, starting with Jeb Reed, David Haskell, Ann Clarke, and Nick Summers. I'm fortunate, too, to have shrewd colleagues perpetually willing to talk through baroque political questions, and whose occasional counsel has always pointed me in the right direction in tricky moments, including Ben Hart, Ed Kilgore, Andrew Rice, David Wallace-Wells, and Reeves Wiedeman.

I researched and wrote this book almost entirely in 2021, but it is in many ways informed by the breadth of my time reporting in Washington and around the country, and I owe countless compatriots from *New York*, *Politico*, and Reuters for continually teaching me how it's done for many years now. I'll get the hang of it one of these days. To Marilyn Thompson and Adam Moss, especially, thanks for taking chances on me, and thanks to Jack Shafer for keeping me on my toes.

This project also owes much of its depth to friends and peers who engaged when they heard me ramble about the topic ad nauseam. Julian Debenedetti, Spencer Gaffney, Ariel Green, and Jeff Nunokawa provided specific insight and perspectives that advanced my understanding and portrayal of several crucial sagas and dynamics recounted in these pages. Adam, Ari, Chris, Dash, Evan, John, Katie, Louisa, Luciana, Lukasz, Mike, Pam, Pete, Pete, Piper, Ryan, Sam, Simon, Teddy, Tobi, Vikram, Zac, and Zach: you may not have known it in the moment, but your friendship also helped make this book possible. (That's alphabetical. Don't any of you read into the order.) Thanks, too, to Debbie, Eric, and Archie for their frequent hospitality and support. And—Why not?—thanks to Max, Barry, and the *Guardian Football Weekly* podcast for keeping me mostly sane.

Dina Debenedetti's persistent calls, joie de vivre, and ability to reset my frame of mind have been indispensable for as long as I can remember. She has my gratitude for always being on the other line. It's no exaggeration to say Silvia Strauss-Debenedetti and Pablo Debenedetti are responsible for all this. They've kept me going as inspirations, moral pillars, maestros, and sources of unending assurance, and I'm proud to call them my parents.

Finally, Rebecca Welbourn, you are the ultimate partner, coconspirator, advisor, and motivator. I still don't know how you do it. But I'm endlessly grateful that you do.

INDEX